CITY OF NEIGHBORHOODS

PHILADELPHIA

CITY OF NEIGHBORHOODS
1890–1910

PHILADELPHIA

BY JOSEPH MINARDI

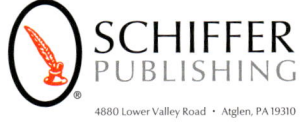

SCHIFFER PUBLISHING

4880 Lower Valley Road · Atglen, PA 19310

Designed by Ashley Millhouse

All photos are from the collection of Joseph Minardi unless otherwise noted.
Type set in Adobe Caslon/EngravrsRoman Bd BT

ISBN: 978-0-7643-6059-6
Printed in China

Published by Schiffer Publishing, Ltd.
4880 Lower Valley Road
Atglen, PA 19310
Phone: (610) 593-1777; Fax: (610) 593-2002
Email: Info@schifferbooks.com
Web: www.schifferbooks.com

For our complete selection of fine books on this and related subjects, please visit our website at www.schifferbooks.com. You may also write for a free catalog.

Schiffer Publishing's titles are available at special discounts for bulk purchases for sales promotions or premiums. Special editions, including personalized covers, corporate imprints, and excerpts, can be created in large quantities for special needs. For more information, contact the publisher.

We are always looking for people to write books on new and related subjects. If you have an idea for a book, please contact us at proposals@schifferbooks.com.

Other Schiffer Books by Joseph Minardi:

Historic Architecture in Northwest Philadelphia, 1690 to 1930s, ISBN 978-0-7643-4198-4

Historic Architecture in Philadelphia: East Falls, Manayunk, and Roxborough, ISBN 978-0-7643-4512-8

Historic Architecture in West Philadelphia, 1789–1930s, ISBN 978-0-7643-3771-0

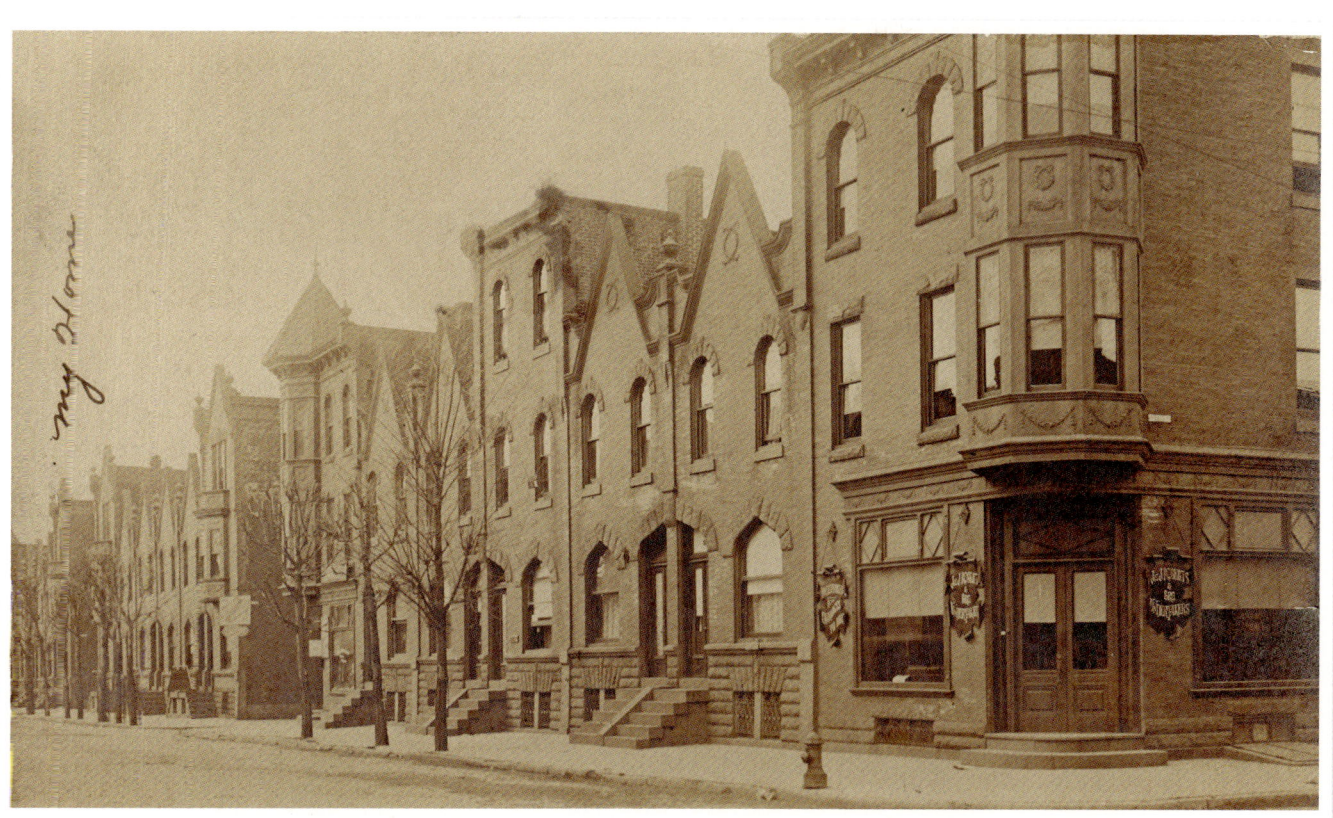

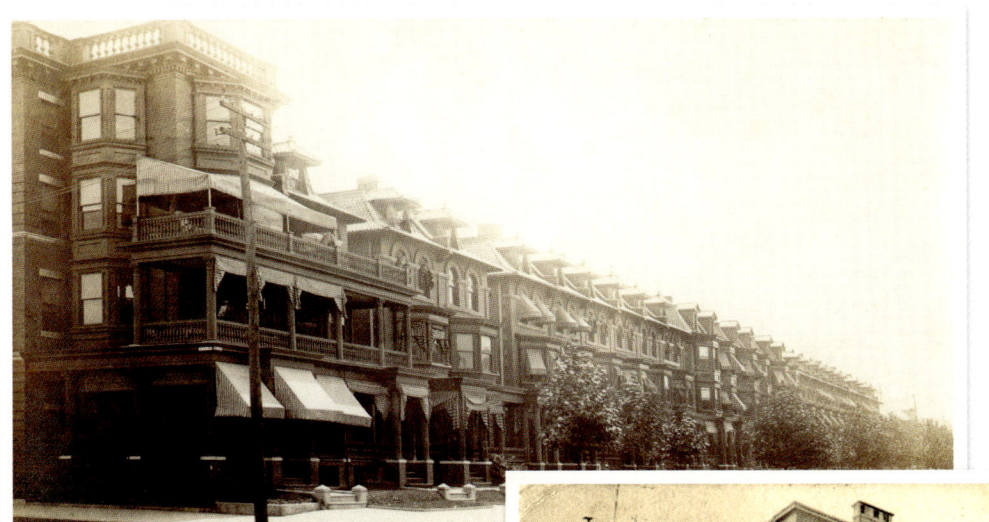
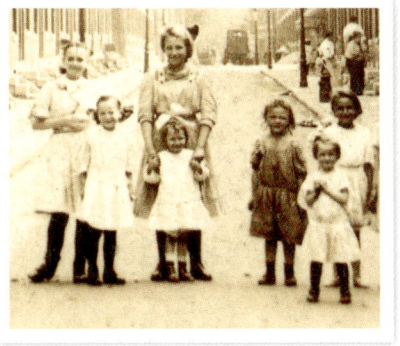
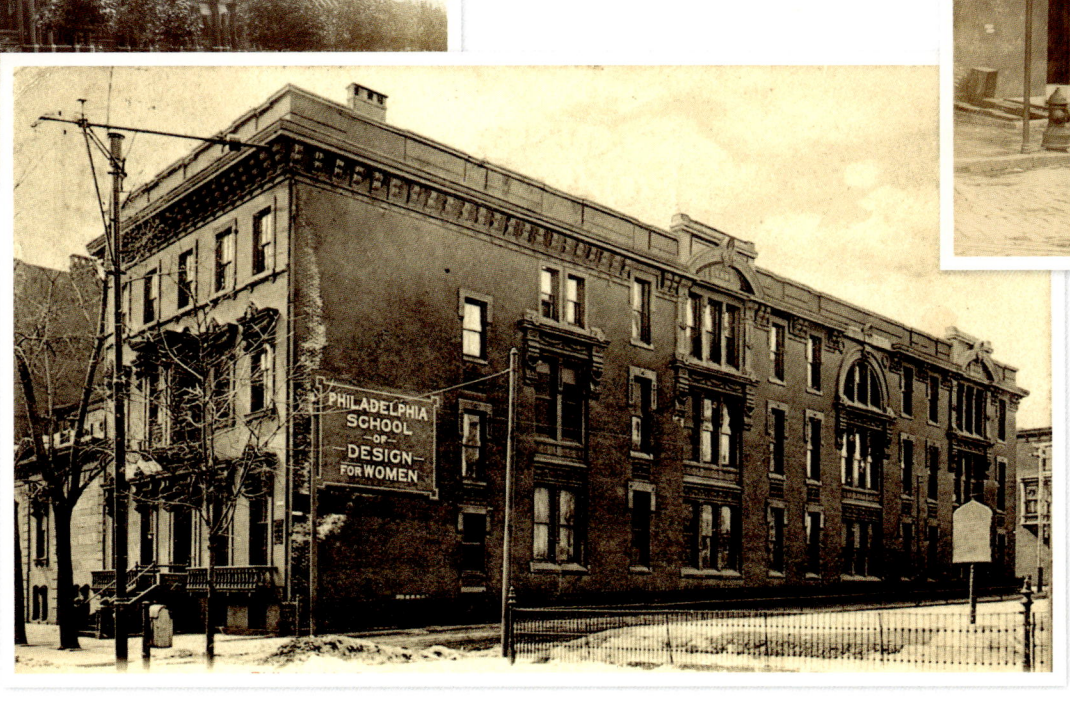

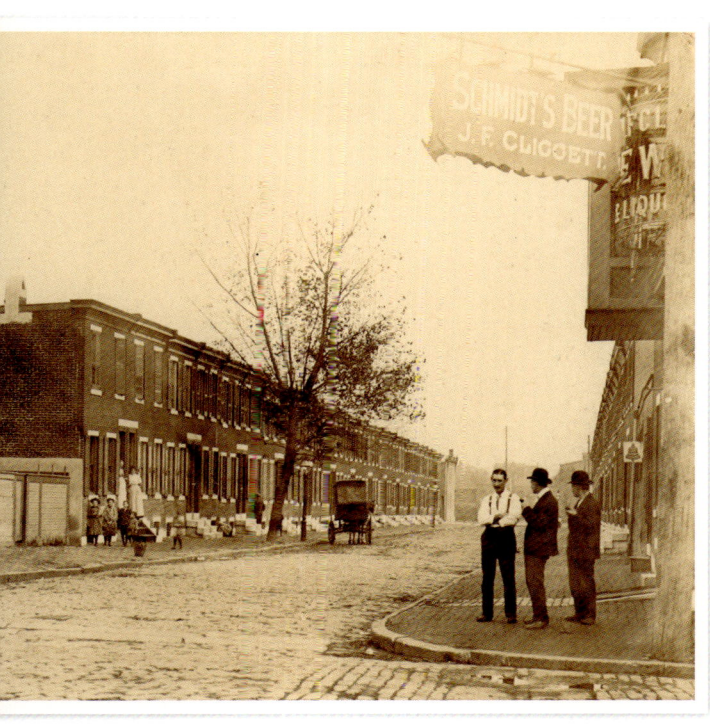

CONTENTS

Foreword by David S. Traub 8

Preface 10

Acknowledgments 17

Introduction 18

CHAPTER 1. Lower North Philadelphia 24

CHAPTER 2. Upper North Philadelphia 40

CHAPTER 3. Northeast Philadelphia 56

CHAPTER 4. Greater Kensington 72

CHAPTER 5. South Philadelphia 90

CHAPTER 6. West Philadelphia 106

CHAPTER 7. Southwest Philadelphia 126

CHAPTER 8. Northwest Philadelphia 138

CHAPTER 9. The People 152

Notes 164

Bibliography 168

Index 171

When commercial photographers at the end of the nineteenth and beginning of the twentieth centuries documented newly built houses stretching along Philadelphia streets, they would have had no idea that more than a hundred years later their photographs would come into the possession of Joseph Minardi and that he would present them in a book. Those photographers also could not have imagined that their work would show twenty-first-century Philadelphians a cityscape that has vastly changed and in some instances disappeared.

The photos were to be turned into postcards intended to publicize the houses for sale. Minardi uses these images to show us a view of the city that no longer exists in pristine form. The mills and factories that supported the neighborhoods have closed, the original inhabitants in many cases have moved away, and the houses have become occupied with peoples who are often of different backgrounds. Though fortunately there now are some reviving neighborhoods, sadly much of the urban fabric has frayed; many buildings have been demolished and the character of community life altered.

Minardi also wants to show us quite simply the artistic quality of the photographs made by anonymous craftsmen of another time. The photos were not made to hang on a gallery wall and be admired, but rather to be employed in a utilitarian way. Still, they stand as artifacts of considerable aesthetic value.

In many ways the photos remind us of the work of the famous French photographer Eugéne Atget, who documented Paris in the same era depicted in this book. But in Atget's case, he knew that his beloved city would inevitably change. Another difference between Atget's photographs and those in this book is that Atget's images generally do not show people. Atget's streetscapes are mysteriously empty, while the streetscapes here usually contain people, revealing a resonance between the human and architectural.

For example, the photograph of a thoroughfare in South Philadelphia shows a group of well-dressed children standing in the middle of the street. An adult, probably a parent, looks on. The photographer stands dead center in the street, taking a photo that shows the handsome three-story row houses embracing the children, while the row houses extend out, apparently to infinity.

Another photo shows houses in the more affluent area of Upper North Philadelphia. Rows of eight elegantly proportioned houses are framed between corner turrets topped by conical roofs. Together with the turrets, finials placed between the houses above the elaborate cornices give the composition the appearance of a medieval castle. Again, the street is filled with children who look delighted to be in the frame.

A photo of more-modest two-story houses in Southwest Philadelphia asserts front porches, a special feature of the western parts of the city. From the second floor, angled bay windows project in contradistinction to the flat-fronted row houses that spread over much of the city. The view down the block is terminated by a dense cluster of trees, telling us that much of Philadelphia housing adjoins green places, squares, and parks as William Penn envisioned his "Greene Country Towne."

A photo of similar porch-fronted row houses with second-floor bay windows in Germantown is included, but in this case the dwellings trickle down steep Lena Street, which is characteristic of that part of the city.

In the newer northeastern reaches of the city, single-family detached houses are featured as an exception to the many row houses pictured. Neighborhoods more distant from the city center tended to be built less densely. For example, a photo shows large, detached houses with porches fronting an unpaved street rutted with the traces of carriage wheels and lined with mature trees, giving the impression of a more suburban environment.

Paging through the book, one might wish to magically return to the Philadelphia of 1890–1910 and walk through the neighborhoods photographed by the unknown artisans. Taking such an imaginary stroll, the reader would see a Philadelphia largely unaltered by the dynamic forces of the twentieth century. Gazing off in the distance, few if any high-rise buildings would appear. Philadelphia then was a city enjoying a low profile, with all buildings rising below the height of the statue of William Penn atop City Hall. "Walking" through the streets, one wonders whether Philadelphia was a better city in that era than it is now.

Minardi is himself a photographer. He has produced three marvelous books, one showing the architecture of West Philadelphia and two more showing different sections of Northwest Philadelphia. He offers us both examples of individual buildings and rows of them forming streetscapes, some of which are similar to those that appear in this book. In presenting literally hundreds of historic places, his books takes on an encyclopedic dimension.

In *City of Neighborhoods*, Minardi has humbly put aside his own work and conjoins with unknown photographers of the past to offer us a view of the city that might be overlooked, given the plethora of material concerning architecture, housing, and historical preservation that is offered to us. Typically the photographs in the book might have been stored on the closet shelves of an unappreciative recipient or, at best, in an archive of one of our city's institutions, but Minardi has rescued the material from obscurity, making it available for all to see in superb book form.

There cannot be enough books illustrating Philadelphia's cityscape of the past and present. All such books, each in their own way, advance the important cause of preservation. With *City of Neighborhoods*, Minardi has placed one more book into that important library that shows us where we have been, where we are, and where we might proceed in preserving and re-creating the Philadelphia of the future.

—*David S. Traub is an architect and planner, author of two books about Philadelphia architecture, and cofounder of Save Our Sites, a local organization dedicated to preserving Philadelphia's rich architectural heritage.*

PREFACE

Why is Philadelphia a "City of Neighborhoods"? It has been known by many names over the years: Cradle of Liberty, City of Brotherly Love, City of Beautiful Buildings, Quaker City, City of Homes, Workshop of the World, City of Neighborhoods.

Those last two nicknames are most relevant to the subject of this book. Philadelphia's moniker "Workshop of the World" was richly deserved, since a person of limited education or skill level could find work in the city's many mills and factories. To be sure, the work was grueling and dangerous, with low pay and irregular shifts, but by working enough weekly hours, an average laborer could earn enough to afford a decent house and raise a family. It was hoped that with the right kind of education (and a little luck), his children could have a better life. For some, Philadelphia during its "workshop" period was the embodiment of the American dream. For others it was an endless cycle of poverty with almost no hope of advancement. Still, the average Philadelphia worker was much better off than his counterparts in other major American cities, largely due to the city's ubiquitous and affordable row houses.[1]

The neighborhoods where workers lived sprang up quickly, as if by magic. Builders worked furiously to keep up with the housing demand, which reached a fever pitch as the city's population ballooned from 1,046,964 to 1,549,008 between 1890 and 1910.[2]

But why is Philadelphia, in particular, a city of neighborhoods? Couldn't the term apply to other American cities such as New York, Boston, Baltimore, or Chicago? Perhaps, but the distinction is particularly applicable to Philadelphia.

Before the Consolidation Act of 1854, which united the city and county of Philadelphia into one governing body, many neighborhoods were sparsely populated villages with their own municipal identity. For a long time after the consolidation, residents continued to identify with their township or borough, rather than as a Philadelphian.

Another reason Philadelphia is a city of neighborhoods may have to do with its incredible walkability. The ancient grid of streets connects neighborhoods; a person can walk around the city and meet others on the street in casual encounters that can't be had when everyone drives from place to place. To put it another way, Philadelphia is a small place with lots of people in it.[3]

Row houses on the 1800 block of East Huntingdon in Kensington, ca. 1907. These houses were built in the latter half of the nineteenth century.

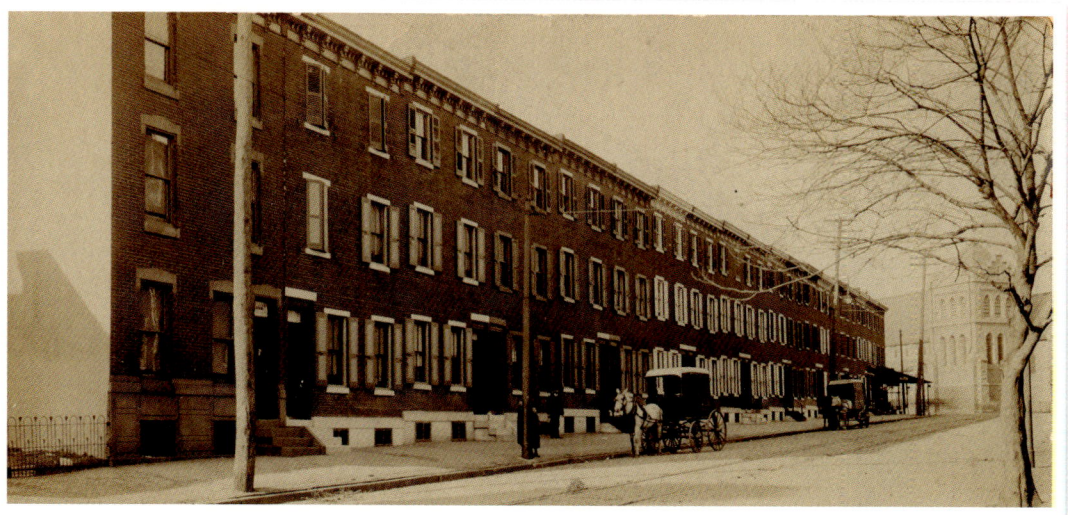

Sketches, left to right: a typical row house, St. Monica's Parish in South Philly; row house with a second-story bay window, Point Breeze in South Philly; a row house in the Tioga/Nicetown section of North Philly; a bay and porch row house in the Roxborough neighborhood

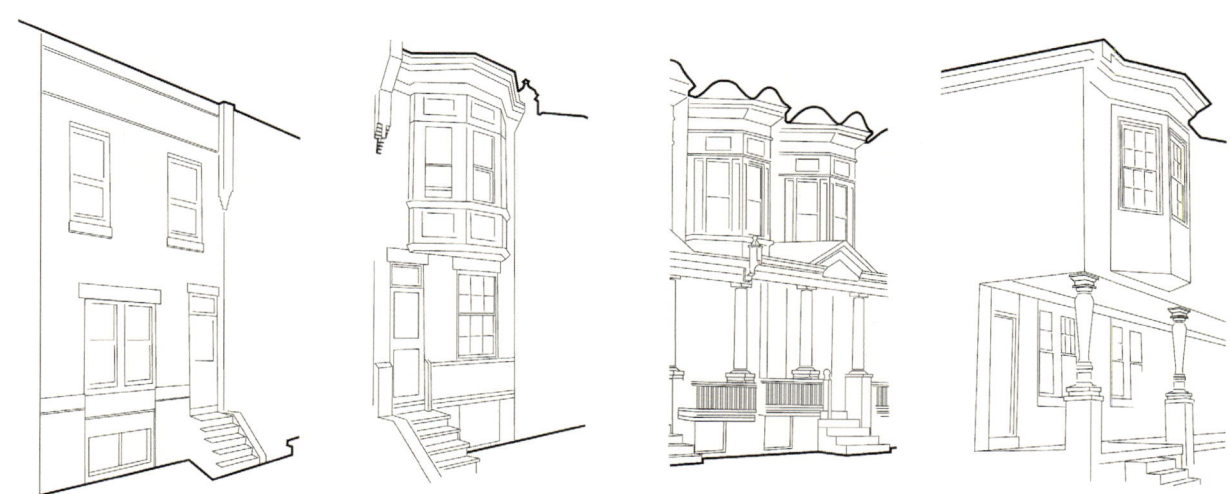

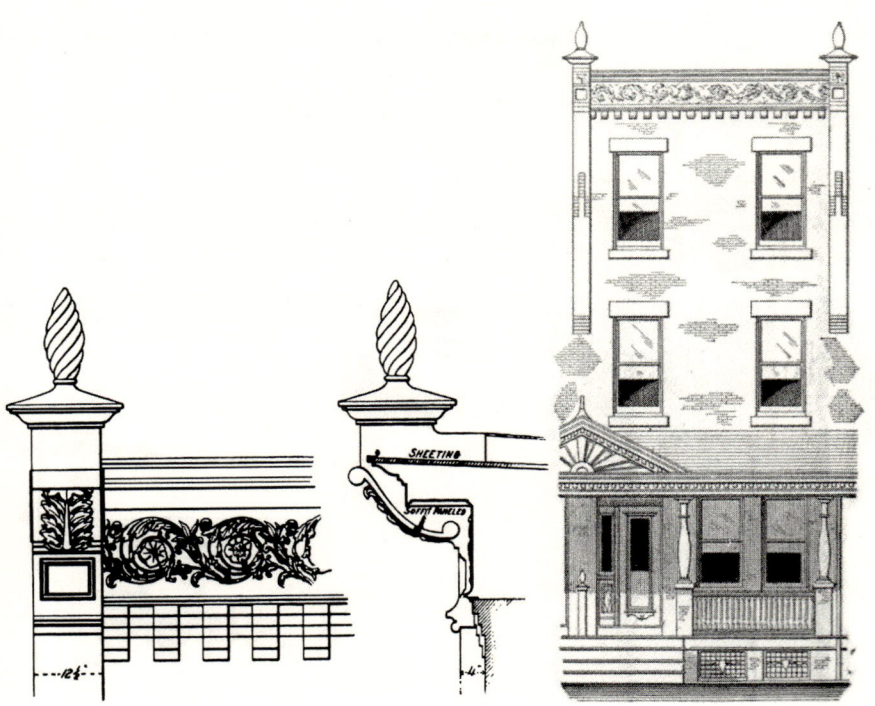

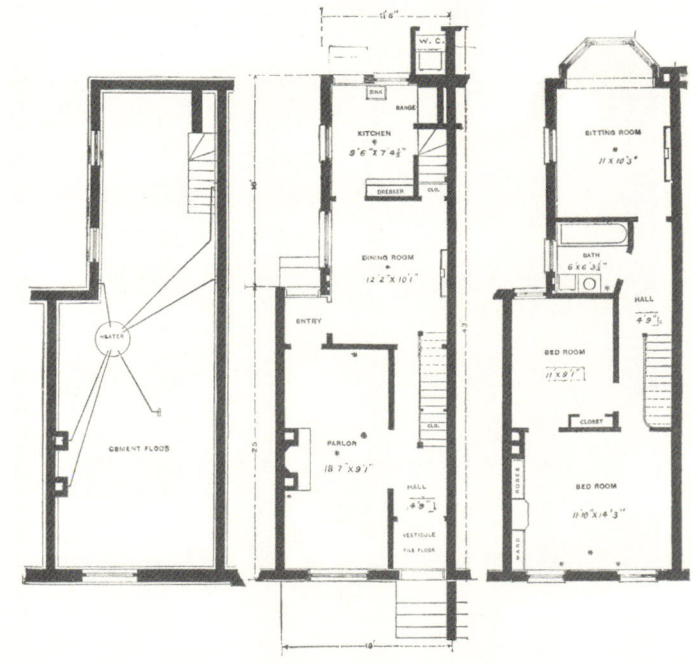

Front elevation and floor plan of a three-story row home built by Otto A. Guenthoer in 1899 on Thirty-Third Street and Ridge Avenue. The homes had a frontage of 15 feet, 6 inches, with a depth of 48 feet, excluding the front porch. The cornice was made of painted galvanized iron. These drawings were from plans by architect E. Allen Wilson, who designed hundreds of similar houses throughout Philadelphia.

Research

Much of the information in this book pertaining to construction dates, builders, and architects was obtained by researching building permits issued between 1890 and 1910. There are thousands of permits, and it took years to comb through the multitude of boxes containing these documents,

Building permits were issued for any new structure, from miniscule to monumental. Information on the earliest extant permits is rudimentary: date of application, builder or owner's name, location, dimensions, type of structure, building materials, date of construction, construction cost, and permit fee. Before 1895, a single permit covered any new building or alteration to an existing structure. Post-1895, new buildings and alterations/

additions were issued separate permits.

These documents are on file at the Philadelphia City Archives; they have not yet been digitized and therefore are not available to a mass audience. Permits issued prior to July 1889 were destroyed and are lost forever, and those that still exist are in varying states of preservation. Some are in excellent condition, while others are crumbling. Although this is the most reliable source of information relating to building activity in Philadelphia from this period, it is far from perfect. The permit forms were filled out by the builder or owner in cursive handwriting with pen and ink, so the researcher is at the mercy of the applicant's penmanship. One also has to factor in clerical errors, and in some cases the permits having gone missing. Still, the documents provide a fascinating insight into how builders and owners conducted business during the busy decades that straddled the year 1900.

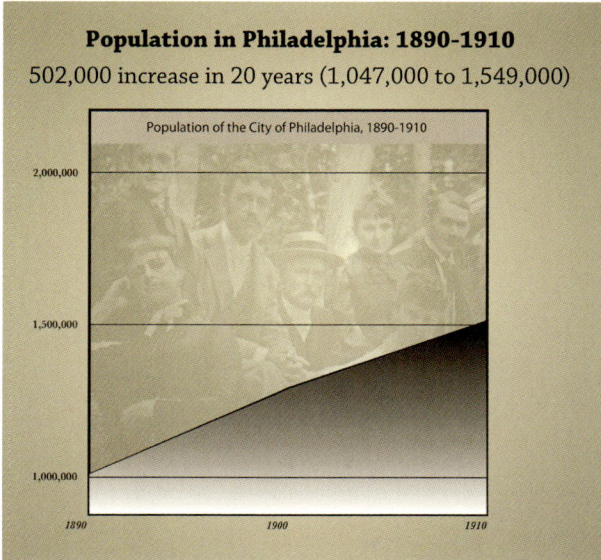

Chart of the city's population growth between 1890 and 1910

Why This Book?

Philadelphians have always had a keen interest in their city's history and traditions. However, the twenty-first century has brought rapid changes to the landscape, wiping out much of its history before we realize what has been lost. Like other major cities, Philadelphia is undergoing a residential boom as Americans rediscover urban living. This phenomenon may be just a taste of what occurred here more than a century ago, when factories and mills dotted the landscape and seemingly endless rows of houses were built to fill ever-increasing demands for housing.

The purpose of this book is to illustrate what the city's neighborhoods looked like when they were freshly built: a time before the view became obscured by automobiles, overgrown trees, and utility wires; a time before the homes' facades were altered beyond recognition; a time when they appeared exactly as the builder and the architects envisioned. Some of the buildings depicted here have been demolished. Thank goodness we have a good visual record by which to remember them.

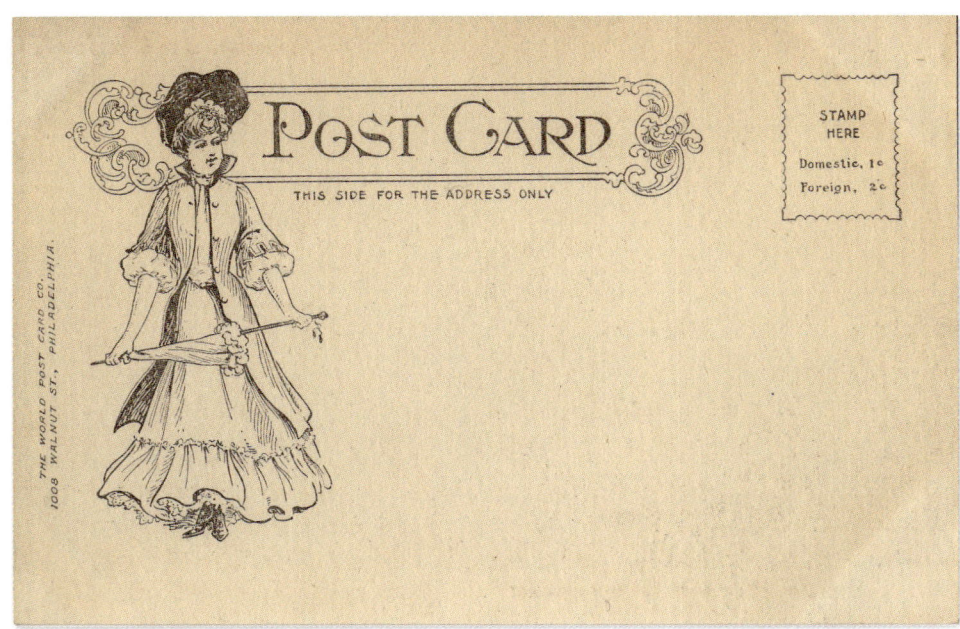

Reverse of a typical postcard (with a lovely Victorian motif) from the 1898–1907 era. Postcards from this time period are known as undivided backs, since the back was used for addresses only.

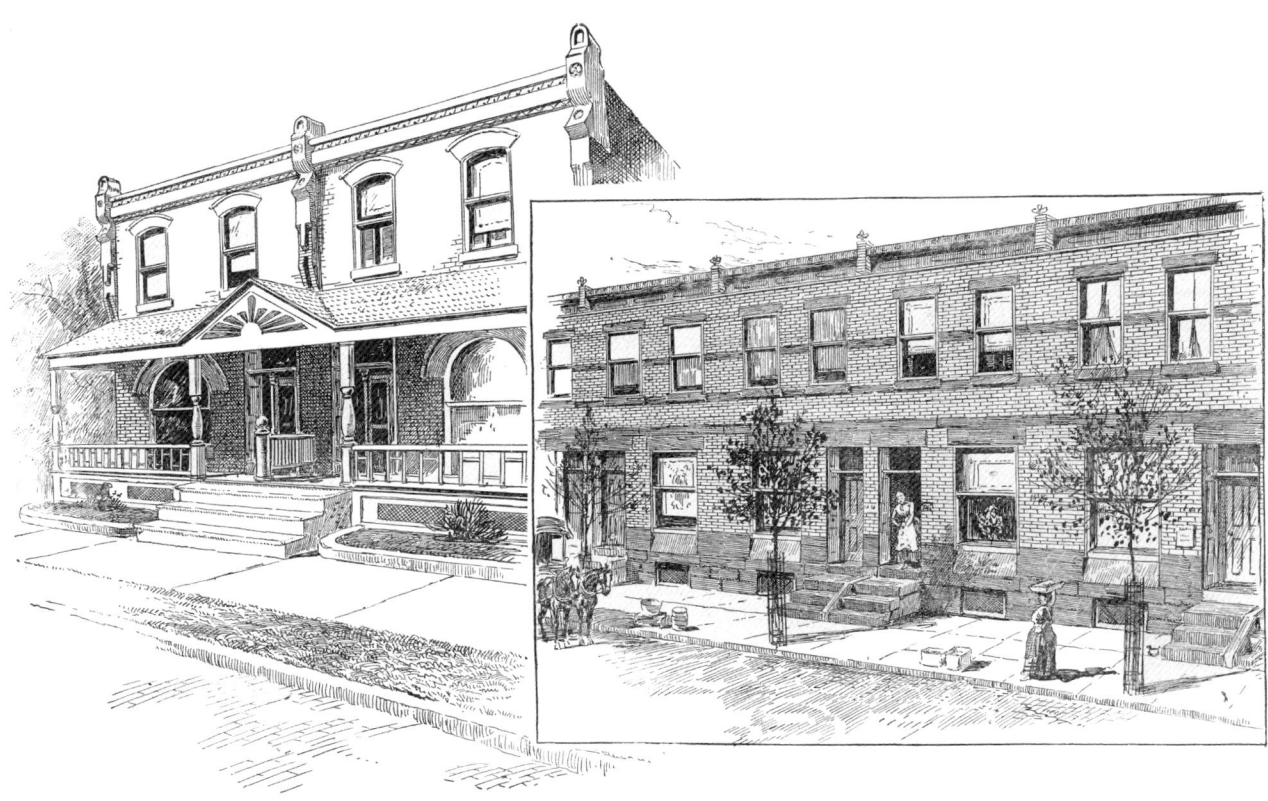

Two examples of typical Philadelphia dwellings from around 1891. The house on the left was 17 feet by 40 feet with seven rooms plus a bathroom; these homes were a ten-minute train ride from Center City and rented for about $23 per month. The house on the right was more suited for laborers and rented for $12 to $20 per month. Despite their plain facade, these workers' houses had six to eight rooms and contained all of the modern conveniences. This illustration appeared in an issue of *Harper's Weekly* of 1891. Reproduced from *The City of Philadelphia: As it Appears in the Year 1894*.

Photographs

The archival images are from a variety of sources, including glass plate negatives, cabinet photos, and stereoviews—a rectangular card with two nearly identical images side by side that appeared to be three-dimensional when viewed through a stereopticon.

The most common type of photograph is the real photo postcard (RPPC), a sharp photographic image printed on the front, with the backside containing space for the postage stamp, address, and a short message (this was after March 1, 1907; earlier, only the address was allowed on the back).[4] The location was handwritten on the front near the bottom or below the image; sometimes it was omitted, leaving researchers with a riddle to solve.

The RPPC provided a convenient way for homeowners to show off their new houses (usually identified by an "X") to friends and family far and wide. And it was an ideal way for builders to advertise their new offerings to prospective buyers.

RPPCs were produced by a handful of local studios: Creely & Sykes, the Douglass Post-Card Co., Pennant Studio, Royal Publishing Co., Slutsky's Studio, Tanguay Studio, the World Post Card Co., X-Ray Studios, and William B. Cooper of Medford, New Jersey. The three most prolific postcard producers in Philadelphia were William K. Swint of 1306 Columbia Avenue in North Philadelphia, the William H. Sliker Art Studio of 4758 Mercer Street in Bridesburg, and Mercantile Studio of 4130 Haverford Avenue in West Philadelphia and, later, 911 South Twentieth Street in South Philadelphia. Beginning in 1904, Mercantile Studio cranked out hundreds (if not thousands) of RPPCs during its seven years of existence. This visual record is of great value to researchers, since many of the houses have been demolished or drastically altered.

The photographers of yore liked to take panoramic views of the block, straight down the middle of the street and showing both sides. Sometimes they opted for an oblique view of one side, usually including the corner property, which was in most cases a grocery store.

Photographers also captured, either inadvertently or purposely, little slices of daily life, such as women diligently scrubbing their marble front steps or a horse-drawn wagon plying the cobblestone streets. Then there were the flocks of children who would quickly assemble and mug for the camera. It must have been an exciting event when a photographer showed up with his exotic equipment. Getting the children to remain still for the long exposure was a bit of a challenge. Some of them would run off while the photograph was still exposing, creating bizarre ghostly images.

All the photographs depicted in this book are from the collection of Joseph Minardi unless otherwise noted.

ACKNOWLEDGMENTS

A special thanks to the following individuals and institutions, whose help was invaluable:

Philadelphia City Archives staff members David Baugh, Ken Rice, Raven Darkholme, Robin Davis, and Jill Rawnsley for their help with going through dozens and dozens of heavy boxes of old city permits, and their general help in the microfilm department and looking up old deeds.

The Pennsylvania Historical Society, the Free Library of Philadelphia, David S. Traub and Save Our Sites, Lassiter Williams, Jennifer Loustau and the University City Historical Society, Steve Filmore, Carolyn Filmore and *East Falls Local*, Elizabeth Stegner, and Barry Grosbach.

INTRODUCTION

Philadelphia: 1890–1910

Philadelphia has been in existence for more than three centuries, but a two-decade period transformed it into an industrial powerhouse that spurred exponential population growth. Builders rose to the challenge by producing thousands of houses, many of them the familiar Philadelphia row house. Seemingly overnight, fields and farms were transformed into densely populated neighborhoods.

Prior to the Consolidation Act of 1854, Philadelphia County consisted of nine districts, six boroughs, and thirteen townships. The built-up urban core was centered in the original boundaries of Philadelphia, from the Delaware River to the Schuylkill from Vine Street to South Street, and the districts of the Northern Liberties and Southwark.[1]

On Philadelphia County's extremities were small, self-contained villages and towns. Many of them have faded into history: names such as Branchtown, Pittville, and Milestown are virtually unheard of today. Other town names such as Olney, Kensington, Germantown, and Bustleton have survived as urban neighborhoods.

These place names are tied directly to their unique histories or industries and had their own way of life and architecture. As the population swelled, the grid pattern of streets expanded accordingly, eventually overrunning many of the old districts.

GROWTH AND DEVELOPMENT

More than 50,000 houses were built between 1863 and the centennial year of 1876. By the closing decade of the nineteenth century, the metropolis boasted some 200,000 houses.[2]

> There is, probably, no city in America that can show more than one-third of the building operations of Philadelphia for 1889.
>
> —*Philadelphia Real Estate Record and Builders' Guide*, January 8, 1890

That prideful quote was merely a harbinger of things to come, as a tsunami of new construction was about to wash over the city. The housing demand was so out of hand that many architects were refusing small jobs because their plates were full.[3]

At the beginning of the 1890s, the two-story, single-family row house was the dominant housing type and would come to typify residential construction throughout the city's long history. In 1890, 9,281 houses were built, 7,301 of them two stories tall.[4]

Some of the swankier houses had amenities such as a front porch, fancy brickwork, bay windows, and small front and back lawns. Semidetached houses started to appear in the prosperous new streetcar suburbs, such as those of West Philadelphia.

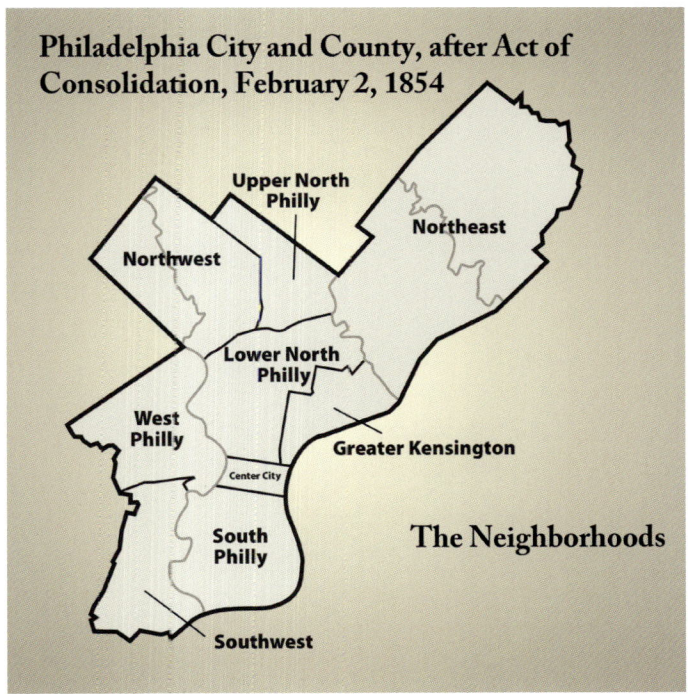

Map of Philadelph a and the major sec:ions featured in this book

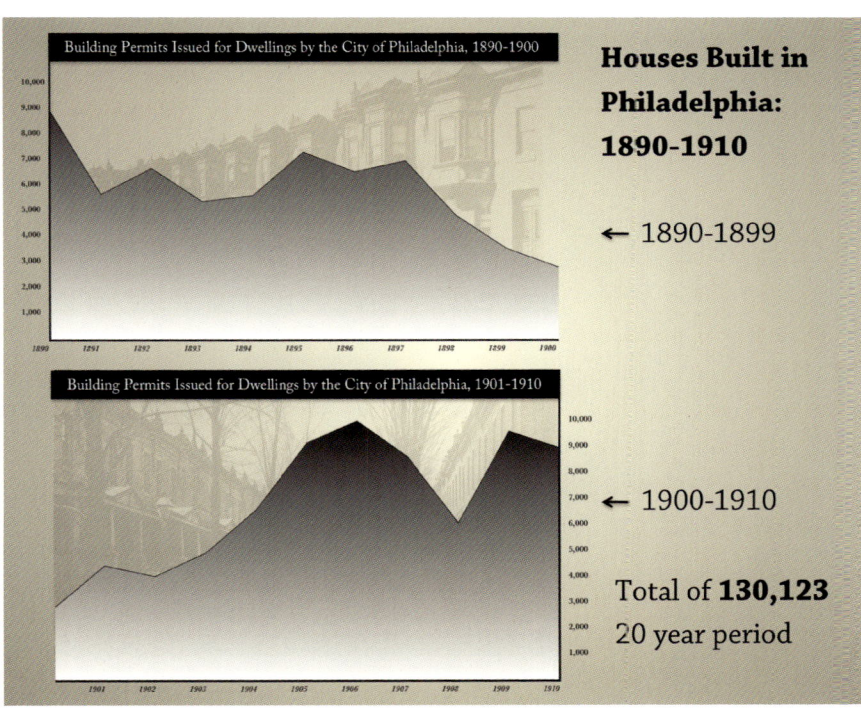

Charts showing the number of new houses built in Philadelphia between 1890 and 1910

A total of over 86,000 dwelling houses in thirteen years [1887–99], sufficient to house comfortably a population of over 400,000 persons, represents development and growth of a single city without a parallel in the world.

—*Philadelphia Real Estate Record and Builders' Guide*, January 3, 1900

Philadelphia's population explosion between 1890 and 1910 was tied to its reputation as the "workshop of the world." Factories produced virtually everything under the sun, from locomotives, steel ships, and streetcars to hats, sugar, and cigars. Philadelphia produced 211 of the 264 items listed by the US Manufacturing Survey of 1910. Most of these jobs required little or no formal education. They were often dirty and dangerous, with long hours and low wages. Most of the workers sought simple houses near their place of work.[5]

Although the houses were built in repetitive rows with scant open space or parks, this was still a great deal better than in New York, where tenement dwellers endured the tortures of living in cramped, dark, and stifling conditions. Luckily for Philadelphia, the city's infrastructure and well-established street grid aided in the construction of block after block of row houses. Horse-drawn streetcars, later replaced by electrified streetcars and an extensive passenger rail system, allowed workers to live on the rural fringes.

In 1890 the city encompassed approximately 800 farms on 33,000 acres. By 1920 that number had dropped to roughly 400 acres because of the insatiable appetite for buildable land. Former farmers became wealthy real estate developers almost overnight, and home building outpaced the city's population growth.[6]

Between 1890 and 1910, an average of more than 6,500 homes per year were being built in the city. Many included the luxury features of the day: indoor plumbing, gas and electrical fixtures, steam heat, and hardwood flooring. Low-skilled workers could not afford to live in such luxurious digs. The average annual salary of a manual laborer in the early twentieth century was between $500 and $1,000, while the cost of most new homes averaged around $2,000. The practice of redlining made sure that "undesirables" were shut out. However, there were enough members of the rising white-collar class and skilled laborers to keep the boom rolling along, with help from the city's building and loan associations.[7]

Improvements in mass transit meant a greater expansion of suburban living. Electrified trolley lines totaled more than 400 miles of track by 1897, and 600 miles by 1915, with eighty-six routes. The Market Street Elevated line, which opened on March 4, 1907, spurred development in West Philadelphia. The quaint streetcar suburb of Victorian twin homes quickly turned into a booming bedroom community. Starting at Fifteenth Street, the Market Street "El" was built all the way to Bridge Street in the Frankford section of Northeast Philadelphia.[8]

By the late nineteenth century, Philadelphia's residential architecture was the envy of the civilized world, according to city officials and other civic boosters. One writer, flush with pride (and a touch of hyperbole), exclaimed,

The two-story dwellings of this city are, beyond all question, the best, as a system, not only owing to the single family idea they represent, but because their cost is within the reach of all who desire to own their own homes.[9]

This was an early expression of what would later be known as the American dream.

ROW HOUSE PHILADELPHIA

The row house is among the most common and earliest housing modes in America and can be found in the older sections of many American cities, particularly in the northeastern quadrant of the US. A row house shares a party wall, or firewall, with a house on either side. This dwelling type is durable and adaptable to any climate, architectural trend, or price range. If properly cared for, a row house can last for centuries.

Philadelphia's founder, William Penn (1644–1718), was a proponent of the row house. Horrified by the dense living conditions that allowed the London Fire of 1666 to claim so many lives, he hoped for Philadelphia to grow from both ends of the two rivers between which it was planned—the Delaware on the east and the Schuylkill on the west. But the Delaware was far more navigable for big ships, and the city's eastern shore developed quickly while the Schuylkill side languished for decades. Budd's Long Row, a group of ten houses, appeared as early as 1691 on Front Street between Walnut and Dock Streets. It has long since been demolished, but one early row house example can still be found on historic Elfreth's Alley, a collection of contiguous houses built between circa 1724 and circa 1830 in Old City. A testament to Philadelphia's practicality, Elfreth's Alley's houses are owner-occupied and can be purchased by anyone (with enough money, that is).[10]

Four basic row house types became popular in early Philadelphia: the bandbox, the London house, the city house, and the town house. The first of these, the bandbox, or Father–Son–Holy Ghost house, is the smallest and most basic, usually consisting of two floors with one room per floor. Some of the earliest examples, collectively known as the "Fourteen Chimneys," appeared in 1759 on the west side of Fifth Street north of Arch.[11]

The London house is rectangular, two rooms deep, and typically three stories tall. The London house and the town house were larger variations of the bandbox and city house, respectively.[12]

Philadelphia's love affair with the row house continued into the 1800s, with noted architects such as John Haviland (1792–1852) and Thomas U. Walter (1804–1887) designing fashionable homes for the city's elite. Proving how adaptable the row house model was, they were built in every prevailing architectural trend, reflecting the popular tastes of the time.[13]

Philadelphia row houses were typically built of red or beige bricks but were sometimes constructed of fieldstone, locally known as Wissahickon schist, primarily in the city's northwestern section. The photos in this book depict a wide array of architectural styling such as gables, finials, parapets, and terra-cotta reliefs. Even the plainest row house could be enhanced with an elaborate iron cornice and marble steps.

In their original state, these row houses were quite attractive.

Over the years, many were neglected, abused, or altered beyond recognition, while others were covered in aluminum siding. Architectural details, added solely for aesthetic appeal, were removed due to the prohibitive cost of upkeep.

Not all of the houses built between 1890 and 1910 were row houses. Some were semidetached houses, or twins, as they're known in Philadelphia. Twins were considered a cut above the common row house, with a wee bit of space separating neighbors. Twins appeared in virtually every section of the city, with exceptional examples in West Philadelphia. A handful built during the two-decade boom were detached homes, from capacious mansions on Rittenhouse Square and North Broad Street to humble cottages in suburban outposts such as Olney and Oak Lane. But the row house is found in every section of the city, from car-oriented Northeast Philadelphia to the marshy lowlands of Southwest Philadelphia near the Philadelphia International Airport.

WHO BUILT PHILADELPHIA?

In the late nineteenth century, the line between builder and architect was often blurred. In many instances, the builder was also the designer. Prolific architects such as E. Allen Wilson, James Fernald, and Robert A. Pitts became speculative builders, no doubt after becoming familiar with the construction process and recognizing that it was more lucrative to be on the contracting side of the ledger.

During this period there were certain builders who figured prominently in creating entire neighborhoods. Their names are mostly forgotten, but without them the city would be very different today. Men such as Solomon Greenberg, Otto Guenthoer, Ludwig Lambrecht, the O'Brien brothers, and Antonio Donato all played a role in Philadelphia's residential construction. George Young, Richard Vancleave, John Stafford, and Charles Prettyman also built thousands of homes as the twentieth century turned. It wasn't always great architecture, but the houses were well made and a solid value for hard-working Philadelphians.

SECTIONS COVERED

The chapters in this book are organized by long-standing geographical boundaries, although some explanation of the divisions are necessary.

Roosevelt Boulevard divides the upper and lower sections of North Philadelphia, with Upper North Philadelphia consisting of larger, suburban-style stone homes and Lower North Philadelphia made up of familiar red-brick row homes.

The Greater Kensington section includes Kensington and contiguous neighborhoods such as Hartranft, Harrowgate, and Port Richmond.

The Northeast section includes the Bridesburg neighborhood, which some consider a River Ward.

As important as Center City is to Philadelphia's economic, political, historical, and social life, it is not included because it has been thoroughly covered in other books. As much as I love the individual neighborhoods that make up Center City, the focus here is on the city's lesser-known residential sections.

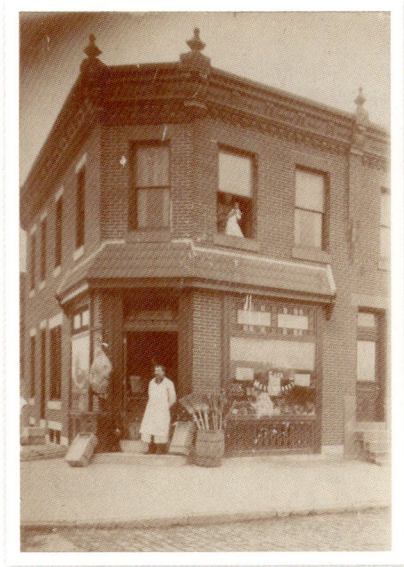

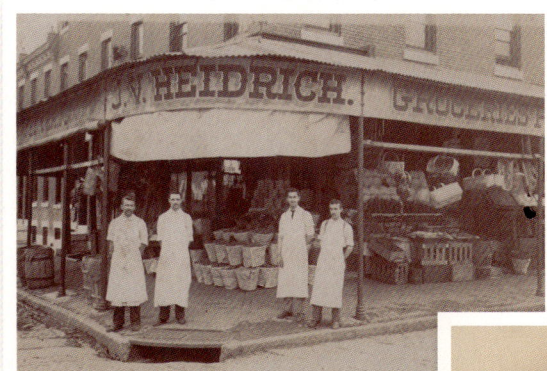

Left to right: Abraham L. Yoder would eventually own his own corner store (pictured here at 4657 Fairmount Avenue around 1897). The woman in the second-story window is likely his wife, Rosa (Rosie) Yoder. Abraham and Rosie were married in 1895. Tragedy would befall them on January 21, 1899, when twenty-eight-year-old Abraham was shot and killed at his corner store, likely in an armed robbery. Rosie would remarry and pass away in 1953 at age seventy-nine.

A ca. 1895 photo of the J. V. Heidrich corner store, at 2870 North Lawrence Street in North Philadelphia. Standing in front are a few of the employees, including a young Abraham L. Yoder at far left.

Photo of Abraham L. Yoder, taken while in the employ of J. V. Heidrich

THE CORNER STORE—A PHILADELPHIA TRADITION

One feature common to virtually all residential blocks built during this period was the corner property, designated as a commercial establishment with a dwelling above. This type of arrangement was called a "store/dwelling," typically one story taller than the residences in the middle of the block. In the time before automobiles, a corner store within close walking distance was an essential element of urban living. Most were highly specialized, selling just meat, dairy products, or sporting goods. Busy homemakers shopped on foot and carried a wicker basket for gathering the day's goods. A handful of general stores, forerunners of the department store, sold a broader range of goods.

Chapter 1.

LOWER NORTH PHILADELPHIA

With its sprawling suburban campus, Temple University is the big player in Lower North Philadelphia today. The school has taken over such large swaths of North Philadelphia that the neighborhood surrounding the college is known as Templetown, a moniker rejected by many longtime residents. Huge university buildings are rising, giving this part of the city a new skyline that can be seen for miles. Despite the fact that Temple demolished a number of historic row houses over the years, North Philadelphia still has outstanding examples of late Victorian dwellings.

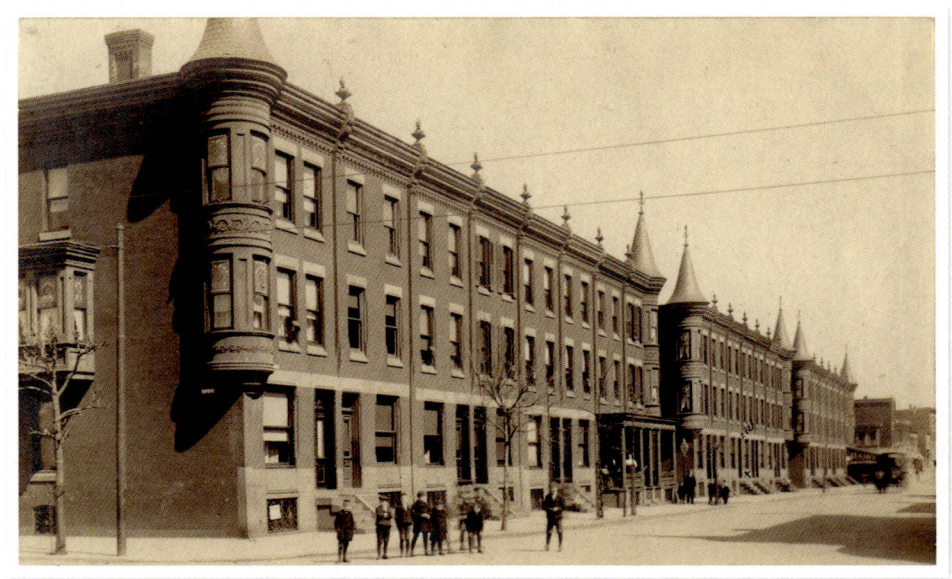

**Oxford Avenue east of
Twenty-Ninth Street, 1910**

Huntingdon Station (Broad and Huntingdon Streets), ca. 1905. This classical revival–style station of the Philadelphia & Reading Railroad stood at the intersection of Broad and Huntingdon Streets until it was replaced by a much-larger station in 1928. The upgraded station was also designed in the classical revival style by Horace Trumbauer and is still standing. The Baker Bowl, the ballpark of the Philadelphia Phillies, was directly across Broad Street.

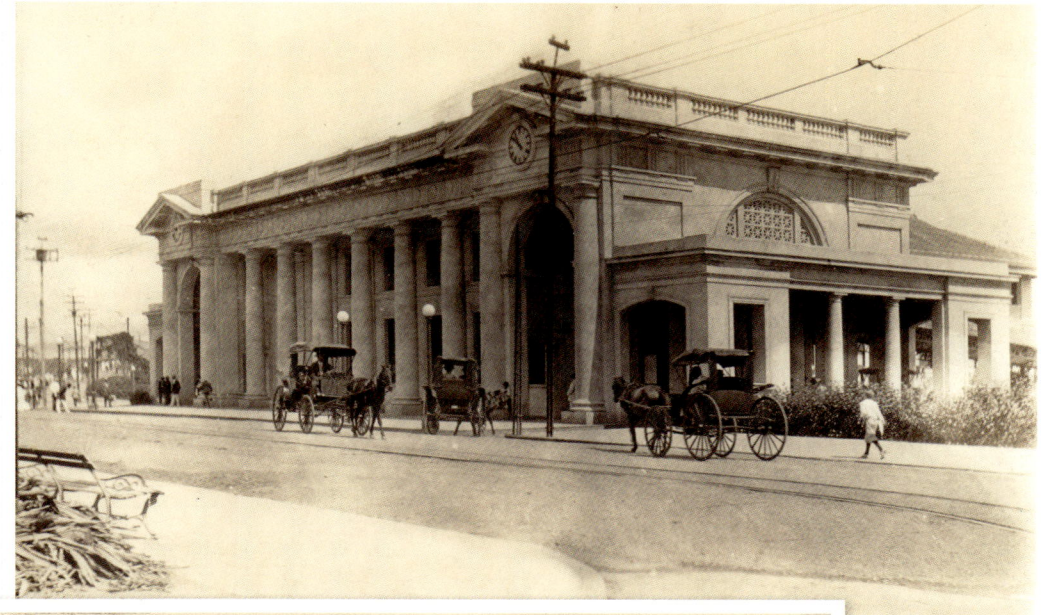

Tioga Station (Twentieth Street and Tioga Avenue), 1910. Tioga Station, a stop on the Germantown & Reading branch of the Philadelphia & Reading Railroad, was essential to the residential growth of Tioga/Nicetown. This section was once known as Kenderton, named after the home of a wealthy landowner. Due to confusion with Kensington, the station was renamed Tioga after the nearest street.

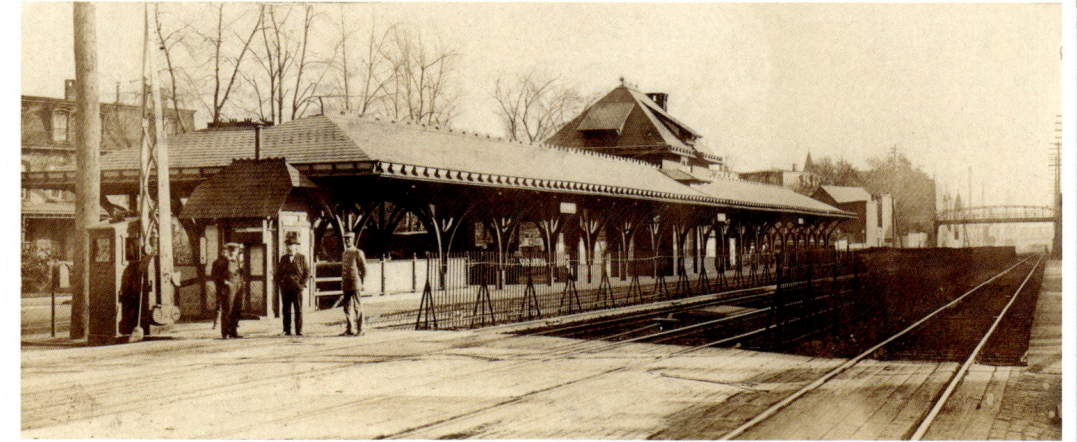

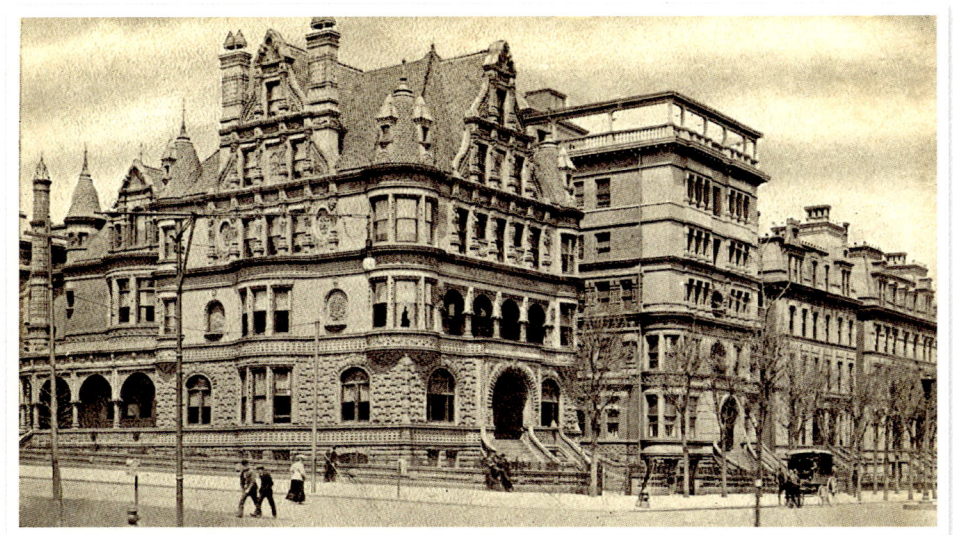

Broad Street and Girard Avenue, 1910. The west side of Broad Street is shown here looking north from Girard Avenue, with the châteauesque mansion of Gilded Age magnate Peter A. B. Widener (1834–1915) occupying the northwest corner, along with three other fabulous dwellings to the north. North Broad Street was one the places where Philadelphia's aristocracy built their architect-designed dream homes. For the design of his conspicuous palace, Widener selected Willis G. Hale (1848–1907), a socially connected architect renowned for his flamboyant style. All the houses in this photo have been demolished.

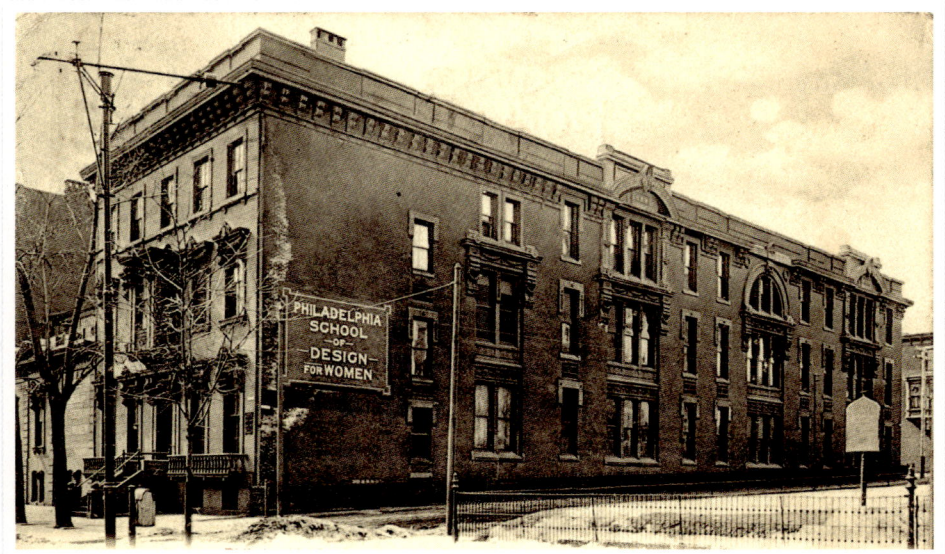

Broad and Master Streets, 1906. Nineteenth-century Shakespearean actor Edwin Forrest (1806–1872) built this fantastic house on Broad Street in 1854. The Forrest Residence is a rare survivor from the early suburban development of North Broad Street and has undergone a series of additions and alterations. It has also been repurposed by a number of institutions over the years (pictured here as the Philadelphia School of Design for Women, which it remained from 1880 to 1959). It now houses the New Freedom Theater, an African American theater company in residence.

Landmarks of North Philadelphia's glorious past are in varying degrees of preservation. Girard College, the Philadelphia Opera House (recently refurbished as the Met), the Divine Lorraine Hotel, and the Freedom Theatre (formerly the residence of actor Edwin Forrest) all speak to a prosperous history. North Broad Street was once the Fifth Avenue of Philadelphia, with commodious mansions of wealthy industrialists on both sides of the wide thoroughfare. North Philadelphia was also the site of industrial complexes on a truly heroic scale. The Baldwin Locomotive Works, once located on North Broad Street in the Spring Garden neighborhood, was a manufacturing behemoth. It was, in fact, the largest such factory of its kind in the United States, occupying a 17-acre site at its zenith. At its busiest, the locomotive works employed nearly 20,000. When business dropped off, however, the number of employees fell to about half that number. The Baldwin Locomotive Works gradually moved from Broad Street to Eddystone, Pennsylvania, where the company took over more than 225 acres and produced its last locomotive in 1956.[1]

Fairmount and Spring Garden

North of Vine Street are the Fairmount and Spring Garden Districts, each with rows of two- and three-story brick houses. Spring Garden was incorporated in 1813 and extended in 1854 from Vine Street to a line 200 feet north of Poplar Street, and from Sixth Street to the Schuylkill River. The annalist John F. Watson (1779–1860) claims that it was named for a spring near Ninth and Spring Garden Streets, and that young people boated to this spring on Pegg's Run, then beautifully rural and lined

with trees. The Spring Garden District included Fairmount, the nucleus of the park, where in 1819 Frederick Graff (1774–1847) built the dam and waterworks, now restored to its original appearance. The city's reservoir stood on a natural rise where the Philadelphia Museum of Art was built in 1928, giving the prestigious museum an advantageous perch. The name "Fairmount" was later applied to the neighborhood that grew up on the western side of the Spring Garden District.[2]

Brewerytown

Long before Milwaukee was the beer-brewing capital of the US, Philadelphia had more than 700 operating breweries. Most of the brewing activity took place in North Philadelphia, with much of it in the Brewerytown neighborhood, bounded by Cecil B. Moore Avenue on the north, Parrish Street on the south, and Twenty-Fifth to Thirty-Third Streets on the east and west.

With the prohibition on "intoxicating liquors" (the Eighteenth Amendment, 1919), the city's stills and brewhouses were forced to close. Even after the repeal of Prohibition (the Twenty-First Amendment, 1933), Brewerytown's suds production never recovered, and the neighborhood fell on hard times. The reminders of the brisk brewing business lingered on. A few of the breweries and secondary buildings designed in the robust Germanic style remained intact. Residential Brewerytown was represented by richly detailed Queen Anne–style row houses and simpler workingman's homes. In time, many of Brewerytown's architectural gems were abandoned or demolished. It was declared blighted in 1991—oddly enough, that same year the Brewerytown Historic District was certified by the National Register of Historic Places.[3]

As the twenty-first century dawned, developers again began focusing on the neighborhood due to its location and superb (and affordable) housing stock. Things are hopping again in Brewerytown, with rehabbed old homes, new construction, and a revitalized commercial corridor along Girard Avenue. Some of the remaining breweries are being converted into apartments.

Not everyone is happy with the dizzying pace of change. Some of the older African American residents are feeling the financial pinch of rising rents and a sense of alienation.[4]

Strawberry Mansion

North of Brewerytown is Strawberry Mansion, named after the justly famous house of Judge William Lewis (1752–1819) in nearby Fairmount Park. The neighborhood is bisected by Sedgley Avenue and abuts Fairmount Park on its western side. Much like Brewerytown, Strawberry Mansion is filled with fine examples of late Victorian architecture, although decades of neglect have left many houses in tumbledown condition. In the early twentieth century, many Jewish people moved to Strawberry Mansion, seeking greener pastures.[5]

The northern part of Strawberry Mansion, continuing into the current neighborhood of Allegheny West, was Swampoodle, a name that has largely passed into history. The boundaries of Swampoodle were roughly from Nineteenth to Thirtieth and from Cambria south to Cumberland. Over a century ago it was a largely Irish neighborhood brimming with colorful characters.[6]

Swampoodle's pride and joy was the steel-and-concrete Shibe Park (built in 1909 for $300,000) at Twenty-Second and Lehigh, home to the Philadelphia Athletics baseball club. Enterprising residents living along the east side of the stadium would set up bleachers on their roofs for fans looking for tickets to sold-out games. Their entrepreneurial spirit was crushed when the Athletics erected an obtrusive "spite fence" in 1935.[7]

Eleventh and Green Streets, ca. 1906. One of the several dozen grocery stores owned and operated by Irish immigrants Samuel R. Robinson and Robert H. Crawford. These two entrepreneurs christened their first grocery in South Philadelphia at 1214 South Second Street in 1891. They merged their enterprise with four other local chains in 1917 to become American Stores, the forerunner of Acme Supermarkets.

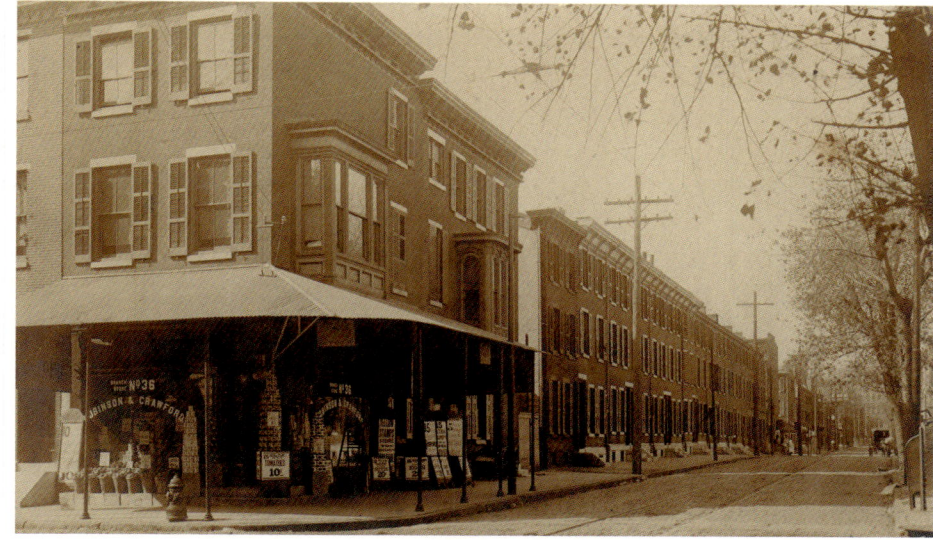

1400 block of Mt. Vernon Street, looking east toward Broad Street, 1907. Eight stately Victorian row houses stand in proximity to a rapidly industrializing North Broad Street, with J. S. Ivins Cracker Factory visible in the distance. The church at the far right is the Trinity M. E. Church. All of these buildings have been demolished.

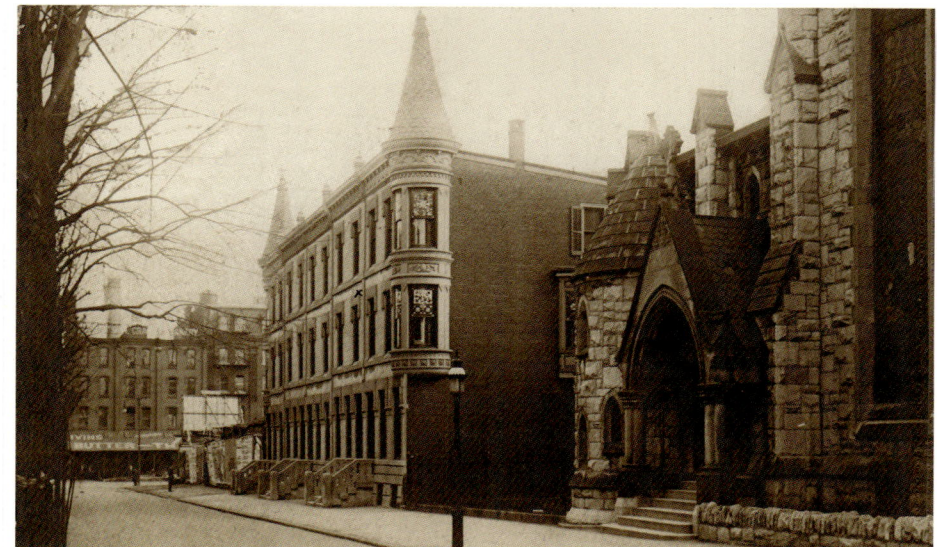

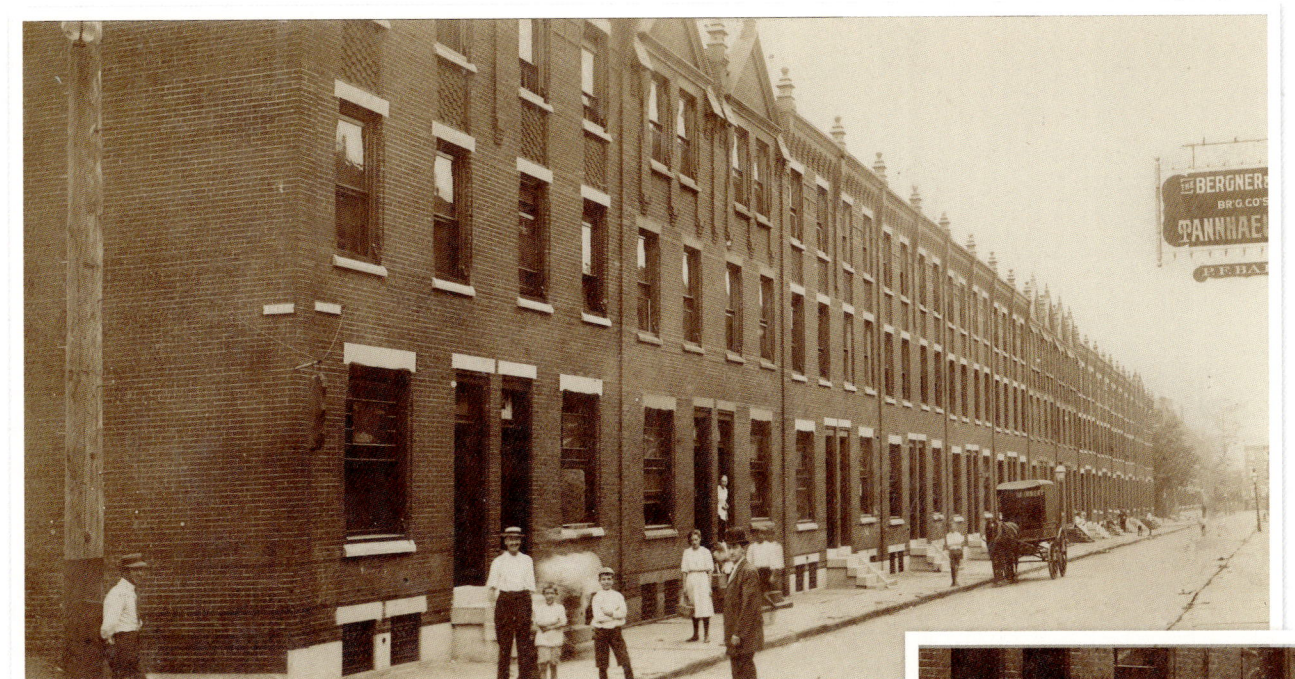

Nicholas Street east of Twenty-Fourth Street, ca. 1907. This
photo depicts a typical street in Brewerytown, with three-story late
Victorian row homes and a tavern sign advertising local brews.

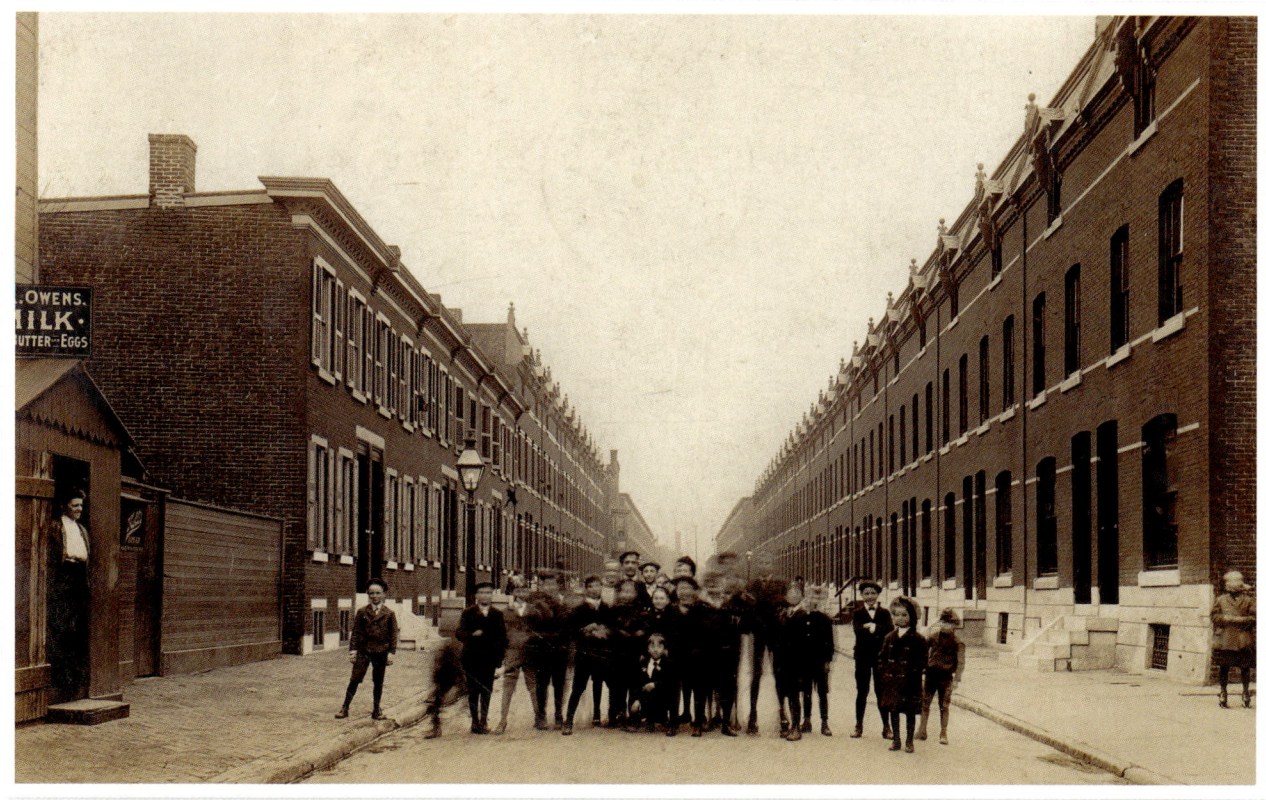

Turner Street east of Twenty-Sixth Street, 1907. Typical of row house construction in the latter part of the nineteenth century, narrow Turner Street is lined with brick-faced homes with marble steps and scarcely any trees in sight. Just visible on the horizon is the smokestack of the Pennsylvania Lawn Mower Works. In the middle of the street, a gang of young boys mug for the camera.

Twenty-Ninth Street north of Jefferson Street, ca. 1907. Albert C. Menger's Pharmacy in Brewerytown. Menger was a local purveyor of drugs, toilet articles, perfumes, ice cream sodas, soda water, cigars, and other assorted goods. A horse-drawn carriage and neighborhood children pose outside the entrance. This photograph is looking north along Twenty-Ninth Street. Prolific builder John Stafford built the east and west sides of Twenty-Ninth Street north of Jefferson in May 1895.

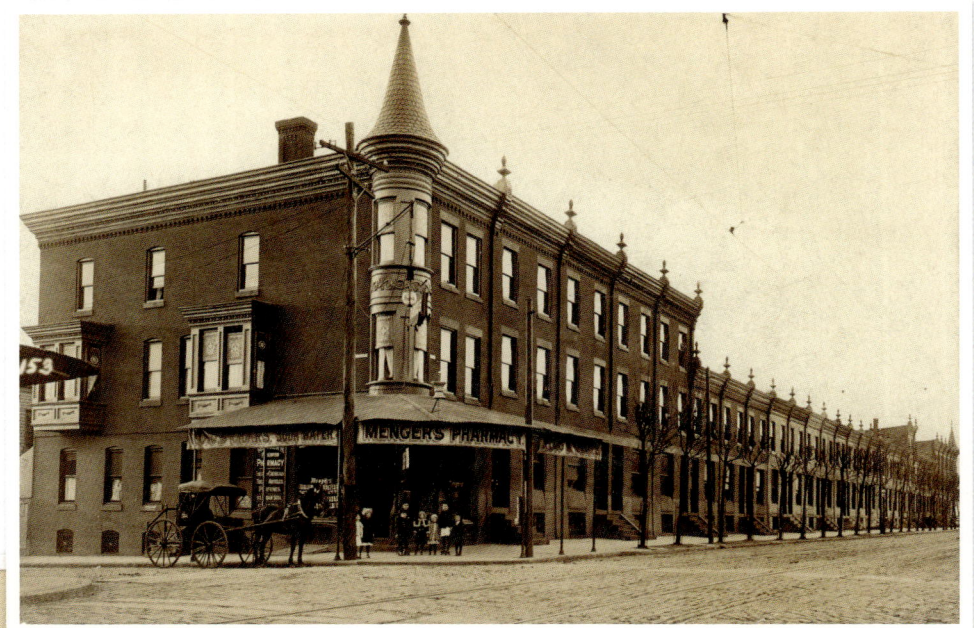

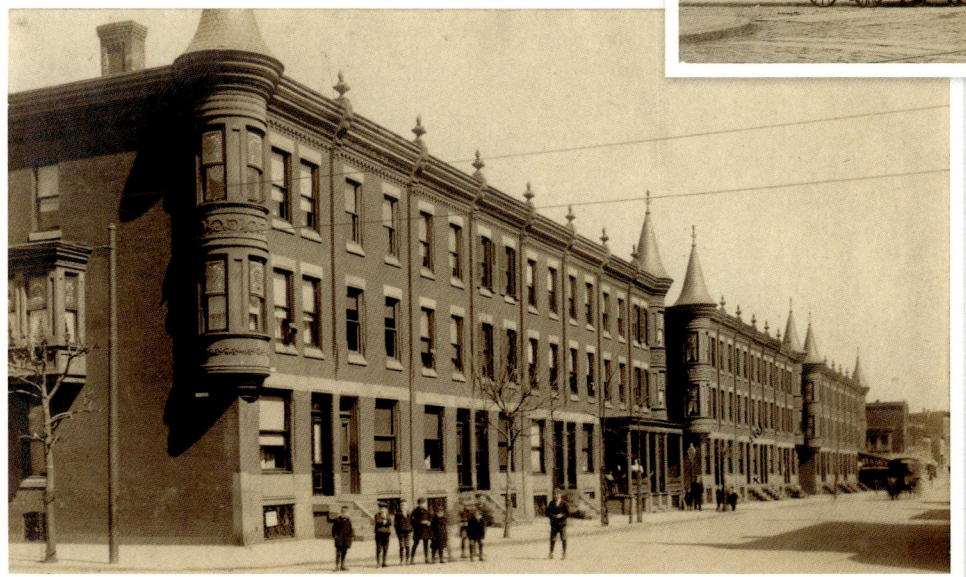

Oxford Street east of Twenty-Ninth Street, ca. 1910. Brewerytown in the days before Prohibition was quite the boomtown, with stylish new residences. The three-story row homes were built ca. September 1894 by John Stafford and are mostly still standing, although the conical roofs and finials are gone.

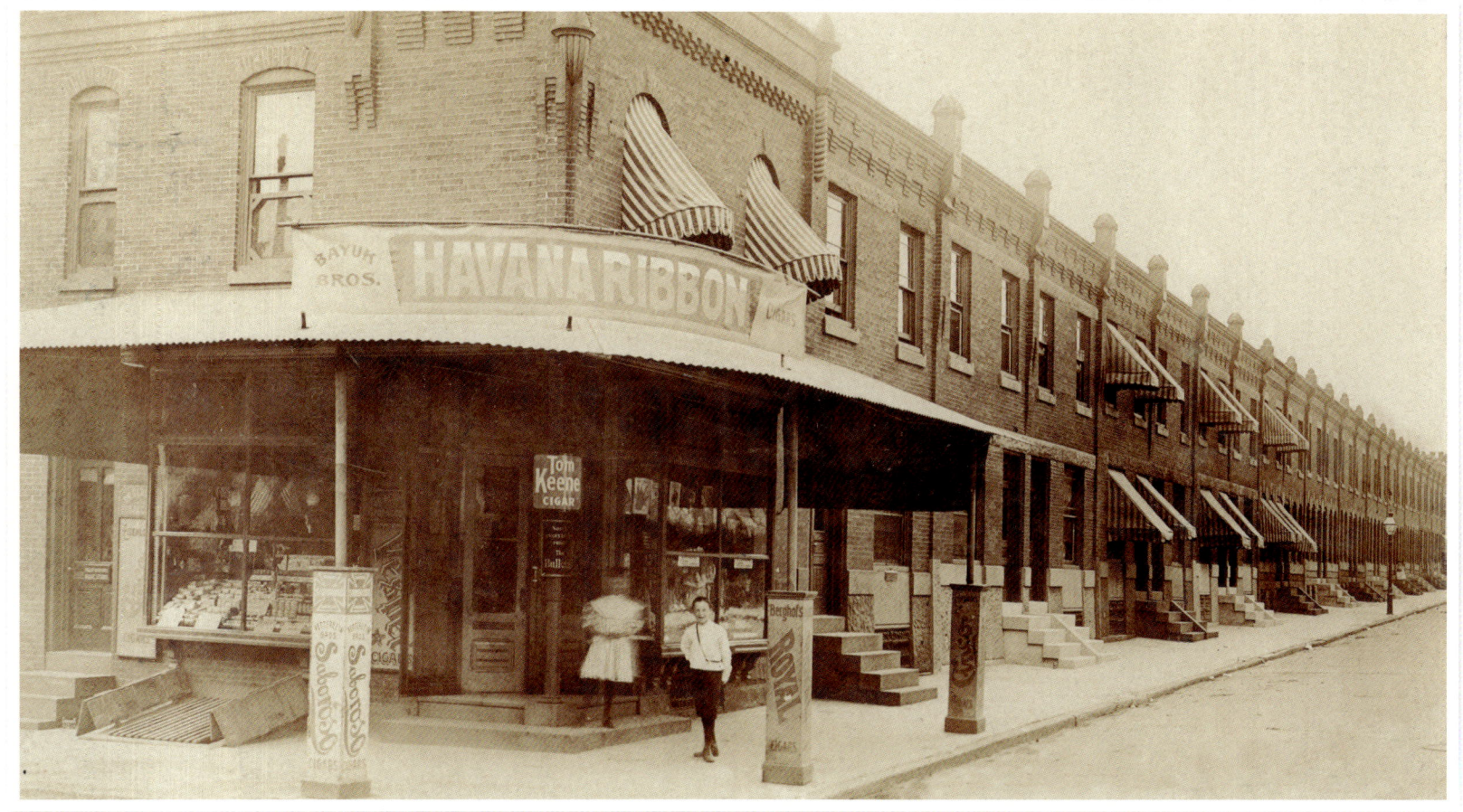

Woodstock Street south of York Street, 1908. Two-story brick row homes make up this block of 2300 North Woodstock Street. The Bayuk Brothers (Samuel, Meyer, and Max) operated this cigar shop at the corner of Woodstock and York Streets. Samuel lived at 3106 Berks Street in Brewerytown, while his brother Max lived in Atlantic City and Meyer Bayuk resided in Jenkintown. This store, and a few others owned by the Bayuks, sold a variety of popular cigars, including the Eisenlohr Cinco, the Vetterlein Brother's Saboroso, the Vesper, Berghof's Royal, the Tom Keene, and their own brand, the Havana Ribbon. The brothers not only distributed cigars but also manufactured them. A few years after this photo was taken, the Bayuk Brothers would enter cigar-making history with the introduction of the Philadelphia Hand Made Perfecto, later known as Phillies.

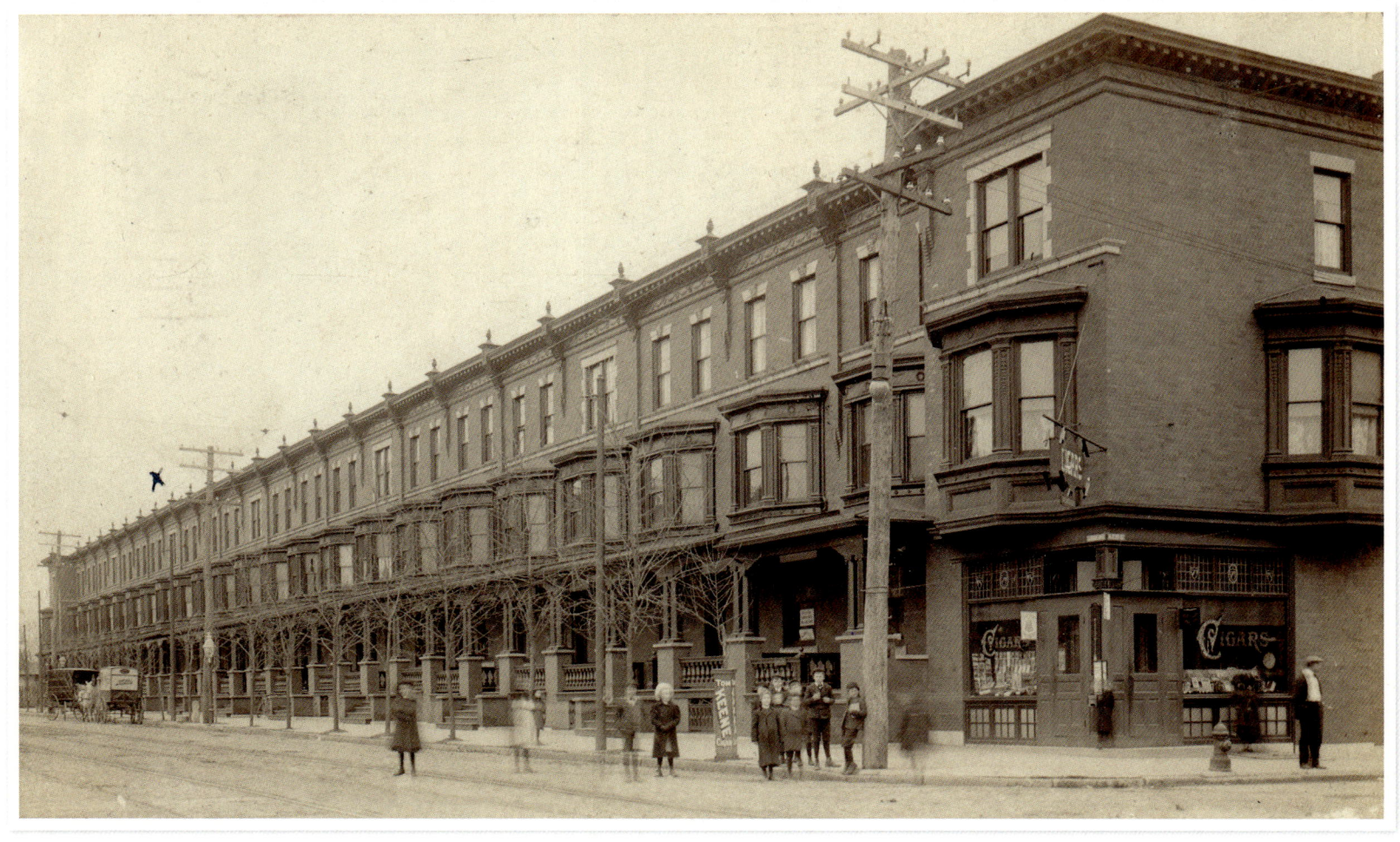

Lehigh Avenue east of Twenty-Third Street, 1908. A neat and uniform (if not monotonous) row of three-story dwellings line the 2200 block of Lehigh Avenue. Developers G. W. and J. M. Zane built these homes in spring 1903 for about $4,000 apiece, a costly sum during this period. This intersection was near the center of Swampoodle, once a mostly Irish neighborhood with a small Jewish section. Twenty-Second and Lehigh was the place where trolley routes 54 on Lehigh Avenue and 33 on Twenty-Second Street intersected. It was there in 1909 that Philadelphia Athletics manager Connie Mack (1862–1956) built the fabulous concrete-and-steel Shibe Park for his dominant ball club. Enterprising youngsters would stand outside the right-field wall during batting practice and collect balls that sailed out of the yard, selling them to "tourists" as home run balls.

Hagert Street east of Twenty-Sixth Street, ca. 1908.
The modest row houses in this photo postcard were built in July 1904 on the former site of the James E. Dingee brickyard. At the height of its operation, Dingee's brickyard employed 285 people and produced 125,000 bricks per day. Philadelphia's building boom was likely the cause for the yard's expansion in 1890, just sixteen years after it opened for business. Eventually he sold it to real estate developers. The young trees in the photo are a testament to the newness of this street.

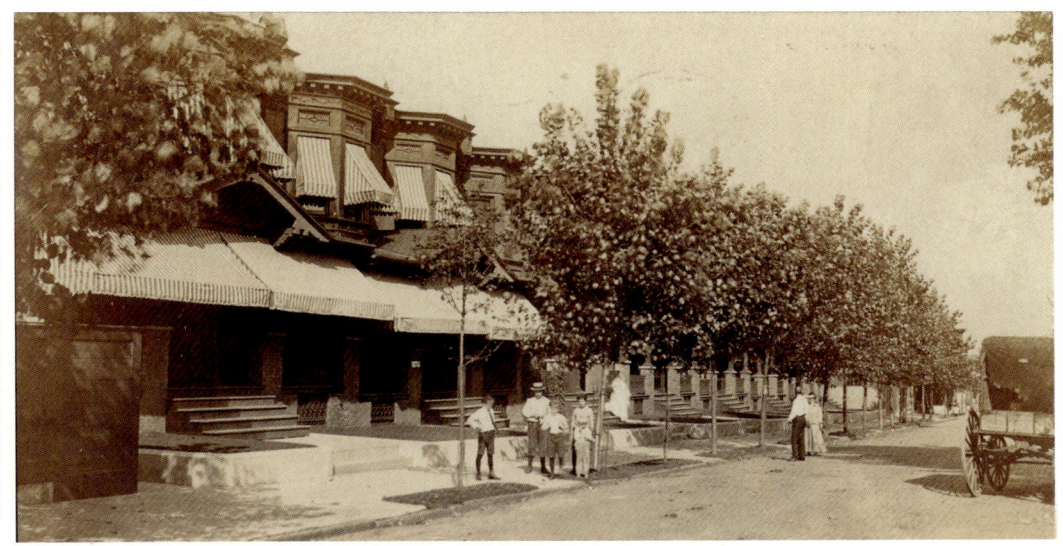

Thirty-Third Street south from Dauphin Street, 1906. Thirty-Third Street between Dauphin Street and Susquehanna Avenue is lined with extraordinary houses facing Fairmount Park. Builder and contractor John Stafford built fifty-seven homes in the area beginning in March 1906, all designed by architect Carl DeMoll.

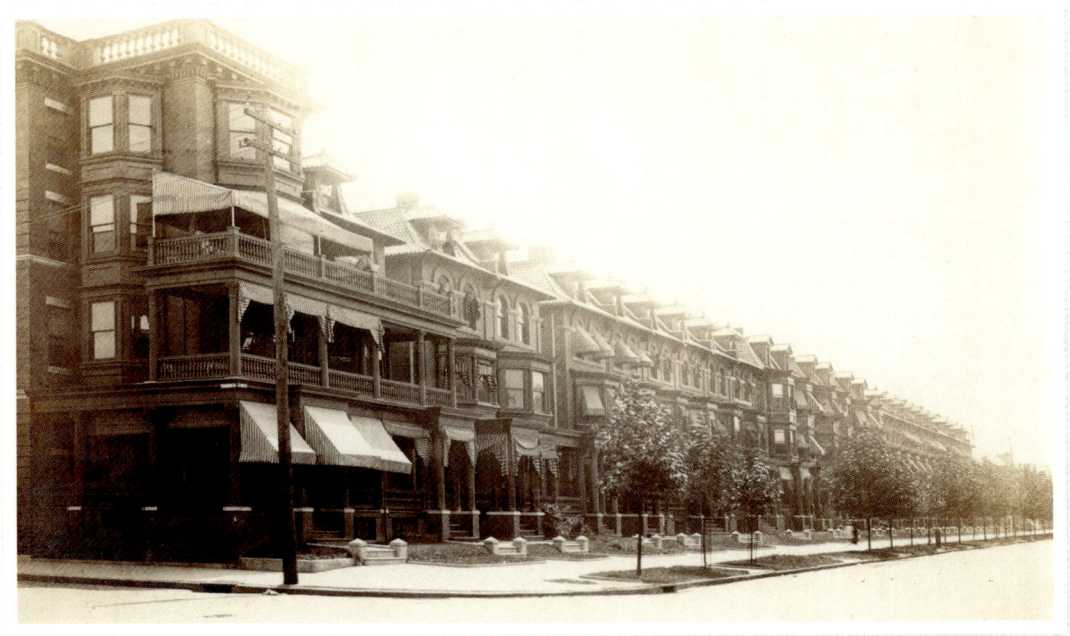

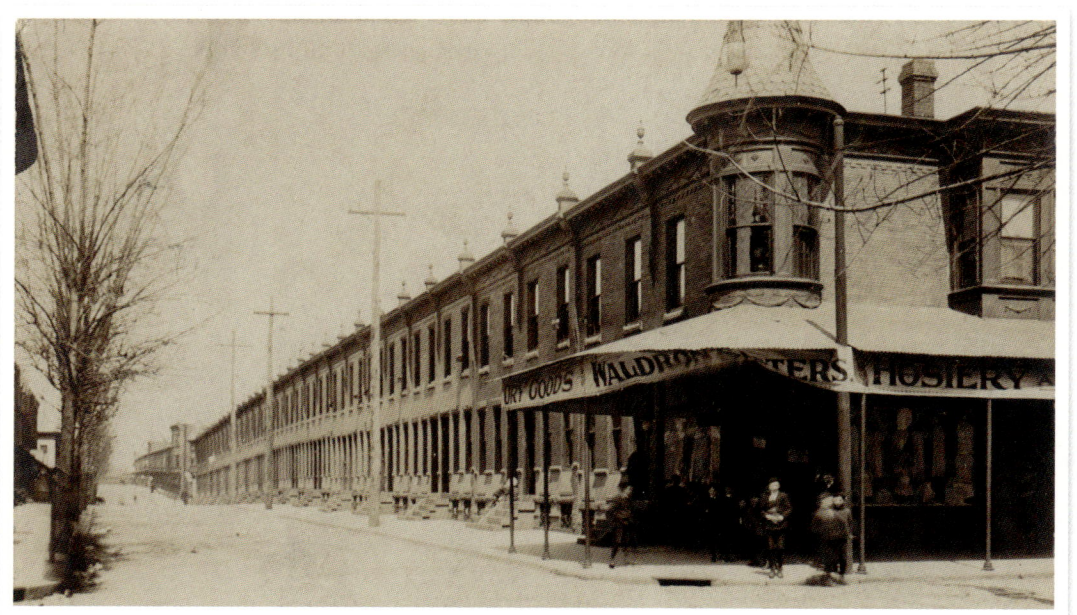

Thirtieth Street north from York Street, 1907. The Waldron sisters, Alice, Clara, and May, owned this dry-goods shop at the corner of Thirtieth and York Streets. It is an early example of a female-owned business and was a boon for residents of Strawberry Mansion who didn't have time to trek to Center City's big department stores. The corner store and the two-story row houses extending northward along Thirtieth Street were constructed in the spring of 1897.

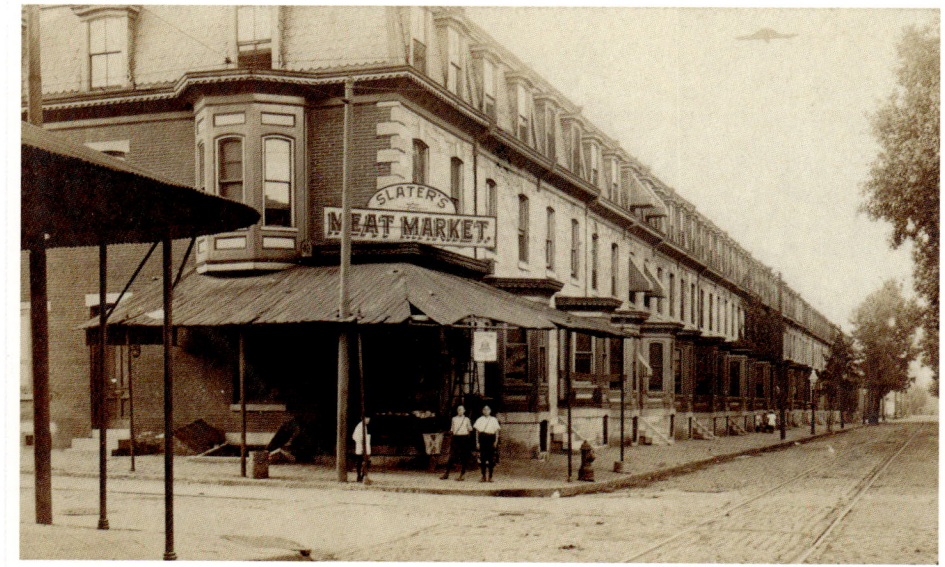

Eleventh Street north of Somerset Street, 1906. Row houses with stone facades were unusual in this part of Philadelphia. These two-and-one-half-story mansarded affairs were somewhat extravagant for their time, suggesting a more well-to-do neighborhood than most. The meat market and grocery store of Frank C. Slater occupied the corner of Eleventh and Somerset Streets.

Eighth Street south of Allegheny, 1910. Two compatible businesses face off on the corner of Eighth and Allegheny, a bar and a cigar store. John Hagan's bar sold C. Schmidt's & Sons pilsner and Puritan beer, as well as pure rye whiskies and gins "for family use." H. D. Fisher's Cigars & Tobacco sold all the popular brands of the day, such as Tom Keene, Vesper, Cinco, and Lipschultz's 44. In the distance on the left is the George H. Thomas Public School (1901). The row houses on the right were built in August 1898 and July 1901 by John Loughran.

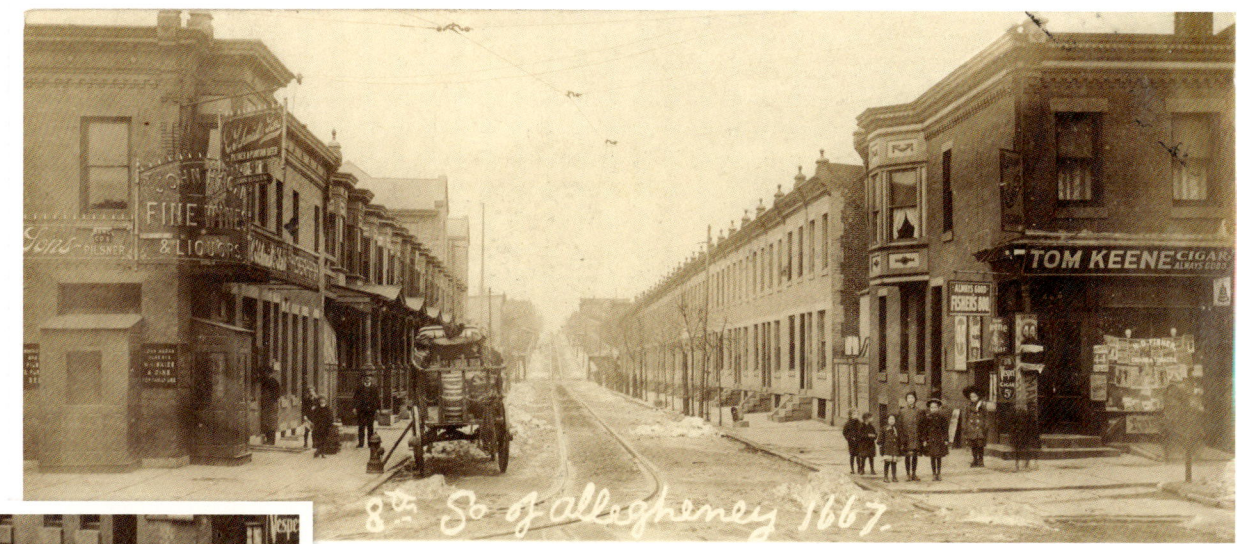

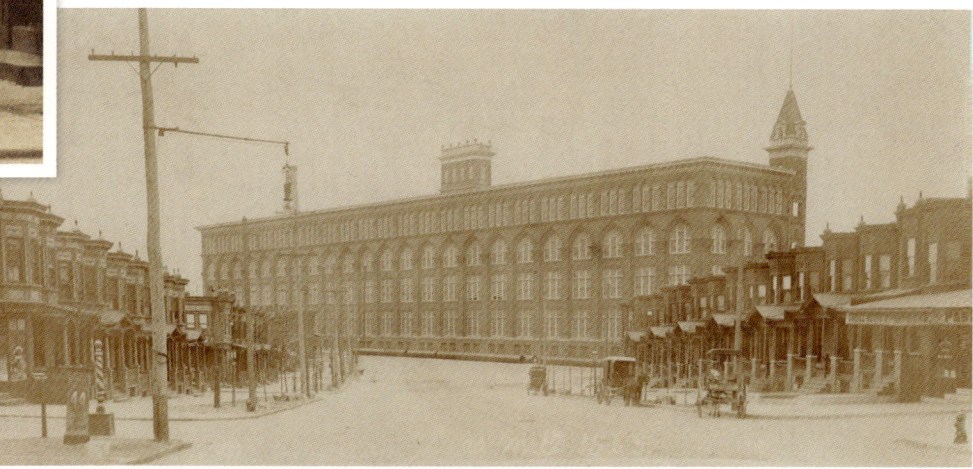

Ninth Street north from Clearfield, 1907. The immense mill of the North American Lace Company is seen here in all its glory at Glenwood and Allegheny. Completed in 1903, it was one of the many textile mills in North Philadelphia. The architecture firm William Steele & Sons built the gargantuan mill and numerous others. The houses on the west side of Ninth Street (*on left*) were built in May 1896, while the east side was built in February 1898. The firm of John Loughran, one of North Philadelphia's biggest developers, designed and built all the homes pictured here.

Fifth and Luzerne Streets, 1913. A gathering of local residents (and a fancy new automobile) pose on the corner of North Fifth and Luzerne Streets in what was then known as Franklinville in North Philadelphia. Today this is just inside the Hunting Park neighborhood. The three houses, built in January 1908 by John Schmunk, housed businesses as diverse as a saloon, an oyster café, and the dry-goods store of Mary A. Blaisdale.

The name "Franklinville" is hardly ever used these days. The Franklin Land Company laid out the former village in 1852 on the estate of Coleman Fisher. The center of Franklinville was near the intersection of present-day Fifth and Butler Streets.

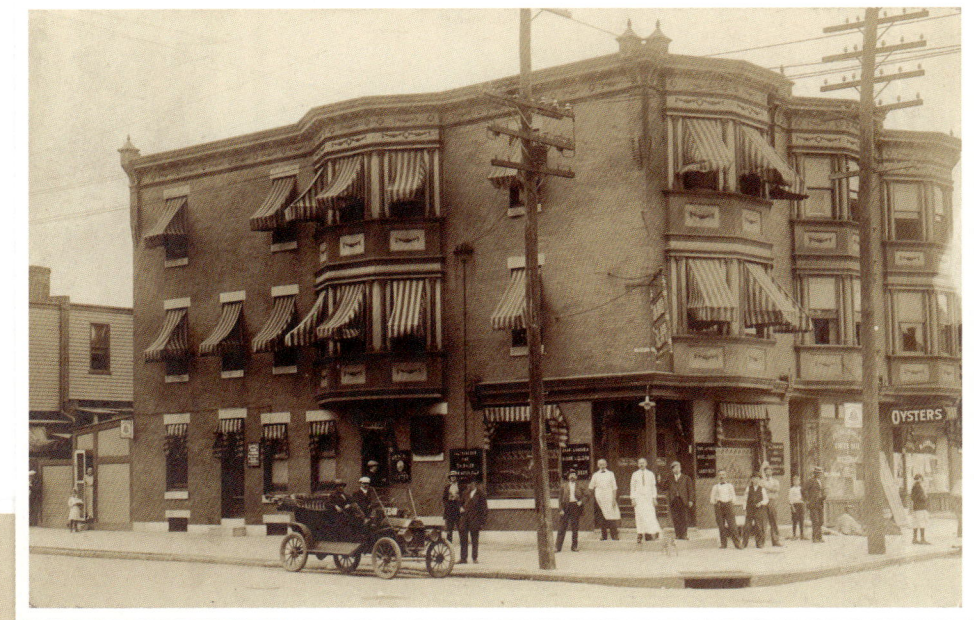

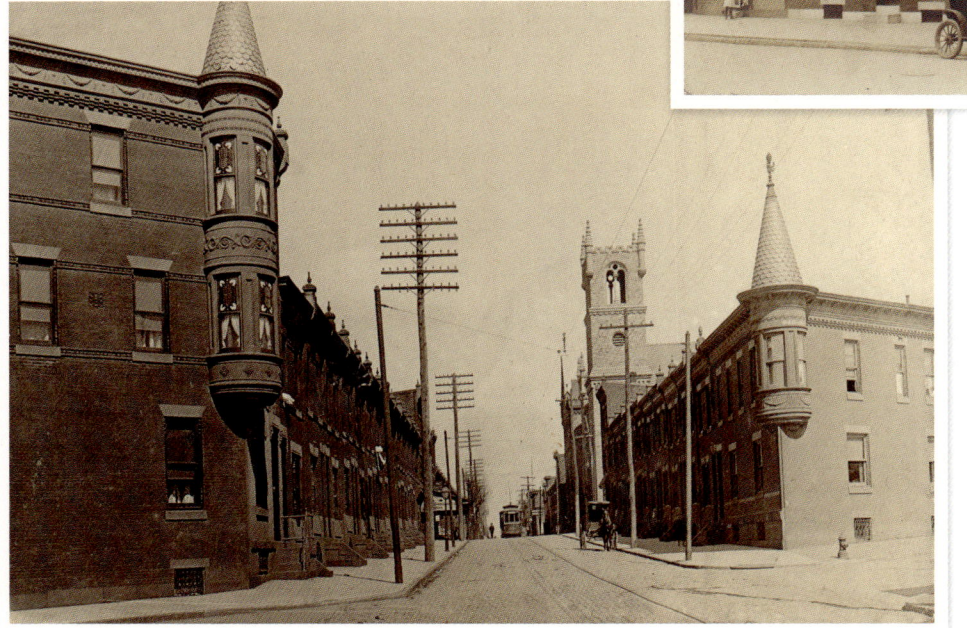

Sixth Street north of Sedgley Avenue, ca. 1908. In the 1890s, North Philadelphia was rapidly filling in with Victorian row homes, often with corner properties sporting "witch hat" roofs. Sixth Street at Sedgley Avenue contained two capped turrets at opposite corners. Houses on the west side of Sixth Street were built in March 1894 by J. B. Vanderslice. The homes on the east side of Sixth Street (*right*) were built in June 1893. The bell tower in the distance belongs to St. Monica (now St. Veronica) Roman Catholic Church at Sixth and Tioga Streets.

1620–1642 Erie Avenue, ca. 1906. Henry G. Schultz & Son built many houses in North Philadelphia, including these distinctive three-story houses and many more just like them on Erie Avenue. This row of houses was built in the spring of 1906.

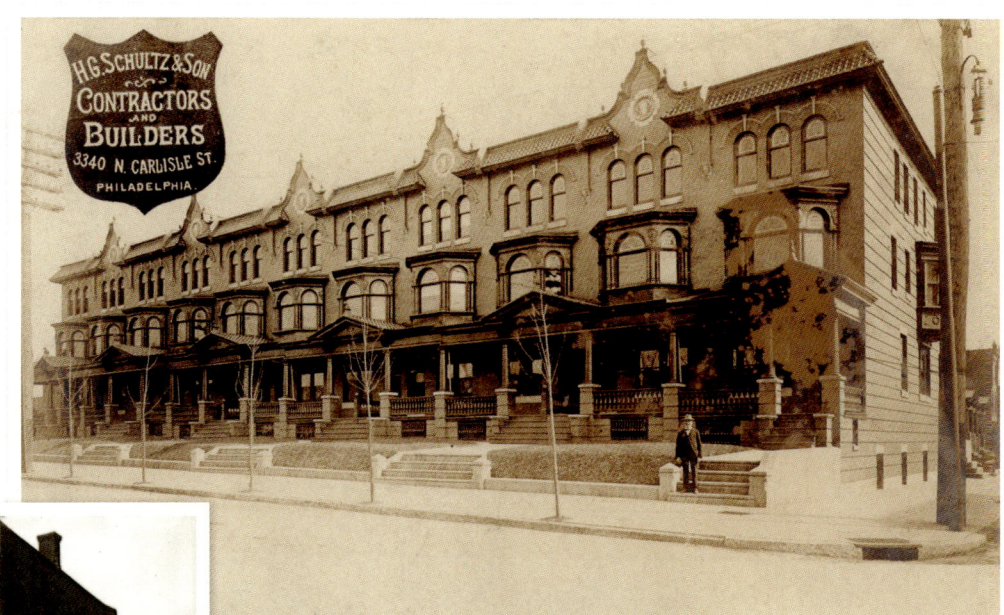

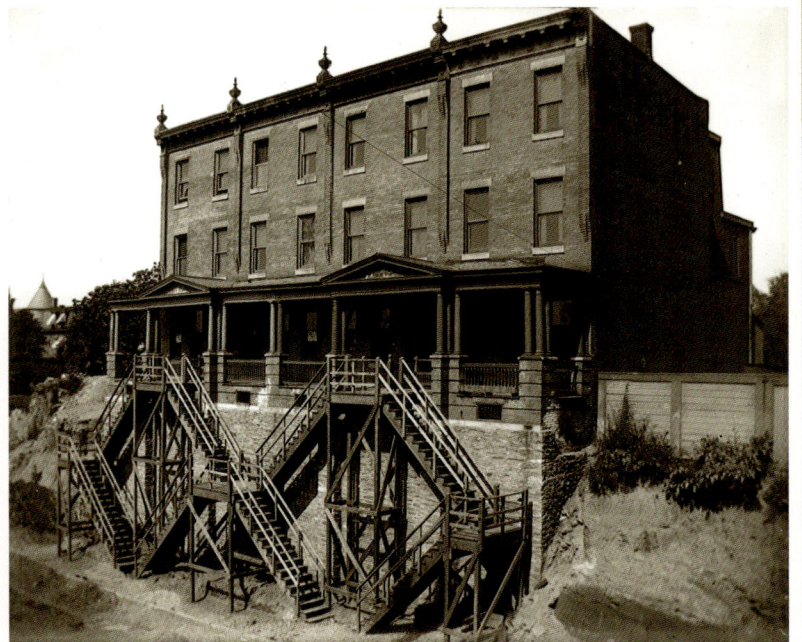

Twentieth and Ontario Streets, ca. 1900. This glass-plate negative depicts a large excavation project, a great inconvenience to residents of these four row houses.

Chapter 2.

UPPER NORTH PHILADELPHIA

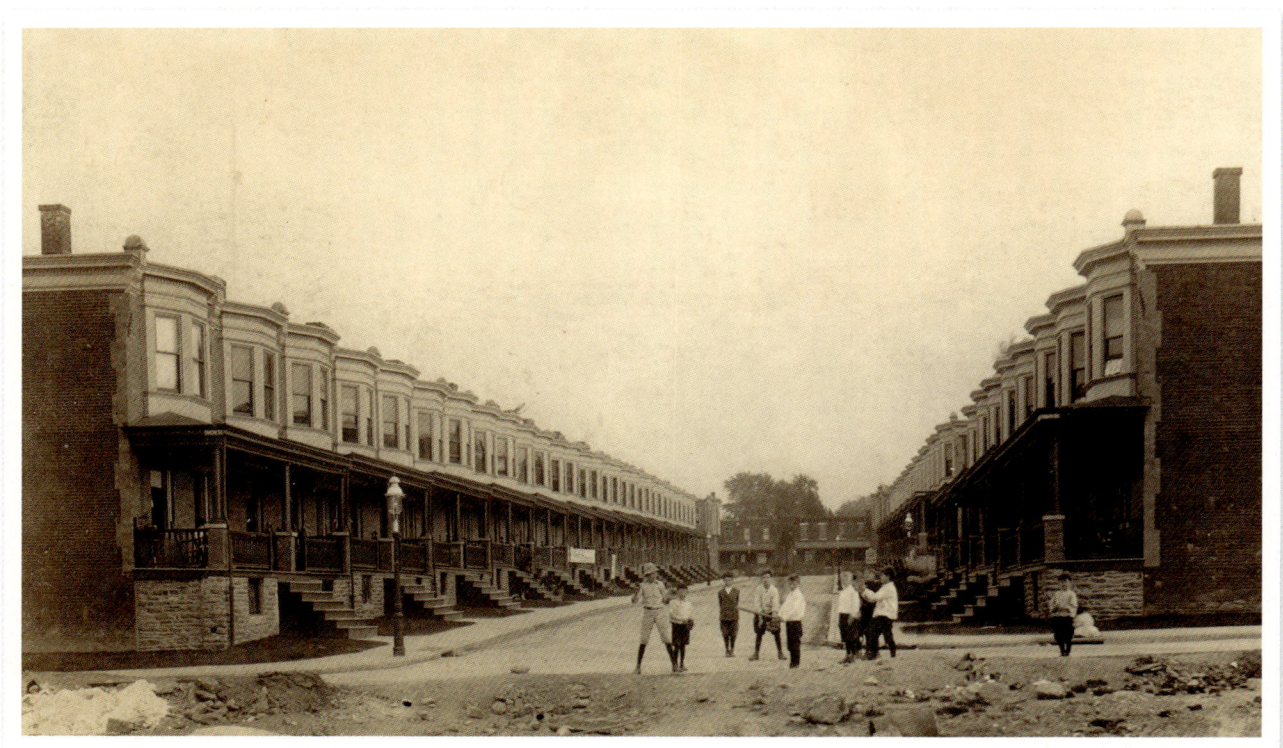

Beechwood Street south of Conlyn Street, ca. 1910

Upper North Philadelphia was sparsely populated at the dawn of the twentieth century, with only a handful of villages connected by unpaved roads. It was an ideal setting for suburban housing developments, and builders were eager to accommodate. Building conglomerates such as the Olney Mutual Land Association, the Fern Rock Land Association, and the Reading Terminal Land Association were busily putting up pretty suburban houses as quickly as demand warranted.[1]

Commuting by rail to Philly's green pastures was quite the romantic experience for the travelers in the 1890s. The urban core's characteristic red brick gradually gave way to irregular suburban lots and detached dwellings whose brick facades recalled the city buildings.[2]

By 1892, the suburbanites were commuting into the city on the Philadelphia and Reading Railroad Company's new suburban branch lines into Frankford, Olney, and Crescentville.[3]

Logan

The Logan neighborhood derives its name from James Logan (1674–1751), a prominent citizen who resided at a famous mansion known as Stenton. Still standing on 4601 North Eighteenth Street, Logan's stately brick home is approaching its third century of existence. But what was once a verdant country setting is now a dense urban neighborhood. After the turn of the twentieth century, the immediate region around Stenton Park looked like the other middle-class neighborhoods cropping up throughout North Philadelphia. Logan's Georgian mansion and its immediate environs were a shrinking, remnant patch of green, a reminder of long-ago days when this part of Philadelphia was a country retreat for the colonial aristocracy. Even the beautiful Wingohocking Creek was subjugated, walled in a tomb of concrete under the street level.[4]

The homes in Logan were finer than most, complete with second-story bay windows and ample front porches. Some of the more upscale residences were twin homes, also accompanied by bay windows and porches. The spaces between the semidetached houses were often little more than breezeways but gave the homes an added touch of class.

The new residents of Logan commuted to downtown Philadelphia by way of trolleys and the Philadelphia and Reading Railroad. Logan Station, near Broad and Lindley Streets; Fishers Station; and Wayne Junction all served the Logan neighborhood. Olney residents had their own station near Tabor Road.[5]

Another game-changer was the subway extension of the Broad Street Line. This allowed developers to expand the suburban dwellings farther north of the Center City business core. When completed in 1928, the Broad Street subway could deliver a worker from Olney Avenue to a downtown office in thirty minutes or less. In time, the northern extension of the Broad Street Line would reach up to Fern Rock.[6]

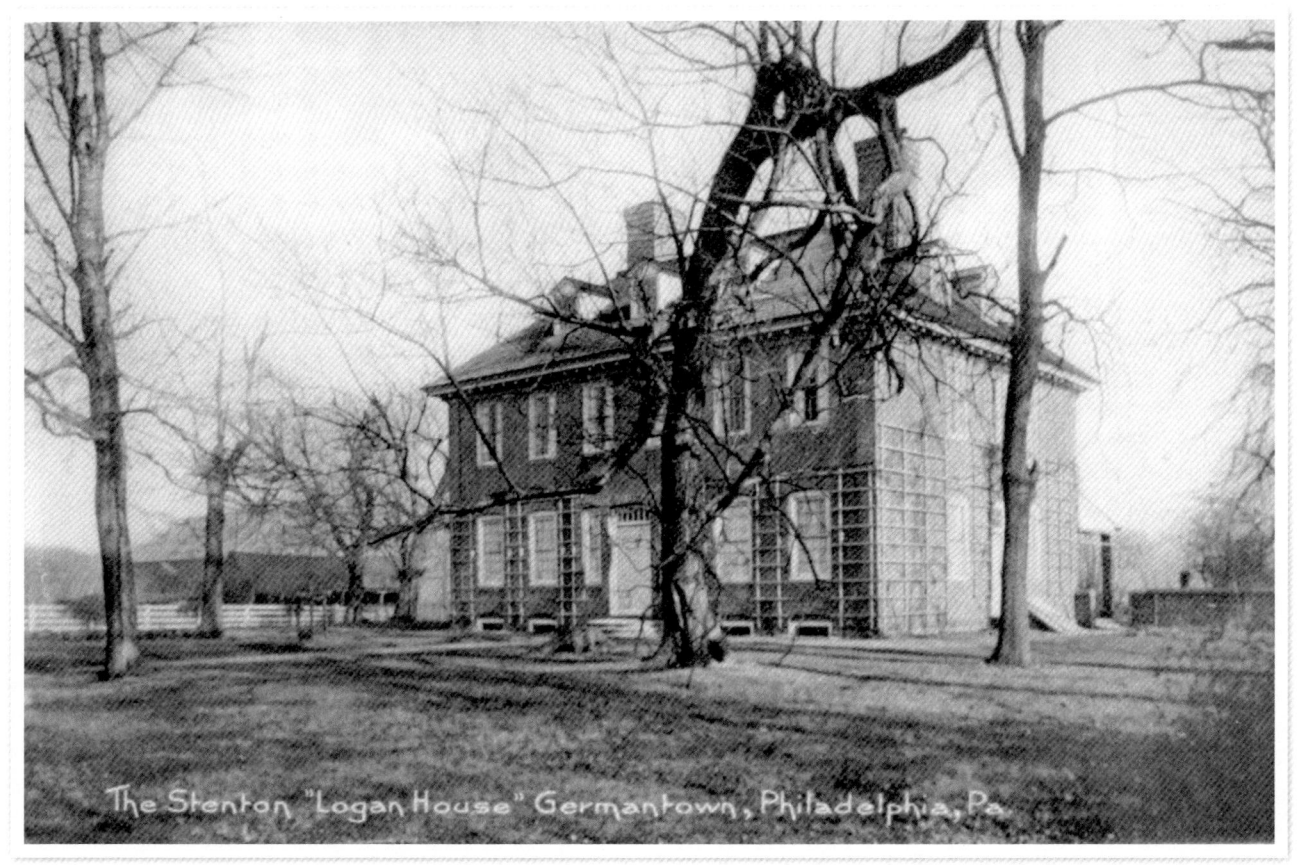

The Stenton "Logan House" Germantown, Philadelphia, Pa.

Stenton, Eighteenth and Courtland Streets, ca. 1900. The lovely country home of James Logan was completed around 1730. Seen here in an early-twentieth-century view, the part of North Philadelphia surrounding Stenton was still somewhat rural, a situation that would soon change.

Olney

Olney was named for the home of an Alexander Wilson, formerly located east of Old Second Street Pike and overlooking the Tacony Creek. Wilson's mansion stood for eighty-four years before being demolished in 1924. He settled on the name Olney because of his fondness for English poet William Cowper (1731–1800) from Olney, Buckinghamshire. The name "Olney" was attached to a tiny village centered near Old Second Street Pike (later renamed Rising Sun Avenue) and Tabor Road. The name later became associated with the area around the train station and then spread to the entire neighborhood, whose boundaries are Route 1 (Roosevelt Boulevard) on the south, the Tacony Creek on the east, Godfrey Avenue on the north, and the railroad right-of-way from Fifth Street to Eighth Street on the west.[7]

One of the big developers was the Olney Mutual Land Association, building hundreds of homes, mostly west of Mascher Street and north of Tabor Road, and transforming the rolling farmland into attractive suburban enclaves.[8]

Ogontz

Ogontz was named after the private estate of financier Jay Cooke, Esq. (1821–1905), which itself was named for a Lenape Indian chief. Ogontz was previously known as Shoemakertown Village for an early resident, George Shoemaker.[9]

The main thoroughfare, Ogontz Avenue, was created by subjugating the Wingohocking Creek into an underground sewer. The avenue roughly follows the course of the former surface stream.[10]

Oak Lane

Modern-day Oak Lane is divided into East Oak Lane and West Oak Lane, with Broad Street marking the line between the two. Before 1900, Oak Lane was a rural hamlet of greater Philadelphia, a far-flung village at its periphery. But even then, city folk were starting to take notice of Oak Lane's "pretty and comfortable cottages." Builders such as Thomas Henry Asbury (1838–1907), president of the Enterprising Manufacturing Company, is credited with building many beautiful homes there in the early 1890s.[11]

> Mr. Asbury found this section an uncultivated waste, and has so exercised his taste and judgment that all are gratified with the present condition of things. He has constructed many architectural cottages; and has studied the art of building in order to make them as convenient and comfortable as possible.[12]

Two commuter stations on the Philadelphia and Reading Railroad served Oak Lane residents: Lawnton Station just south of Sixty-Sixth Avenue and Old York Road, and Oak Lane Station just south of Cheltenham Avenue.[13]

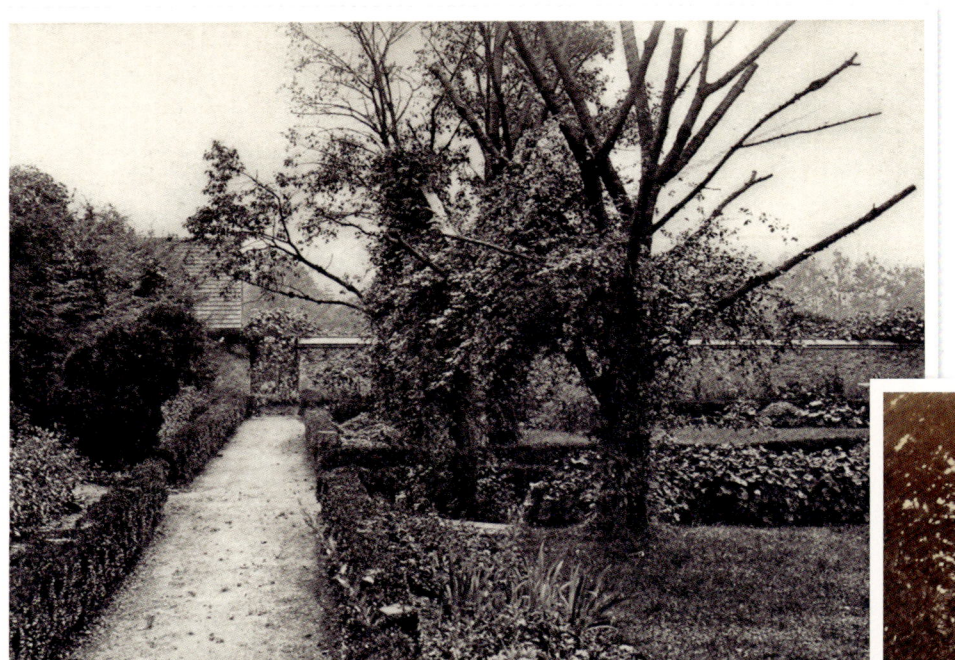

Butler Place, Branchtown, ca. 1906. Butler Place, once a magnificent home and grounds enclosed with a high stone wall, extended along Old York Road from Church Lane.

Townsend's Mill, near Church Lane and Wingohocking Street, ca. 1870. Robert Townsend's gristmill was believed to be the first such mill in Pennsylvania, built in 1683. The Wingohocking Creek provided the waterpower, seen here in a lovely cascading waterfall. A group of local youth are casually perched on the retaining wall of the millrace. When Robert Newell took this photo, the mill was way past its prime and was demolished in 1873. This part of Branchtown is now the Ogontz section of Philadelphia.

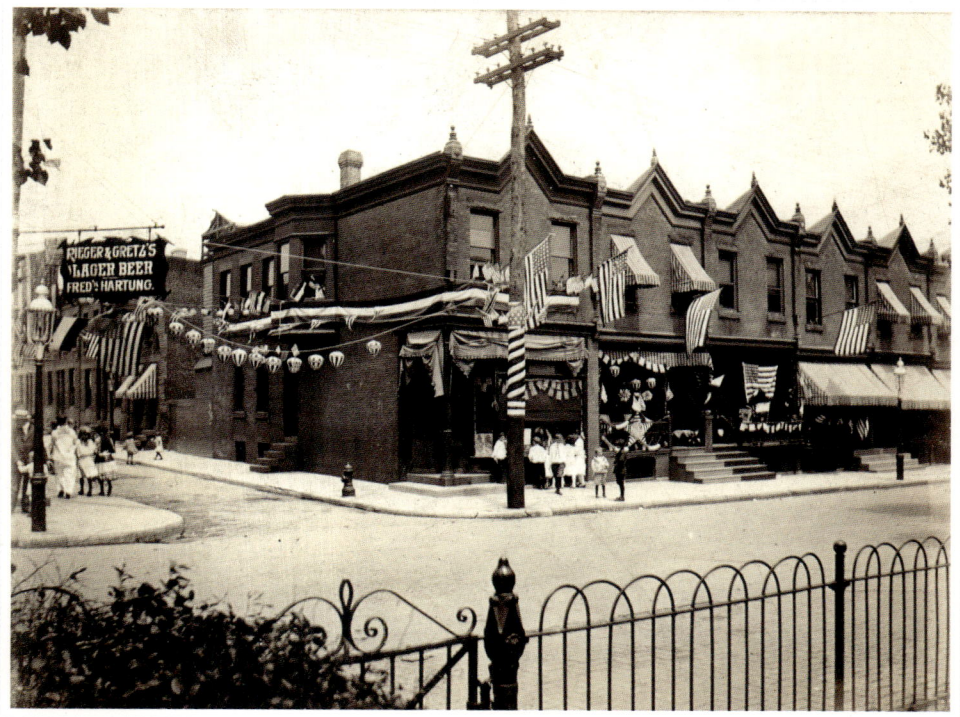

West Cayuga and Gratz Streets, ca. 1910. The patriotic display of flags and bunting is likely for a Fourth of July celebration. On the far left is a sign for the drinking establishment of Frederick K. Hartung, who lived at 1831 Cayuga Street. The houses shown here were built in 1897.

Branchtown

Branchtown, once a village of some note, was located on the Old York Road where it crossed over the west side of Broad Street. The center of the village was the Branchtown Hotel, built in 1790 by Joseph Spencer. This famous inn was also known as the Drovers Hotel and was one of many inns along the heavily traveled road. Another landmark was the home of Mr. Spencer, a colonial-era building renamed Silver Pine Farms when it came into the DeBenneville family. The son of Dr. George DeBenneville named it for a group of nine white pines that rose to a height of 80 to 100 feet, and whose highly visible limbs gave the town its name.[14]

West of Old York Road, near Church Lane, stood the magnificent Butler Place. Frenchman Fredric Boulanger built the mansion in 1791. Pierce Butler (1744–1822) purchased the house in 1810, and its vast grounds extending out to Thorpes Lane (now Olney Avenue) in 1812. Butler Place was demolished in 1924 after being sold to the Fern Rock Building Association. The Ogontz Manor Apartments (three towers in all) were built on the Butler Place grounds in 1940, as well as Kemble Park, named for Pierce Butler Jr.'s wife, the famous actress "Fanny" Kemble (1809–1893).[15]

The village of Branchtown has largely passed from memory, as "progress" in the twentieth century eradicated all traces of it. However, as late as the 1950s, there was a police station at the crossroads of Old York Road and Church Lane known as the Branchtown Station.[16]

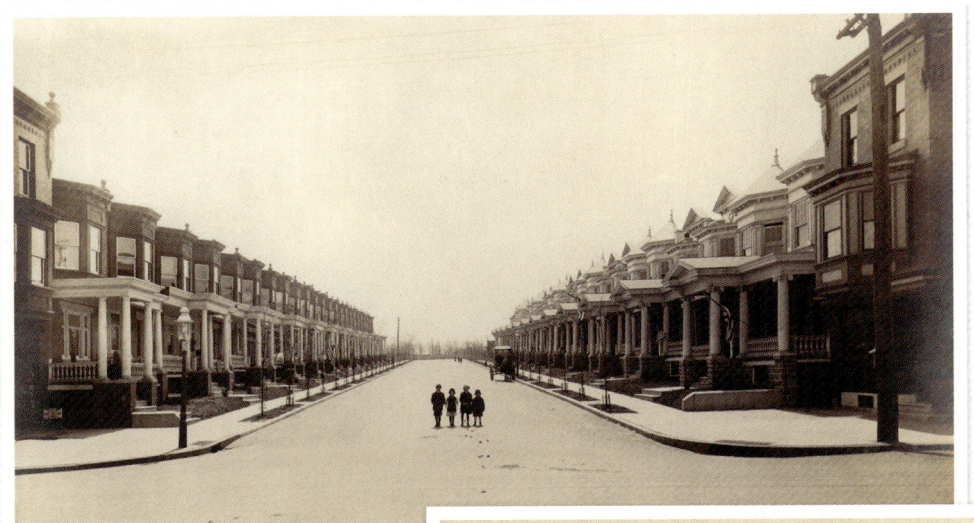

Thirteenth Street south of Courtland Street, ca. 1915. Four children stand smack dab in the middle of the 4500 block of North Thirteenth Street. The row houses on the left were built in 1914, while the houses on the opposite side of the street were built in 1915. All have lovely front porches supported by wooden Tuscan and Ionic columns. The trees and hill on the horizon are part of Hunting Park.

Old York Road north of Courtland Street, ca. 1911. Not all of the row homes built in Logan were of the cookie-cutter variety. Some were real standouts, such as these Tudor Revival homes in the Gables development on the Joanna Wharton Lippincott estate. Harold C. Irvin developed and built these elegant houses, which were completed in June 1911 and cost $6,000 to build, far more than a row house. The old Wingohocking Creek once flowed just south of this intersection.

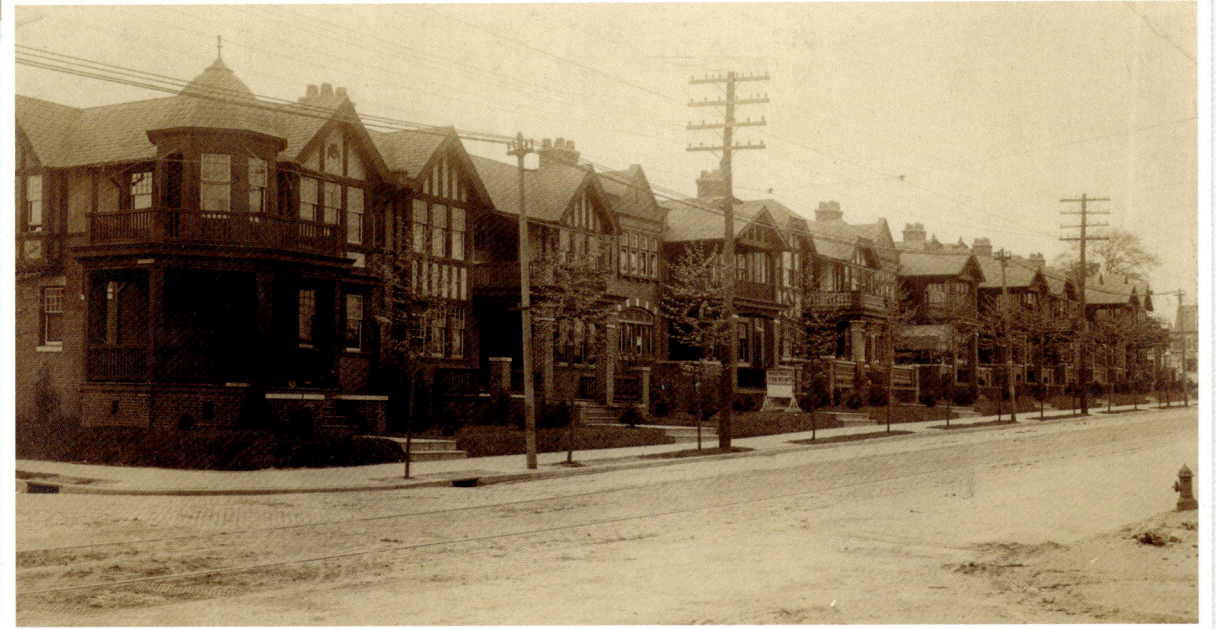

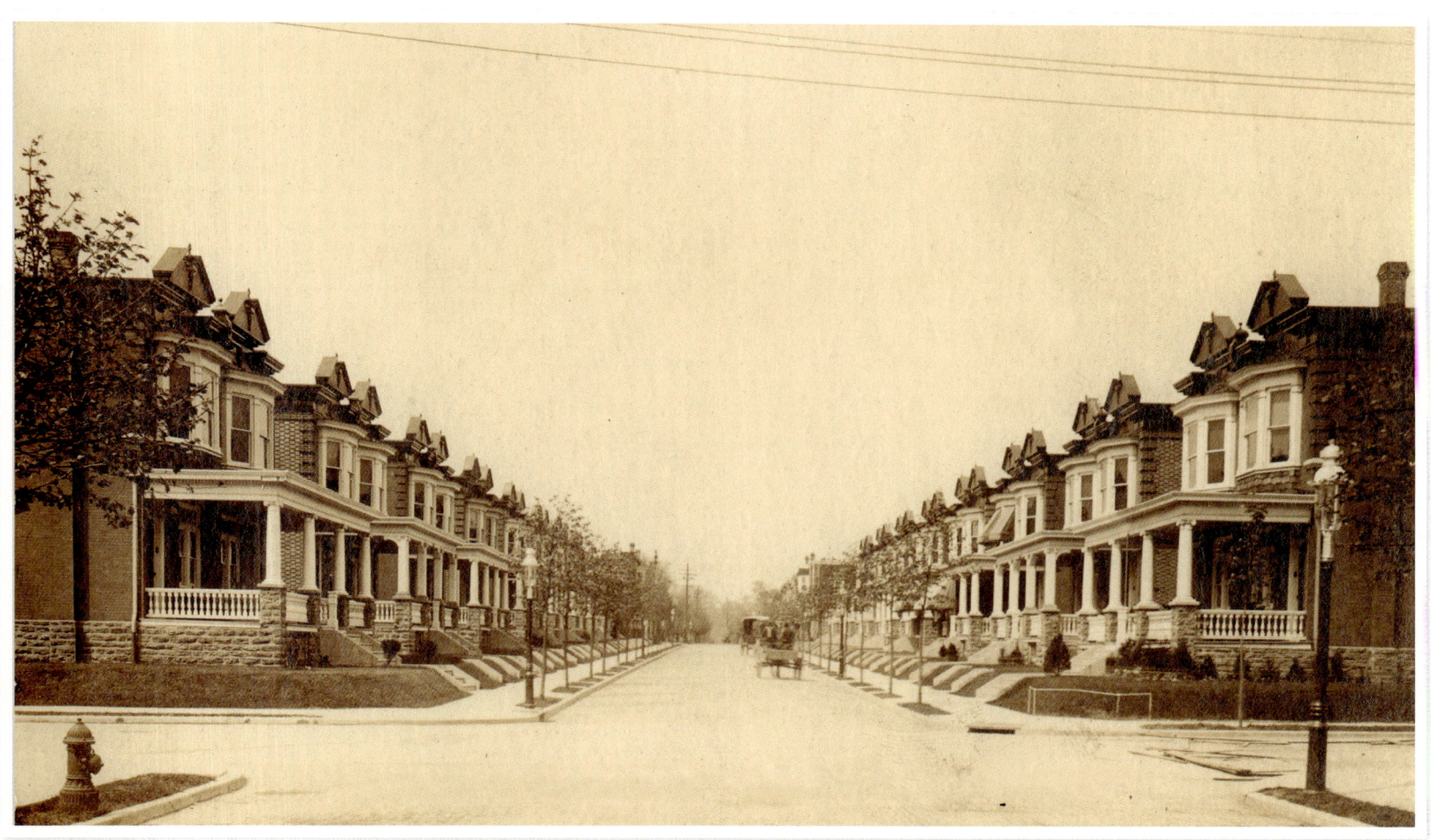

Eleventh Street north of Ruscomb Street, 1911. Tidy twin houses occupy a block of Eleventh Street in Logan. These homes were apparently built for buyers who were moderately well off. The most prominent feature, typical of the era, is the large colonial revival–style crest. Columned porches and manicured front lawns complete the semisuburban setting. A. B. & C. F. Millett Construction began work on these homes in late November 1910. The remaining twenty-four houses were built in March 1911.

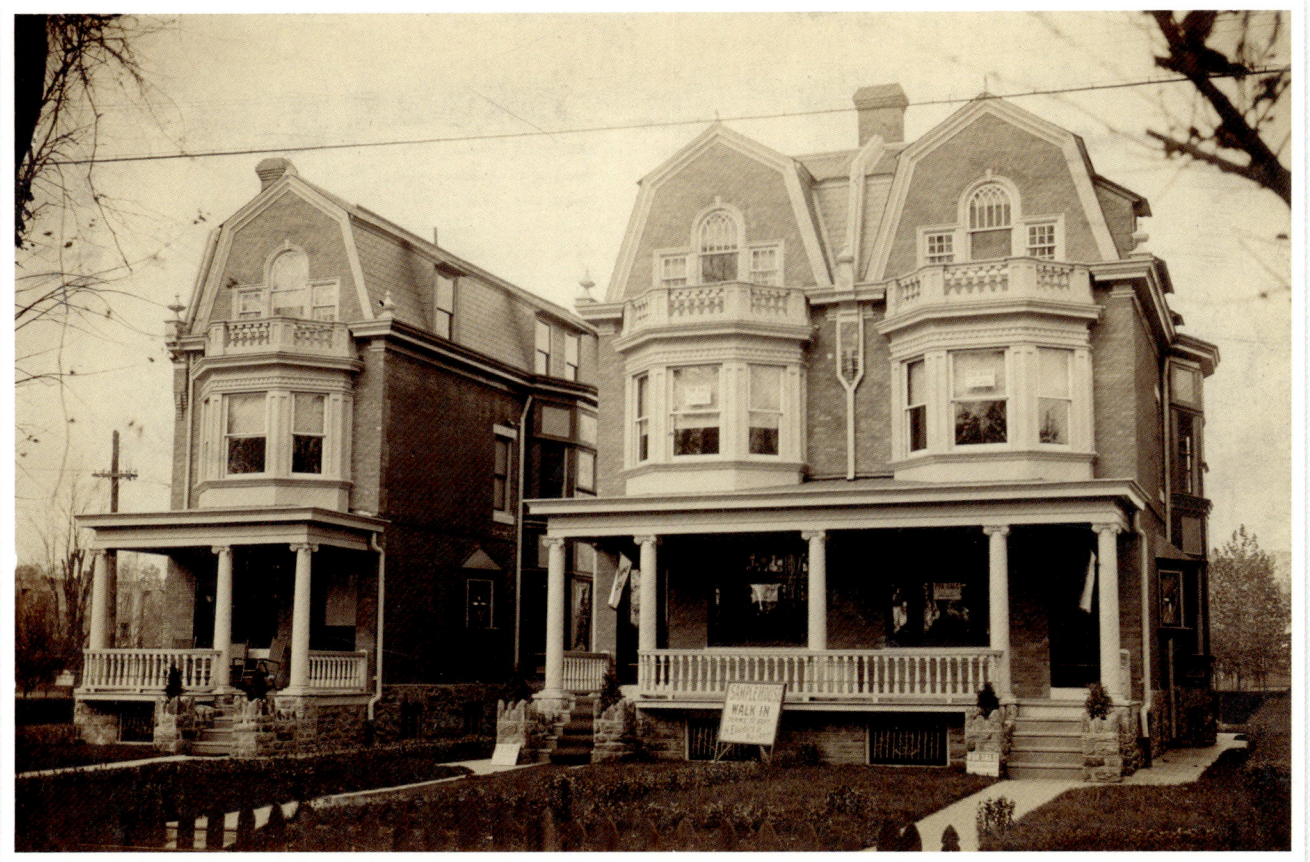

1223–1227 Fishers Lane (Lindley Street), 1916. Large colonial revival twins occupy the 1200 block of Lindley Street, formerly Fishers Lane. Built in March 1910 and January 1911, the houses were designed by architect Charles S. Parker and built by Harry Ellenberg Jr. Oddly, the house on the left (1227 Lindley) has been demolished, while its twin, which hadn't been built yet when this photo was taken, is still standing.

Beechwood Street south of Conlyn Street, ca. 1910.

Neighborhood children, some with baseball equipment, pose on the corner of Conlyn and Beechwood Streets. Conlyn Street is in a rough, unpaved state in this photograph. Both sides of Beechwood Street are lined with small, neat row homes with front porches and bay windows, making them more desirable than many built at the time.

On August 18, 1909, Robert Killough Construction began work on the houses on the east and west sides of the 5700 block of North Beechwood Street.

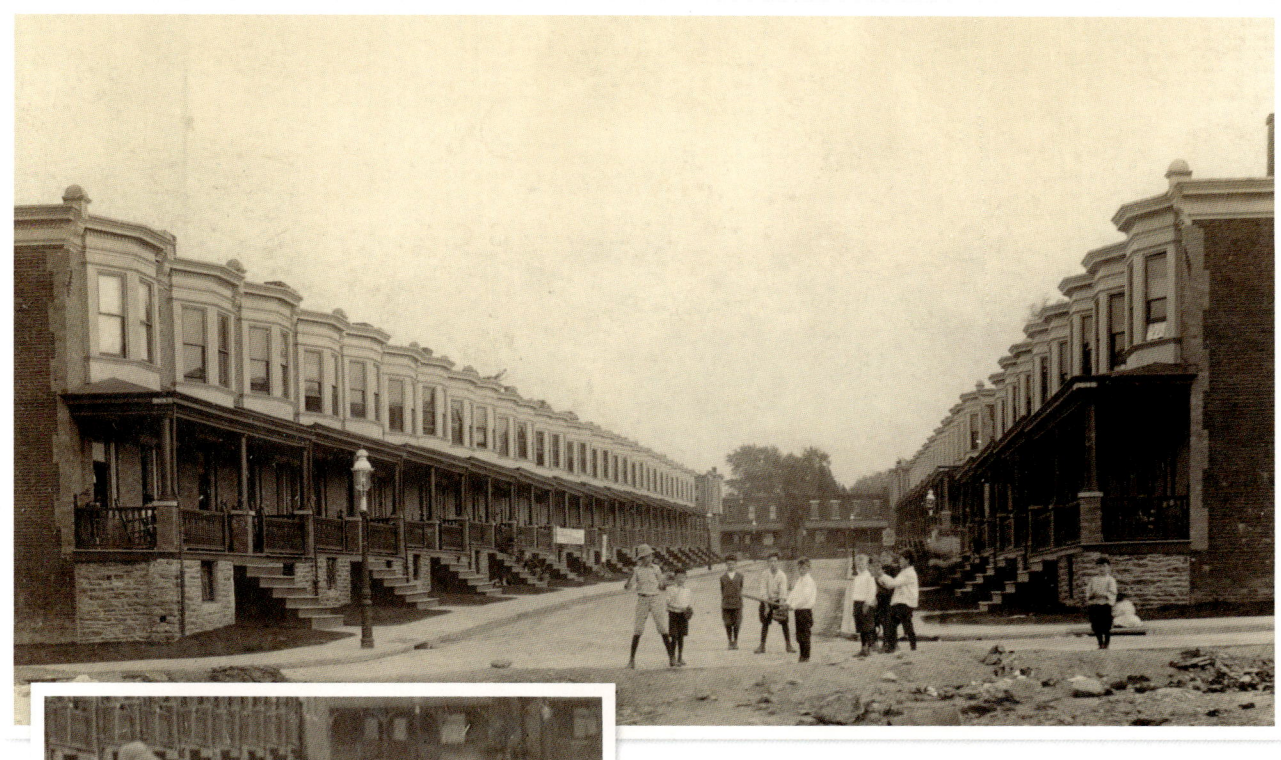

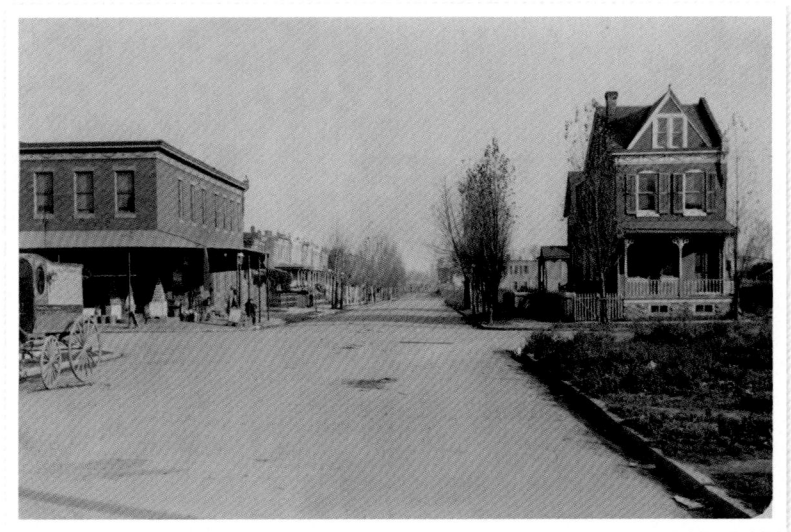

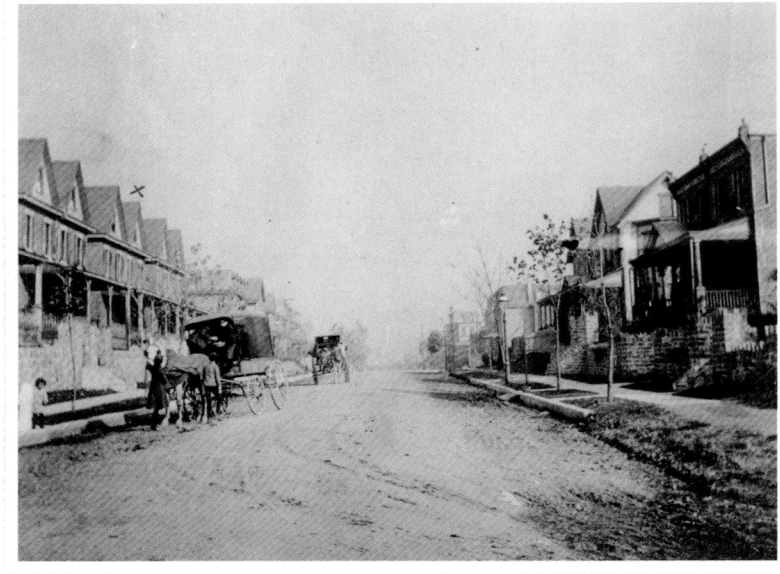

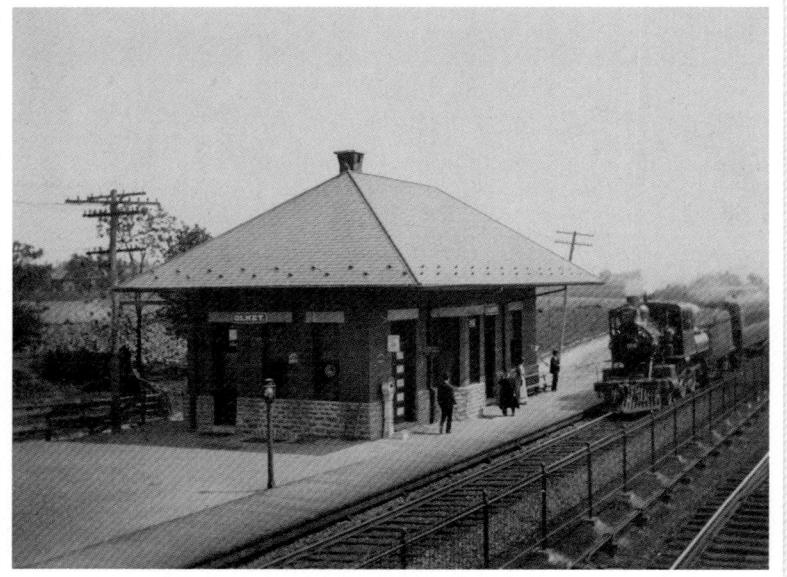

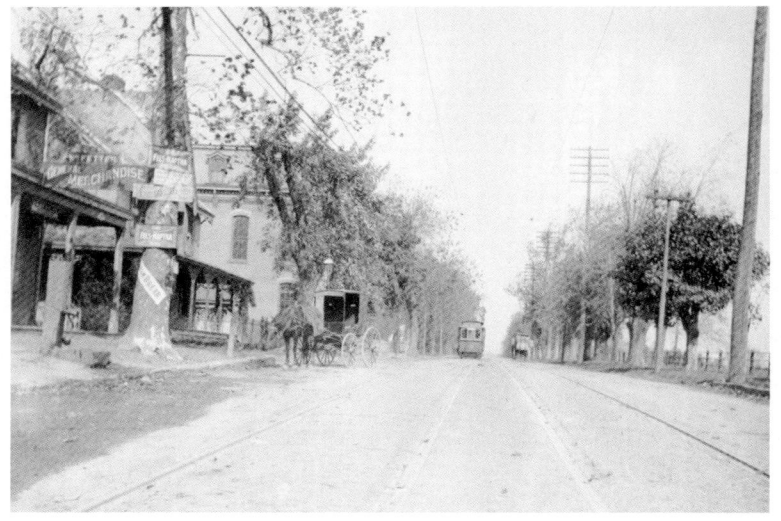

Clockwise from top left: Louden Street east from Second Street Pike (Rising Sun Avenue), 1906.
The Feltonville section of Philadelphia was still mostly rural, looking more like a frontier village than part of the city. Feltonville was founded in 1815 by John Felton (1788–1865), assemblyman, sheriff, and hero of the War of 1812. The village was centered on Second Street Pike and Fishers Lane. The single house on the right was designed and built in April 1900 by Harry Fatz, whose occupation was given as carpenter. The houses and corner store on the left were built in August 1899 and are still standing, as is the Fatz house.

Front Street north of Wellens Street, ca. 1906.
The Olney section of the city was mostly unpaved in this period. The view is of Front Street looking north from Wellens Street, named for Jules Wellens, lace manufacturer and landowner.

Second Street Pike (Rising Sun Avenue) north of Tabor Road, 1911. The general store of William Fetter was on the west side of Second Street Pike, north of Tabor Road (5310 Second Street Pike). Fetter's store supplied necessities including Fels-Naptha, a popular laundry soap first manufactured in Philadelphia in 1893. The estate of William Burk was on the east side of Second Street Pike.

Olney Station, near Tabor Road and Mascher Street, ca. 1910. A key to Olney's growth was the availability of reliable passenger railways. The Olney Station, near Mascher Street and Tabor Road, fit the bill nicely.

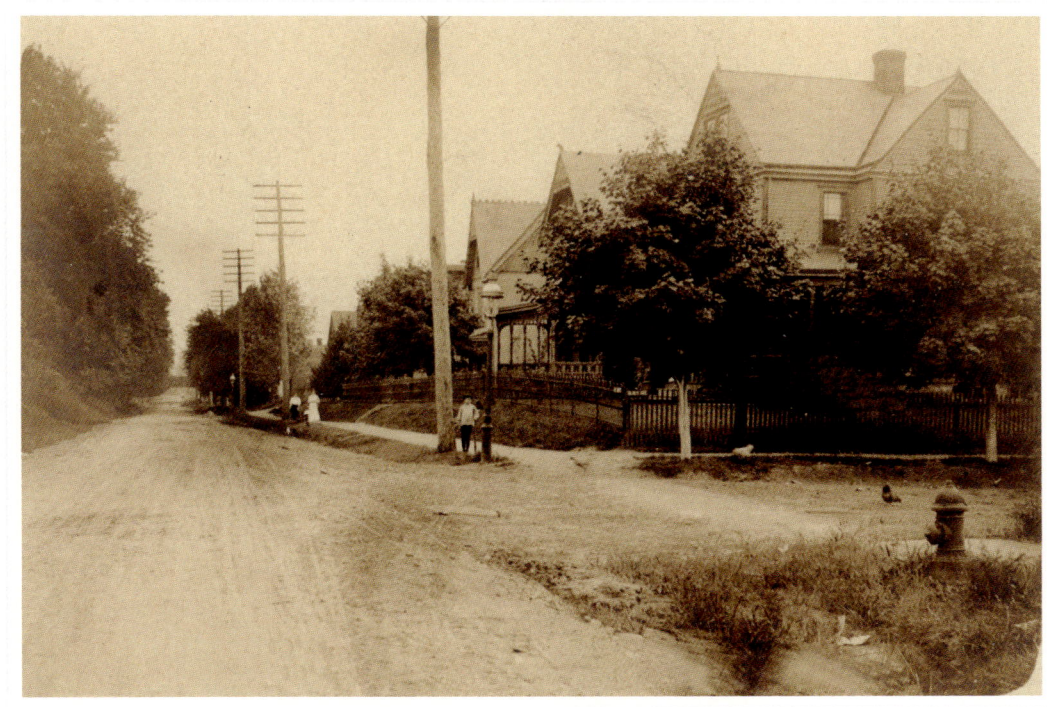

Clinton (Mascher) Street south of Olney Avenue, ca. 1910. Clinton Street, later renamed Mascher Street, was unpaved and rural in this part of Olney. The three houses on the right were built in 1889. The overgrown lot on the opposite side of Clinton Street belonged to Jonah Wentz, for whom Wentz Street is named.

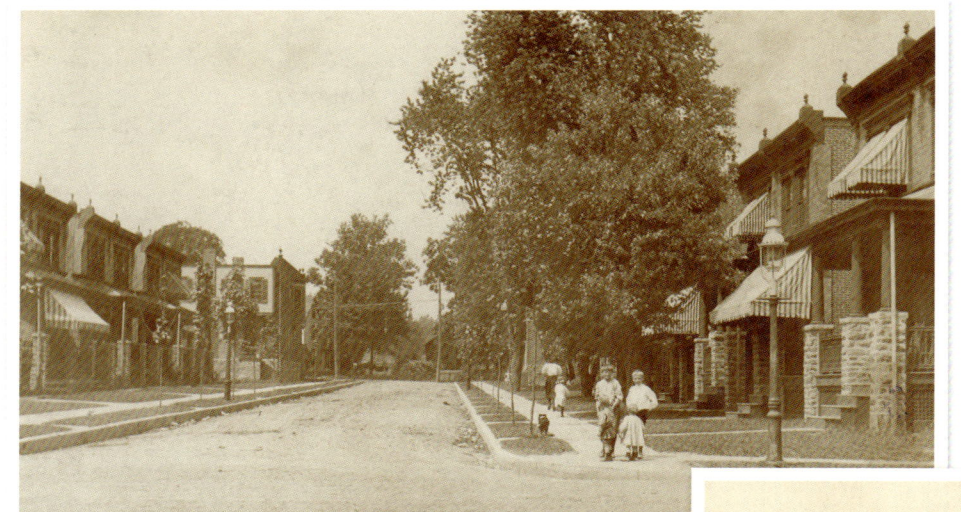

Fourth Street north of Somerville, 1909. These twin homes were built in June 1906 by Jonathan P. Nyce, a builder and developer who worked exclusively in the Olney and Oak Lane sections of Philadelphia.

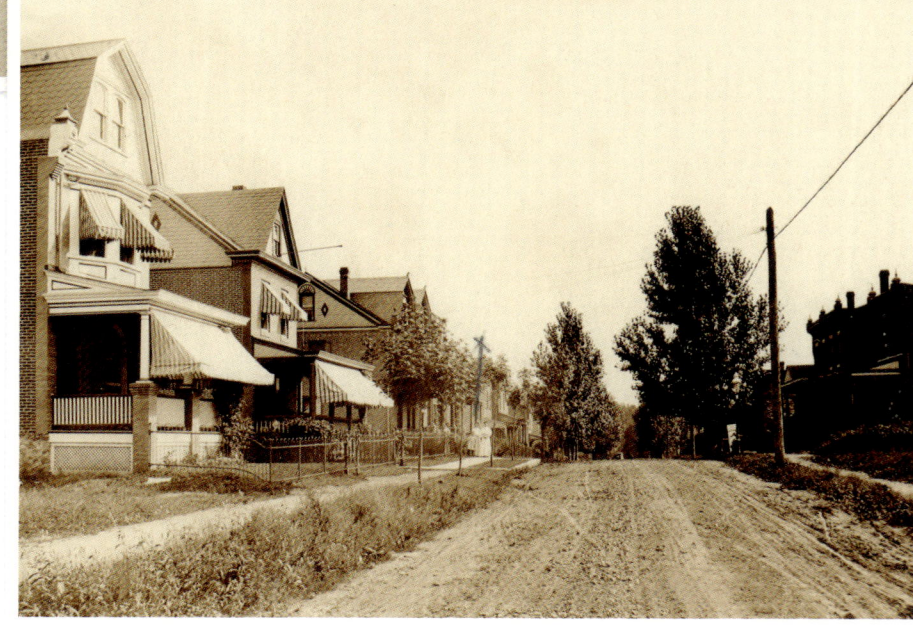

Third Street south of Olney Avenue, 1908. This unpaved street of attractive single and twin houses was built on land owned by the Olney Mutual Land Association.

Third Street south of Olney Avenue, 1908. The opposite side of Third Street is pictured here.

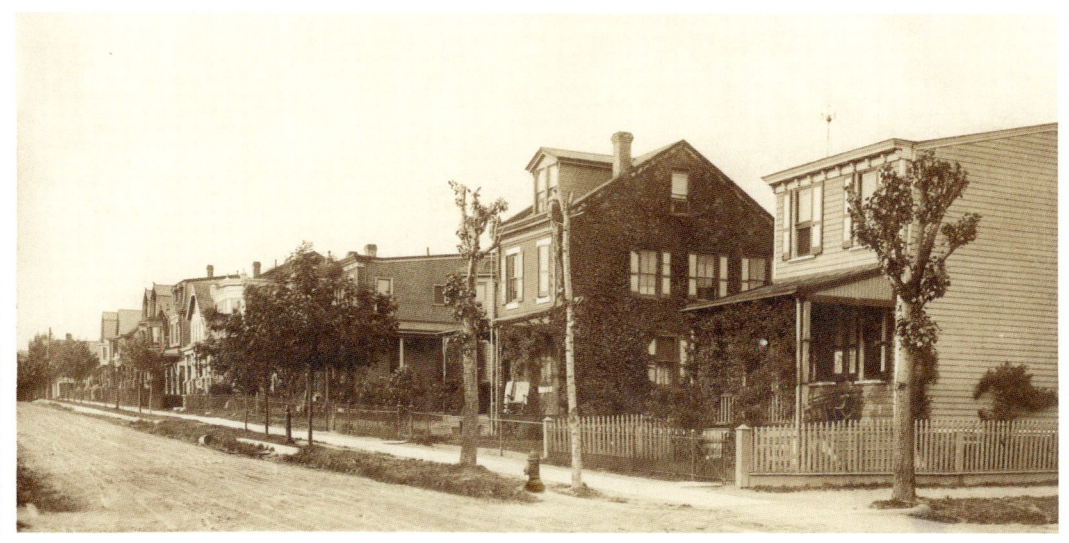

Fairhill Street north of Tabor Road, 1909. Residential development on Tabor Road and Fairhill Street was less than a decade old when this photo was taken. Fairhill Street was unpaved and deeply rutted.

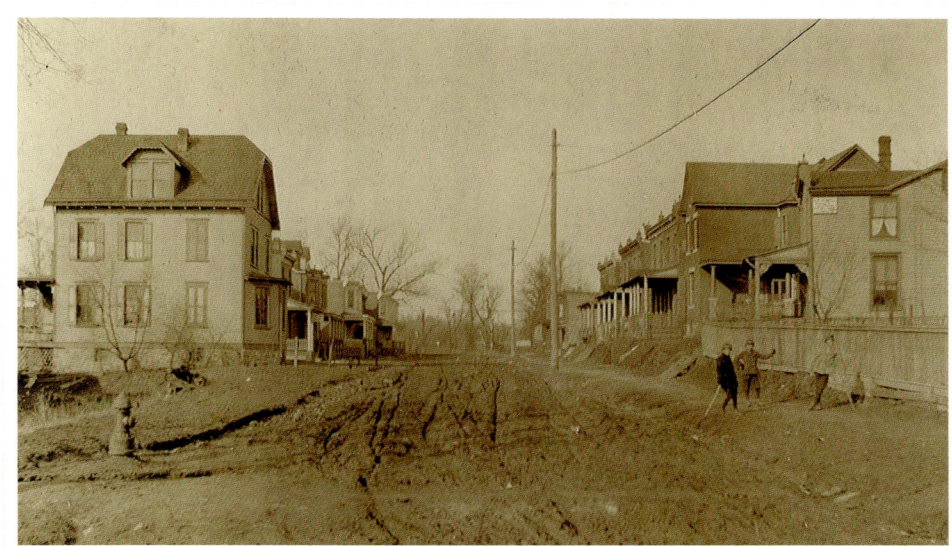

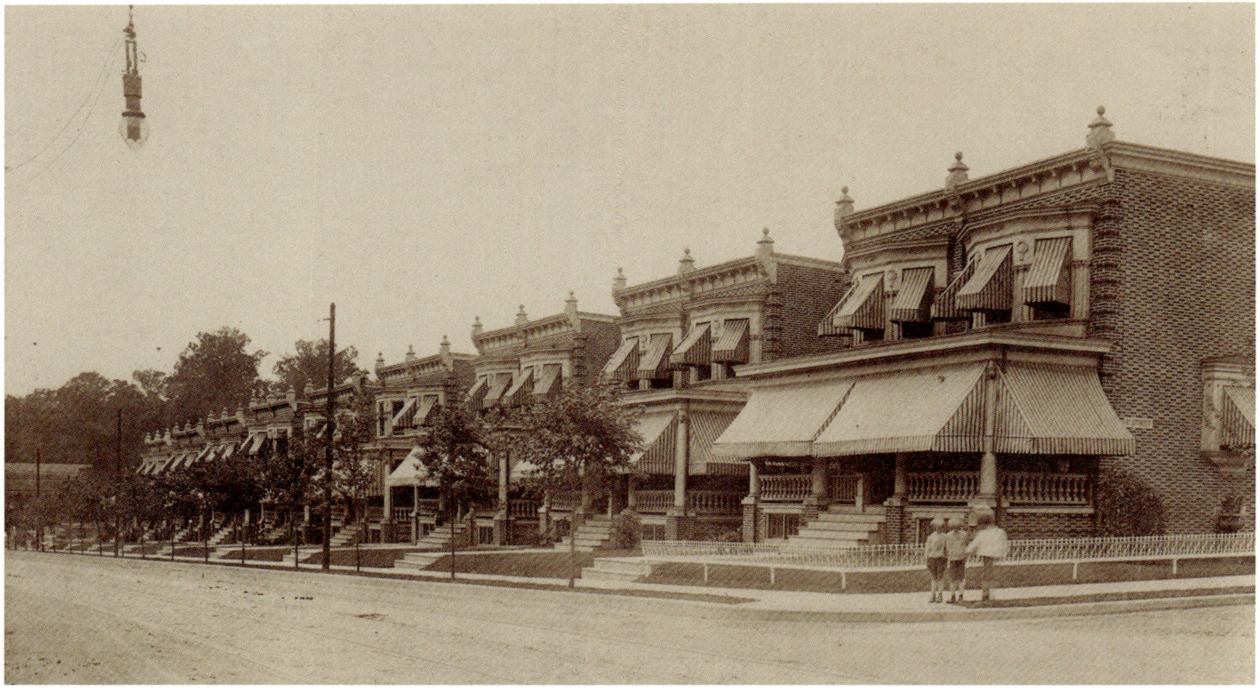

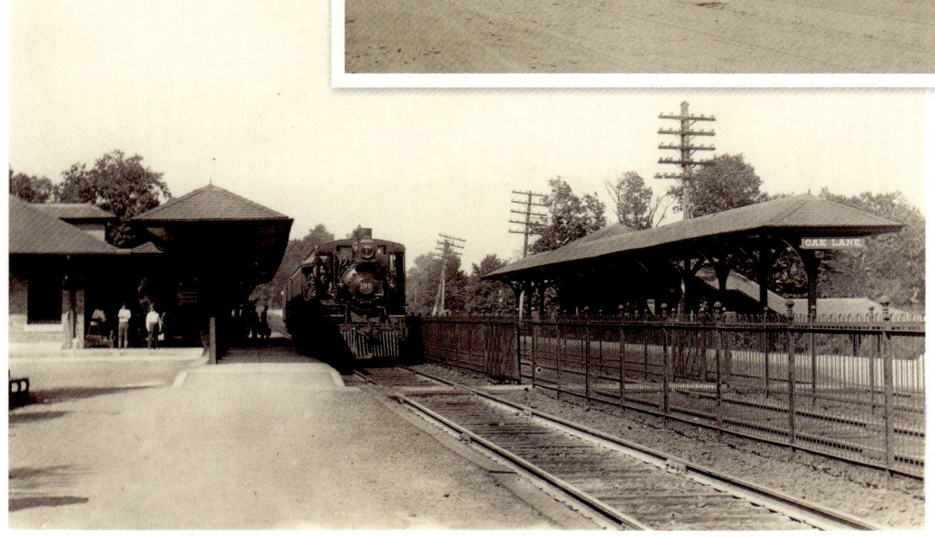

Olney Avenue west of Sixth, ca. 1910. Twins homes are found throughout Philadelphia. Harry Schmitt built these eighteen houses in 1909 and 1910.

Oak Lane Station, ca. 1910. Just south of Cheltenham Avenue, Oak Lane Station was the last stop within city limits for the Philadelphia & Reading Railroad.

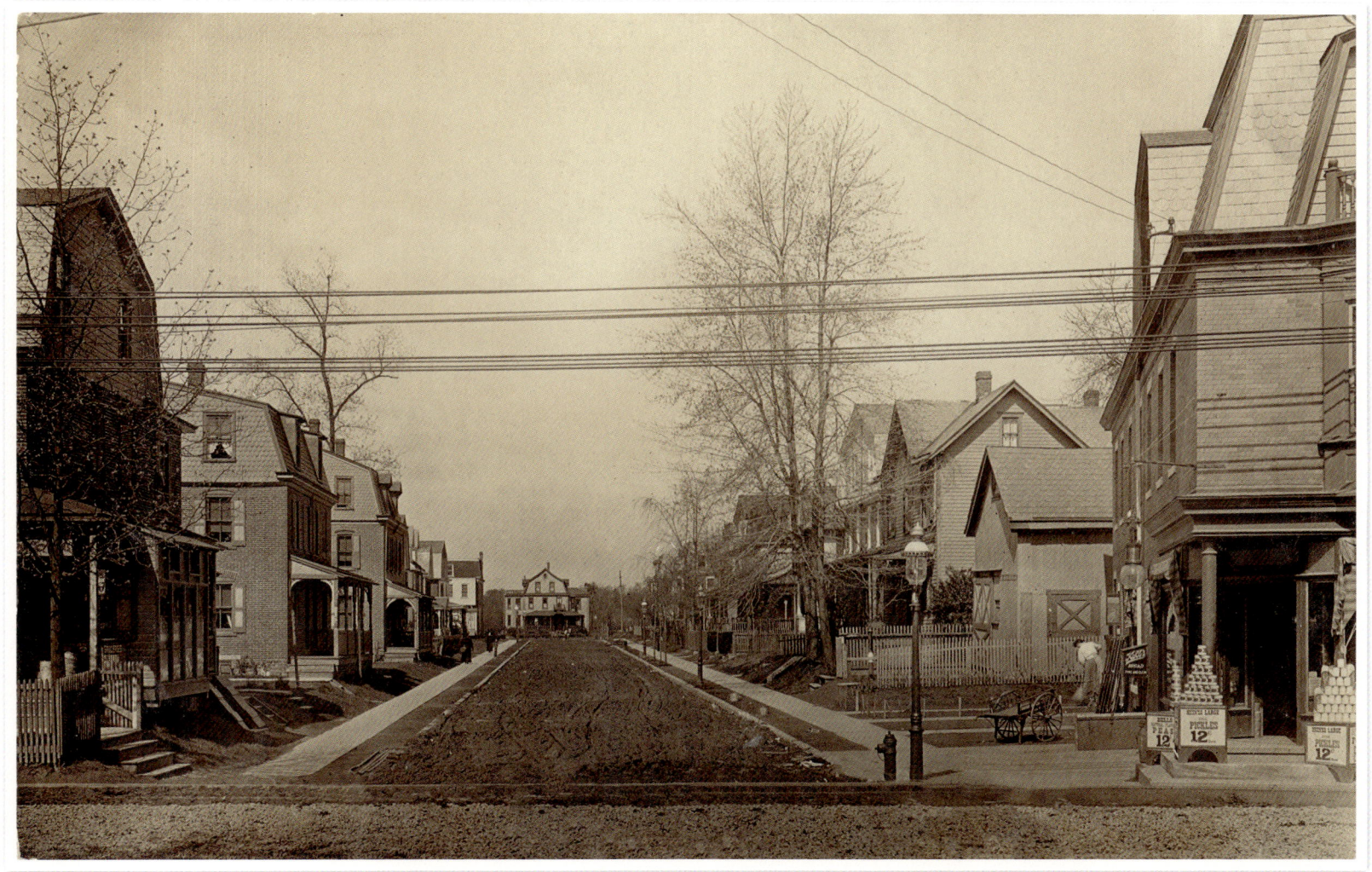

Fracker (Seventy-Second) Street west of Old York Road, ca. 1910. Tiny Fracker Street ran for only one block, terminating at Cheltenham Avenue. The twenty houses are a hcdgepodge of styles, built between 1896 and 1909. The store on the right sold Heinz large sour pickles for twelve cents.

Chapter 3.

NORTHEAST PHILADELPHIA

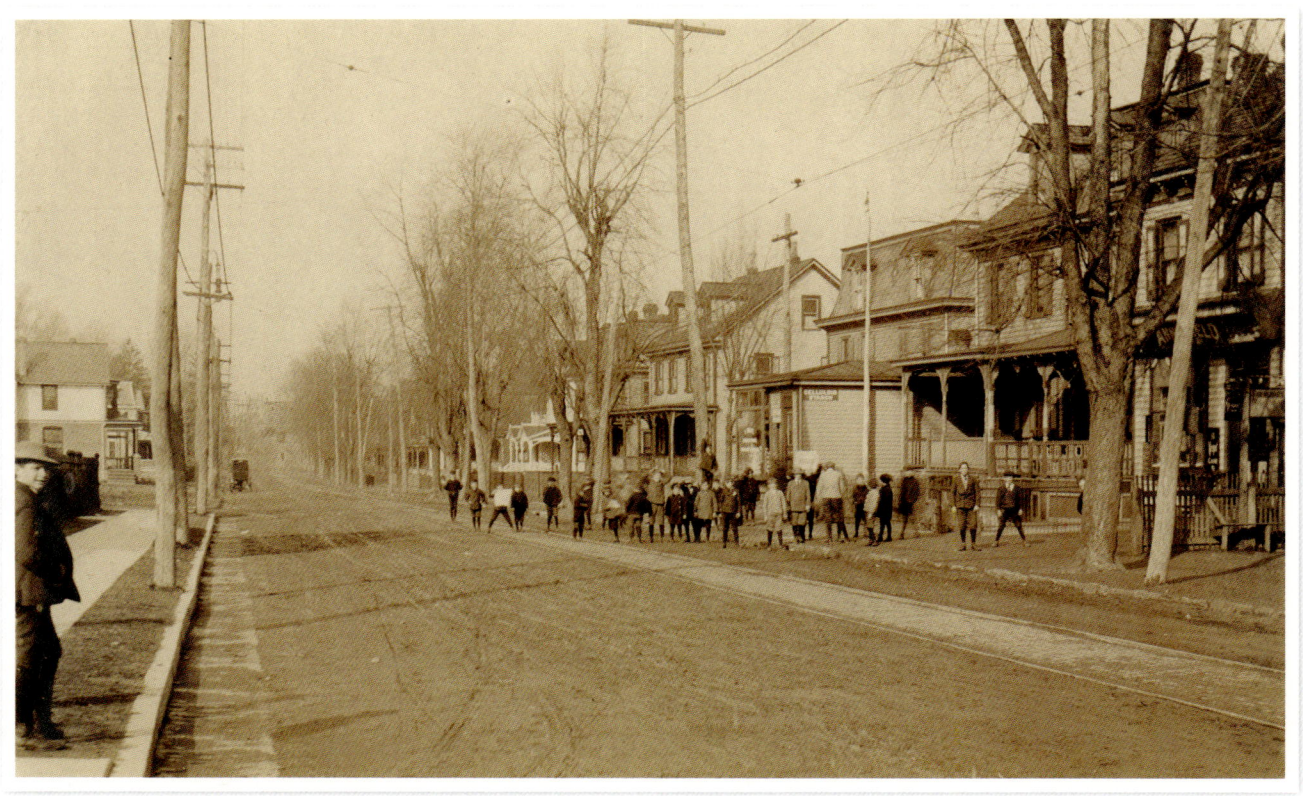

Rhawn Street looking west, 1907

Northeast Philadelphia has long felt like the neglected stepchild. Residents were paying high city taxes with little to show for it. So strong was this feeling of being disregarded by City Hall that there was a serious move afoot in the 1980s to secede from the city and become Liberty County. But the secession scheme fell through, and the Northeast is still an important part of the city. Today nearly one out of three Philadelphians call the Northeast home.[1]

There was a time, not that long ago, when Northeast Philadelphia saw some of the most explosive residential growth in the city's history. The completion of the Frankford Elevated in 1922 and the Roosevelt Boulevard in the 1930s was just the trick needed to turn this once-remote part of the city into a fashionable new suburb. Development slowed dramatically during the Great Depression and then World War II. After the war, residential construction boomed, continuing into the 1980s. But for most of Northeast Philadelphia's history, it consisted of farmland and dirt roads connecting ancient towns. These old-time villages were more or less self-contained communities, with nearly all the necessities of life close at hand or a short carriage ride away. The names of these hamlets—Bustleton, Holmesburg, Fox Chase, Wissinoming, etc.—live on as neighborhood names.[2]

Frankford

The neighborhood of Frankford got its name from the Frankford Creek, once a branch of the Wingohocking Creek that originated in the lands of the Frankfort Land Company, a German company organized for promoting settlements in the new colony of Germantown. The first European to occupy land in what would become Frankford was Henry Waddy, a London milliner who was granted a patent for 750 acres in 1682, known as Waddy's Grange. It was said that the native Lenni Lenape tribe still dwelled in the area as late as 1755, but in time the number of European settlers would swell. Growth was slow at first, with only twenty-six taxables in 1693, increasing to just twenty-nine by 1734. Things began to pick up after 1756, when Germans began to buy in Frankford's Oxford Township. By 1769 there were ninety-eight taxables, twenty-four of whom were German, and in 1783 there were 167 taxables, with forty-seven Germanic names among their ranks. Frankford benefited from the outbreak of yellow fever in 1793, when the city's denizens sought refuge in the relative safety of outlying areas. On March 7, 1800, Frankford incorporated as a borough in Oxford Township and had a population of about 1,000. In 1830, the population was 1,843, and by 1840 it was 2,318. Between 1840 and 1850, Frankford's population soared by 130 percent, fueled by the industrial manufacturing boom.

After the consolidation with the City of Philadelphia in 1854, Frankford continued to grow rapidly. By 1870 it had around 12,000 inhabitants, and by 1910 its population stood at around 35,000. During the late Victorian era, developers began to build on the farmlands of Frankford. Row houses were constructed for mill workers, while the burgeoning middle class was purchasing new Victorian twins. By the twentieth century, Frankford was ready for its next big innovation, the Frankford Elevated.[3]

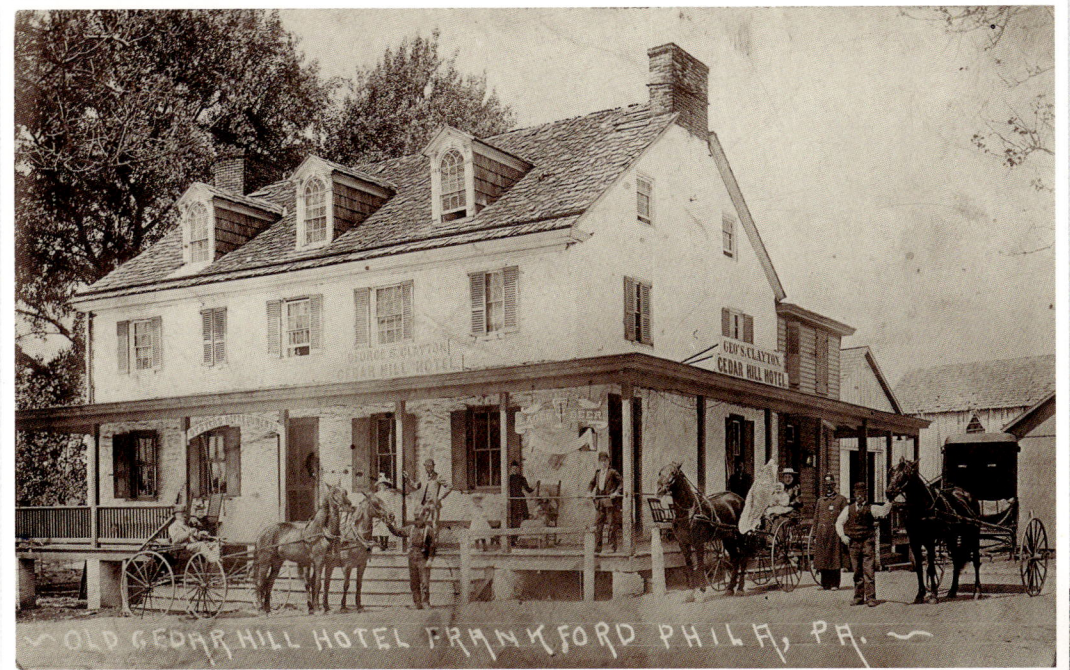

Cedar Hill Hotel (5287 Frankford Avenue), seen here in an early-twentieth-century photograph, when it was operated by George S. Clayton. It was demolished in 1903.

Old Jolly Post Tavern (4608 Frankford Avenue) began welcoming travelers (including George Washington) in 1680. The venerable old inn bit the dust in 1912.

Stagecoaches ran frequently between Frankford and Philadelphia by the 1840s, departing from such former landmarks as the Eagle Hotel, the Seven Stars, the Cedar Hill Hotel, and the Jolly Post. The fare for these rides was twenty-five cents. Stage lines also connected Frankford to the outlying communities of Fox Chase and Bustleton. By the 1850s, a more reliable and faster method of transportation between Frankford and the city was needed. Much to the consternation of stage and omnibus operators, horse-drawn streetcars, or horse cars, were introduced on January 20, 1858, by the Frankford and Southwark Philadelphia Passenger Railroad Company.[4]

The horse cars glided smoothly on rails and were a huge improvement over omnibuses, whose cacophonous rumbling over deeply rutted streets and cobblestones disturbed the peace. The new cars were immediately popular, but horror stories abounded. African Americans were denied ridership until 1867. The early horse cars were uncomfortable and filthy, hot in the summer, and cold in winter, and the overworked and malnourished horses were cause for revulsion. It wasn't until 1893 that electrified trolley cars were introduced in Frankford, supplanting the horse cars. The following year, the Philadelphia and Reading Railroad began running trains from a station just north of Unity Street and Frankford Avenue to the Reading Terminal at Twelfth and Market Streets.[5]

In time, a new form of rapid transit would help define Frankford. The extension of the Market Street Subway-Elevated was completed in 1922, which meant that for a single fare, one could travel from the line's terminus at Sixty-Ninth and Market Streets in Upper Darby all the way to the end of the line at Bridge Street in Frankford.[6]

Bustleton

The pretty yards adorned with flowers, and the well-painted houses of [Bustleton] deserve a word of commendation, for they add to its attractiveness and draw the notice of those who walk or ride through its streets.

—Rev. S. F. Hotchkin, 1892

How Bustleton got its name has been the subject of some speculation. The earliest reference is a deed conveying 198 acres in Cheltenham Township, Philadelphia County, known as "Bustilltown," dated January 22, 1745. Another early reference to that name dates to February 18, 1768, when the local tavern "Busseltown" was listed for sale. Nineteenth-century historian Reverend S. F. Hotchkin believed that the name was derived from "Brisslington," formerly "Busselton," a suburb of Bristol, England. Others think the name came from "Bustling Bess," a noteworthy resident of the early settlement. Yet others believe the name is related to Cyrus Bustill (1732–1806), a local African American baker who later became one of the founding members of the Free African Society.[7]

The main access point from the city was the Holmesburg and Bustleton spur of the Pennsylvania Railroad, near the intersection of present-day Welsh Road and Bustleton Pike, close to the center of the primitive village.[8]

Bustleton was the kind of rustic village one imagines from olden times, a veritable *rus in urbe*, exceedingly charming, with the only distraction being the constant rumbling of farm wagons traveling to and from the city.[9]

Cool bowery lanes, 'mong happy hills;

Old groves that shade ancestral eaves;

Farms which the prosperous season fills

With flocks and fruits and golden sheaves.

—Rev. Dr. Powers.[10]

Fox Chase

The name Fox Chase dates to the Fox Chase Inn (1705), at the intersection of Oxford and Huntingdon Pikes. As its name implies, city folk participating in foxhunts made their way up to the rural village in colonial times. As late as 1948, a newcomer to the neighborhood described it as "all wilderness."[11]

The rural nature of Fox Chase is not completely gone, since it contains one of two working farms in Philadelphia (the other is in Roxborough).

County Bridge over Poquessing Creek, a romantic rural scene from the Northeast of over a century ago. The bridge was famed for its single wide arch, and the creek for its picturesque waterfall.

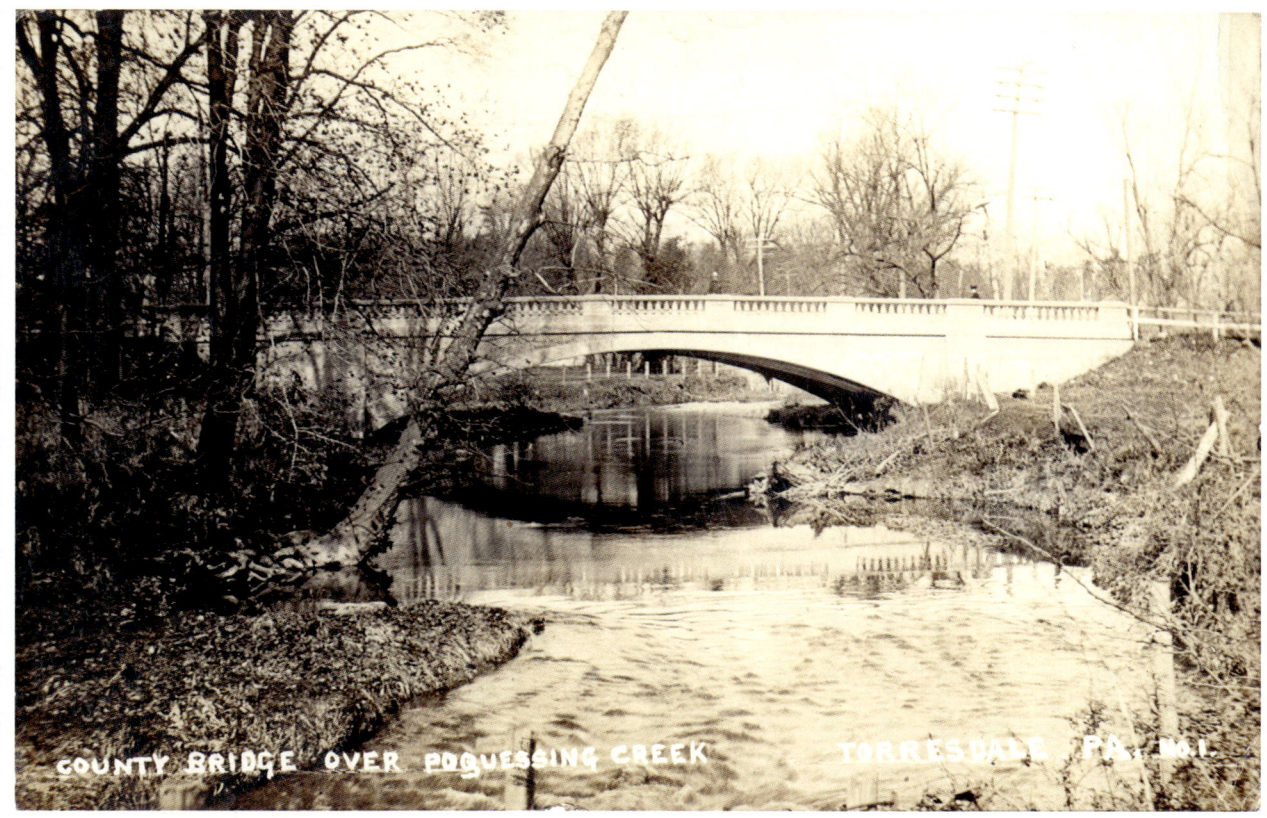

COUNTY BRIDGE OVER POQUESSING CREEK   TORRESDALE PA. 101.

Bridesburg

Modern-day Bridesburg is cut off from the hustle and bustle of the city by Interstate 95 (completed in the late 1960s) on its west side and the Betsy Ross Bridge on its southern boundary. It retains the ambiance of a small town with its own customs and way of life and is one of Philadelphia's leading Polish neighborhoods.

Bridesburg was once called Kirkbridesburg after the town's founder and was shortened for convenience to its present form.

In colonial days it was known as Point-no-Point for the deceptive appearance of the blunt cape at the mouth of the Frankford Creek on the Delaware River. As an old saying goes:

Point look out, point look in,
Point-no-Point, and point ag'in.

—T. Worcester Worrell.[12]

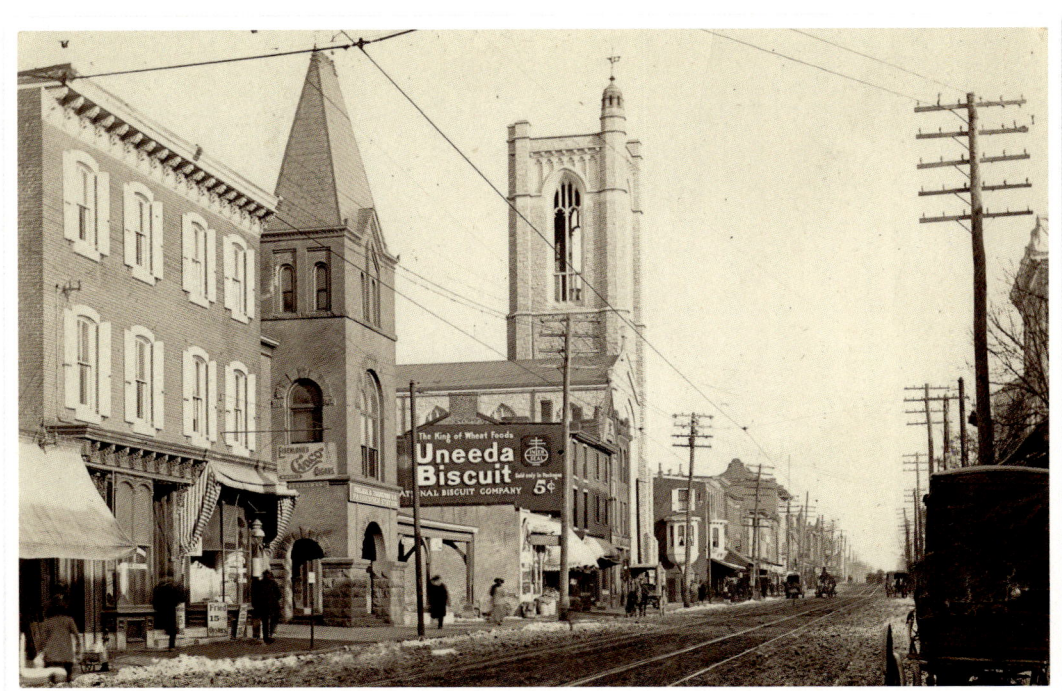

Frankford Avenue north from Unity Street, ca. 1910. A wintry view of Frankford Avenue before the construction of Market Street Elevated Railway's extension through Northeast Philadelphia. As seen here, Frankford Avenue was the "Main Street" of Frankford and remains so today. The Philadelphia and Reading Railroad's passenger station is pictured, as is the bell tower of St. Mark's P. E. Church (still standing) farther along Frankford Avenue. The church of St. Mark's was constructed in 1908 at a cost of $140,000.

Cedar (now Darrah) Street looking north from Margaret Street, ca. 1910. Built around 1900, these row homes with bays and porches are still standing. Cedar Street was renamed Darrah Street about a decade after this photo was taken.

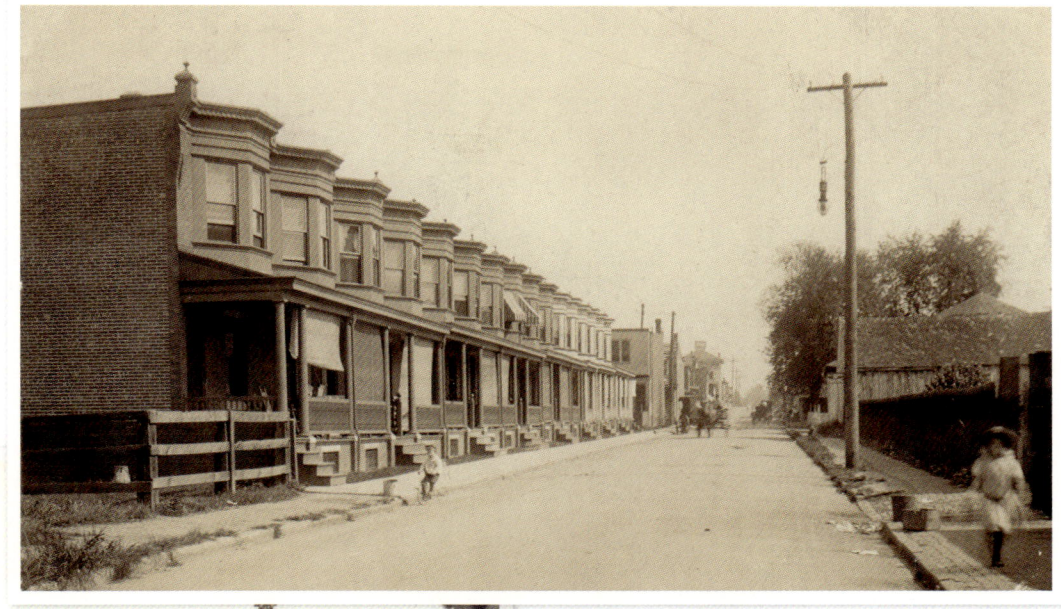

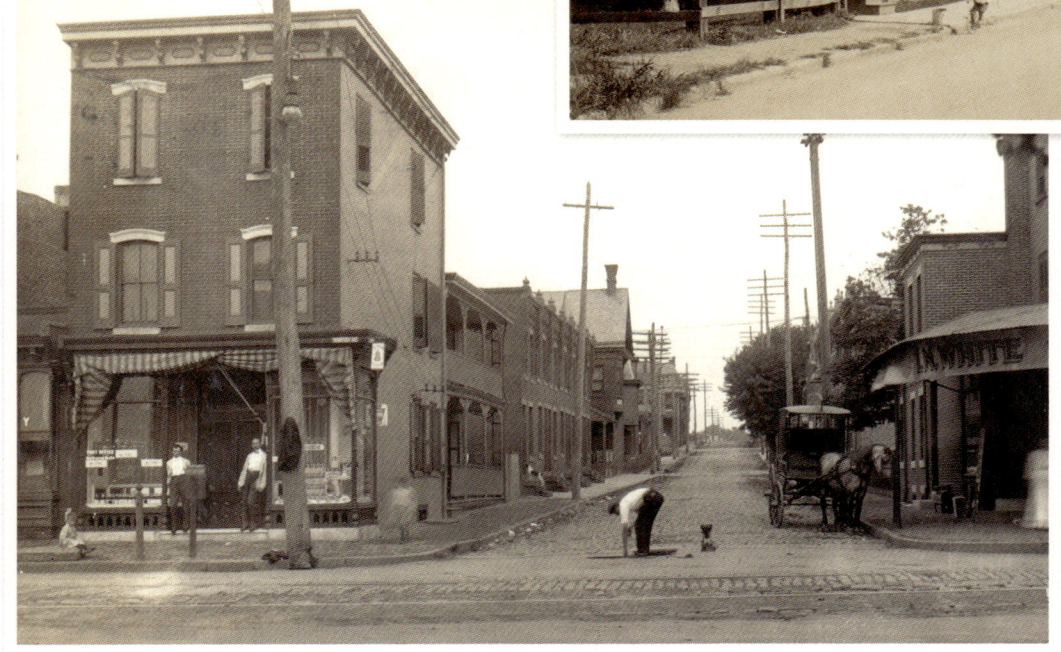

Foulkrod Street west of Frankford Avenue, 1906. The historic community of Frankford developed as a small town within the city, with its own societies, traditions, civic associations, and commercial concerns. This view illustrates Frankford's less hurried pace of life.

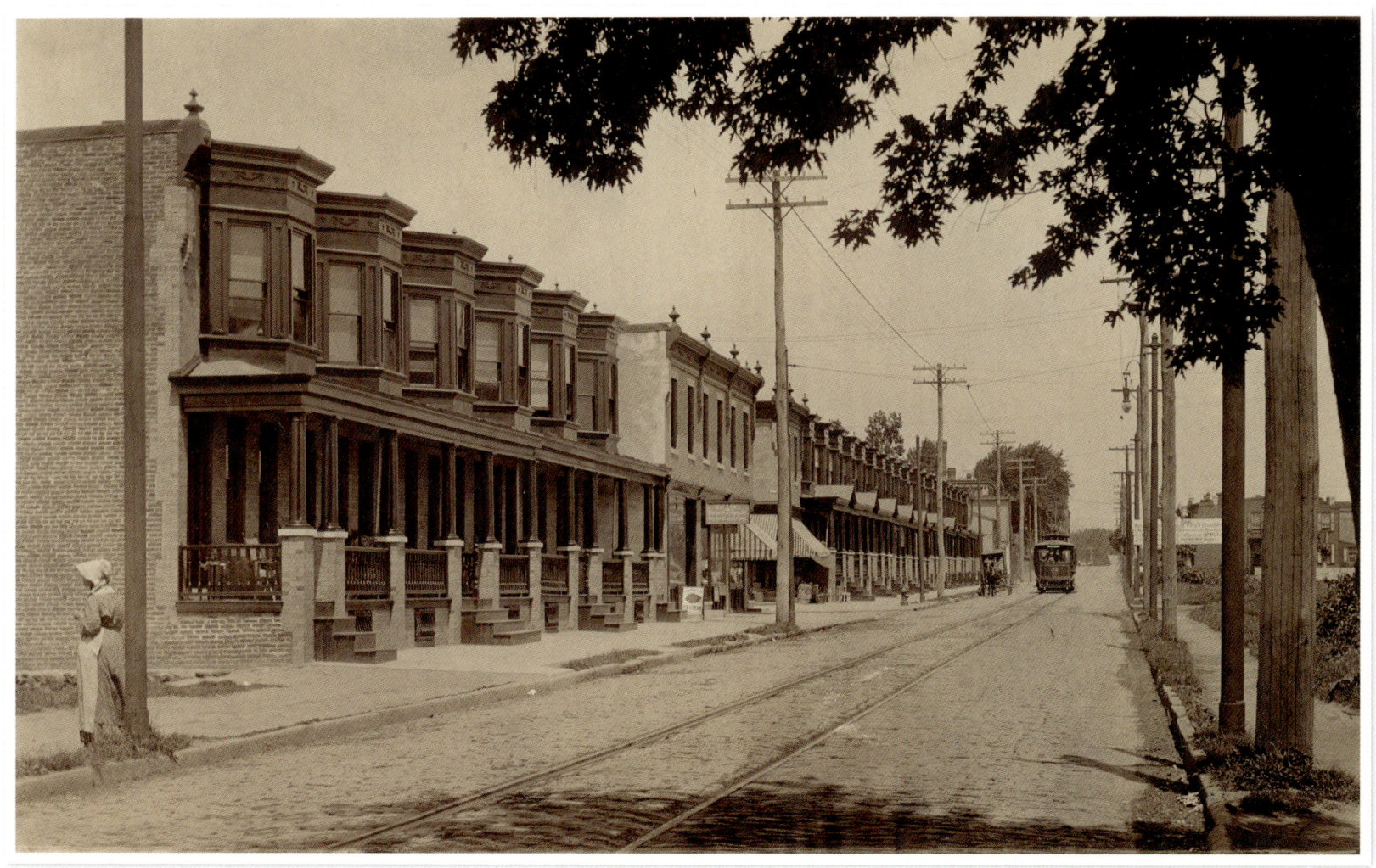

Bridge Street west of Torresdale Avenue, ca. 1910. Bridge Street west of Torresdale Avenue in Frankford is shown here in a transitional phase. The south side of the street, halfway to Ditman Street, was built up with row houses, while the north side was still undeveloped. The same pattern continues to Ditman Street, where a horse-drawn carriage and a trolley head east on Bridge Street. On the corner of Ditman and Bridge Streets is Keller's, offering bargains in remnants, dry goods, and notions.

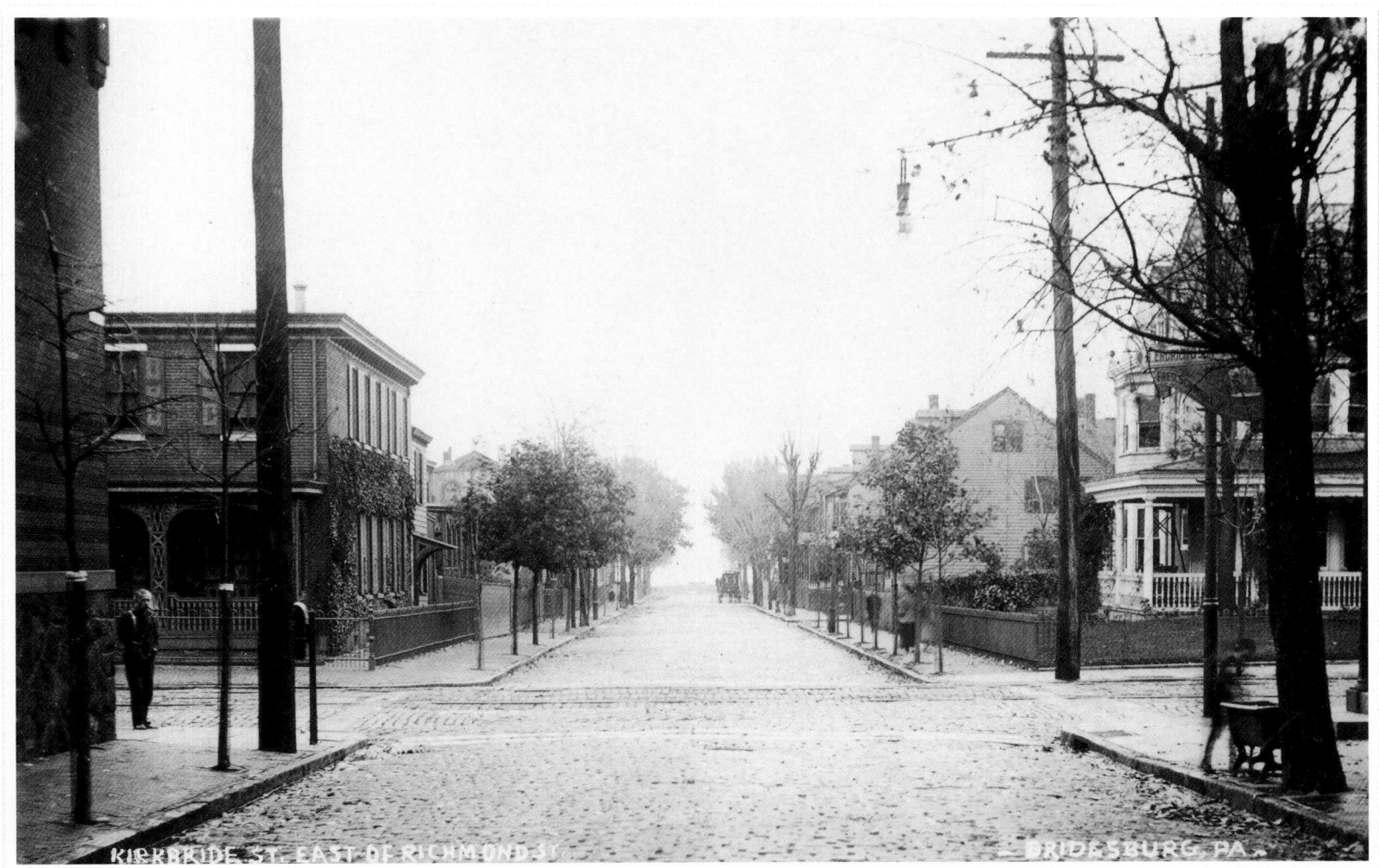

Kirkbride Street east of Richmond Street, ca. 1908. It may be hard to believe, but this quiet residential street scene was the intersection of two of the main streets in Bridesburg. Richmond Street, formerly Point Road, was the major street in the former borough. Kirkbride Street was named for the town's founder, Joseph Kirkbride, who operated a ferry to New Jersey and later built a toll bridge over the Frankford Creek in 1811.

Thompson Street, east of Lefevre Street, ca. 1908.
Thompson Street was another major street in Bridesburg. This photo is looking east from Lefevre Street toward the soaring steeple of All Saints Catholic Church at Buckius Street. The church, built in 1895, is still standing though the tower was shortened after this picture was taken. The simple, two-story dwellings on Thompson Street were built around 1900.

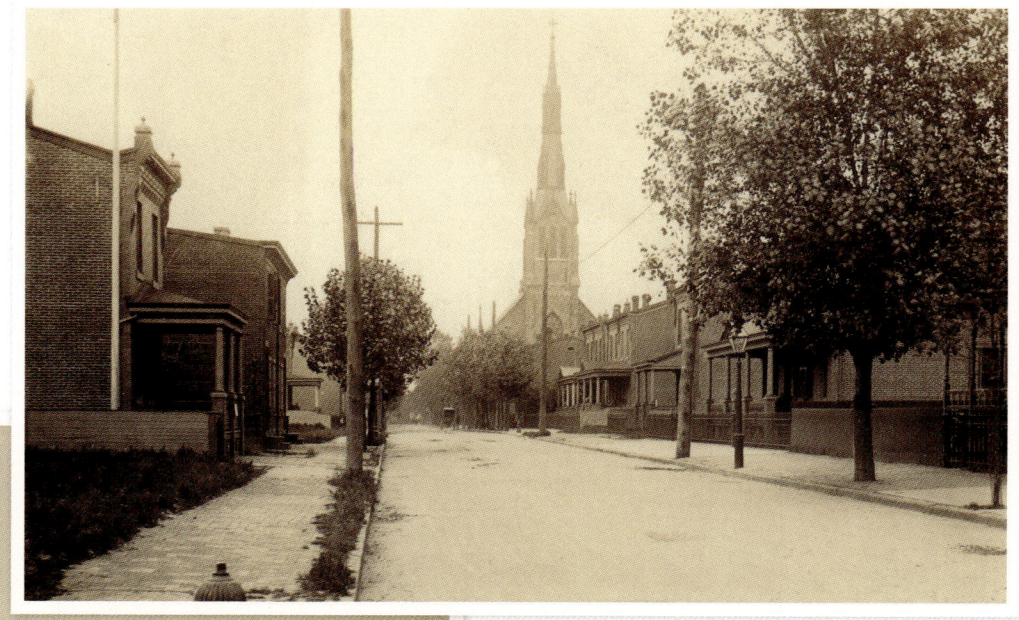

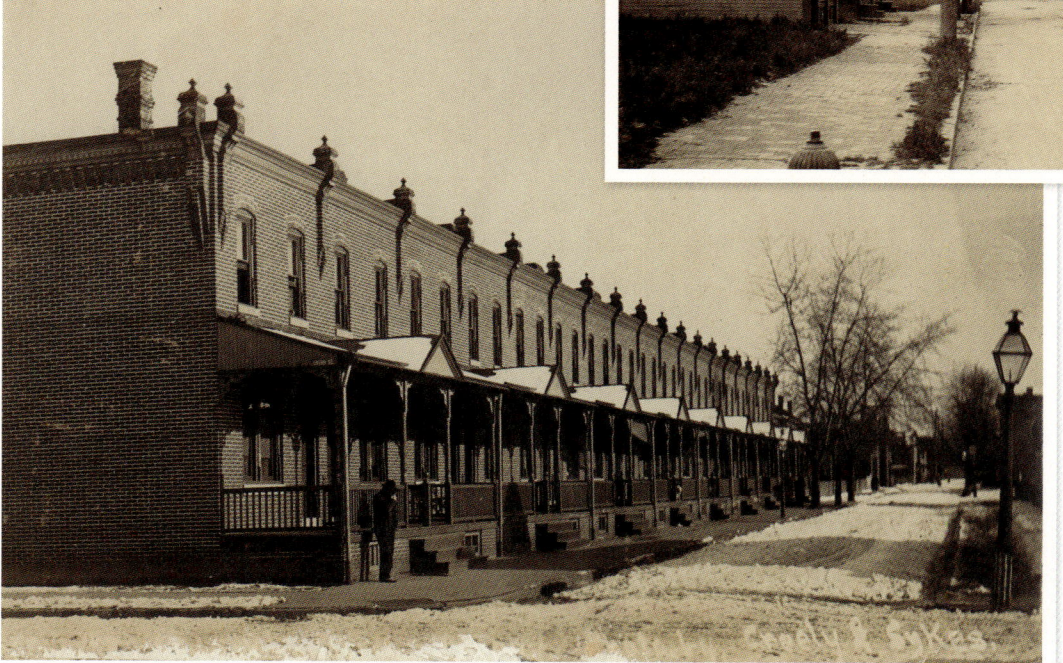

Vandike Street north of Unruh Avenue, 1909. Samuel Paulthese began construction on these utilitarian row houses in the spring of 1908, on the estate of Mary Disston. Her name was very well known in the Torresdale section of Philadelphia.

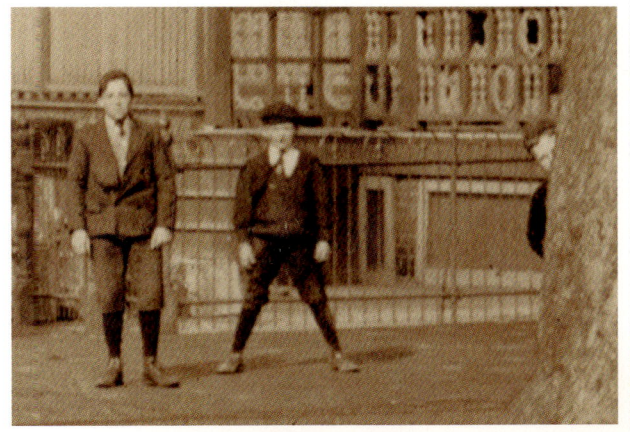

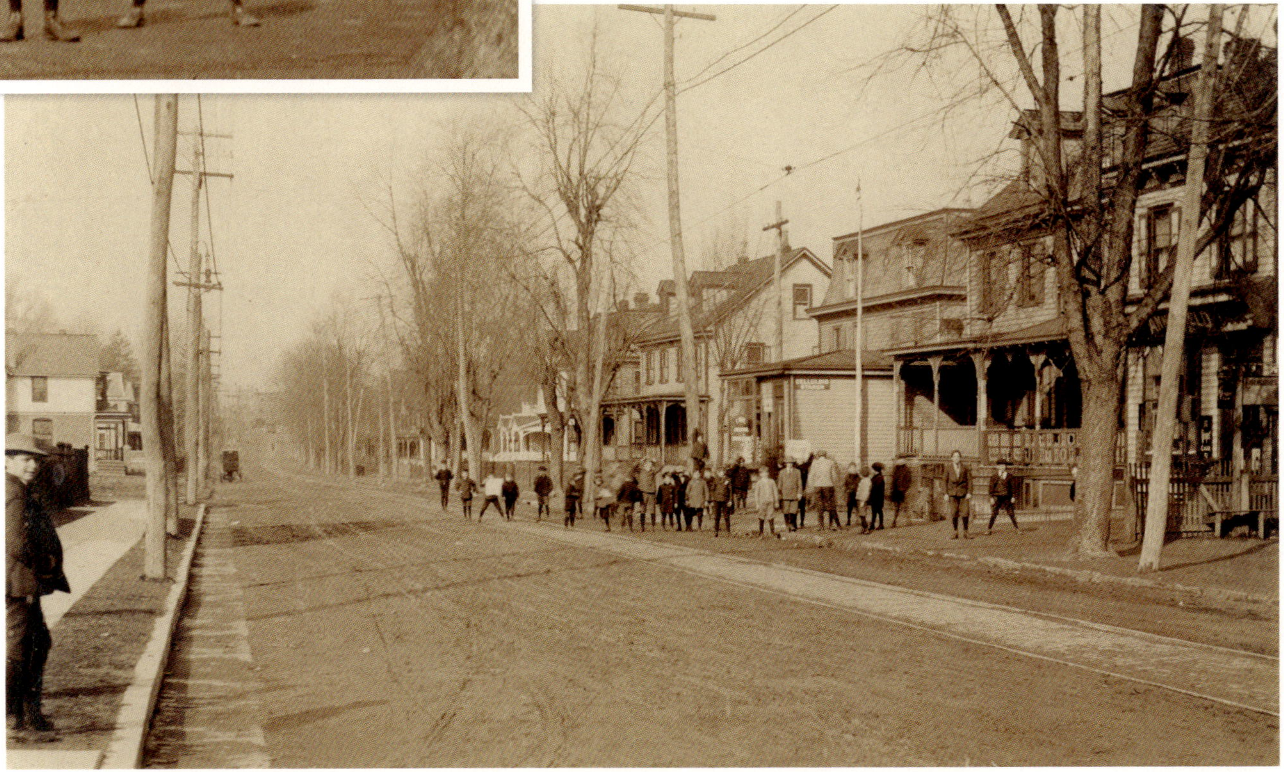

Rhawn Street west of Ditman Street, ca. 1910.
Children stand on Rhawn Street in Holmesburg. Across the street from the older homes stood a public school, now occupied by the Rambler Playground.

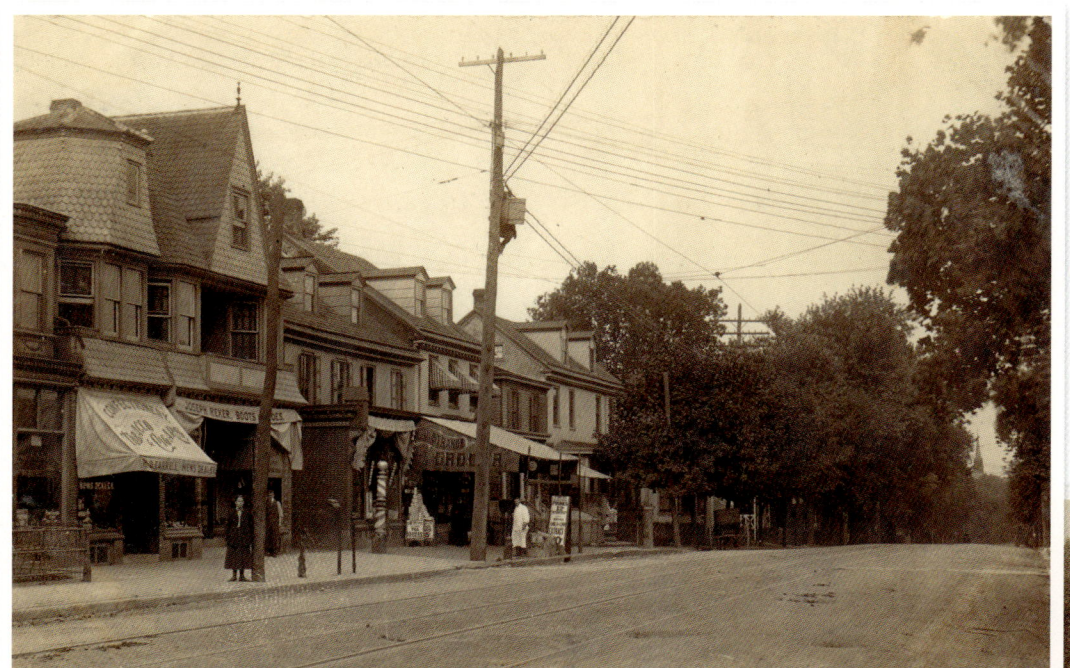

Frankford Avenue north of Rhawn Street, ca. 1909.
An eclectic mix of businesses sit side by side on Frankford Avenue, or Main Street, as it was then known. The setting puts one in mind of a small town center from yesteryear. Among the businesses operating on this stretch of Frankford Avenue are a real estate agent, confectioner, shoe store, barbershop, and grocery store. Note the utility worker at the telephone pole. Few of these buildings are still standing.

State Road south of Ashburner Street, ca. 1910.
Holmesburg was a rural outpost in the early twentieth century, with State Road a country lane fit merely for equestrian traffic. The House of Correction was nearby, as was the Pennypack Creek, and not much else.

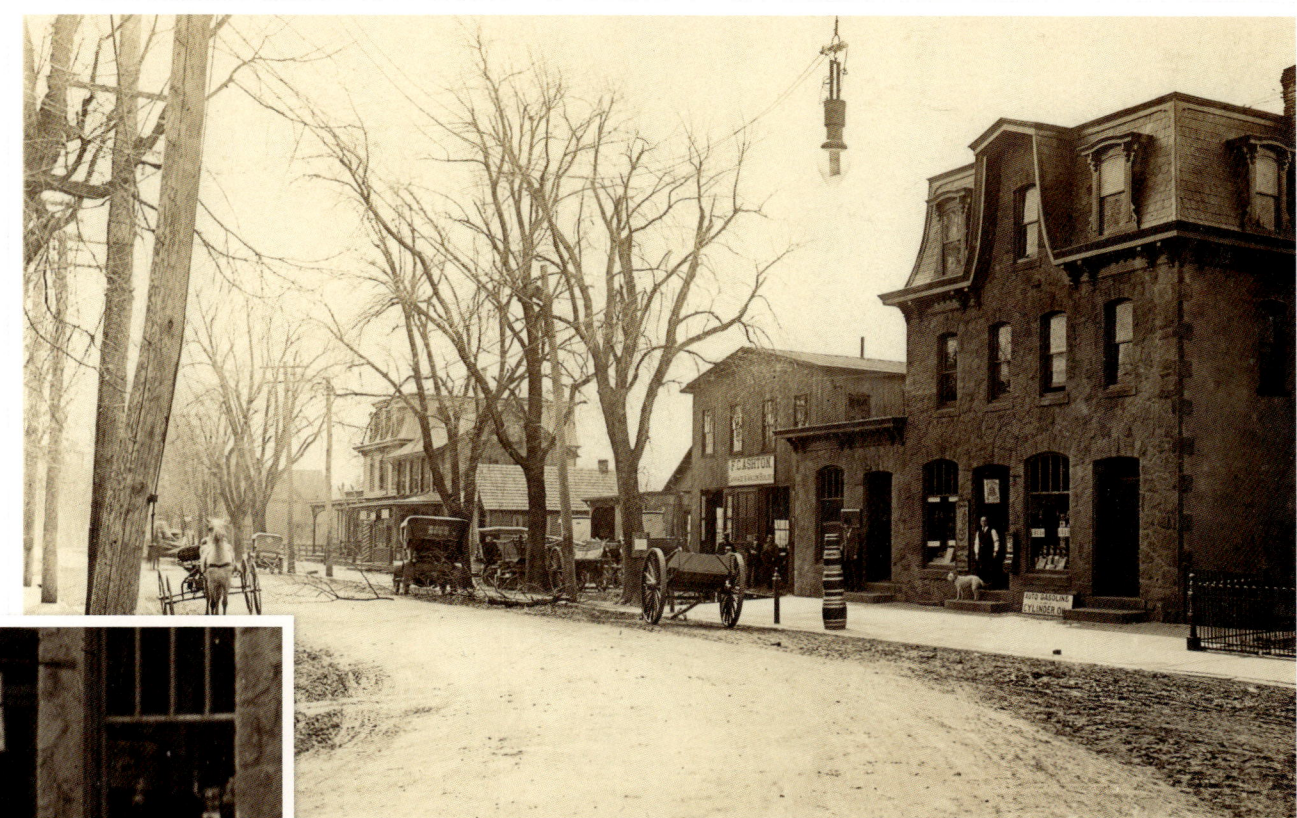

Bustleton Pike at Welsh Road, looking south, ca. 1910. Near the center of the old town of Bustleton was this intersection of two major highways. The carriage and wagon factory of Frederick C. Ashton is to the left of H. L. DeKalb's pharmacy, which serviced that competing new conveyance of the twentieth century, the automobile, with gasoline and cylinder oil. Bustleton had a reputation for fine carriage and wagon building by the late 1800s. In addition to F. C. Ashton's shop, Richard Hall, Thomas Paul, George Northrop, Amos A. Gregg, and Starkey & McDowell all did a brisk trade in the local carriage industry.

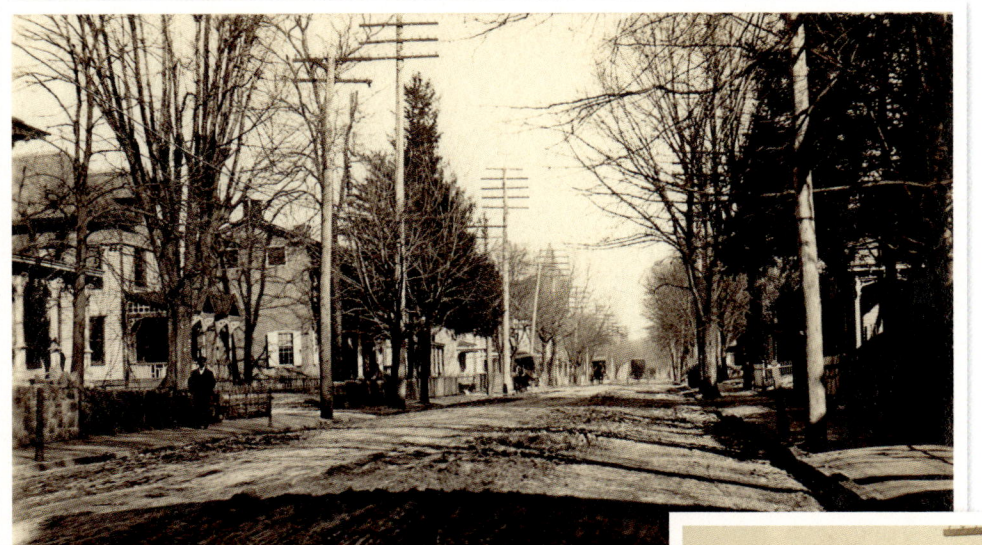

Bustleton Pike north from the Holmesburg and Bustleton Station, ca. 1907. This view depicts a serene suburban setting complete with an unpaved Bustleton Pike and Victorian-era houses on both sides of the road. This photo was taken just north of the local train station, which was the terminus of the Holmesburg and Bustleton Railroad, a branch of the Pennsylvania Railroad. The completion of this railroad spur in May 1870 stimulated development. The Bustleton Station of the New York Short Line was also nearby on Welsh Road.

Bustleton Pike north of Grant Avenue, ca. 1910. This photo of Bustleton Pike is a little farther north from the previous view. The single-family Victorian houses lend a quaint village atmosphere. In the distance is the steeple of the Bustleton Methodist Episcopal Church, whose cornerstone was laid in 1868.

Bustleton Pike and Welsh Road, ca. 1910. The village of Bustleton grew around the Union Hotel, earlier known as the Eagle Hotel. At the time of the photo it was run by William Tillyer and proudly served Arnholt & Schaefer Beer. The hotel also had the seal of approval from AAA (established in 1902). Even in 1910, Bustleton was a sleepy corner of Philadelphia, a community of mostly retired farmers. The only time Bustleton bustled in those days was in September, during the annual mushroom harvest.

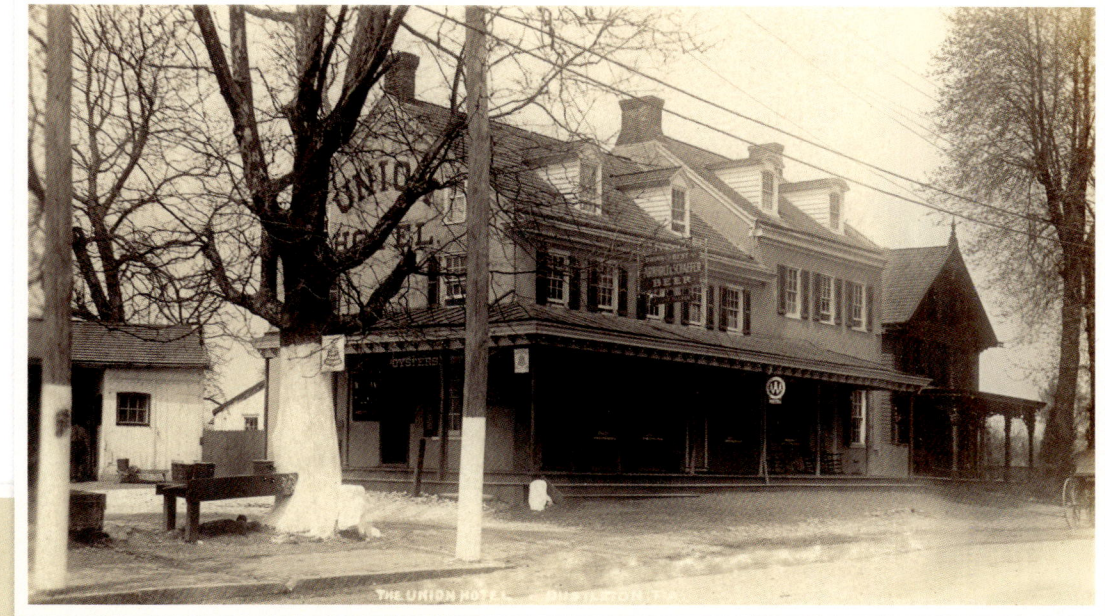

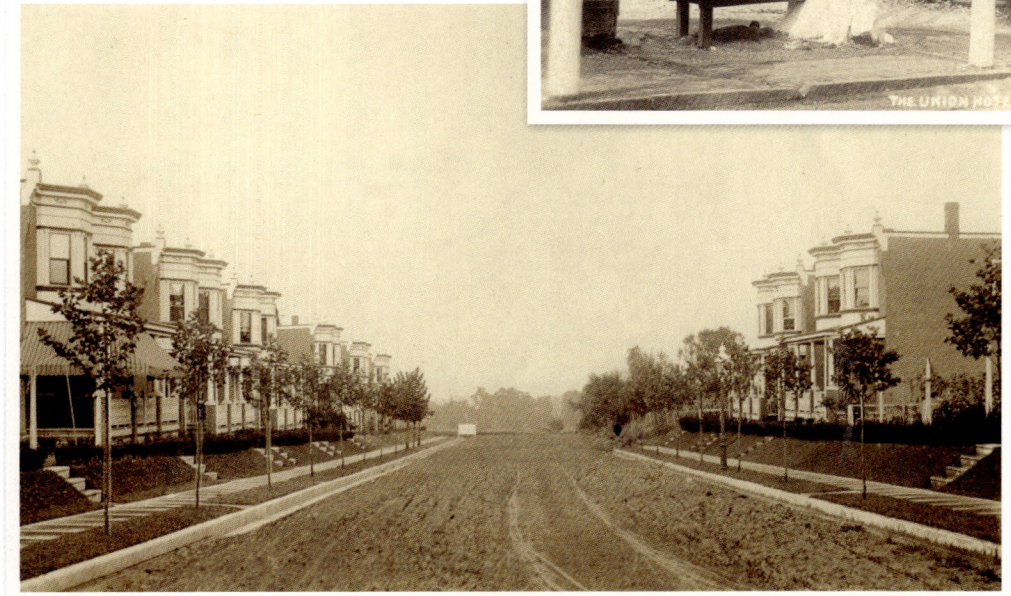

Stanwood Street west of Ridgeway Street, ca. 1912.
Muddy Stanwood Street in Fox Chase is shown here after a heavy rainstorm. These attractive twin houses were built in 1911.

Chapter 4.

GREATER KENSINGTON

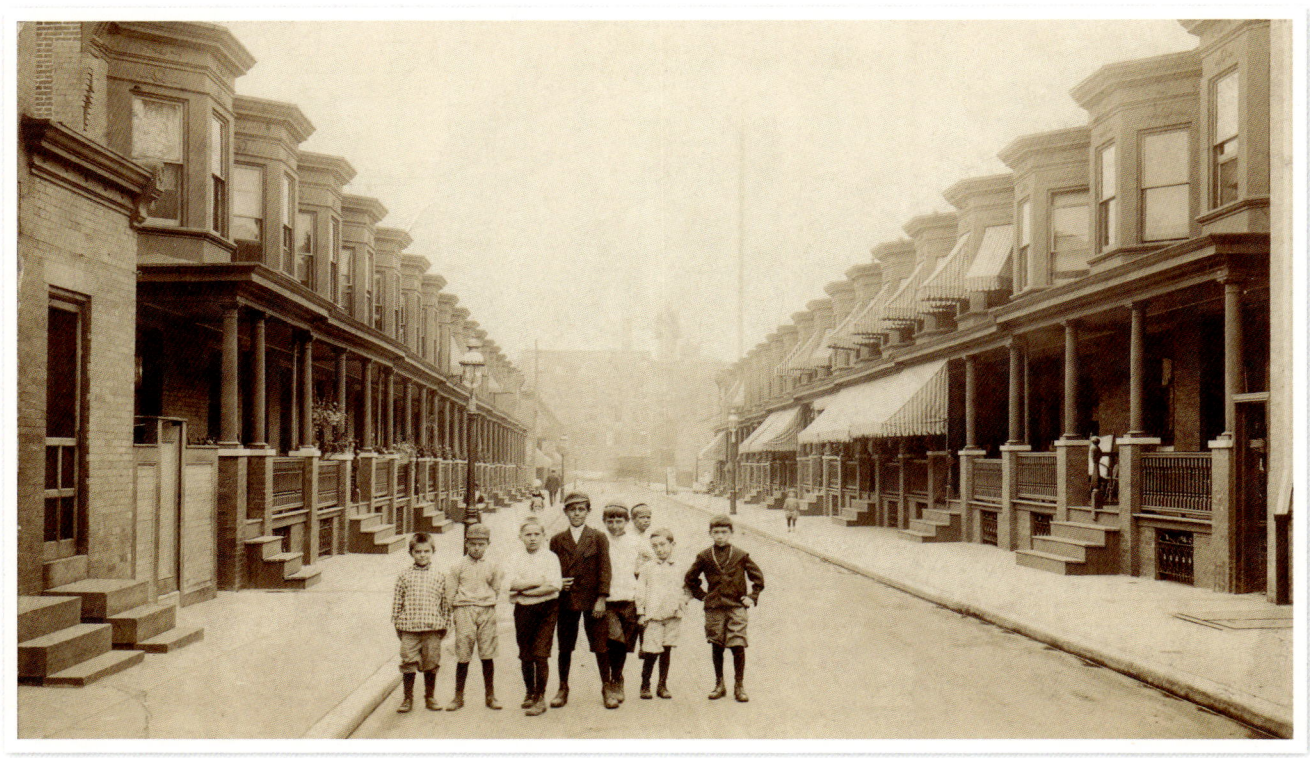

Birch Street west of Frankford Avenue, ca. 1910

Kensington, along with Germantown, Manayunk, and Northeast Philadelphia, was one of the great manufacturing centers of Philadelphia, contributing to Philadelphia's reputation as the Workshop of the World. Most of the Kensington mills were related to the textile industry, with dye works; spinning, worsted, and knitting mills; and hosiery, tapestry, upholstery, carpet, silk, cotton goods, and leather mills. Additionally, sheet iron works, coal, and lumberyards provided ample employment for a large immigrant population, mainly from Ireland, Italy, and Poland. These ethnic groups still populate large swaths of the Kensington, Port Richmond, and Fishtown neighborhoods. Many of the old factory buildings, long since abandoned, now sit vacant. The western edge of Kensington is part of the city's Puerto Rican community, with a commercial corridor known as El Centro de Oro (The Heart of Gold).[1]

The streets of old Kensington are typical of the working-class development that rose during the late nineteenth and early twentieth centuries. Dense blocks of plain-style houses with the neighborhood grocer on the corner proliferated seemingly overnight. Amenities were few, but the homes were sturdy and affordable, selling for as little as $2,200. This part of the city was also shockingly devoid of parks, which meant that the factory workers' children were forced to play in the streets and vacant lots. They faced far fewer hazards on the cobblestone avenues and alleys than children do today. Traffic consisted mainly of trolleys, horse-drawn vehicles, and the occasional automobile.

Mill workers of industrial Kensington endured a hardscrabble existence: backbreaking labor for long hours and little pay, with the occasional pleasure of watching two pugilists beat each other senseless in "the Blood-Pit" section of Kensington Avenue or partaking in a spirited game of quoits with the neighbors. Fisticuffs were common in the old days, fueled by a combination of boredom, bravado, and booze. Nobody got seriously hurt, and the fights usually broke up when the law showed up.[2]

The weary workers dreamed of a better life but had little chance for upward mobility and were forced to accept their dreary lot in life. Even after the industries they depended on for a living moved south, they continued living in their tiny row houses (as narrow as 10 feet) and Father–Son–Holy Ghost houses.[3]

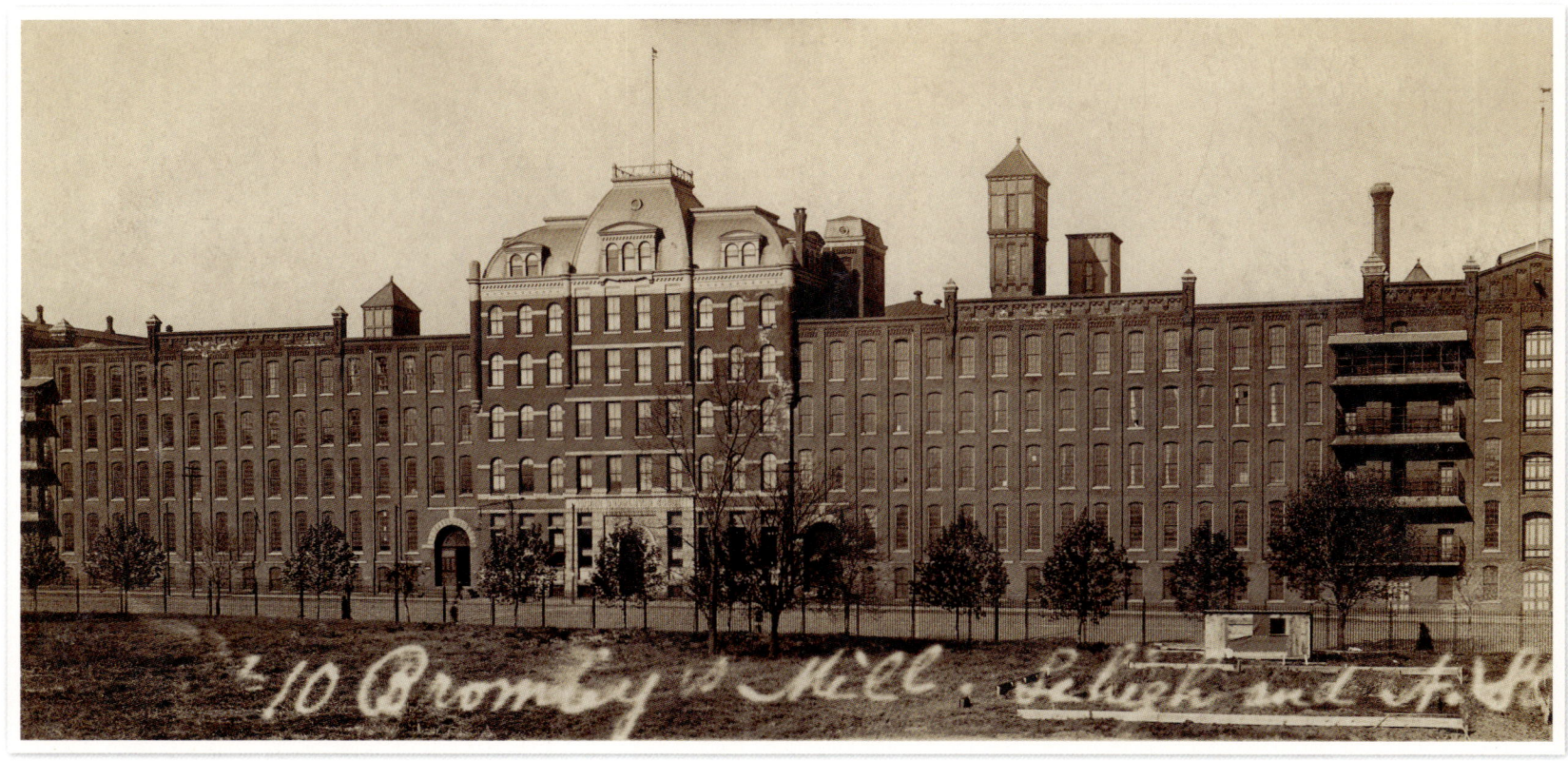

The massive John Bromley & Sons Mill at 201–263 East Lehigh Avenue was once the largest manufacturer of rugs and carpets in the US. Mills like this were commonplace in Kensington. The Bromley complex burned in 1979 and was subsequently demolished.

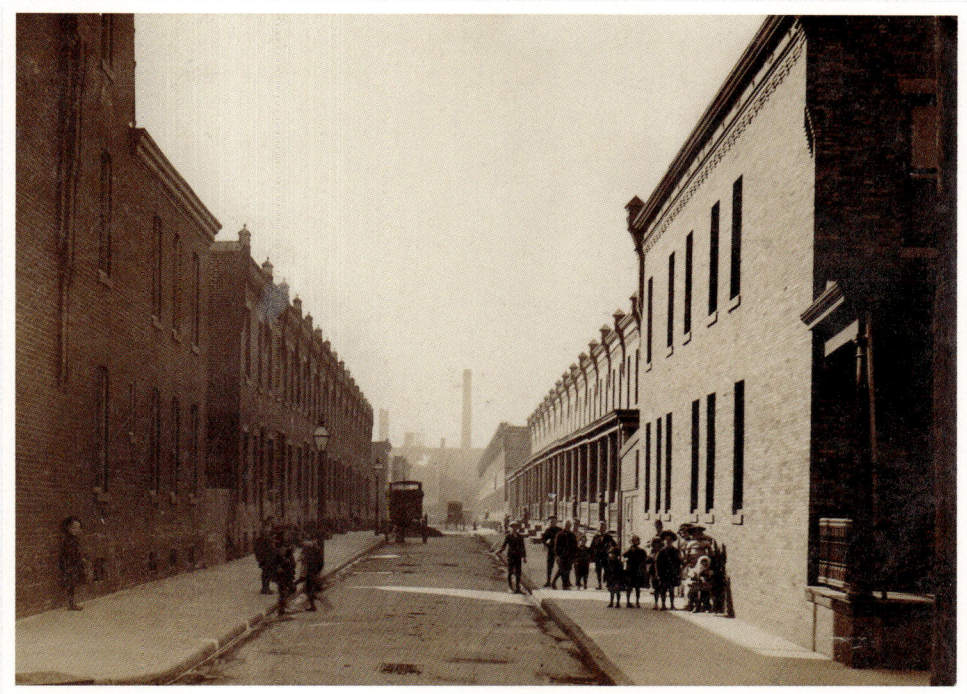

Narrow streets such as Braddock Street (seen here at the intersection with East Tioga Street) were typical of the Harrowgate section of Kensington, with narrow, tightly packed homes. The tall smokestack of the Allegheny Worsted Mills adds to the neighborhood's working-class ambience.

Gentrification is occurring in parts of Kensington and adjacent neighborhoods such as Fishtown and Northern Liberties. The Coral Street Arts House (2515 Frankford Avenue) is one such revitalization project, transforming Beatty's Mill, a one-time producer of cotton and wool yarn, into affordable housing for artists. The massive building was one of many dilapidated factories in the vicinity and is now home to painters, actors, writers, photographers, and graphic designers.[4]

Organizations such as the New Kensington Community Development Corporation are dedicated to revitalizing Kensington, Fishtown, and Port Richmond. Their stated mission is to strengthen the community's physical, social, and economic fabric by being a catalyst for sustainable development and community-building.

Another miraculous transformation is Oxford Mills at Oxford and Howard Streets, formerly a textile mill. The oldest building in the complex dates to 1873, when it was known as the Quaker City Dye Works. During its period of peak performance, it employed about 200 workers. But as time went by, the property changed hands and was nearly abandoned in 2011, when tall weed trees were growing out of its roof. The current owners purchased the moribund assemblage and, with the help of federal historic tax credits and the National Trust Community Investment Corporation, performed a complete resurrection of the Oxford Mills, now bustling with offices and affordable new residences. Such restoration success stories are commonplace in South Kensington.[5]

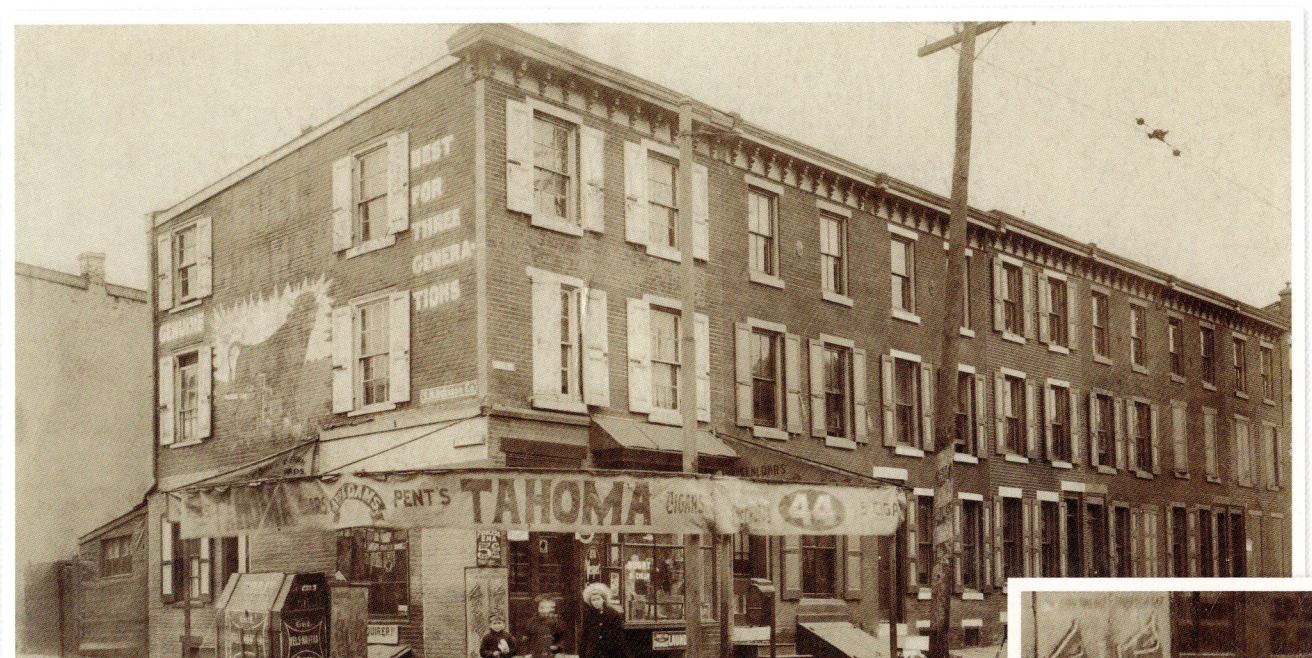

East Hazzard and Coral Streets, 1908. Three children pose in front of a store specializing in tobacco products. This intersection was at the center of Kensington's then-flourishing textile and carpet mill district.

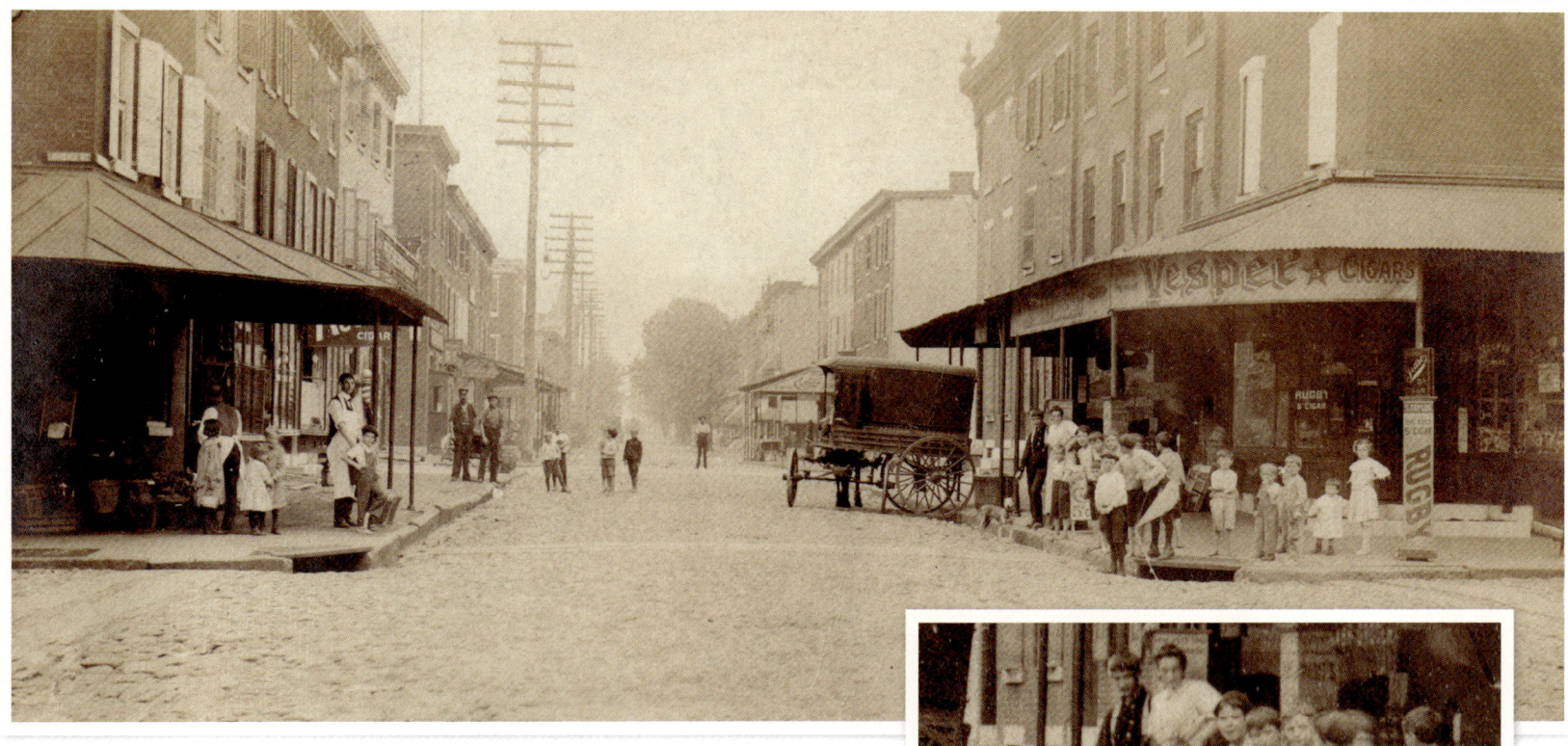

Dauphin west of Lawrence, 1906. This busy intersection of West Kensington is looking west along Dauphin Street. The area was dense with residences and corner stores, many selling popular cigars.

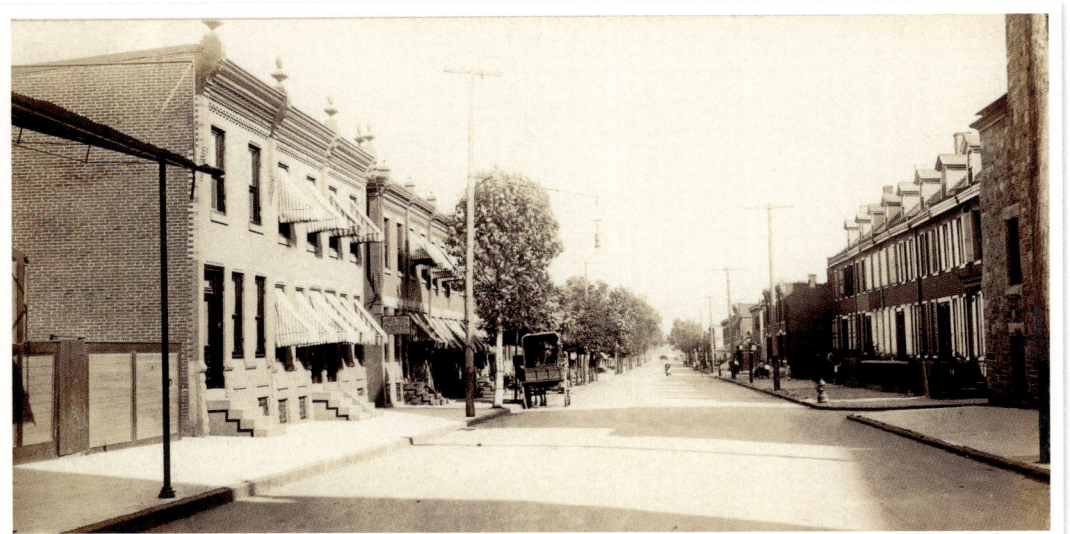

Cambria east of Frankford Avenue, ca. 1907. Row houses on the left of the photo are typical of this area. The three houses on the far left were built in 1895 by Wright & Prentzel, while the remainder of the block was built in late 1891 by Moore & Bro. Across Cambria Street stands a row of late federal-style houses.

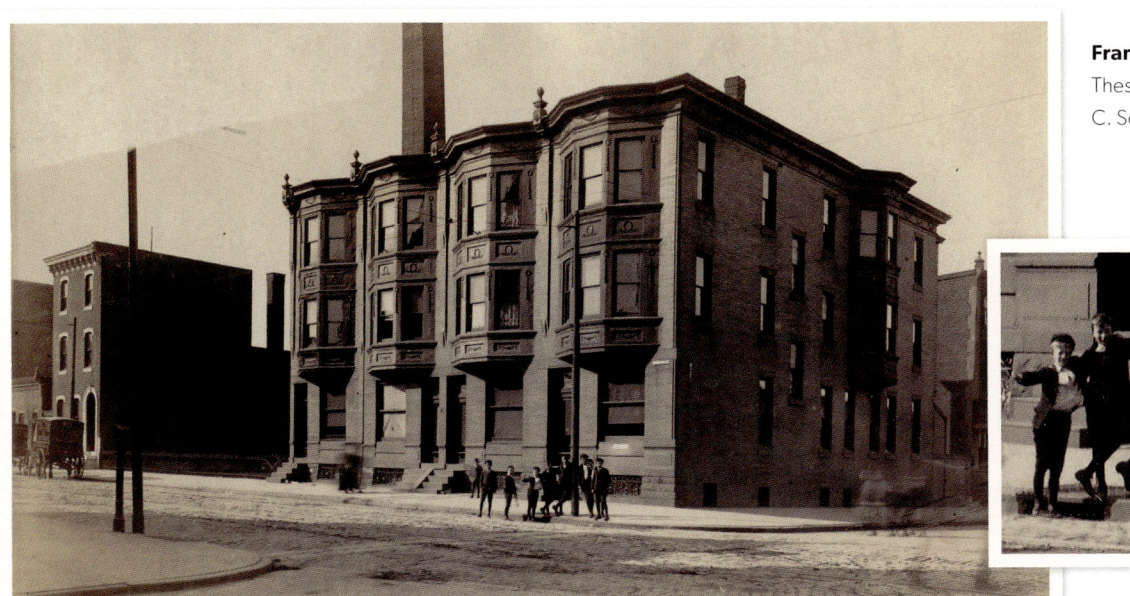

Frankford Avenue south of Cambria Street, ca. 1910. These four stately row houses were built in 1902 by David C. Schuler & Son. Today only the corner house exists.

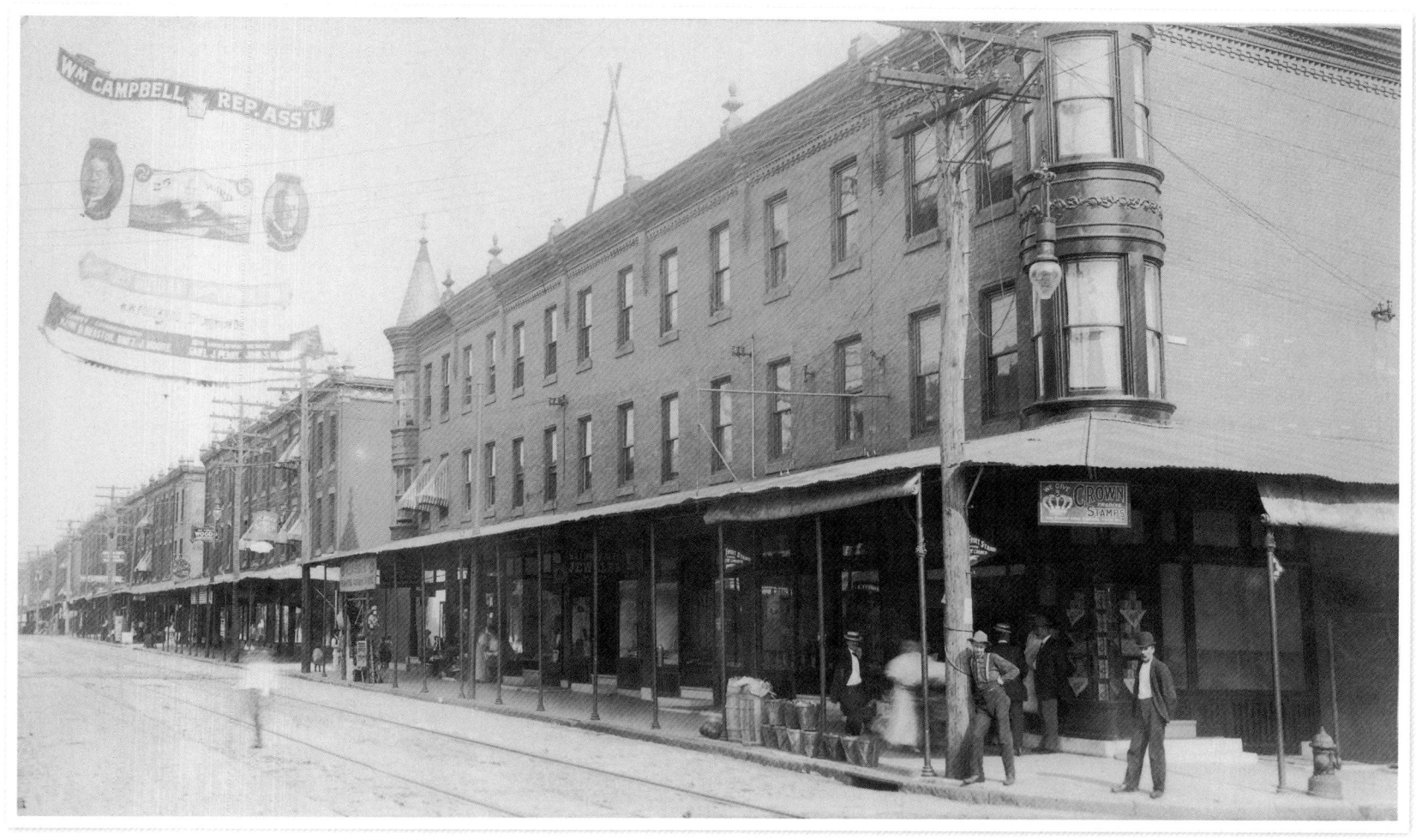

Frankford Avenue north of Cambria Street, ca. 1909. At the dawn of the twentieth century, Frankford Avenue was a bustling commercial district. Beneath the corrugated tin awning, one could find a wide variety of shops ranging from a bargain store to a jewelry store. Wright & Prentzel built the seven properties on the right in the spring of 1895.

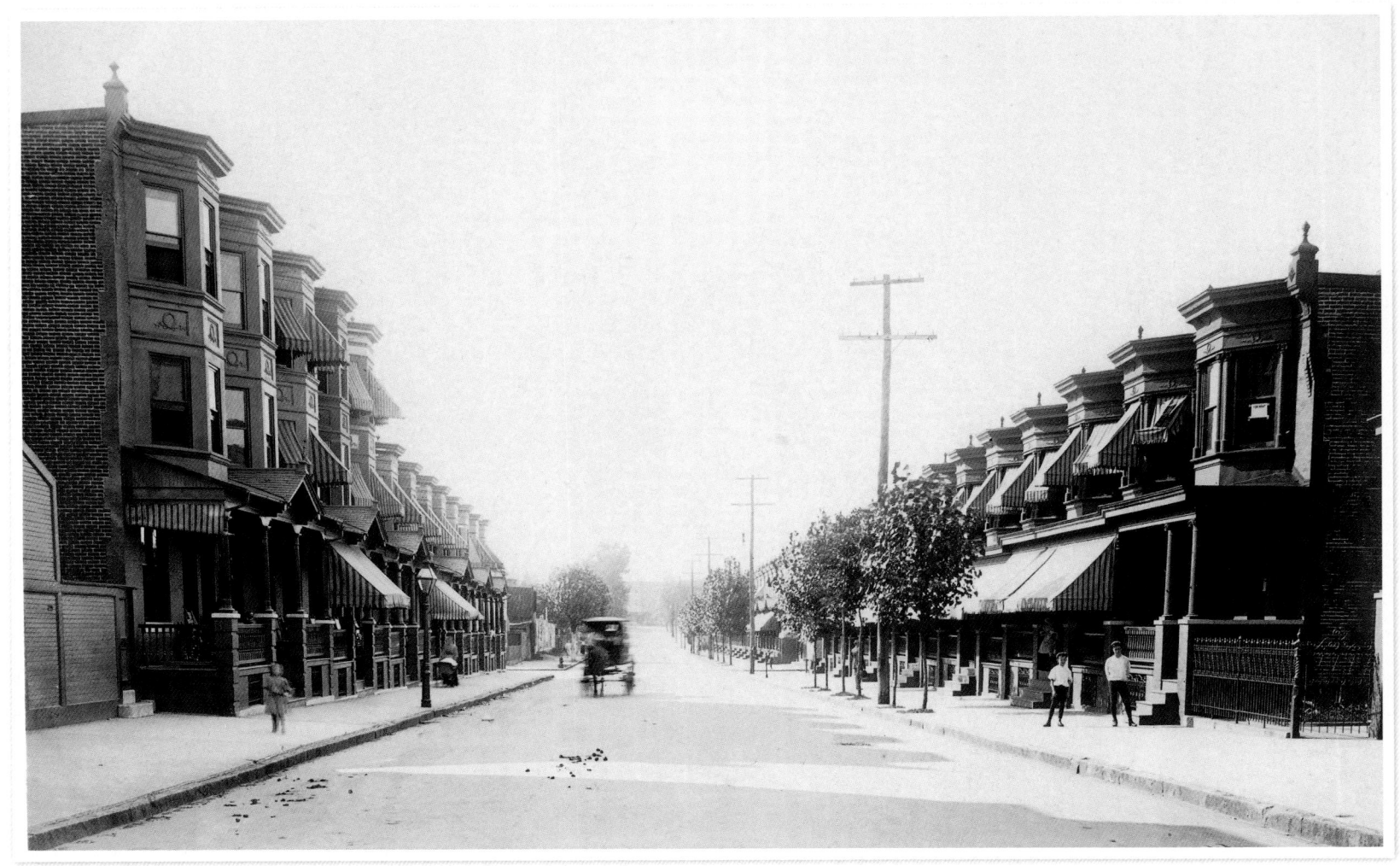

Cambria west of Frankford Avenue, ca. 1907. On Cambria Street west of Frankford Avenue, we find row houses that are a cut above others in this part of Kensington. The homes on the far left, built in 1902 by David C. Schuler & Son, have a two-story bay window and front porches. David McKibben built the houses on the right in April 1905. Cloth awnings indicate that this scene was photographed in summer.

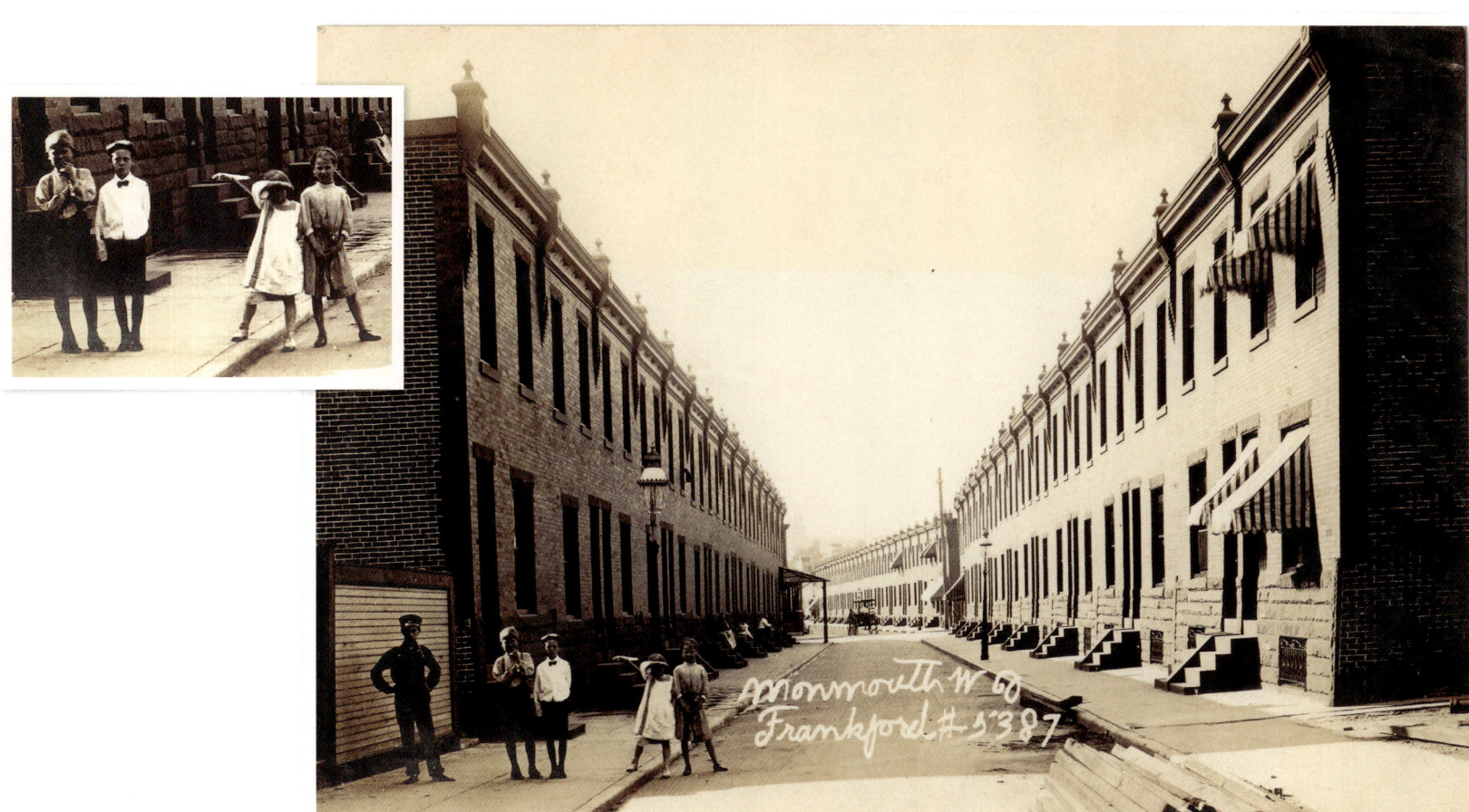

Monmouth west of Frankford Avenue, ca. 1910. Inexpensive, efficient row houses were all the rage in Kensington. The homes on Monmouth Street just off Frankford Avenue fit the bill for the average mill worker. The blocks were dense, the houses were plain and unadorned, the streets were narrow, and nary a tree was in sight. The houses on the left were built in 1905, while the houses on the right appeared in 1906.

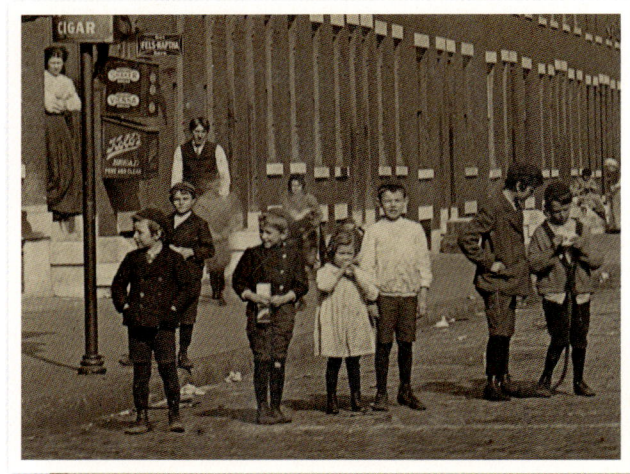

Rosehill Street north from Cambria Street, 1911. These plain houses were typical of working-class Kensington. Homes on the east side of the street were built in April 1890, while construction on the west side of Rosehill began in April 1891. Many of the houses were owned or rented by workers at the John G. Carruth Endurance Mills, which looms over the neighborhood in the distance. The mill, at Rosehill and Indiana Streets, was built in 1894 by Carruth, a Scottish immigrant. The drinking establishment of James H. Rowbottom (*on right*) proudly sold Yuengling's Pottsville porter.

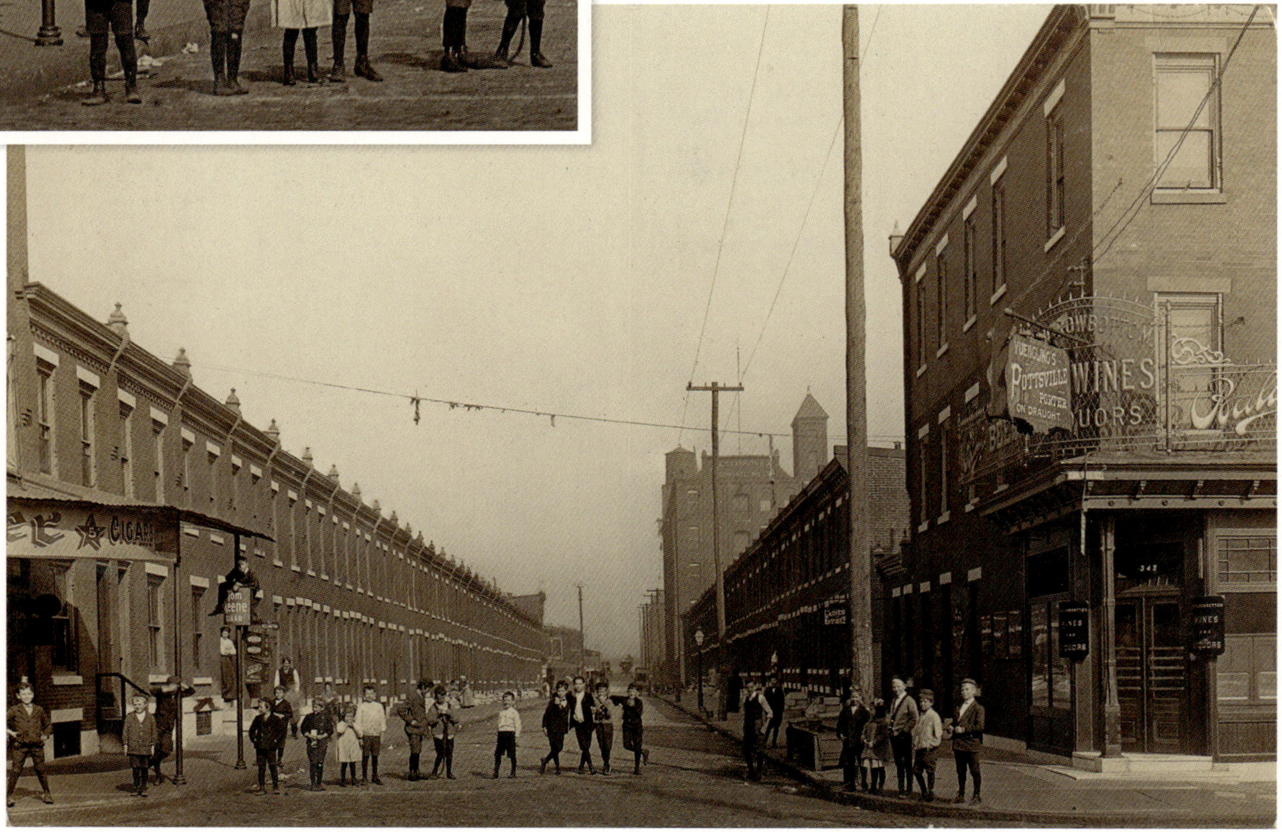

Allegheny Avenue east of Emerald Street, ca. 1907.
The East Allegheny Methodist-Episcopal Church, completed in 1892 at 2021 East Allegheny Avenue, stands out in the middle of this Victorian residential block. It is now the Greater Church Training Center.

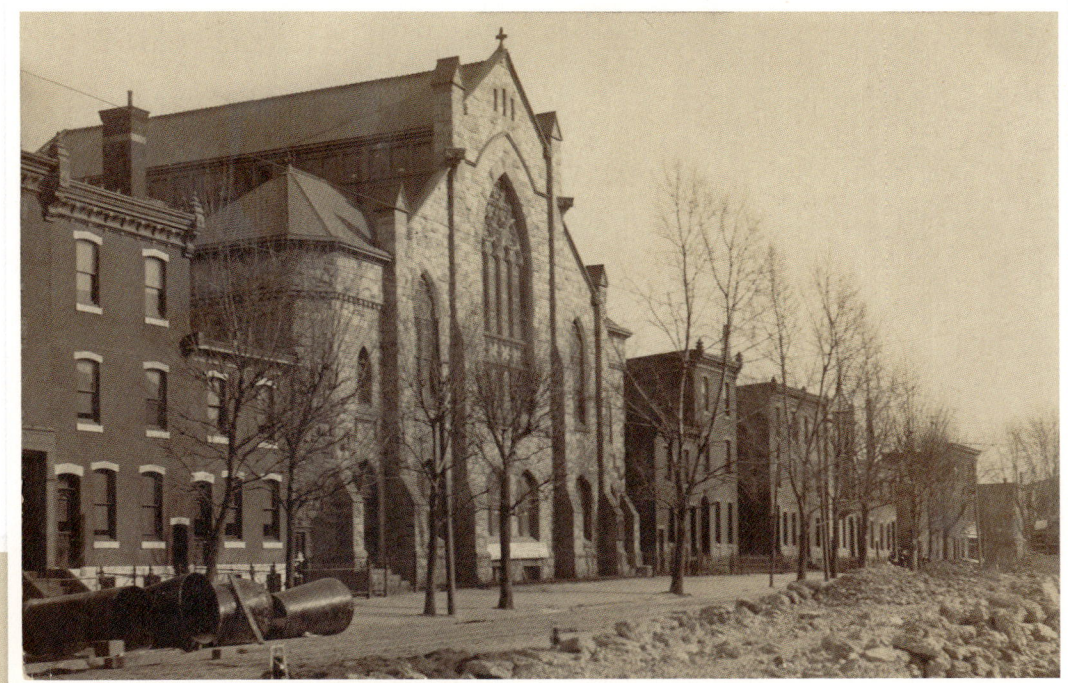

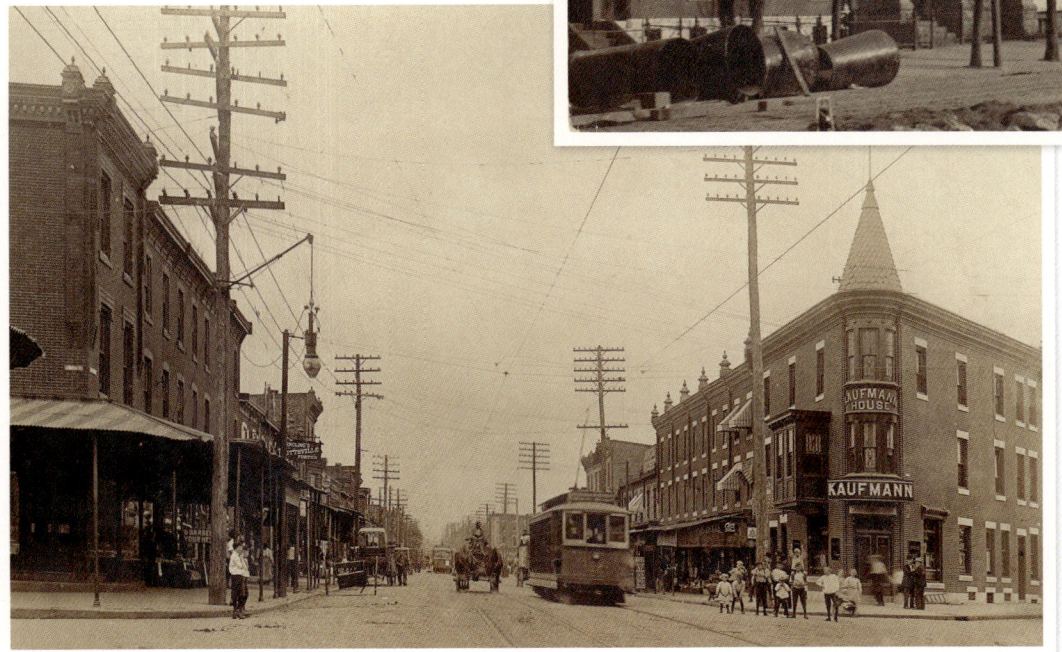

Kensington Avenue south from intersection of E and Cambria Streets, 1911. This early view of Kensington Avenue shows a busy street scene before the construction of the Market-Frankford El. Kensington Avenue was, and remains, a main commercial corridor through the Kensington section of Philadelphia. The three-story Kaufmann House tavern on the right is an unusual wedge-shaped building that still stands, minus the "witch hat" roof.

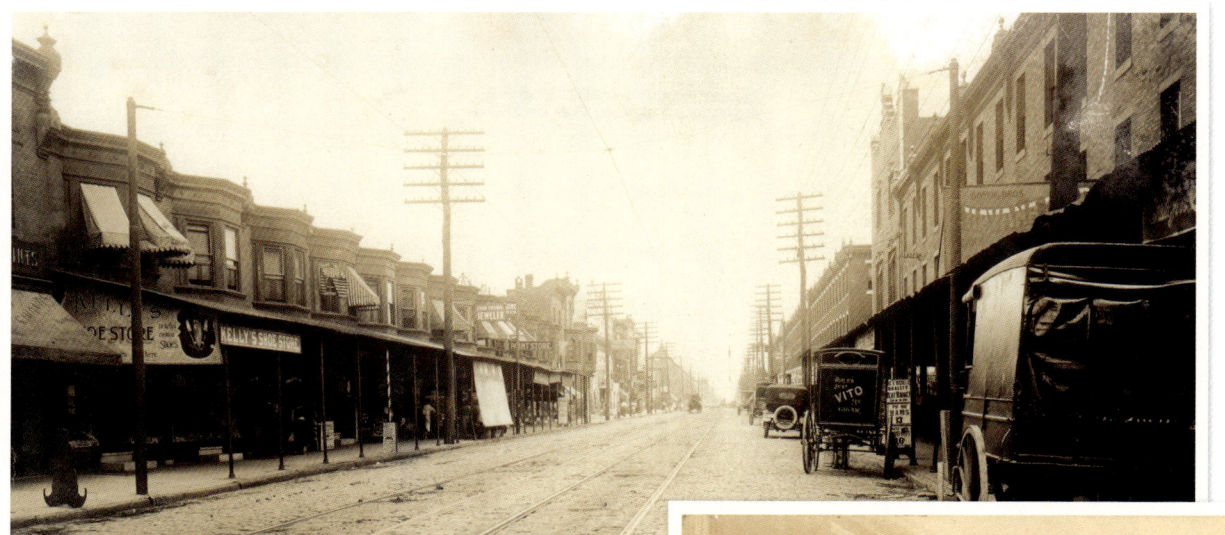

Kensington Avenue north from Clearfield Street, 1913. Well before the construction of the Market-Frankford El, Kensington Avenue was a hub of business activity. A variety of stores, ranging from mundane items such as meat and shoes to John Gund's high-end jewelry store, welcomed shoppers. The Iris Theatre, built in 1910, was also on this block at 3146 Kensington Ave. The Iris closed in 1969, and the building now houses a discount store.

Madison Street east of Emerald Street, 1906. Three well-dressed gents pose casually outside of the bar of John F. Cliggett on the corner of Emerald Street and East Madison. Cliggett lived about one mile away at 2548 Ann Street with his extended family. J. F. Cliggett's tavern was a purveyor of Schmidt's beer, a popular local brew. In time, Schmidt's would become one of the largest breweries in the US.

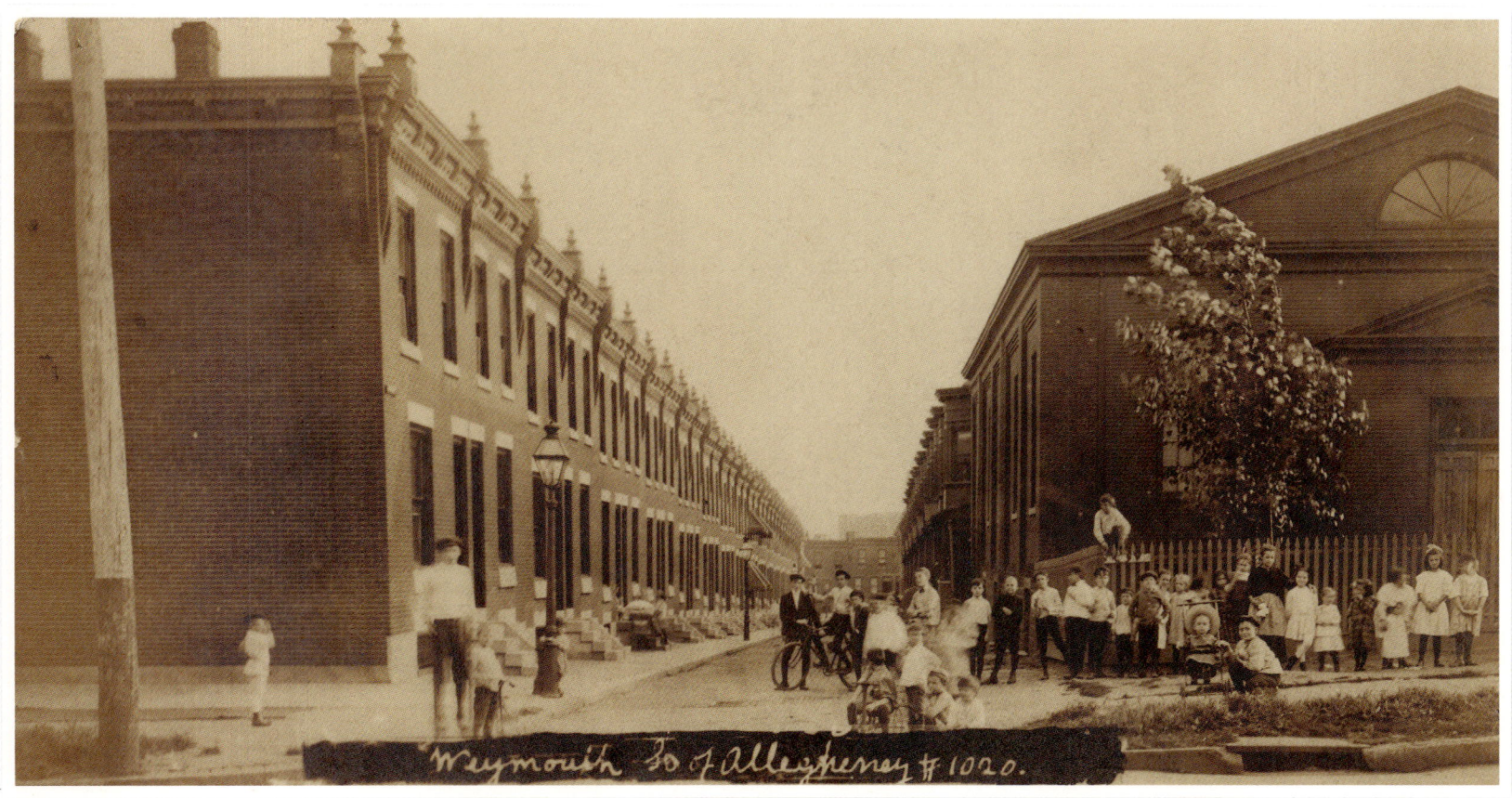

Weymouth Street south from Allegheny Avenue, 1907. Many children came out for this shot of Weymouth Street, formerly Windrim Street, looking south from Allegheny Avenue. The east (*left*) side of Weymouth was built as early as 1893. The west side of the street was begun in March 1896. Trinity Episcopal Church, on the right, was later enlarged and is now Iglesia Adventista del 7mo Día.

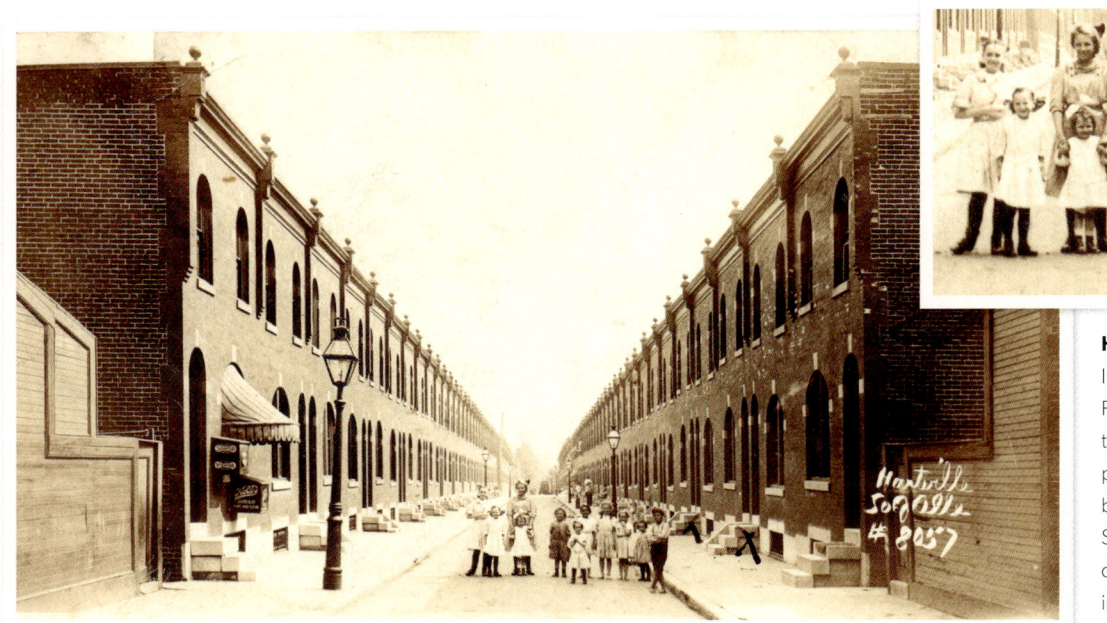

Hartville Street south of Allegheny Avenue, ca. 1910.
In the days before motorized traffic, the streets of
Philadelphia were the domain of children. The houses on
this street were like thousands of others built during this
period. The amenities were few, but the homes were solidly
built and affordable. The east and west sides of Hartville
Street were built in May 1901. The firm of Hales & Ballinger
designed these humble homes and about a hundred others
in the area.

Allegheny Avenue east of D Street, 1907. Allegheny
Avenue is one of the major thoroughfares in North
Philadelphia. This residential block of D Street is lined with
late Victorian row houses, a bit fancier than those found in
Kensington at the time. On the corner of D Street and
Allegheny Avenue is a bakery belonging to F. P. Hofmann,
which doubled as a residence. The bakery is topped with a
conical roof, a common feature on corner properties and a
vestige of Queen Anne–style architecture. This entire block of
Allegheny Avenue between D Street and Rorer Street has
been demolished, replaced by the Lewis Elkin Elementary
School. The house marked with an "X" was owned by R. D.
McRobie.

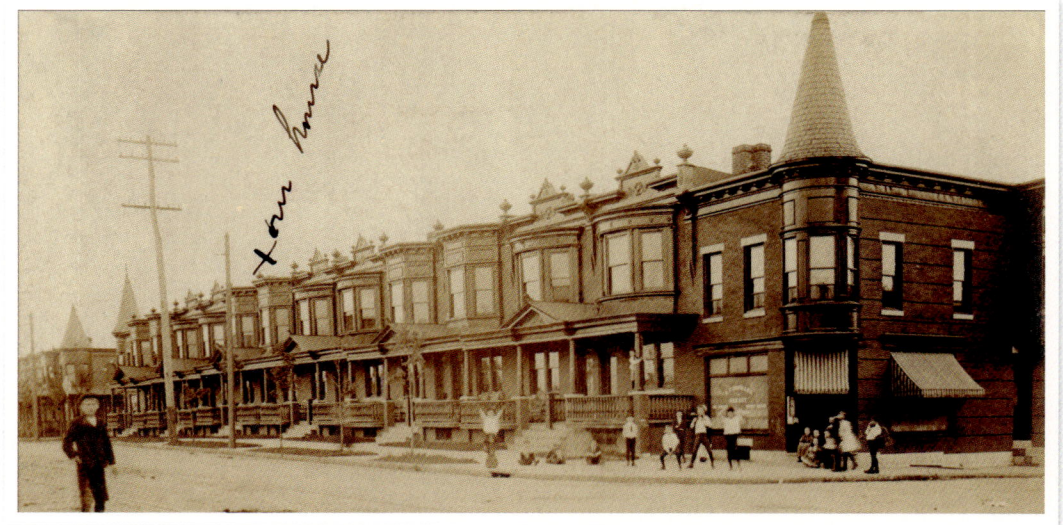

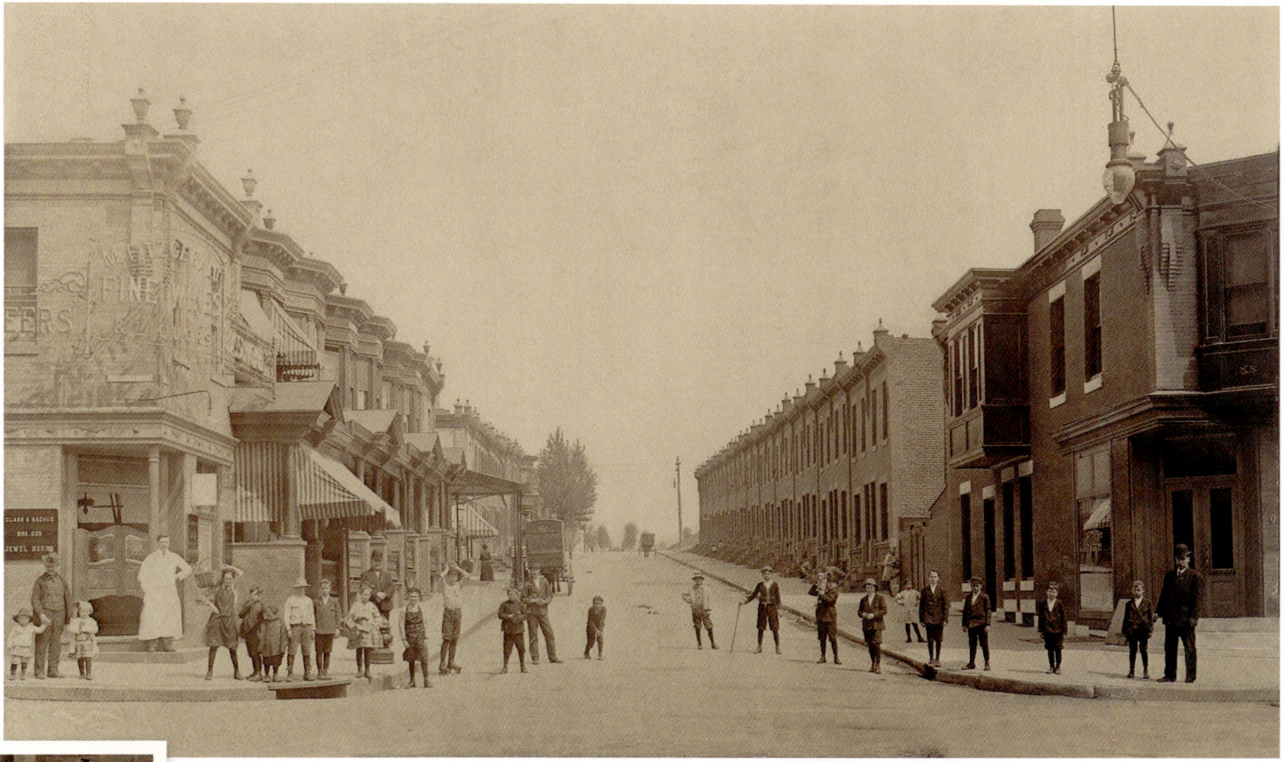

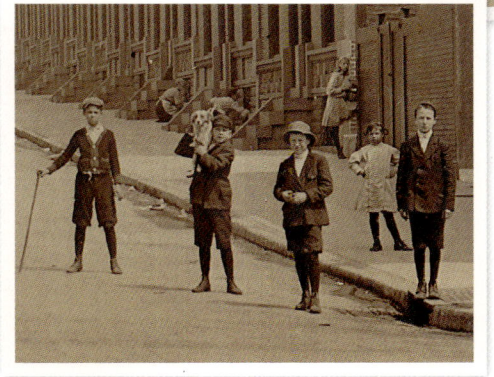

H Street north from Westmoreland Street, ca. 1910. No working-class neighborhood would be complete without a local watering hole, such as Fitzgerald's on the corner of H and Westmoreland Streets. The west side of H Street, including the saloon, was built in February 1906 by James W. Orr and designed by Richards & Son. Builder George W. Shisler and architect William H. Young were responsible for the houses on the east side, begun in February 1909.

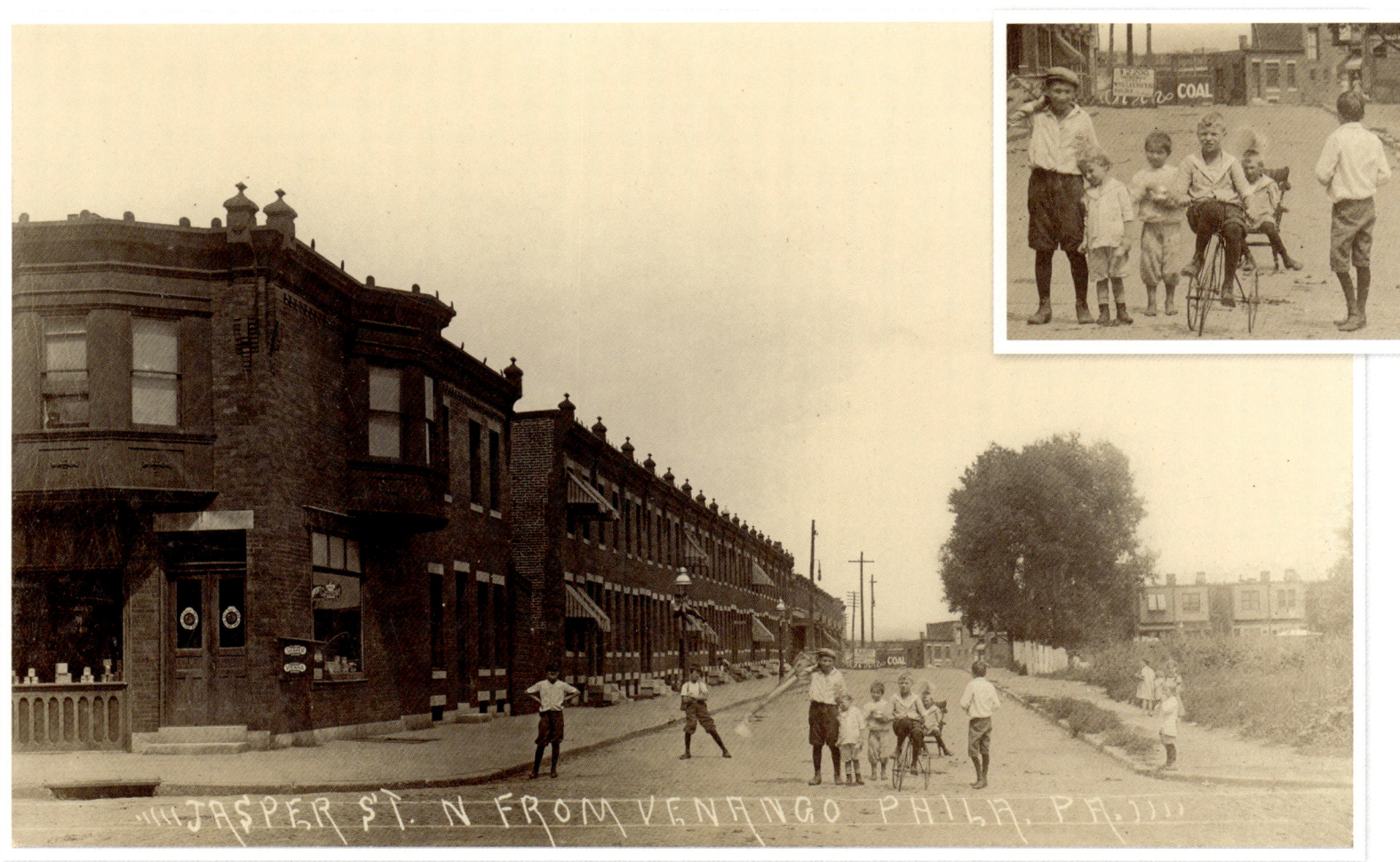

Jasper Street north of Venango Street, ca. 1908. A view of Jasper Street showing vacant lots on the east side of the street. In the distance on the right side, the rear of homes on Pacific Street are visible. Many of the residents likely worked at the Cameron & Co. Spinning Mill on Glenwood Avenue and Pacific Street.

Rorer Street south of Allegheny Avenue, ca. 1907.
A row of nondescript yet comfortable row houses line Rorer Street in Kensington. They were built in May 1901, part of massive development in this part of Kensington.

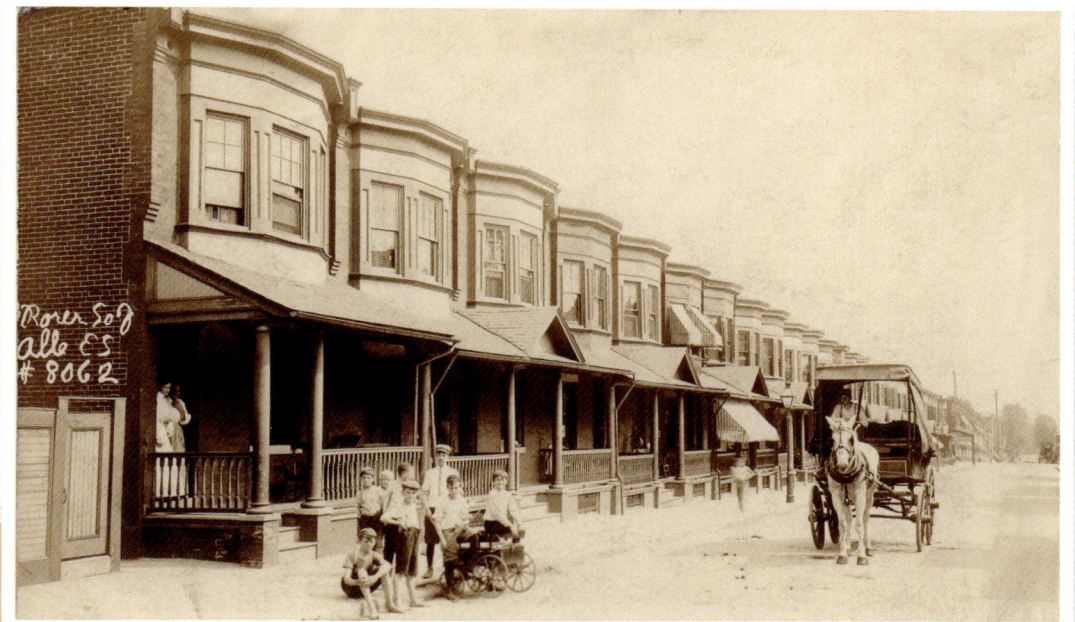

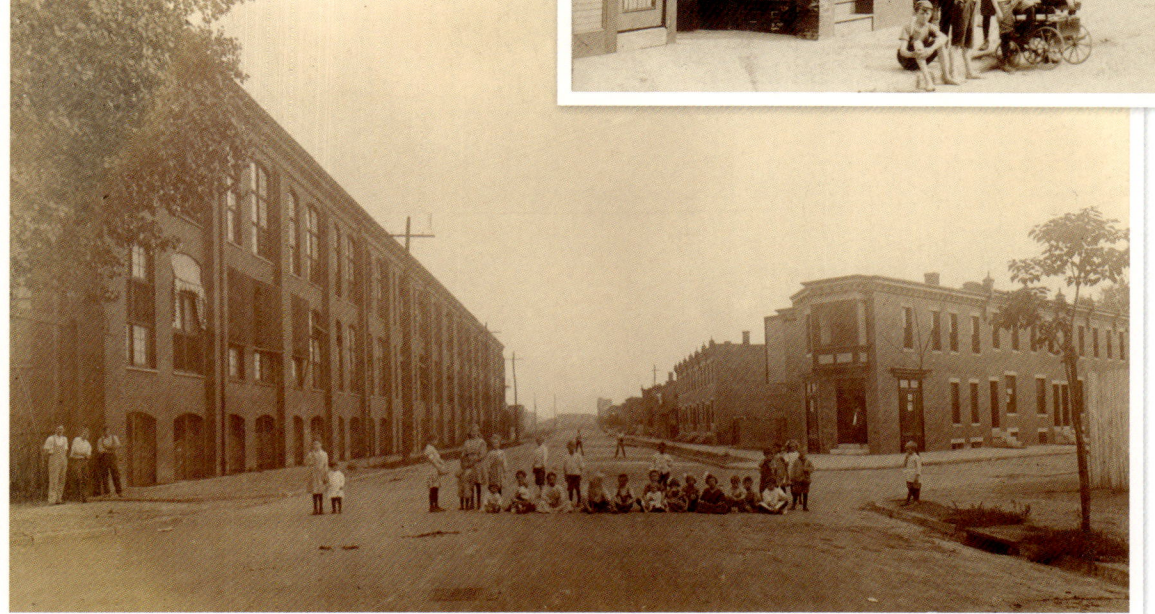

Glenwood Avenue north of Kensington Avenue, ca. 1910. Taken near the intersection with Pacific Street, the three-story building on the left is the A. J. Cameron & Co. Spinning Mills, where the parents and siblings of these children were likely employed. The Cameron Mills produced wool yarn.

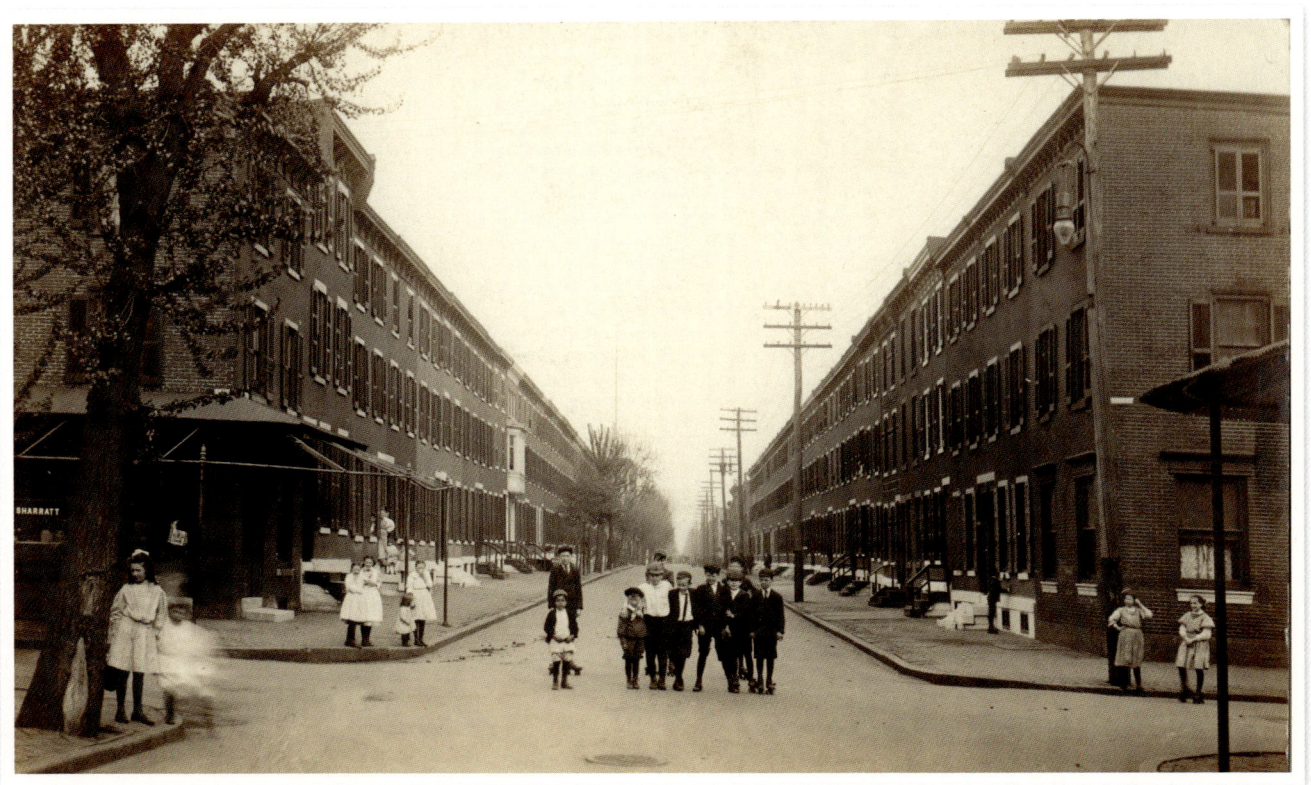

Fitzwater Street east of Twenty-First Street, 1907

South Philadelphia is famous for its cheesesteaks, Mummers New Year's associations, and the Italian Market, but unbeknown to most visitors and residents alike is the fact that the neighborhood is the site of a very early European settlement, even by Philadelphia standards. Passyunk Road (now Passyunk Avenue) is the oldest road in Pennsylvania, written about as early as 1660. Previously it was home to the colony of New Sweden, established to take advantage of the lucrative beaver fur trade. The Swedes built log structures, very few of which are still standing. The Swedes continued to thrive here, even after the Dutch took dominion over the region in 1655. The oldest extant building with a Swedish lineage in Philadelphia is the Church of Gloria Dei (Old Swedes Church, 916 South Swanson Street), built in 1700. The old brick church replaced the earlier Wiccaco Church, built of logs in 1677.[1]

Early South Philadelphia

Early South Philadelphia did not enjoy the greatest of reputations. The name "Moyamensing," one of the townships, is said to have derived from a native phrase meaning "pigeon droppings." The old village of Martinsville, formerly located near the intersection of Water Street and Snyder Avenue, was described in 1866 by the Board of Health as "not fit for dogs to live in."[2]

In 1920, intrepid *Philadelphia Inquirer* writer Christopher Morley ventured into the marshy hinterland of South Philadelphia and reported on his findings as if he were an explorer visiting alien territory. What Morley saw on his treks to South Philadelphia was a landscape completely unknown to his uptown readers. It was a place of canals, pigpens, tar-paper shacks, barefoot children, and customs of its own. It also had foul-smelling dumps and a thin haze of burning waste. The remoteness made it an ideal location for malodorous industries such as slaughterhouses, leather tanning, and fertilizer plants. Despite South Philadelphia's unsavory reputation, the city grid pushed relentlessly southward, eventually consuming rural parts of South Philadelphia.[3]

Immigrant Groups

In the late nineteenth century, South Philadelphia was comparable to New York's Lower East Side. It was a place where the city's ethnic groups, both new and old, lived and worked.[4]

On an autumn evening in 1891, a reporter from a local paper observed:

> In the glare of the electric lights . . . can be seen the peasants of Italy, who, perhaps, a few months ago knew nothing above the light of a candle, walking along in gorgeous purple skirts, green bodices with yellow scarves as head covering. These women carry themselves well and jostle freely with the Russian Hebrews and the Poles and the Hungarians, Scandinavians from the land of the midnight sun, and Turks from the land of the burning noons, and in fact a most motley and conglomerate lot.[5]

Jews, Italians, Irish, and African Americans had their own sections in South Philadelphia, with some overlap. African Americans had been there the longest, and frequently they and the Irish clashed with each other. The Jews, escaping troubles in eastern Europe, came to the ports of South Philadelphia in larger numbers after 1881 and settled in the Jewish Quarter. The Italians were the last group to come over en masse, settling in the Italian District, which would later become the Italian Market area, recently rebranded as trendy Bella Vista ("Beautiful View" in Italian).[6]

The ethnic and racial mosaic of this early period will be discussed in further detail in chapter 9.

Squatterville

Rustic conditions persisted in the deepest parts of South Philadelphia well into the twentieth century. Squatterville, or the Neck, as locals liked to call it, was a village of about 200 families that existed until 1956. People lived there for two primary reasons: it was cheap and they liked it. It was a place that time and regulations forgot. Building permits? Plumbing, sanitation, and fire codes? No one followed these rules in Squatterville. In the absence of indoor plumbing, water was carried or piped from city hydrants. Rookie city inspectors were tasked with inspection tours of Squatterville as a rite of passage or practical joke. The large stack of violations would wind up in the trash. Even the police were not an effective deterrent. Constables went in with eviction notices and were chased away; some were even beaten. An old-time denizen of Squatterville remarked, "We've had inspectors here by the gross. Sometimes we talked to 'em; other times we chased 'em. Either way, we knew nothing would ever come of it."[7]

Then, on May 2, 1955, at 10:38 a.m., a tragedy at 3508 South Seventh Street put a permanent end to Squatterville. On that fateful morning an electrical fire broke out in the four-room frame house of Bertha Ibetson, killing her four children and badly damaging their neighbor's house at 3506 South Seventh (present-day Seventh and Packer Avenue). This was the final straw for city officials, who had been trying to put an end to the South Philadelphia backwater for half a century. Top-level city officials including Councilman Paul D'Ortona and Fire Commissioner Frank McNamee went to inspect the charred remains. They said that some of the houses were nothing but shacks, violated city codes, and should be torn down immediately. The city had finally had enough. In 1956, the last of the shacks and abandoned farms were cleared, replaced by the $100 million Food Distribution Center and the Walt Whitman Bridge right-of-way.[8]

South Philadelphia Neighborhoods

Today, the area once called Southwark is now Queen Village and Pennsport. Some of the neighborhood's more interesting relics are the aforementioned Gloria Dei Church and the highly visible Sparks Shot Tower (1808) near Front and Carpenter Streets.

Southwark was named for the London district, which contained the "southern defense work" (shortened to "south-work") for the London Bridge. Southwark was made a municipality in 1762 and received full incorporation in 1794. Some of the city's earliest row homes were built in this area. They were simple, two- or two-and-a-half-story structures, usually built of brick. The occupants of these humble dwellings were usually employed in the maritime trades, given the proximity to the Delaware River and the Philadelphia Navy Yard, once located in Southwark.[9]

Beyond Southwark, in Moyamensing Township, were the low marshlands of Stonehouse Lane, or the Neck. The area below Hollander's Creek was known as Greenwich Island, and farther still was League Island beneath the southern tip of mainland Philadelphia (the current home of the US Navy Shipyard). Out of this swampy morass was carved the neighborhood of Whitman.[10]

The western half of South Philadelphia was Passyunk Township. This too was sparsely populated before the twentieth century. Aside from Gentilehommiere, the grand house and farm of Stephen Girard (1750–1831), there were a handful of plantations and truck farms. The marshy lands were home to the bygone villages of Martinsville (a.k.a., Frogtown), Eleven-Gun Battery, and the "Ma'sh," noted for large numbers of rails and other small birds. Avid game hunters wound their way down to this largely unknown part of the city to shoot their fill of marsh birds.[11]

The farmland surrounding Stephen Girard's mansion was developed as Girard Estate between 1906 and 1916, a high-class suburb of attractive twin homes designed by James H. Windrim and his son, John T. Windrim. The district, modeled after Ebenezer Howard's Garden City movement, is bounded from Shunk Street to Porter Street and from Eighteenth Street to Twenty-Second Street. North of Girard Estate is Point Breeze, an old neighborhood filled with the familiar red-brick row houses and ethnic enclaves.[12]

North of Washington Avenue is Schuylkill, or South of South, although it is currently referred to as the Graduate Hospital neighborhood, even though that name is no longer applicable because Graduate Hospital became Penn Medicine at Rittenhouse in 2007. The proximity to western Center City, already a fashionable enclave in the late nineteenth century, meant that the South of South area was ripe for development. The interesting garden blocks of Madison Square and St. Albans Place, between Twenty-Second and Twenty-Fourth Streets, are part of the neighborhood. These blocks are closed to traffic and maintain their central "gardens" between the row houses on either side. A tiny fragment of the neighborhood is known as Devil's Pocket, once a working-class Irish enclave.[13]

West of Twenty-Fifth Street is Grays Ferry, yet another densely packed row house section of the city. The area took its name from George Gray, an eighteenth-century innkeeper and ferry operator. The main street in this neighborhood is Grays Ferry Avenue, which runs to the northeast from the Schuylkill River and terminates near Twenty-Third and South Streets in the Graduate Hospital neighborhood.[14]

The Future of South Philadelphia

Big changes have come to parts of South Philadelphia—some of them positive, others with unforeseen negative impacts. Developers with deep pockets and political connections are building on seemingly every available parcel of land, even at the expense of historic buildings. This demand for new houses is driven by arrivals from the suburbs and from outside the Philadelphia metropolitan area. They bring with them a taste for the modern conveniences of yoga studios, cafés, and organic grocery stores. Meanwhile, the ethnic landscape has changed dramatically. Immigrants from Southeast Asia and Latin America are taking up residence in South Philadelphia, imparting their own exotic flavors to the neighborhood.

Older South Philadelphians view the newcomers with trepidation, while others welcome the infusion of youthful energy. Going forward, change may be the only constant in South Philadelphia.

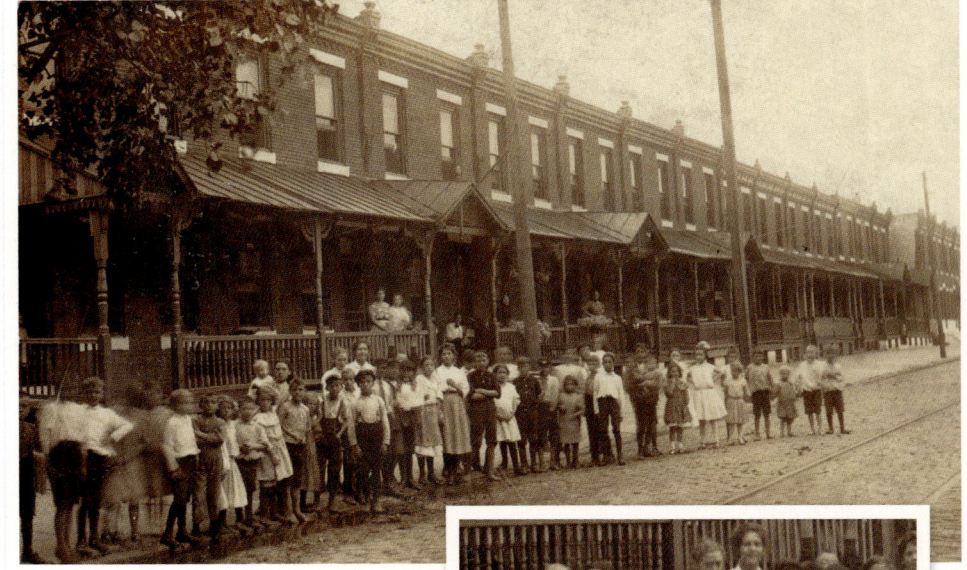

Second Street north of McKean Street, ca. 1907. These houses were slightly fancier than other homes in the area, with front porches facing the trolley line running down Second Street. A gaggle of children, some barefoot, stopped their play to watch the photographer. These houses were built between January 1890 and November 1891.

Buck Road, 1902. View showing Buck Road between Eighth Street and Ninth Street and Shunk Street to Porter Street. Old farmhouses and picket fences are seen on either side of this dusty old road. Development of this area was less than a decade away, and this rustic setting was replaced by the type of urban density for which South Philadelphia is known. The haziness shown here is from a combination of dirt from the road and nearby fields and fumes from the Bauss Fertilizer Plant, which processed horse manure with a phosphate screener. The burning of paper and assorted rubbish from a neighboring dump added to the smoky and malodorous atmosphere.

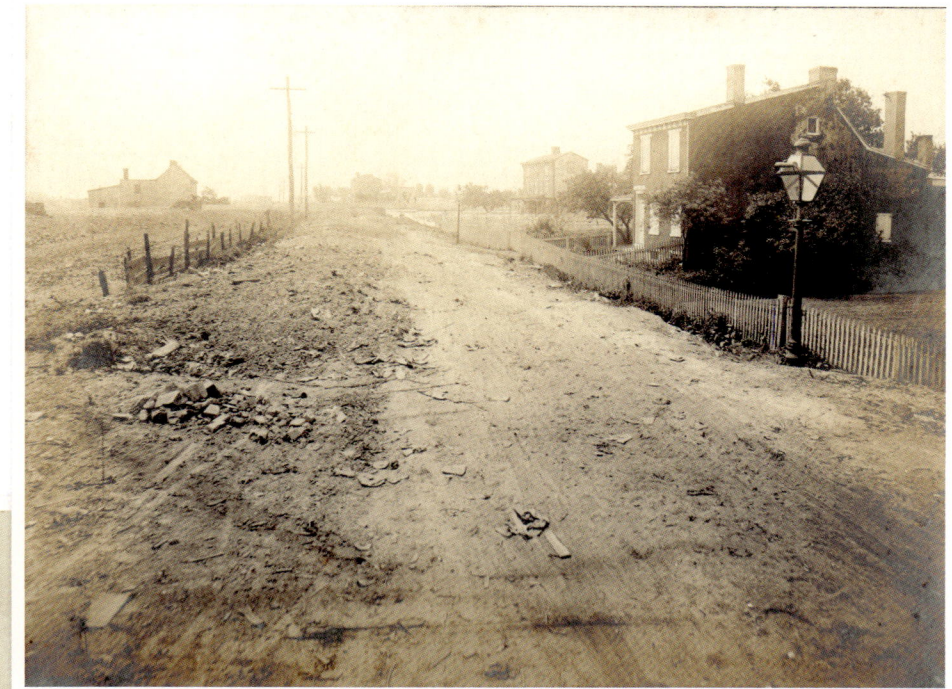

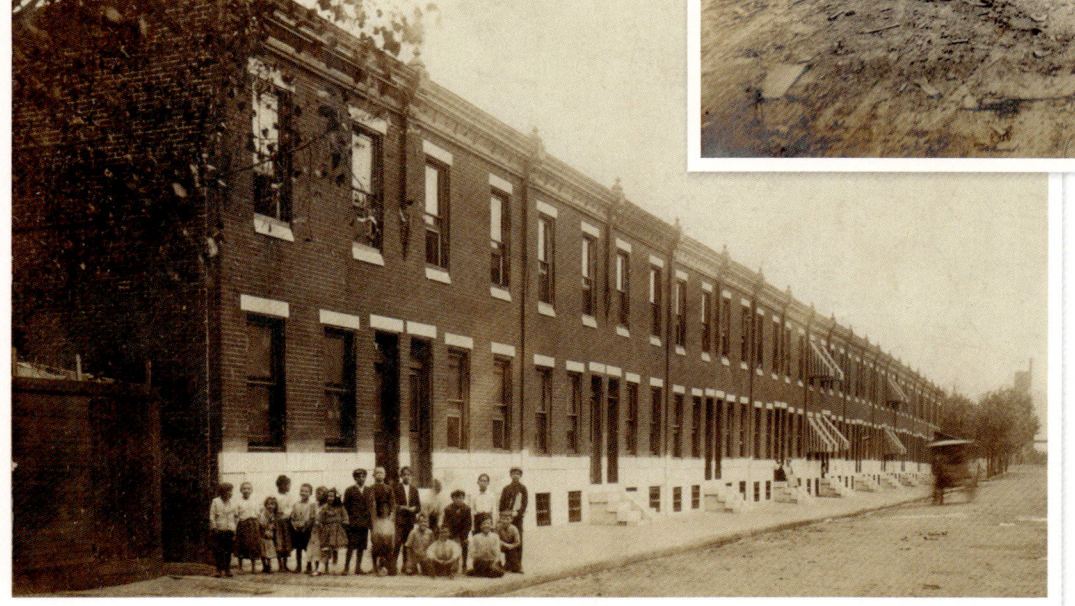

McKean Street east of Second, ca. 1907. In the lower portion of the Pennsport section of South Philly, the houses were simply designed—porchless two-stories with narrow floor plans. Large families with many children were the order of the day. This part of Pennsport was fairly close to the Delaware waterfront, likely the workplace of many male wage earners. These houses were built in January 1890.

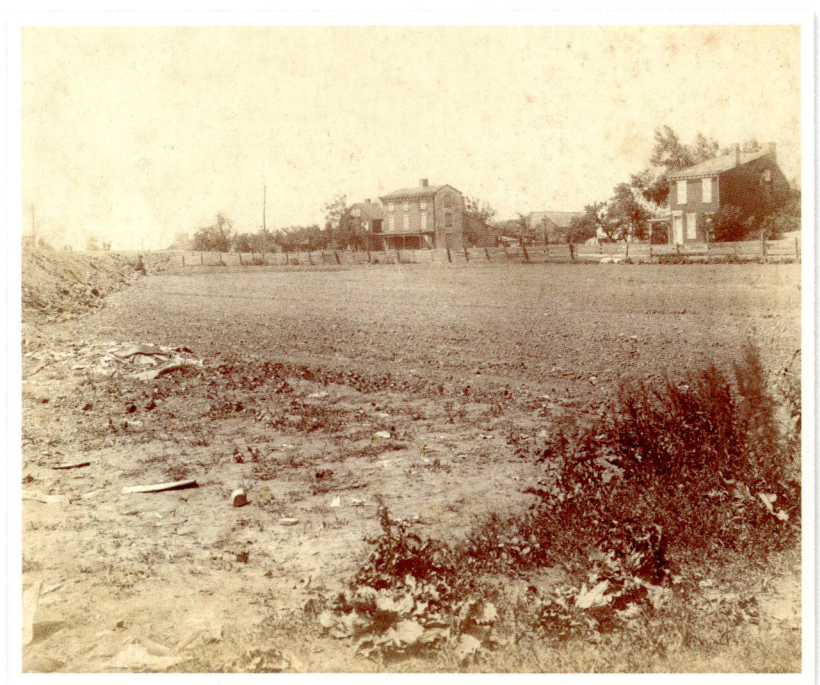

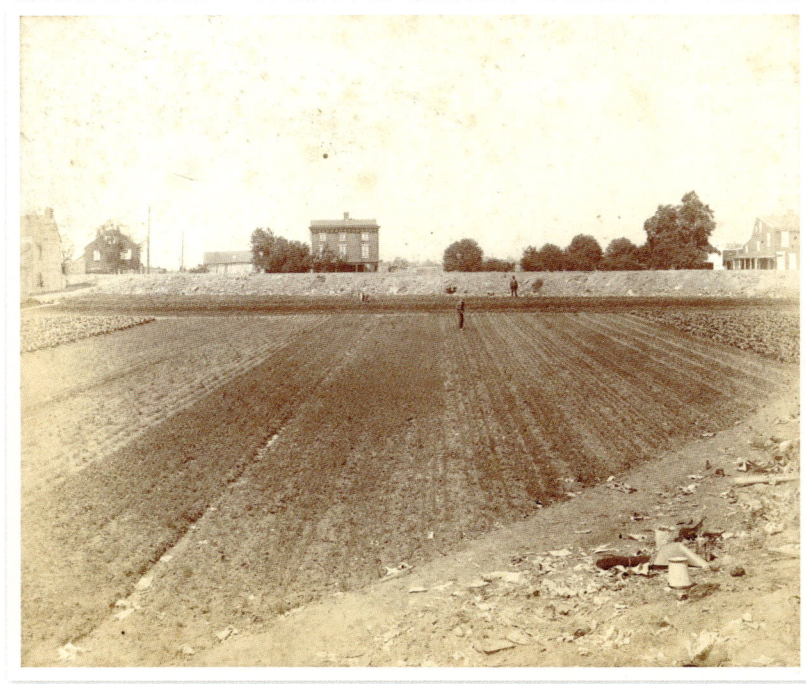

South side of Eighth Street showing Buck Road, 1902. This rare photograph depicts the area of Eighth and Porter Streets before urbanization transformed the region. The farmhouses shown here fronted on Buck Road, a dirt road that ran from roughly Seventh and Oregon Avenues to Tenth and Jackson Streets. It once continued to approximately Broad and Dickinson Streets before the city's grid pattern gradually obliterated Buck Road, like so many other old dirt trails in the Neck. In the foreground are weeds and debris from a nearby dump. The middle ground shows the well-tended fields that once proliferated in South Philadelphia.

Eighth Street north of Porter Street, 1902. A lone farmer toils in his fields in South Philadelphia while a well-dressed Mr. Shetzline stands watch. His office, Charles H. Shetzline & Co., was located at the intersection of Broad Street and Passyunk Avenue.

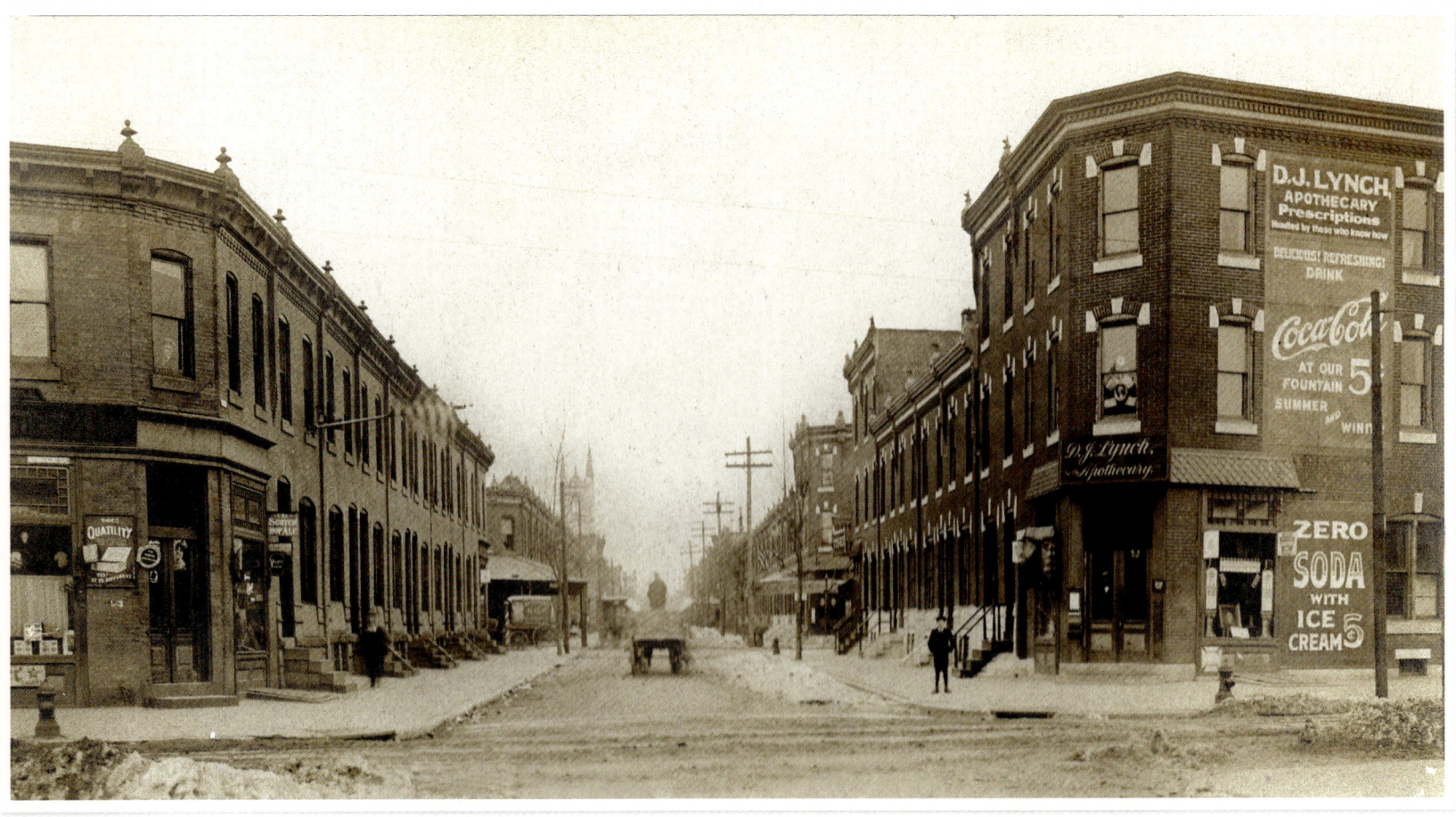

Eleventh Street north from Moyamensing Avenue, 1906. The apothecary and residence of David L. Lynch occupies the northeast corner of Eleventh and Moyamensing Avenue. Lynch's sold Coca Cola and ice cream sodas for a nickel. Harry Koch built these houses in June 1896.

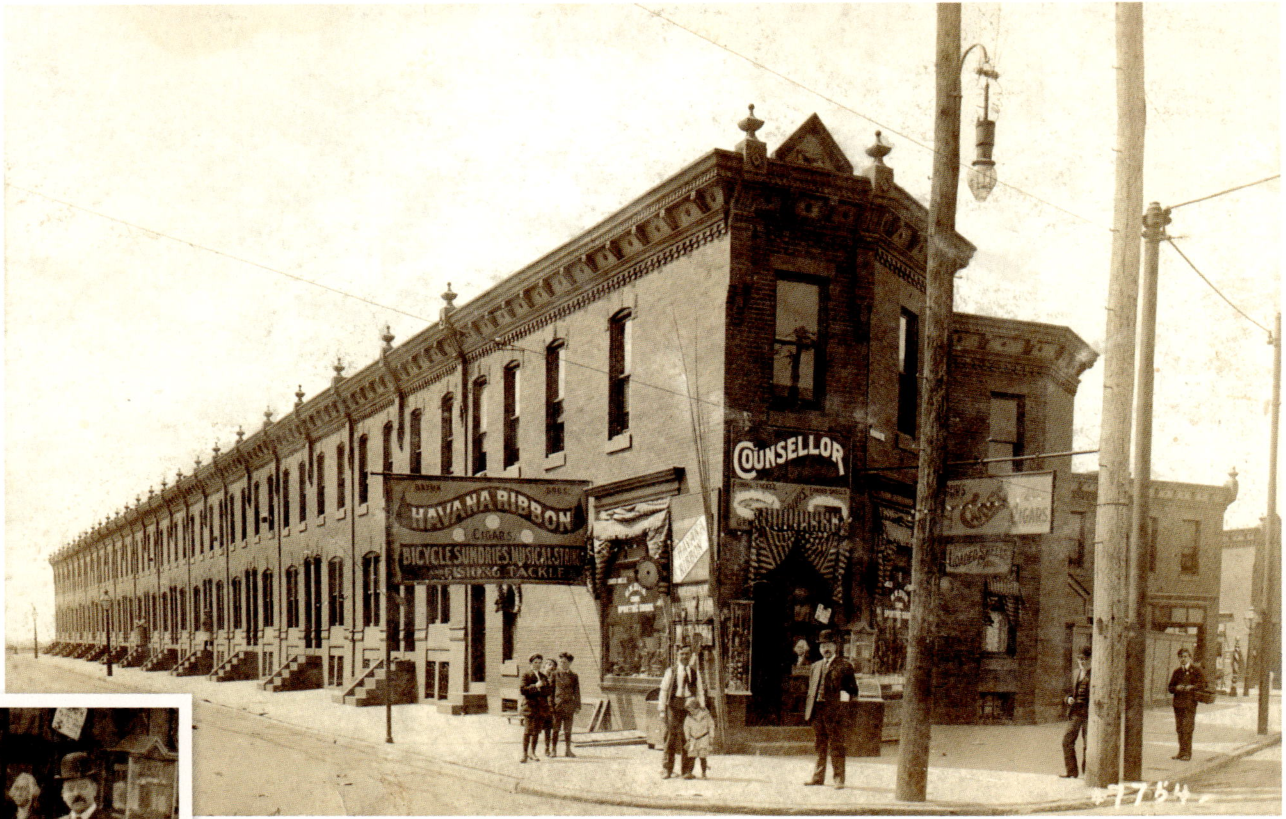

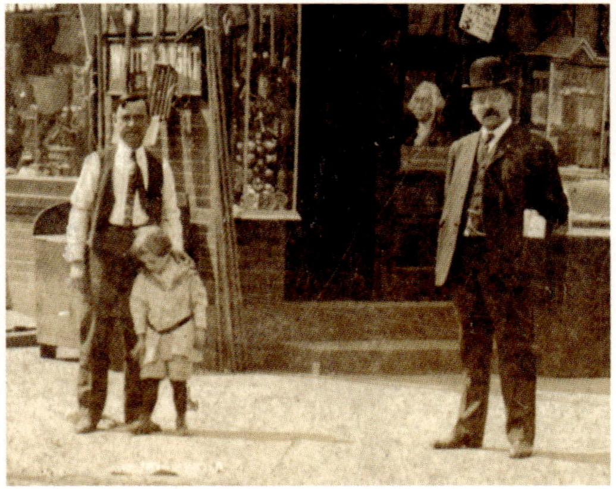

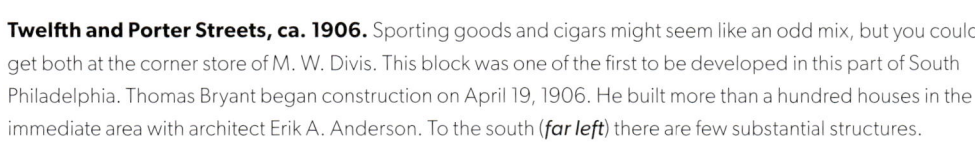

Twelfth and Porter Streets, ca. 1906. Sporting goods and cigars might seem like an odd mix, but you could get both at the corner store of M. W. Divis. This block was one of the first to be developed in this part of South Philadelphia. Thomas Bryant began construction on April 19, 1906. He built more than a hundred houses in the immediate area with architect Erik A. Anderson. To the south (*far left*) there are few substantial structures.

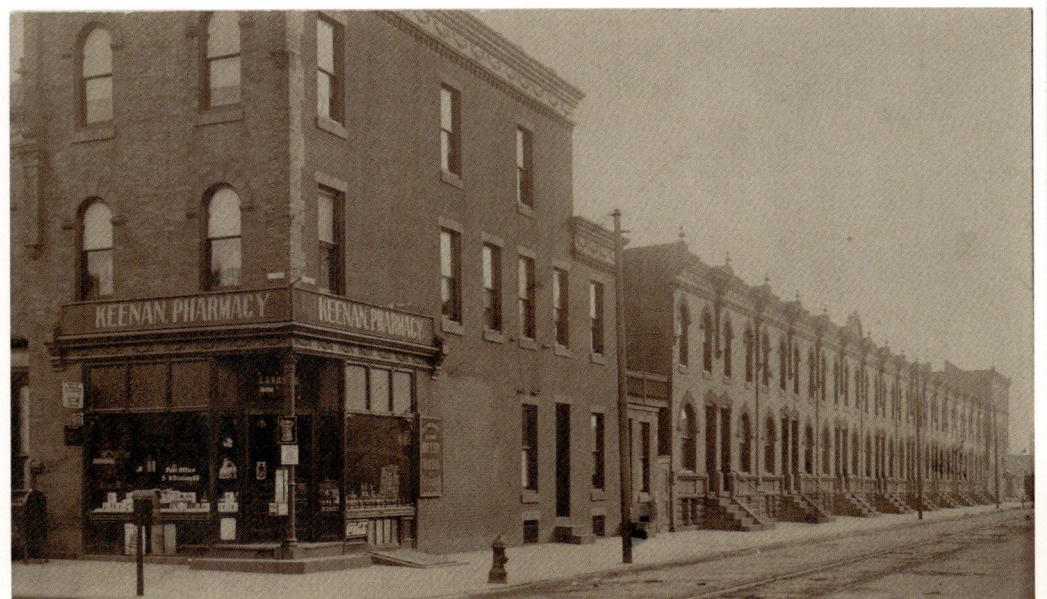

Seventeenth Street south of Ritner Street, 1908.
Keenan Pharmacy, owned by Anna Keenan and Mary Gallagher, occupies the southeast corner of Seventeenth and Ritner Streets. To the south are row houses typical of South Philadelphia. John C. Gallagher built the entire block in 1897.

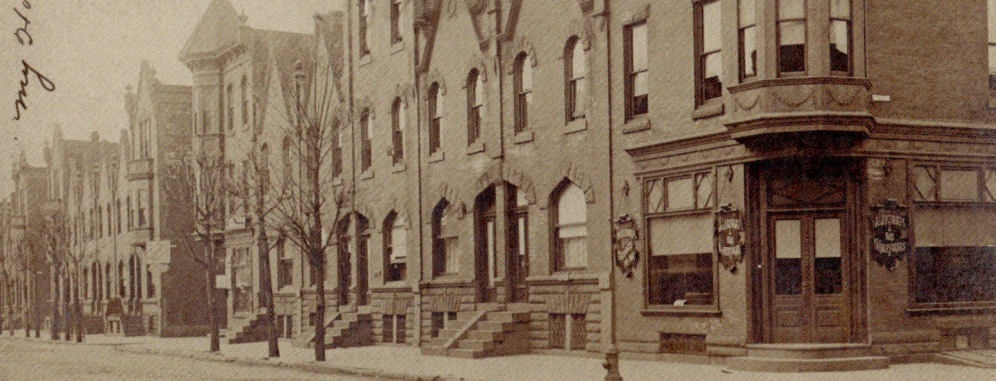

Ritner Street west of Seventeenth Street, 1908. These homes were built in August 1896 by Thomas J. Milnamow, who took up residence at 1715 Ritner Street. The houses are still standing, but many have been stripped of their Victorian features. The property at the corner of Seventeenth and Ritner Streets (*right*) was the undertaker business of Joseph J. Roberts & Bro., conveniently located across the street from St. Monica's Roman Catholic Church.

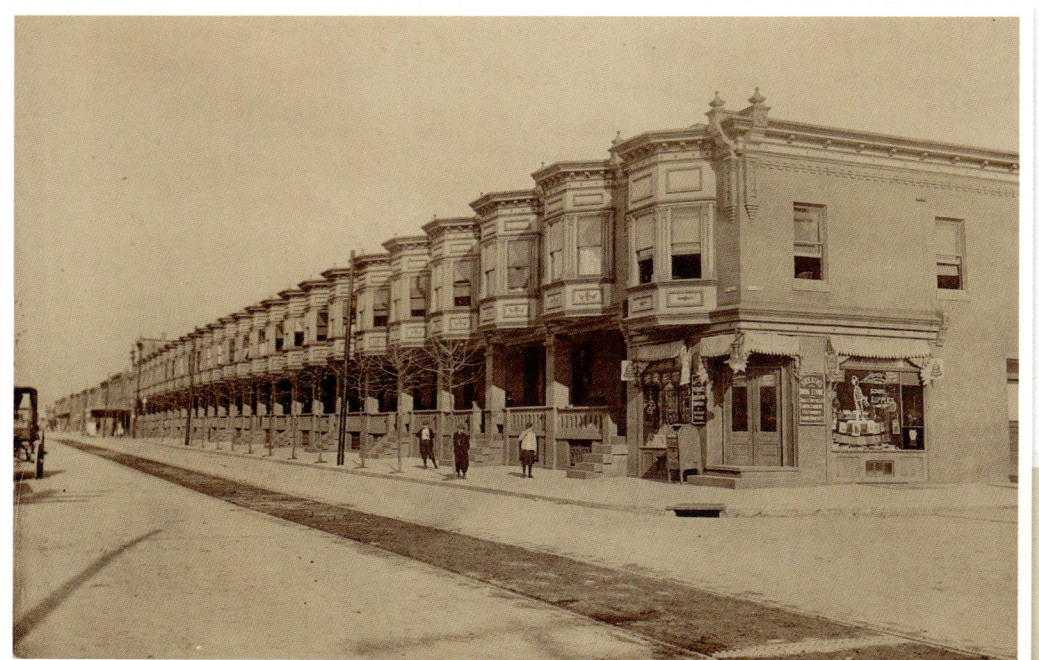

Twentieth Street north of Porter Street, ca. 1909. The near-perfect uniformity of these newly built homes has since been destroyed by unattractive renovations, including aluminum siding on the bay windows. The corner store on the right was Skeath's, a drugstore, confectionery, stationer, and tobacconist. The store portion was recently converted into a dwelling. Built in April 1909 by Barton C. Simon, a builder of hundreds of South Philadelphia homes, the row houses are directly north of the Girard Estate Historic District.

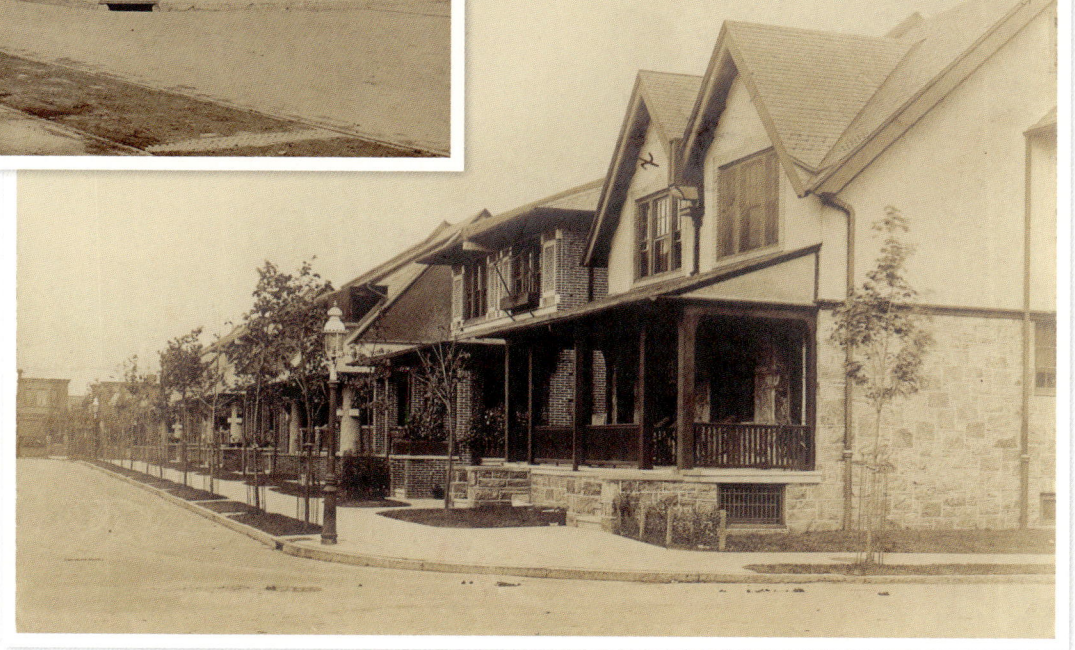

Cleveland Street north of Shunk Street, ca. 1910. Twin homes fill the Girard Estate Historic District, on the east side of Cleveland Street, looking north from Shunk Street. These houses were built in July 1909 and are now part of a historic district created in 2009 to protect the houses from demolition or alterations, but not before some of the houses were changed. In the distance, on the far left, are twin houses on the north side of Porter Street. These were the earliest homes in the Girard Estate; construction began in May 1906.

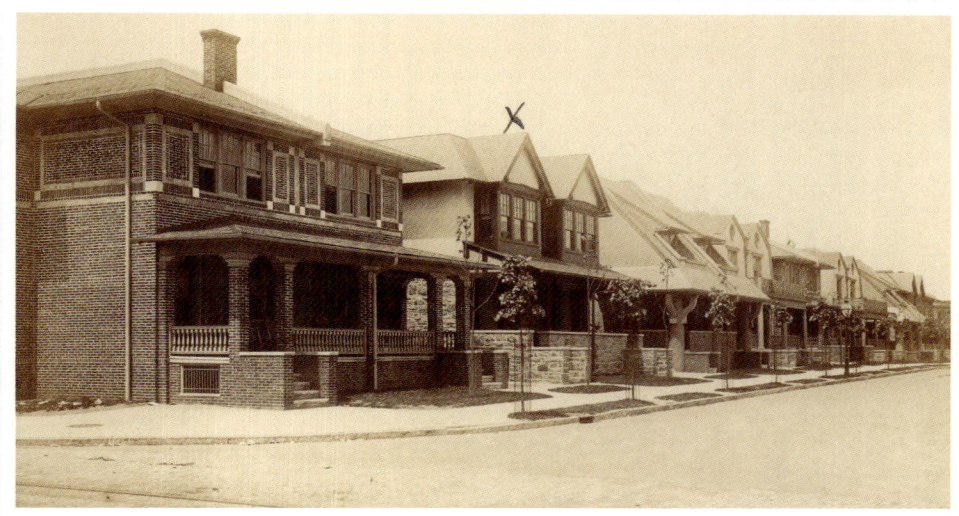

2500 block of South Colorado Street, ca. 1909. Girard Estate in South Philadelphia was inspired by the Garden City movement of Ebenezer Howard (1850–1928). The houses were built between 1906 and 1916 on land owned by the heirs of Stephen Girard (1750–1831). Row homes on the west side of Seventeenth Street south of Porter are the exception in this community of twins. Noted architect James H. Windrim (1840–1919) designed the houses in a variety of popular early-twentieth-century styles: prairie, mission, Jacobean, arts and crafts, and colonial revival. Construction on the 2500 block of South Colorado began on August 17, 1908. The twin homes are better viewed in this photo, taken when the block was new and the trees were saplings. The house with the "X" above it (2530 South Colorado) belonged to Albert E. Burns, a salesman.

Mifflin Street east of Eighteenth Street, 1907. Row houses with gabled parapets were a common sight in South Philadelphia. Many of the open porches of homes on the 1700 block of Mifflin were later enclosed. Bouvier Street (formerly Lingo Street) is the side street on the right. Construction on Mifflin's south side began on May 10, 1897, by developers Henry D. Prettyman and Richard H. Parrish. The east and west sides of Bouvier Street was also built during this time. The photo shows the bell tower of St. Elizabeth Protestant Episcopal Church, now the True Gospel Tabernacle Family Church.

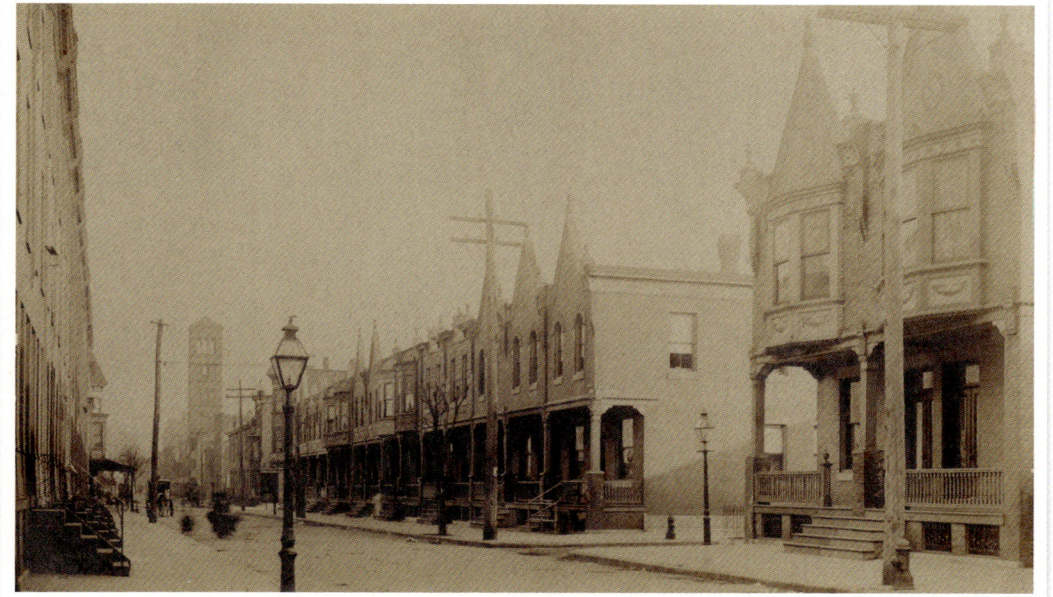

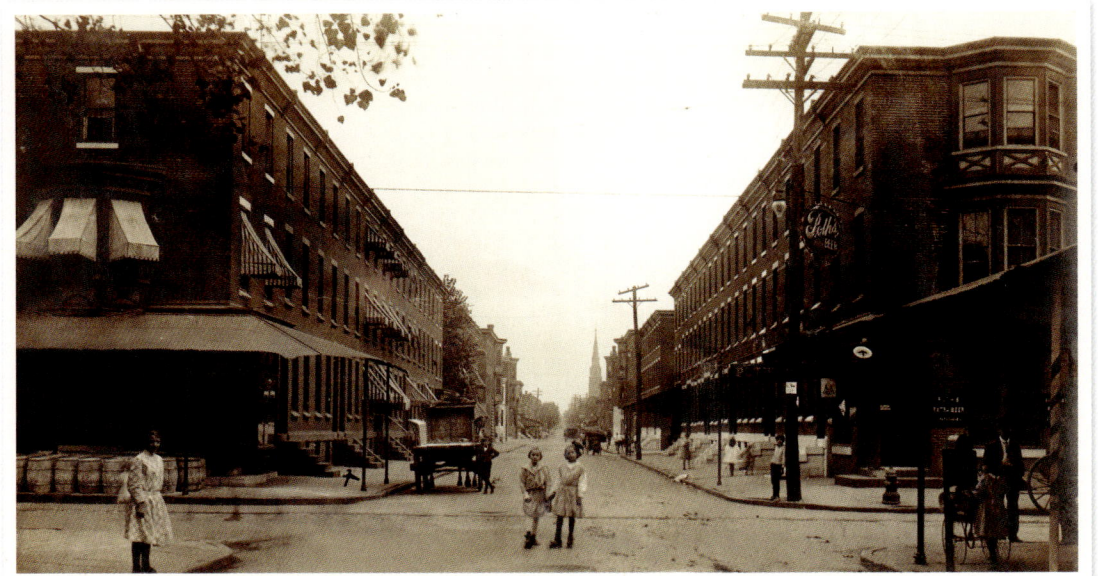

Dickinson Street east of Fifteenth Street, ca. 1907. This photo was taken one block west of the preceding photo. The building on the far right proudly served Poth Beer, while the opposite corner has a sidewalk full of barrels related to the beer distribution industry. In the distance is the steeple of the Annunciation of the Blessed Virgin Mary Roman Catholic Church, built ca. 1863, at the corner of Tenth and Dickinson Streets. The church is still standing, minus the steeple.

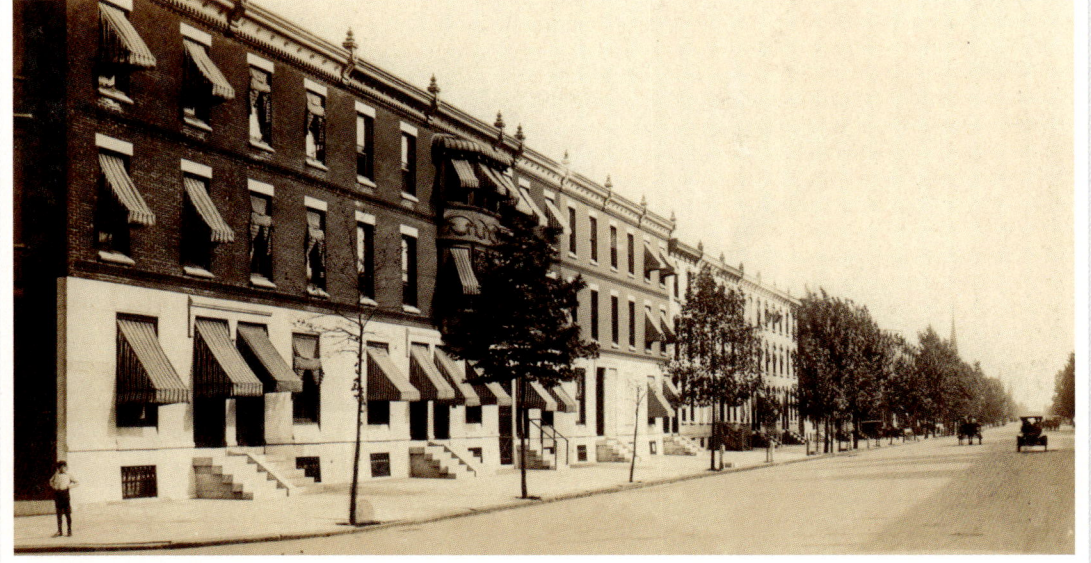

Broad Street south of Dickinson Street, ca. 1910. The 1500 block of South Broad Street is lined with stately three-story town houses. Rural Buck Road once crossed Broad Street near this point. Heading south, Broad Street led to a marshy, rustic section of the city known as the "Ma'sh" or "Neck." This countrified district was long ago developed into middle-class residential neighborhoods such as Packer Park. The open land west of Broad Street and south of Pattison Avenue was set aside as League Island Park, later used as the grounds of the 1926 Sesquicentennial International Exhibition. A large stadium was erected for the event, originally named Municipal Stadium and later John F. Kennedy Stadium. The open space east of Broad Street, where the colossal stadium was built, remained rural until the mid-twentieth century. The area, called Stone House Lane, was cleared by the city and became home to Philadelphia's produce distribution and, eventually, professional sports teams.

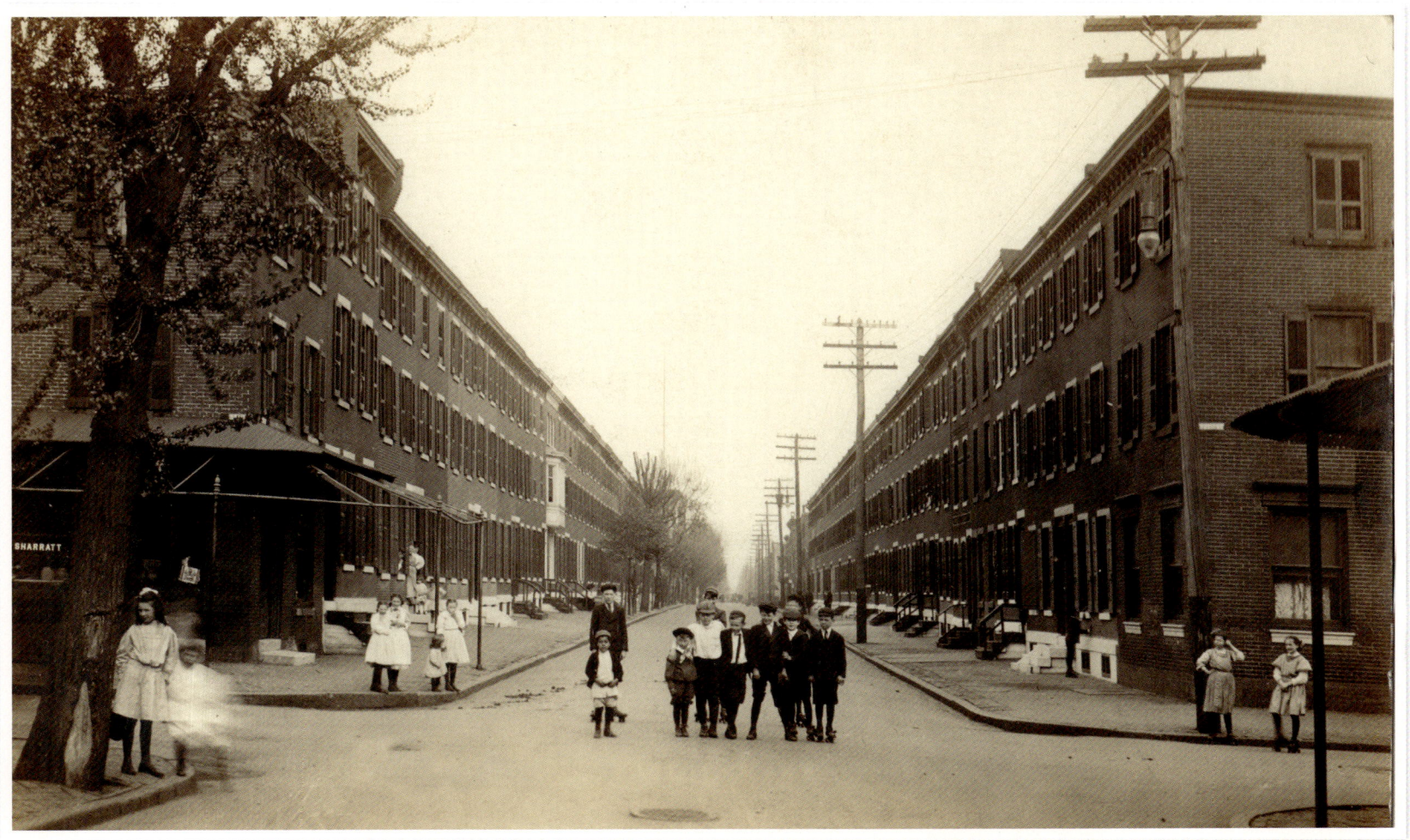

Fitzwater Street east of Twenty-First Street, ca. 1910. Rows of stately three-story Italianate homes line the 2100 block of Fitzwater Street in the Schuylkill neighborhood. As evidenced by the large number of young children in the photo, this was an ideal neighborhood for raising a family. It was also somewhat prosperous for its time, as evidenced by the grouping of young boys posing in the center of the photo, who are dressed in finer attire than usual and are equipped with amenities such as roller skates. These houses were built in the 1870s.

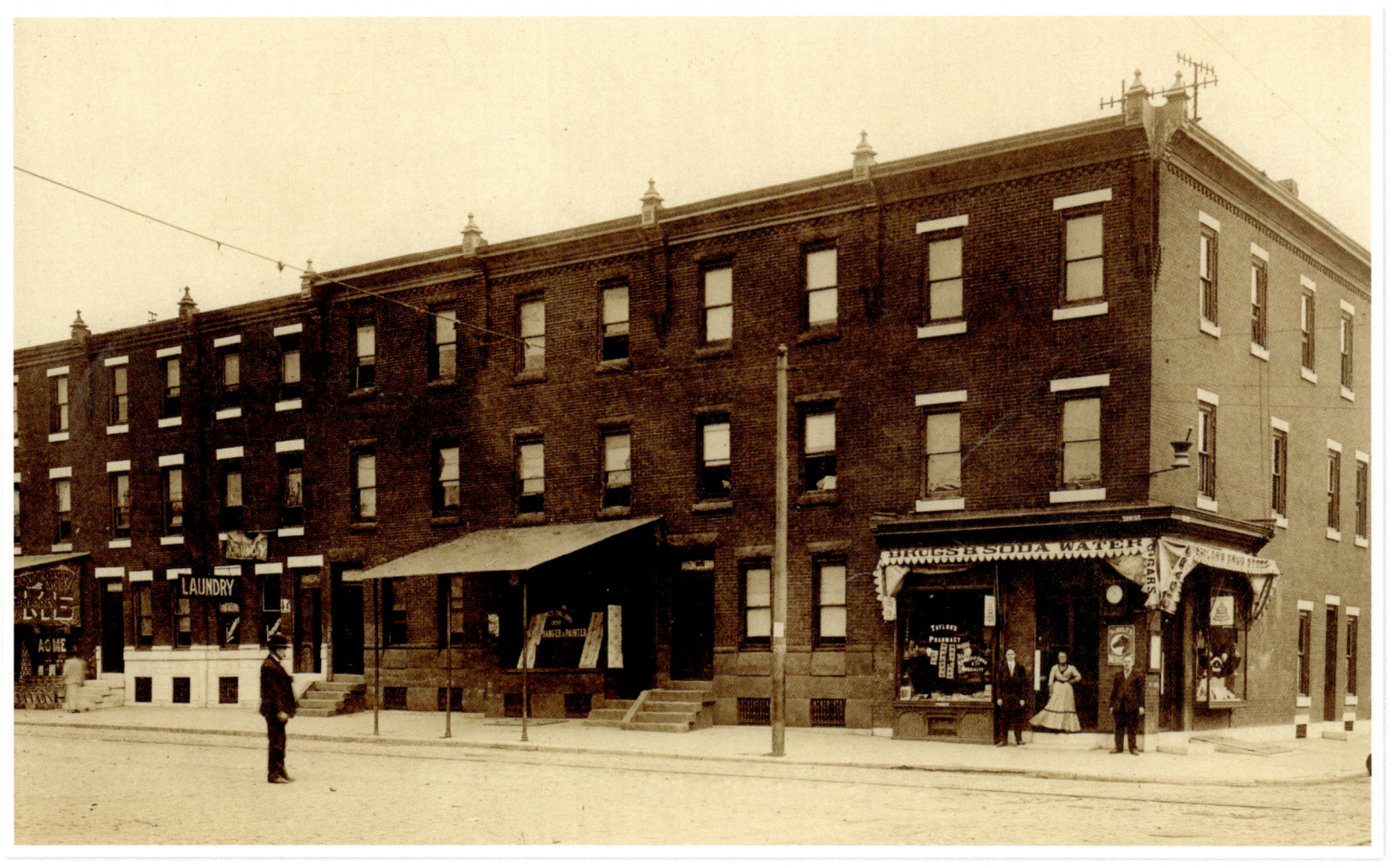

Twenty-Second Street north of Tasker Street, ca. 1910. The 2200 block of Tasker Street in the Point Breeze neighborhood was noteworthy for the number of businesses it contained. The corner property was John D. Taylor's Drug Store. Two doors down at 1537 South Twenty-Second Street was the establishment of Morris Orlow, a paperhanger and painter. A laundry business also inhabited the block, along with an early branch store of the Acme Company (*far left*).

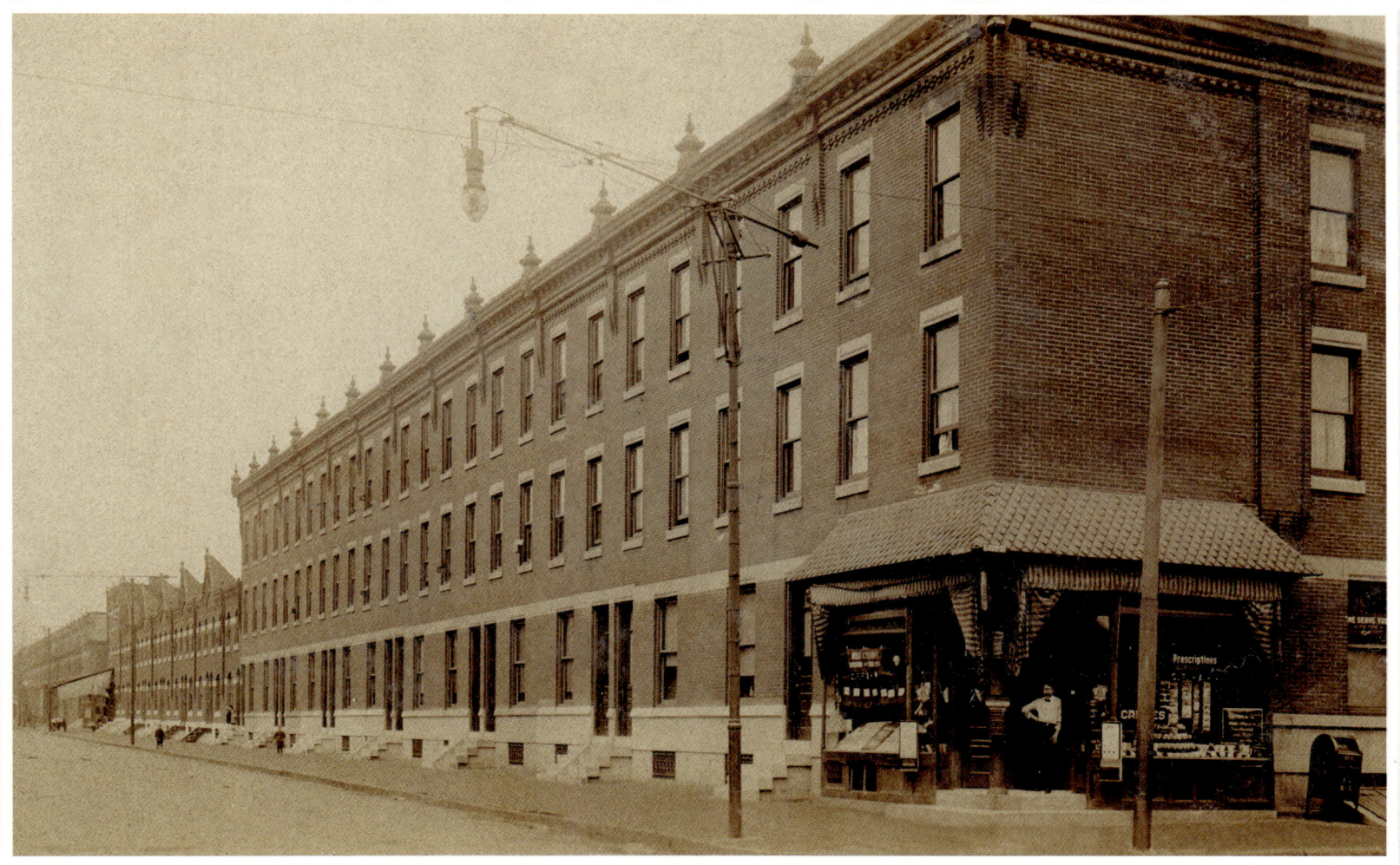

Christian Street west of Twenty-Third Street, 1908. A corner pharmacy served this section of Southwest Center City with potions, elixirs, and candy. This neighborhood would later be known as the Graduate Hospital neighborhood for the large medical facility on South Street. Construction on the thirteen three-story houses on the right side of the photo began on May 25, 1892. The houses on the left are of a slightly older vintage.

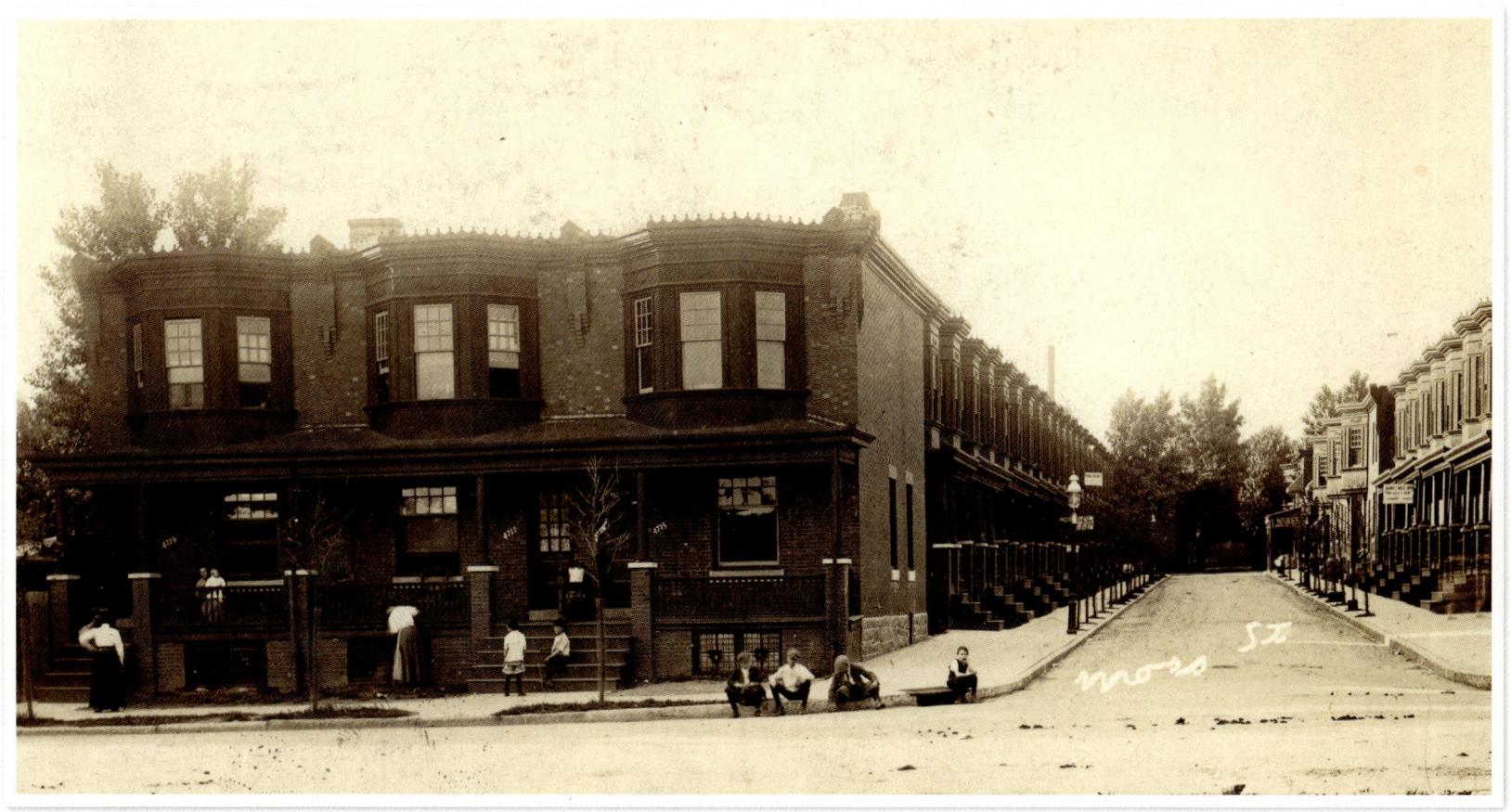

4715–4719 Brown Street, 1911

By the 1890s, practically every part of the city caught construction fever, including West Philadelphia. The newly created districts west of the Schuylkill River appealed largely to the city's middle- and upper-middle-class workers. Builders made every effort to create attractive suburban homes that were spacious enough to accommodate growing families and live-in servants. Reporters gushed over these beautiful new neighborhoods and recorded their progress. On November 6, 1895, the *Philadelphia Inquirer* included a glowing report on the work in West Philadelphia.

No section of this great city of homes has experienced such a wonderful transformation as that lying south of Chestnut Street and from Thirty-fourth Street west. Embraced within a territory covering a little over a mile square are to be found houses such as the early settlers never even dreamed of as possible creations. From an inaccessible suburb the place has become one of the most accessible and most delightful places of residence within the limits of the municipality. The streets are wide and well paved, shade trees abound and the charm of suburban life is fully maintained through the majority of the houses having small lawns in front and further carried out through the open space between the buildings.

Although it has been but a few years since the improvements began, the change is most wonderful. The character of the houses is of the higher grade. Some are built for and are occupied by the well-to-do class and others for the more moderately fixed as to finances. Architecturally the "Colonial" predominate, but it is so varied and interspersed with the fanciful creations of the architect's brains that the neighborhood is made beautiful through its dissimilar similarity, if such a term is permissible.[1]

The anonymous writer's mention of accessibility probably alluded to the many trolley lines that connected West Philadelphia to the Center City business district from Broad Street eastward. The writer also suggests that the homes appealed to a wide range of incomes, but to be sure, these were a cut above the row homes of factory workers. The "open space between the buildings" referred to the semidetached (or twin) houses that proliferated throughout West Philadelphia for many decades. This small bit of separation was a major selling point to potential buyers. Those of more-modest means, however, were also being lured to West Philadelphia. Increasingly, people on a smaller budget could buy into the suburban dream. The writer tells of modern amenities and a front porch, all of which distinguish the new construction from the average row houses in other parts of the city.[2]

The Market Street Elevated Railroad, completed in March 1907, was another impetus for residential growth in Wes-

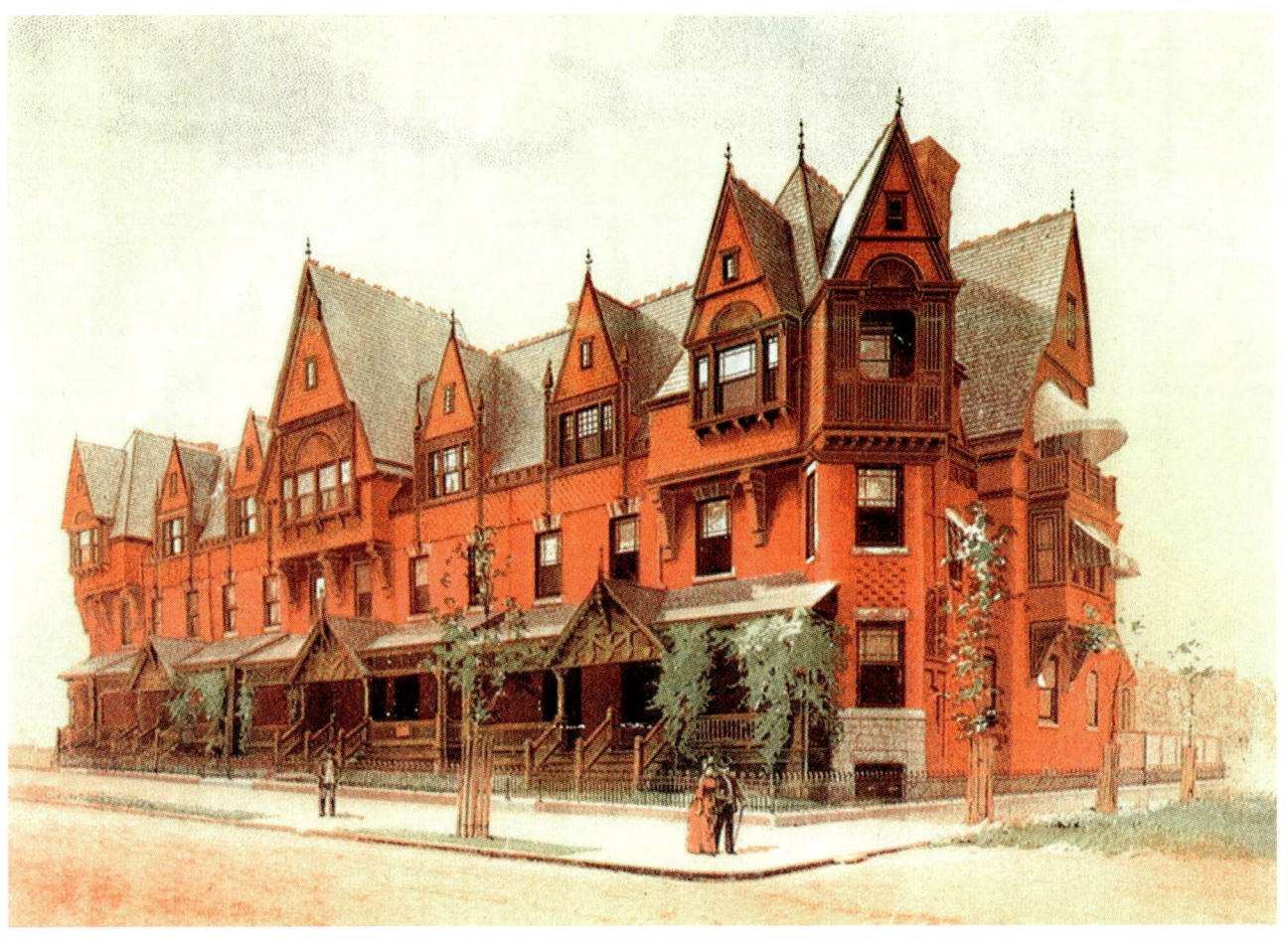

Spruce Street Row (4206–4218 Spruce Street) as it appeared in a July 1891 trade magazine. The Queen Anne–style homes were described as "houses of moderate cost" but were really meant for the nouveau riche suburbanites flocking to West Philadelphia in the late nineteenth century. Happily, Spruce Street Row is completely intact. *Reproduced from* Scientific American, Architects and Builders Edition, *July 1891*

Sixty-First and Haverford Avenue, ca. 1880. This rare photograph of West Philadelphia farmland shows a house and barn, which is now the intersection of Sixty-First and Haverford Avenue.

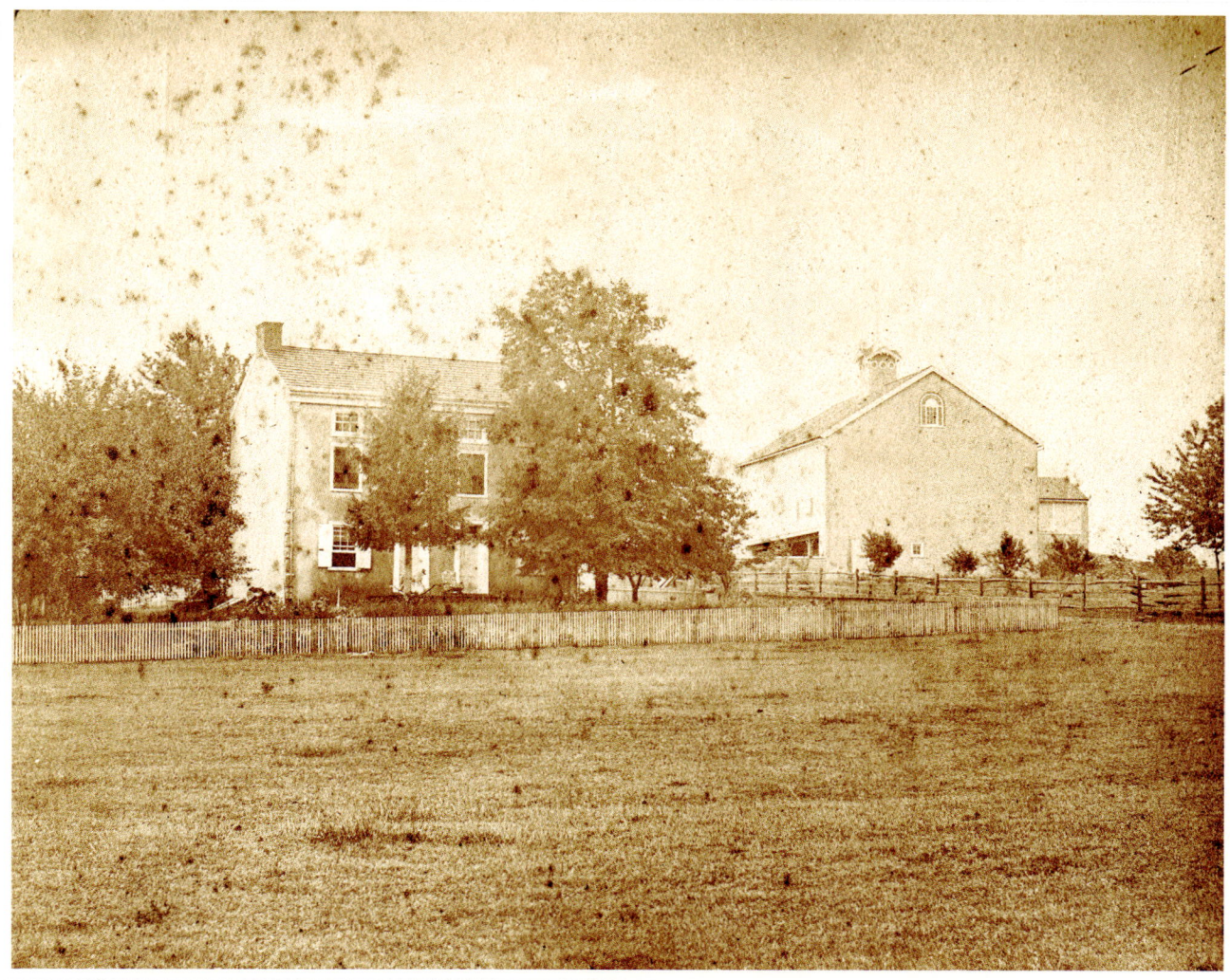

Philadelphia. Many of the blocks depicted here were built as a direct result of this new and modern form of mass transportation. The trains allowed for new houses to be built as far west as Cobbs Creek, the western boundary of Philadelphia in this part of the city. Parts of West Philadelphia were already well established by the time the El arrived. Spruce Hill, Cedar Park, Walnut Hill, and Powelton Village were fashionable neighborhoods made possible by the introduction of trolley lines and bridges spanning the Schuylkill River. But now, with the Market Street line, the newly emerging middle class was able to stake out residence far to the west of central Philadelphia. Row houses quickly overtook the farms and fields of rural West Philadelphia, springing up virtually overnight. Built cheek by jowl, the houses featured minimal ornamentation and the barest necessities, but they had a front porch where one could while away the few idle hours watching the children play in the street. Affordability was the key to these new houses, which sold for as low as $1,850. The American dream of owning a home was now a reality for the growing number of working-class residents flocking to West Philadelphia.[3]

Mantua

Mantua was named for the Italian city of the same name. Mantua Village was first laid out in 1809 by Judge Richard Peters of nearby Belmont. The village was once centered near present-day Thirty-Fourth Street and Haverford Avenue, and later there was a passenger station of the Philadelphia & Reading Railroad near what is now Thirty-Sixth Street and Haverford Avenue. Modern Mantua is north of Powelton Village and is known more for typically Philadelphian row homes than is its neighbor to the south.[4]

Belmont

Belmont briefly became a district within Philadelphia in 1853, one year before the Consolidation Act of 1854. Belmont was named for Belmont Mansion in Fairmount Park, built in 1743 by William Peters. Belmont District was formed from the northern part of Blockley Township and encompassed a large area from the Schuylkill River to Overbrook Farms and from City Line Avenue to Westminster Avenue to the south. The modern boundaries of the Belmont neighborhood, by the broadest definition, are Fortieth Street to Forty-Fourth Streets, and from the SEPTA railroad tracks on the north to Haverford Avenue to the south. Belmont is bisected by Lancaster Avenue, one of its commercial corridors along with Haverford Avenue.[5]

Redfield Street north of Chestnut Street, 1908. The tracks of the Market Street Elevated Line are clearly visible in the distance. At the time, this new mode of mass transit was only a year old.

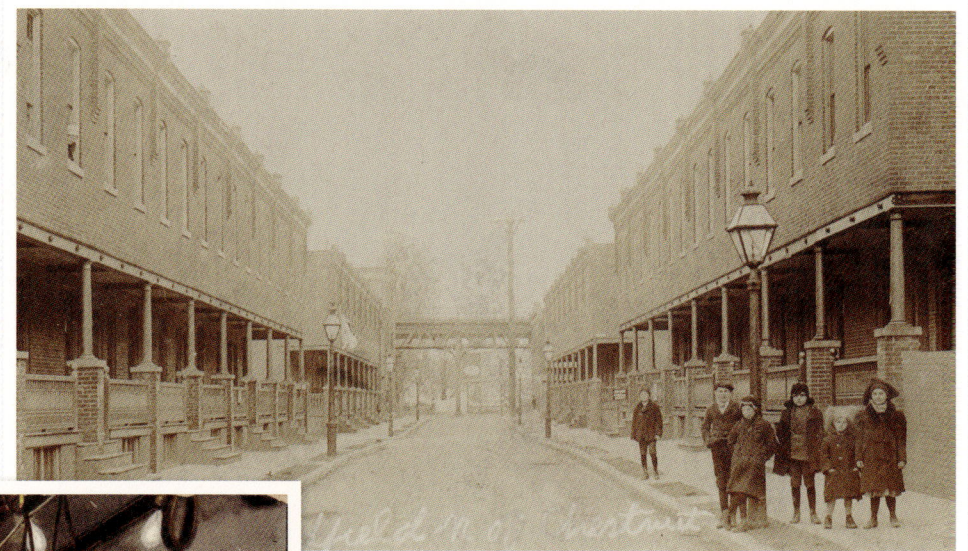

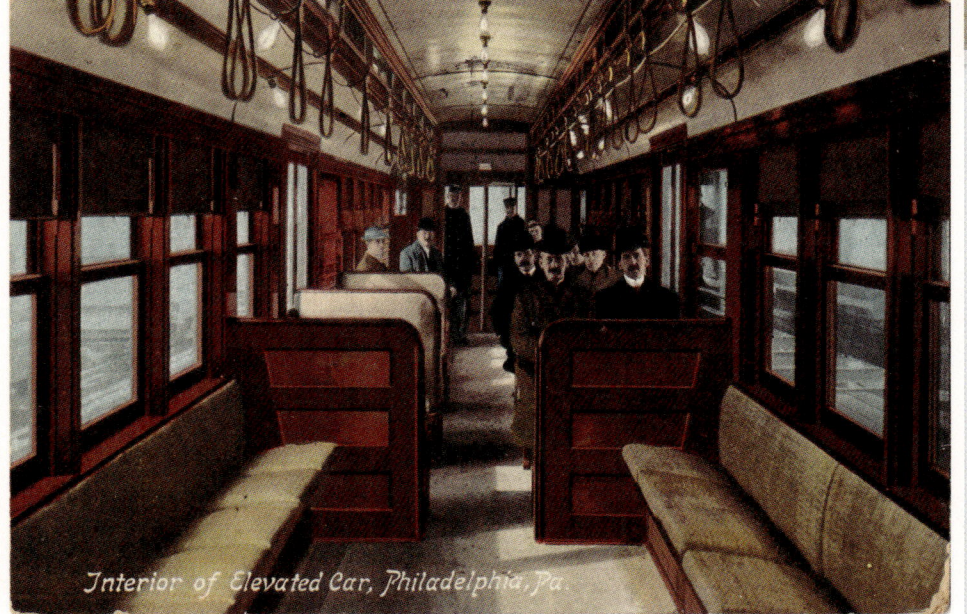

Interior of Elevated Car, Philadelphia, Pa.

Interior of Elevated Car, 1909. Beautiful elevated-subway cars allowed citizens to travel from West Philadelphia to Center City in speed and comfort. The new line led to increased residential development in West Philadelphia and thriving commercial corridors near the passenger stations.

Walnut Street west of Forty-Third Street, ca. 1907.
The two Queen Anne–style twin homes on the left were built ca. 1884 and designed by George W. Hewitt, half of the acclaimed G. W. and W. D. Hewitt Brothers architectural firm. These lovely semidetached homes feature Victorian touches such as Eastlake detailing, fish-scale slate roof shingles, mansard roofs, and a prominent pointed finial atop a large front gable. The homes were demolished long ago, replaced by a four-story brick building. Farther down the block are five impressive late Victorian Gothic row houses built in July 1896 and designed by Willis G. Hale. Only one is still standing and is used as a student dormitory for the Restaurant School at Walnut Hill College. At far right is the Italianate Allison Mansion, the current home of the Restaurant School at Walnut Hill College.

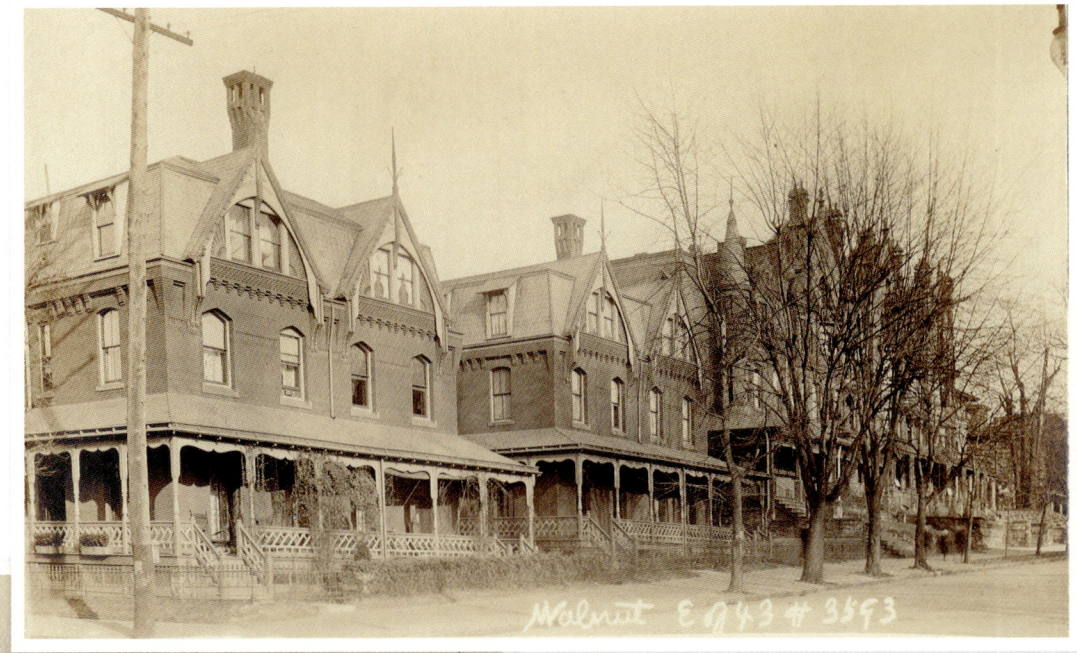

Locust Street east of Fortieth Street, ca. 1905.
These beautiful Italianate houses were typical of West Philadelphia's streetcar suburb, where wealthy folks built expansive mansions far from the hustle and bustle of the urban core. Its proximity to the University of Pennsylvania and Drexel University was a bonus. In time the universities gobbled up more and more of the surrounding neighborhoods to feed their insatiable requirement for land. In an ironic turn, the University of Pennsylvania closed Locust Street to automobile traffic and turned it into a green pedestrian walkway, removing many old mansions. Only St. Mary's Church (barely visible in the photo) still stands.

Baltimore Avenue east of Fiftieth Street, 1907.
Baltimore Avenue was as busy a commercial corridor in the first decade of the twentieth century as it is now. Shown here is the Acme Tea Company store, a forerunner of the Acme Supermarket chain. On the right is the hardware store of Charles W. Flood at 4914 Baltimore Avenue.

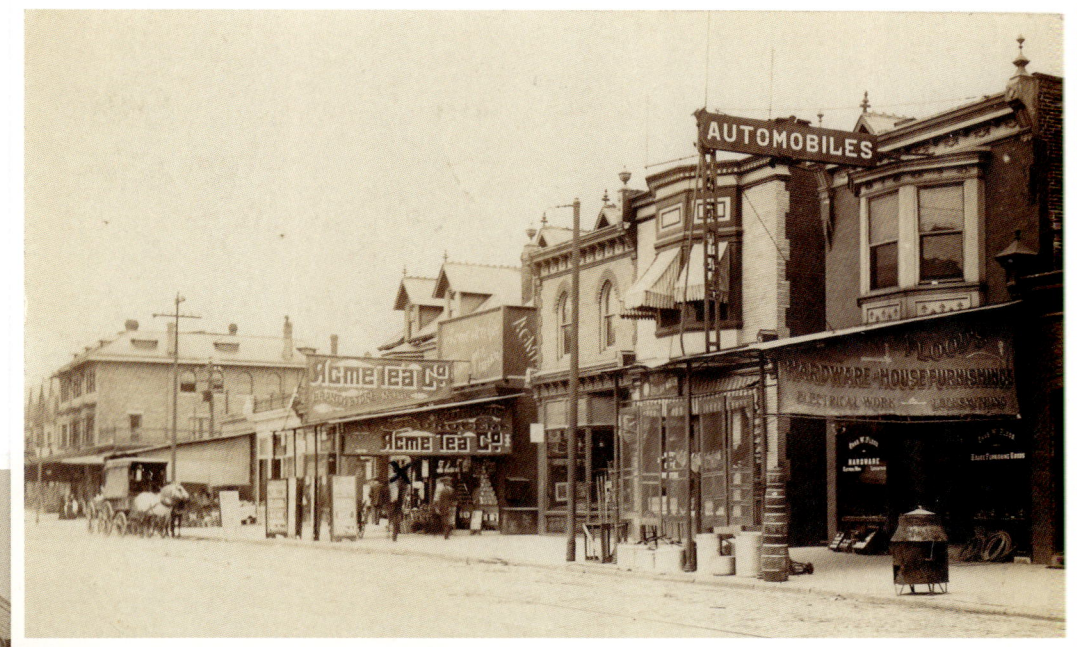

Forty-Seventh and Baltimore Avenue, ca. 1907.
When the Ivan Apartment building was built in 1901, its Queen Anne design was already out of date. It was around this time that a number of apartment buildings began to appear in West Philadelphia, many of them adopting a Romanesque design. This photo was likely taken in the summer, which explains the cloth awnings (also known as bonnet blinds) being opened. The apartment building is still standing as the University Apartments.

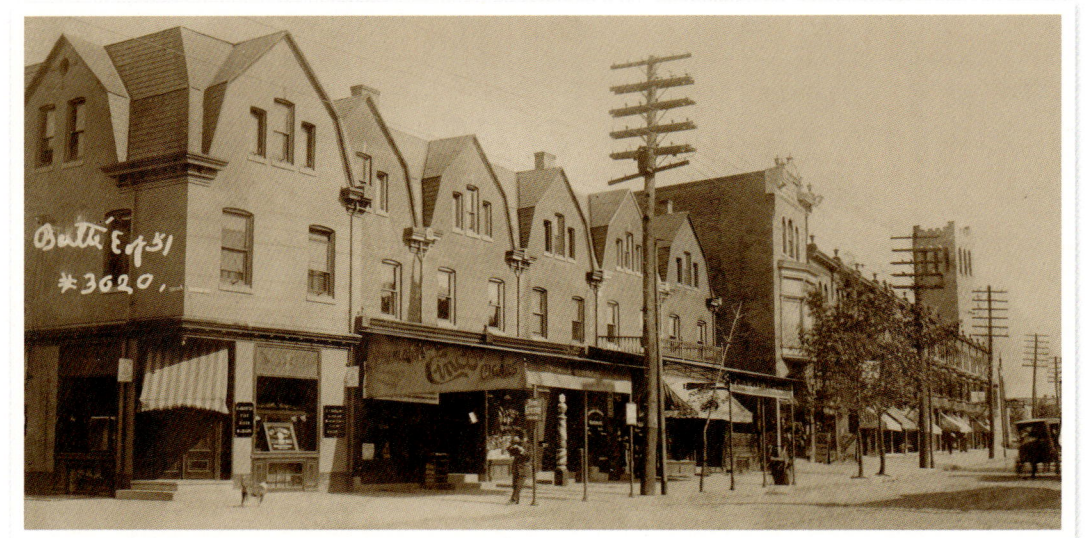

Baltimore Avenue east of Fifty-First Street, ca. 1909. The Dutch colonial revival–style dwellings on the left were built in 1904 by Alexander Wilson Jr., and all have ground-floor storefronts. The shops appeal to manly interests, with a bar, cigar store, barber shop, hardware store, and poolroom. The remainder of the block was built 1905–1906.

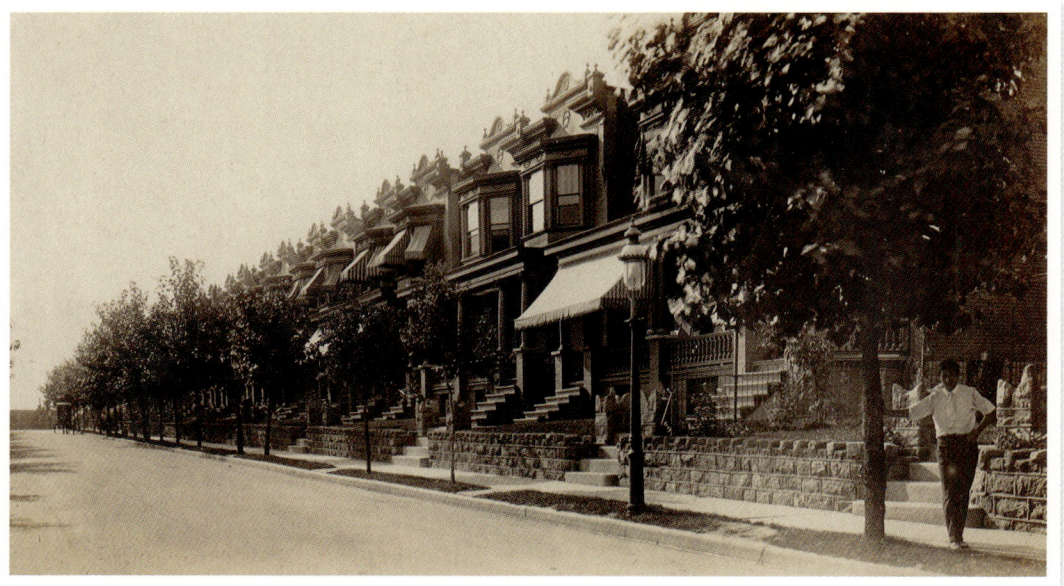

Webster Street west of Fifty-Second Street, ca. 1910. Harrison N. Diesel built these twins on the 5200 block of Webster. Work on both sides of Webster began on June 1, 1903. Diesel was an active builder and developer beginning in 1902, occasionally employing James C. Fernald as his architect. The style of these homes is common for West Philadelphia during this period, with the prominent bay windows and crenelated stone retaining walls enclosing modest front lawns.

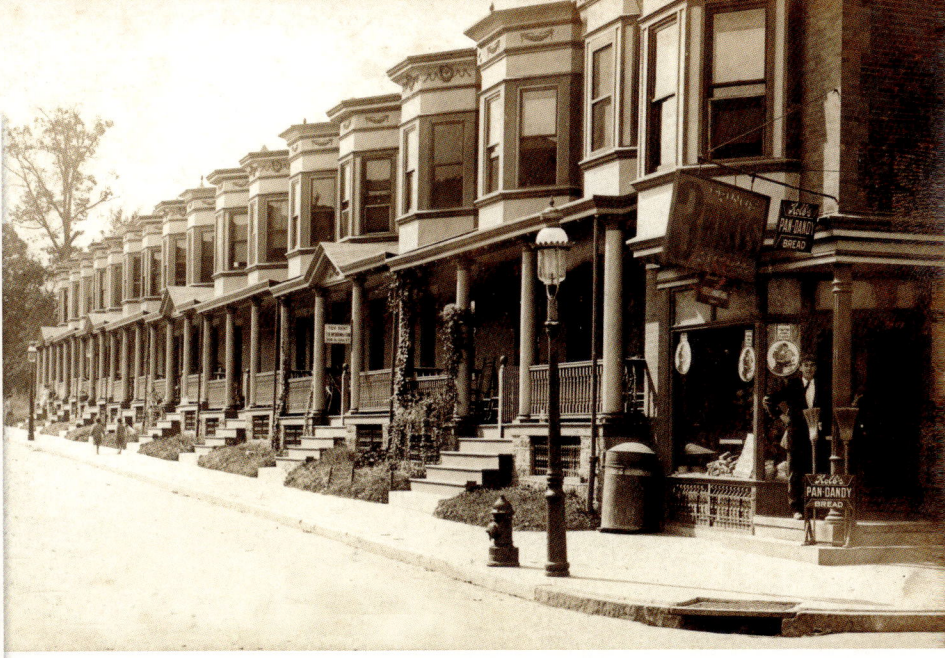

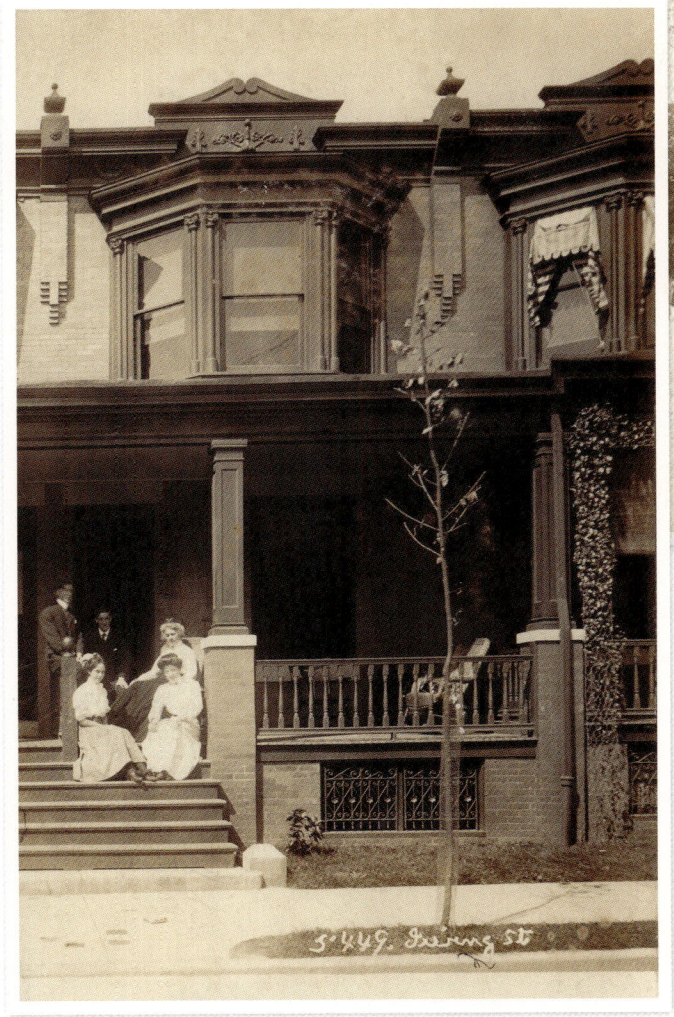

Alden Street south of Washington Avenue, ca. 1910. This freshly built row of bay-and-porch houses on Alden Street represents typical residential construction in this part of West Philadelphia around 1910. The row houses and corner store were built in April 1906 by F. C. Michaelsen. The wreaths and festoons on the bay windows give the homes a colonial revival touch. On the corner of Washington Avenue is the Three Bros. grocery store, selling such sundry items as brooms, cornflakes, and Kolb's Pan-Dandy bread.

5449 Irving Street, ca. 1908. A family poses on the front steps of their new house on Irving Street in West Philadelphia. William A. Patterson built the 5400 block of Irving in spring 1907. James A. Fernald was the architect for these and hundreds of other homes in West Philadelphia.

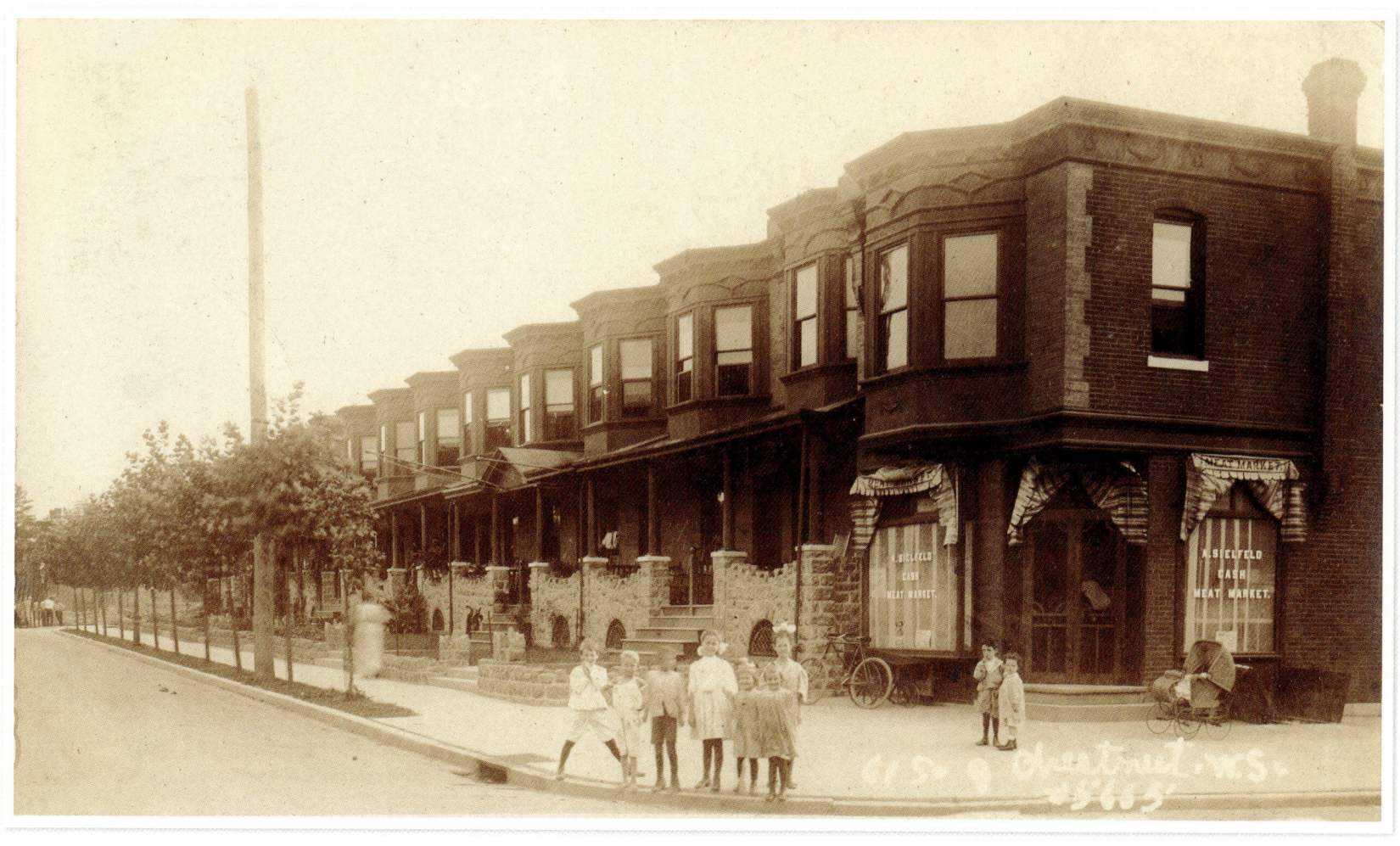

Sixty-First Street south of Chestnut, ca. 1908. Neighborhood children pose on the corner of Sixty-First and Chestnut, next to A. Sielfeld's Cash Meat Market. The houses were built in 1905 by James C. Clarke.

Sixty-First Street north of Arch Street, ca. 1908. The heavy stone porch walls and retaining walls add a sense of strength and permanence to this row of houses. These homes are the most generic type of residential architecture found in West Philadelphia. Small front lawns and Tuscan columns add refinement.

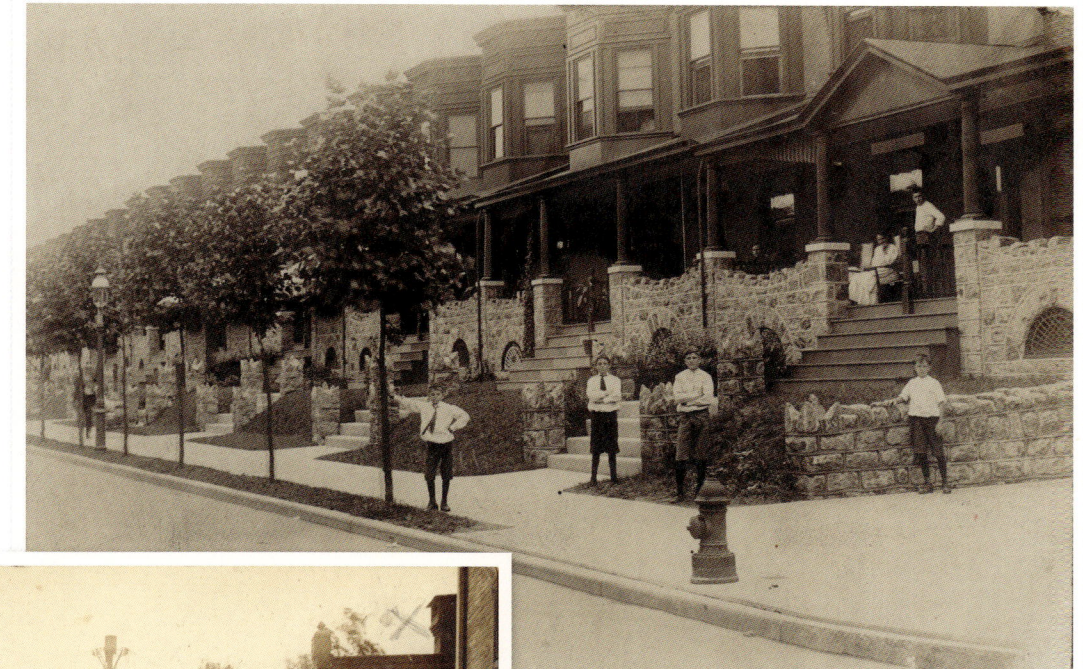

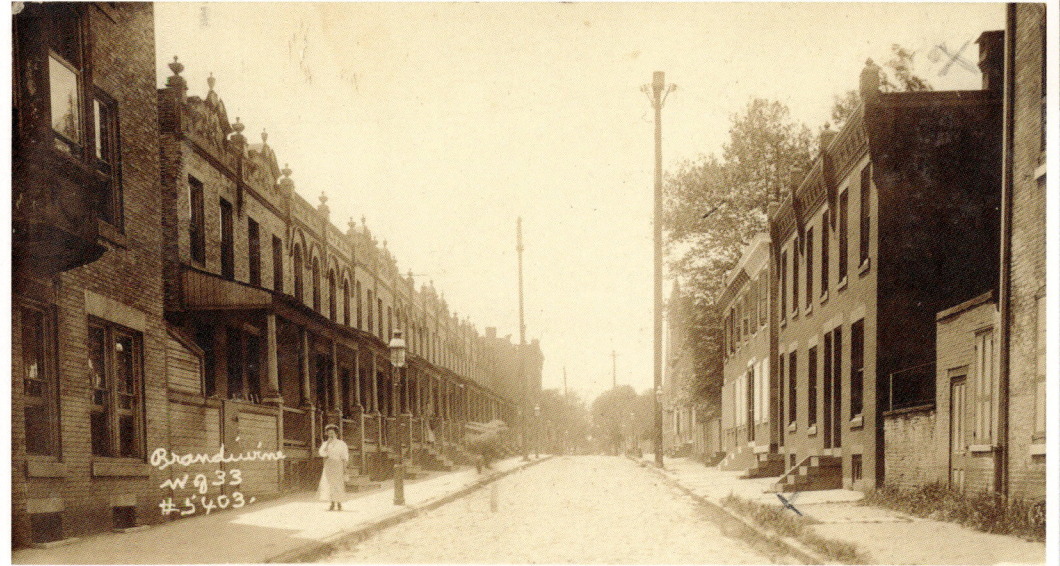

Brandywine Street west of Thirty-Third Street, 1908. Brandywine Street (formerly Rockland Street) west of Thirty-Third Street featured two-story row houses. The homes on the south side of the street (*on left*) were fancier than those on the north side, featuring front porches and ornamental parapets. Built between 1893 and 1897, these houses are still standing.

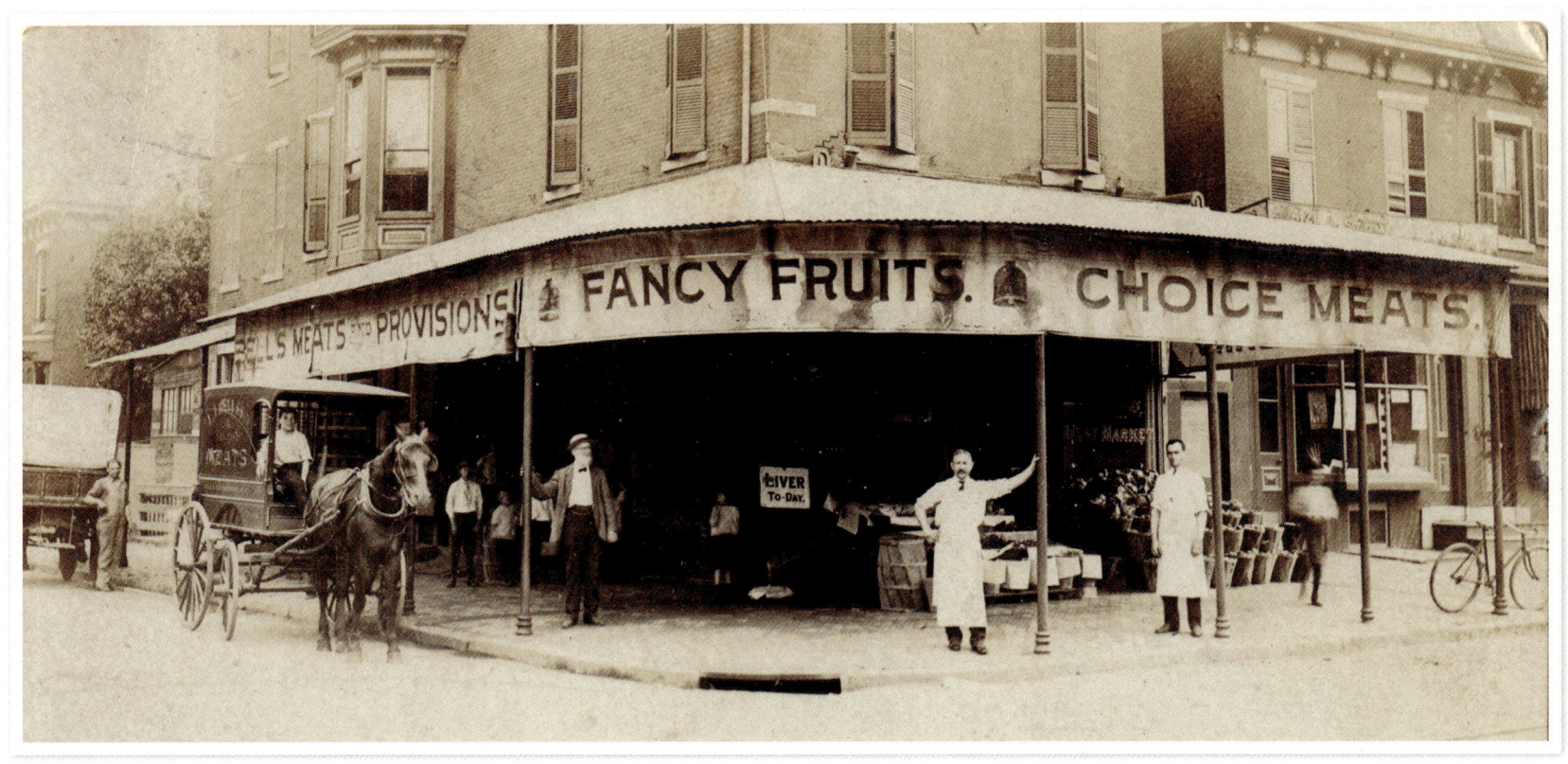

Haverford Avenue east of Forty-Second Street, 1907. One of many groceries in the James Bell & Son empire stood on the corner of Forty-Second and Haverford. Bell Sr. died in 1915, and two years later his chain of 214 stores merged with several other local commercial enterprises to eventually become Acme Supermarkets. Bell's stores specialized in choice meats and poultry, with this particular store boasting "Fresh Liver To-Day."

Forty-Second Street north of Westminster Avenue, 1907.
An interesting study in contrasting styles of architecture is on display in this postcard view. The row homes in the foreground are a plainer style than the turreted Victorian row houses to the north, which were built in August 1891 by James J. Comly. The vintage automobile parked on the east side of Forty-Second Street speaks to the area's former affluence.

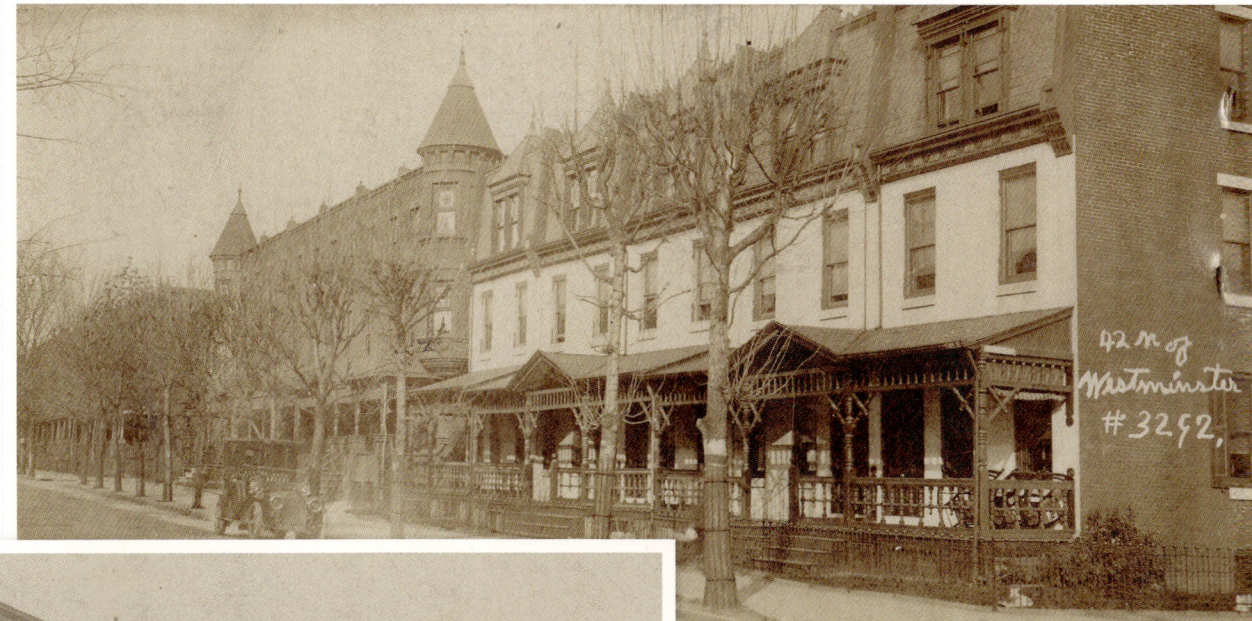

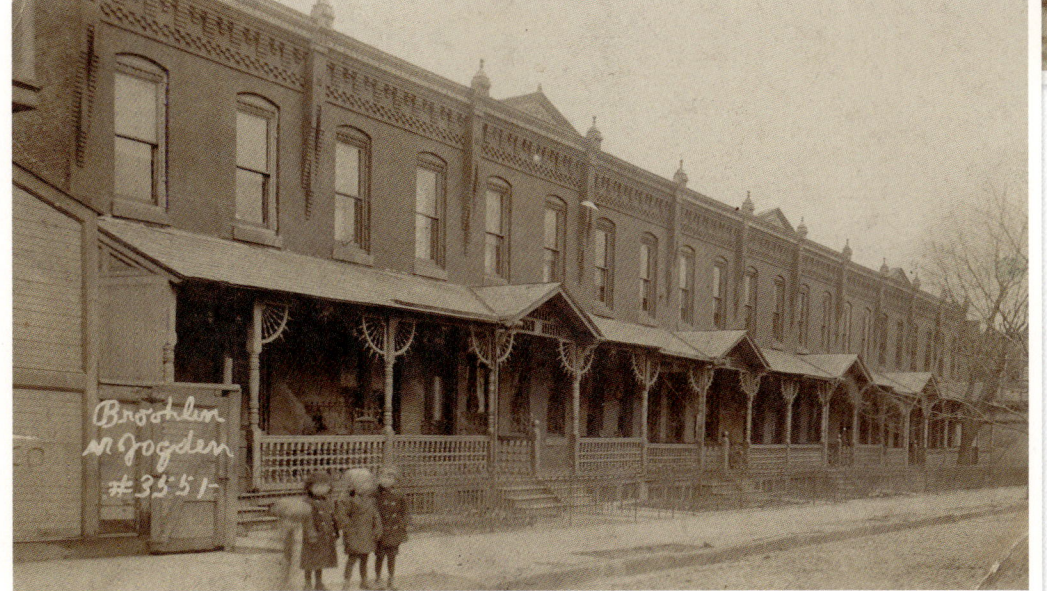

Brooklyn Street north of Ogden Street, 1908. Built in September 1890 by Jacob R. Jordan on the west side of Brooklyn Street in the Belmont section of West Philadelphia, these eleven porch-fronted row homes were more extravagant than those in other blue-collar neighborhoods. These houses had wood mantels, stained and plate glass, and hot-air heat and were fitted with electricity and other modern conveniences. Jordan built twenty-five more houses just like these near Forty-Third and Ogden in August 1890.

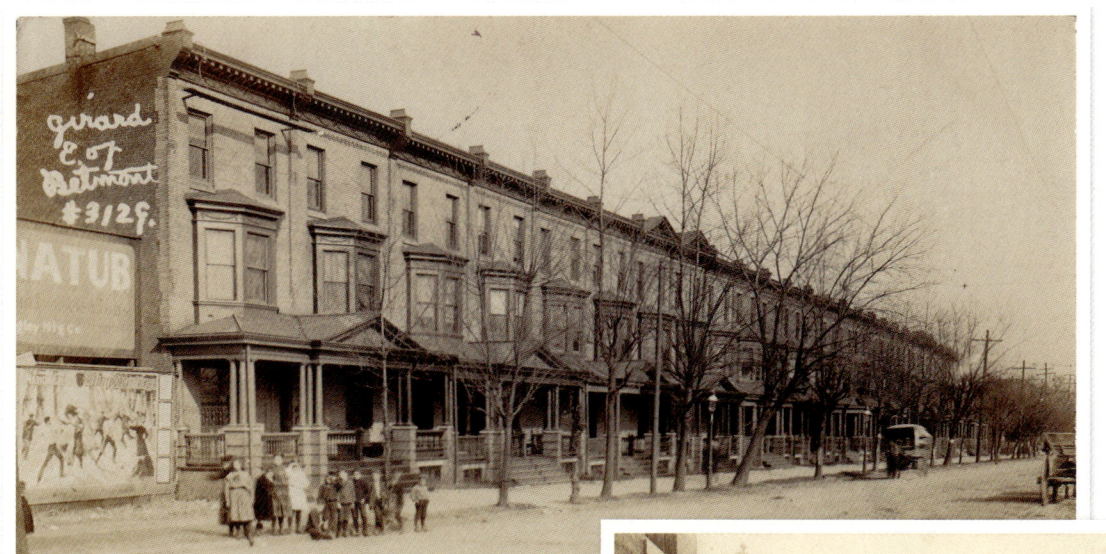

Girard Avenue east of Belmont Avenue, ca. 1907. Angus Wade built twenty-eight row houses on the north side of Girard Avenue in autumn 1897. The three-story homes, with their bay windows and front porches, were more elegant than many other row houses.

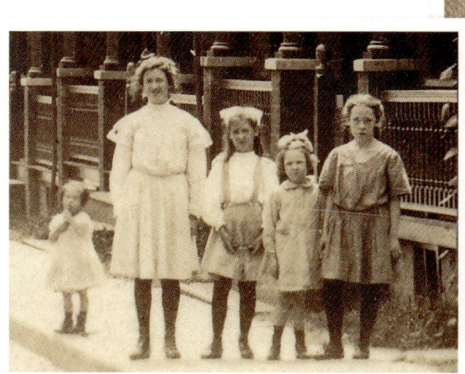

Sickels Street south of Girard Avenue, ca. 1907. A. C. McGill built these houses on North Sickels Street for about $1,000 each; many were rented to factory workers. Oriental Mills, south of Wyalusing Avenue, can be seen in the distance.

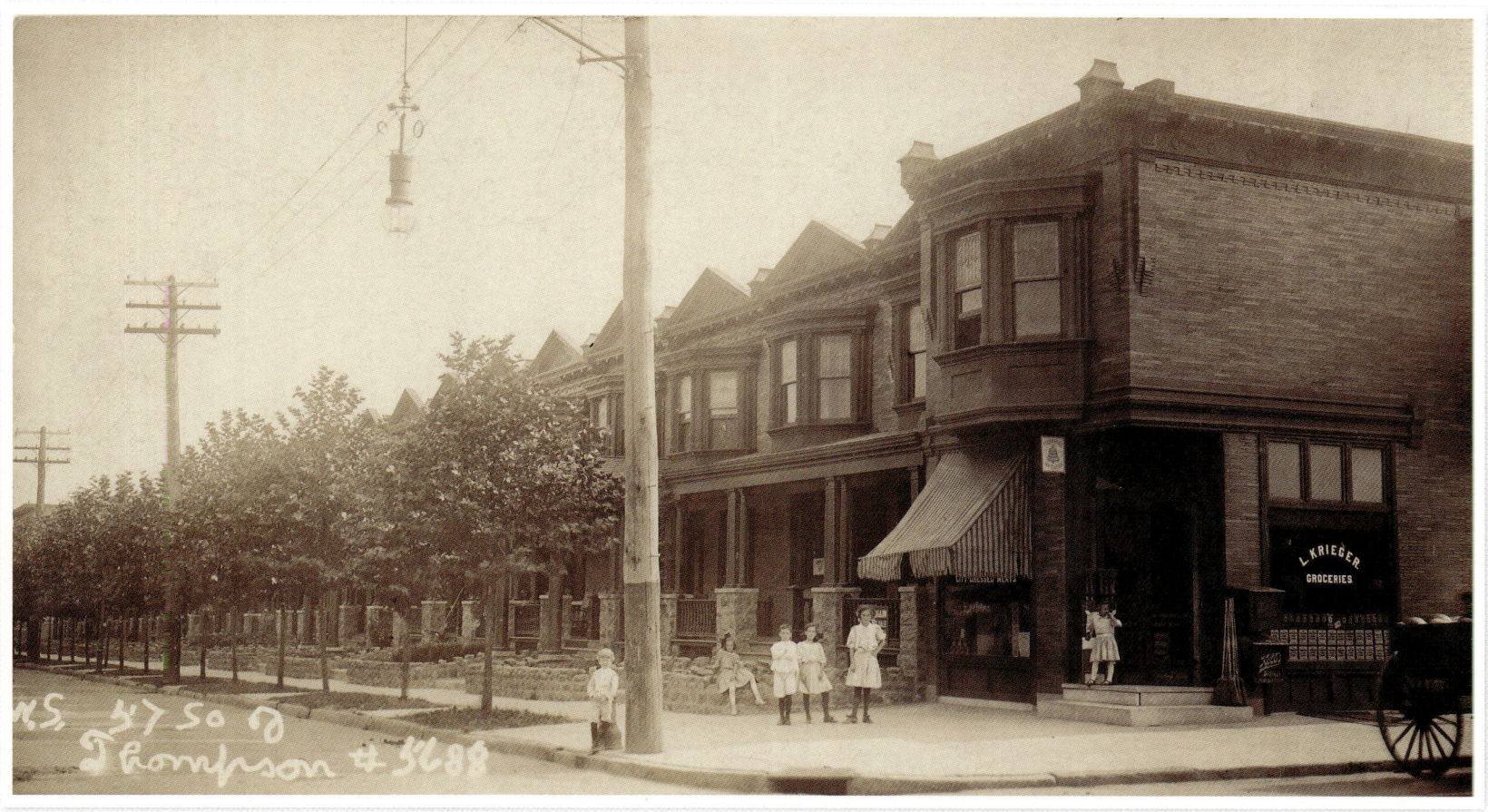

Fifty-Seventh Street south of Thompson Street, ca. 1908. This view of Fifty-Seventh Street in West Philadelphia features children posing near the corner grocer and new houses shaded by young trees. The homes were built in spring 1904 by Pemberton & Co., which played an active role in West Philadelphia's residential boom.

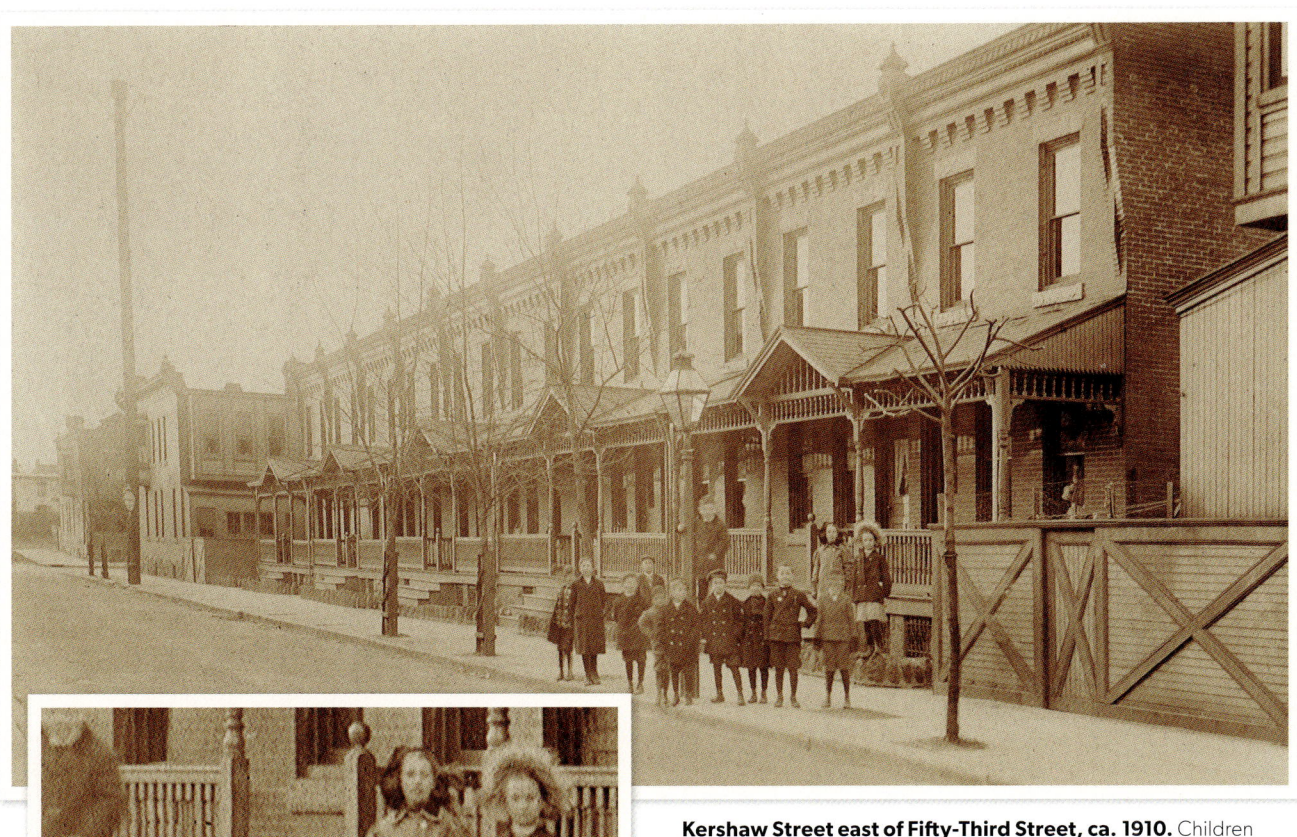

Kershaw Street east of Fifty-Third Street, ca. 1910. Children pose on the north side of the 5200 block of Kershaw Street in the Carroll Park section of West Philadelphia. The ten simple homes featured in this real photo postcard were built in April 1896 and July 1897 by builder/developer George W. Sherman. Hundreds more were built here in the following decades.

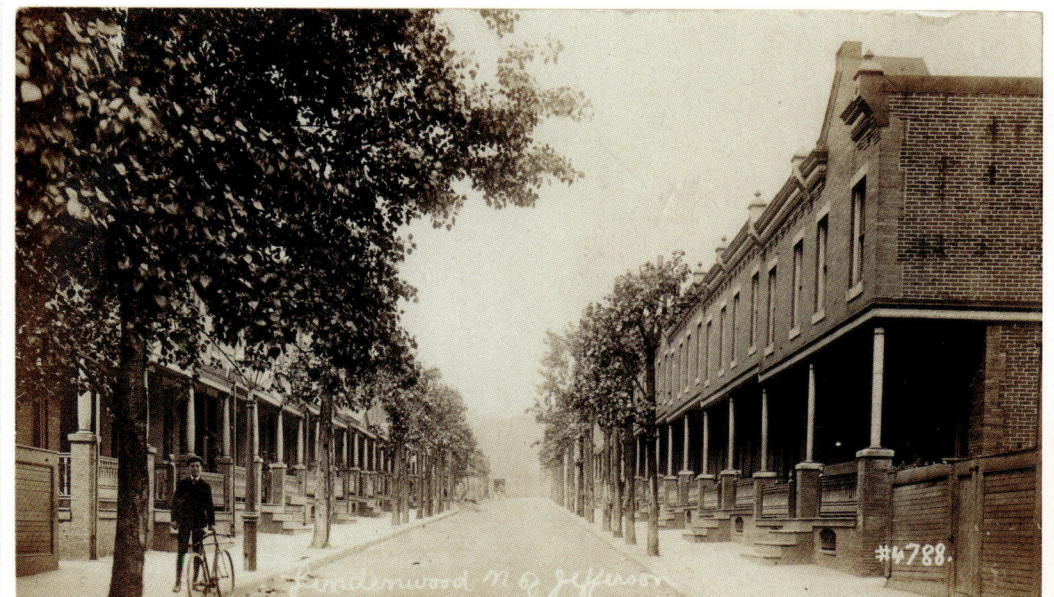

Lindenwood Street north of Jefferson Street, ca. 1908.
Lindenwood Street was laid out around 1900 on land belonging to George A. Fletcher, near a spot named Poplar Grove just south of Parkside Avenue and western Fairmount Park. Lindenwood Street was typical of the red-brick row house construction that proliferated from 1890 to 1910.

Master Street east of Hobart Street, ca. 1909. Local youth stand in the middle of Master Street, with a sign advertising a porch party. A plethora of convenience stores served the neighborhood: a meat store, grocery, bakery, and cigar store are visible. The south side of Master Street (*right*) was built in April and July 1904 by John McConaghy, with Charles J. Brooke as the architect. James J. Harnett built the stores and dwellings on the north side (*left*) beginning in August 1907.

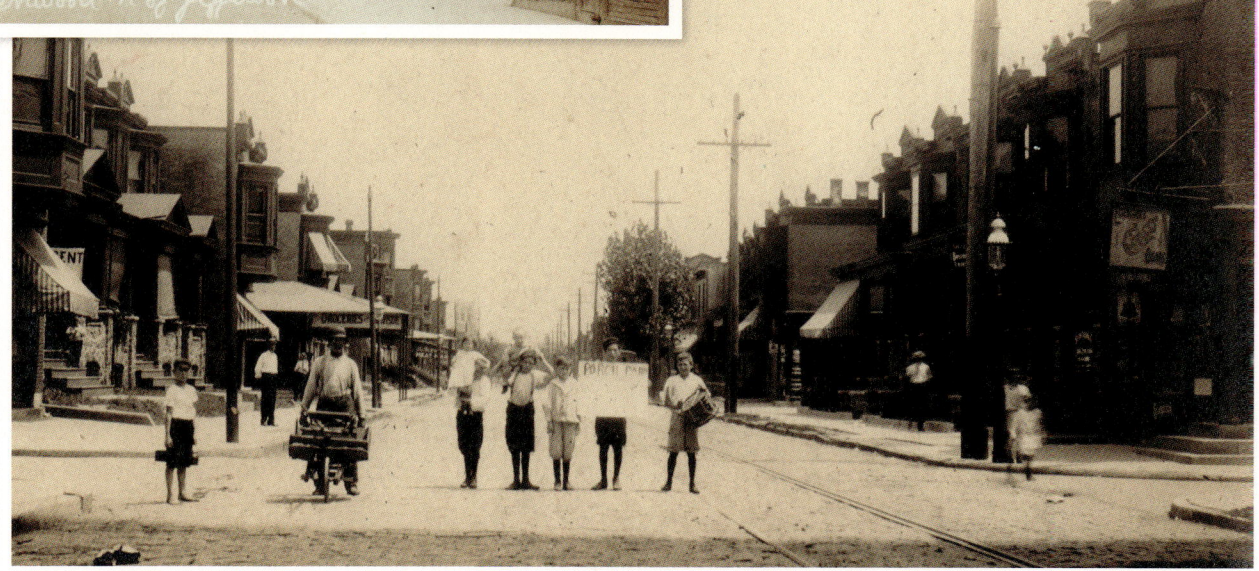

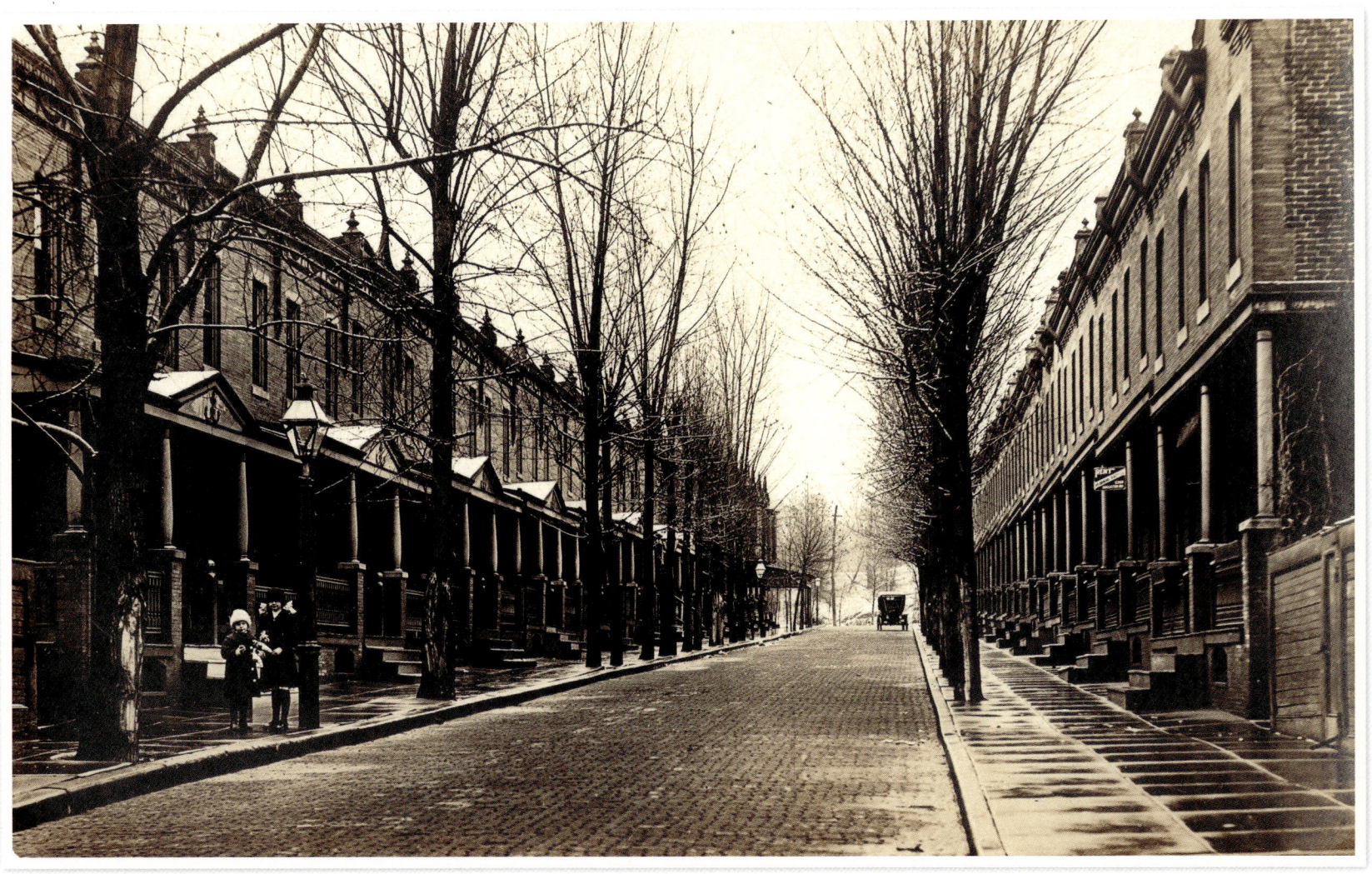

Lindenwood Street north of Jefferson Street, ca. 1912. The same block of Lindenwood Street, seen here several years later on a chilly winter day. This photo shows the west side of the street (*on left*) more clearly. In the time elapsed since the preceding photo, the trees have grown significantly. At the end of the block, a snow-covered slope of Fairmount Park can be seen in the distance. The homes on this block are still standing, in varying degrees of preservation.

Master Street east of Sixty-First Street, ca. 1909. Children pose in front of M. W. Geyer's grocery store in Carroll Park. These handsome, two-story row houses on the south side of Master Street were built by Samuel G. Whittaker in September 1895.

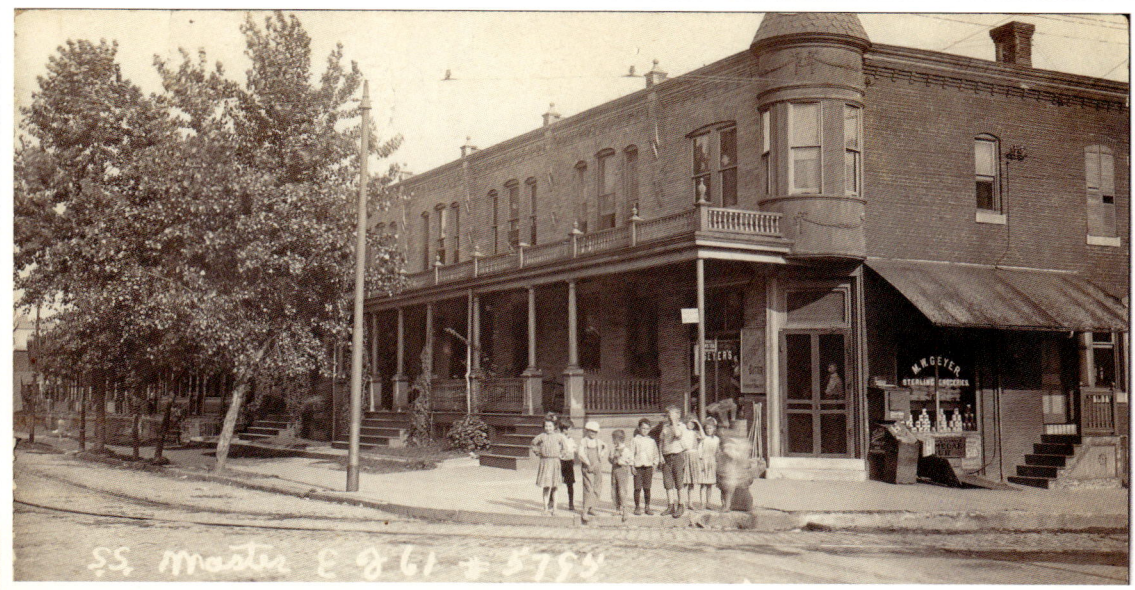

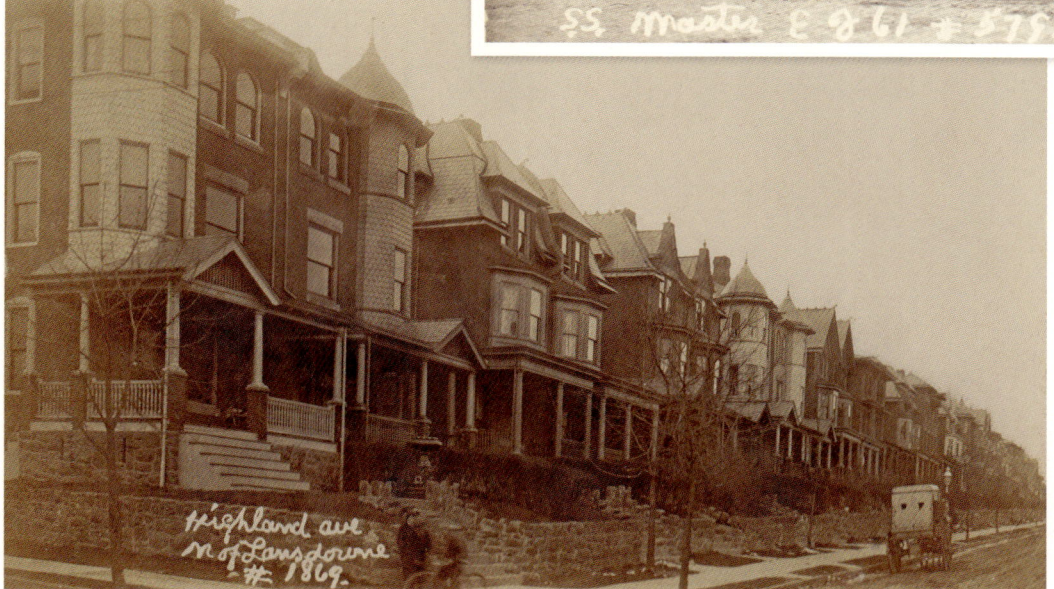

Wynnewood Street north of Lansdowne Avenue, ca. 1907. Wynnewood Street (misidentified here as Highland) is lined with handsome, late Victorian twins built by James Florey and Walter Bevan in 1898. The architectural firm Schermerhorn & Reinhold designed these fine houses and was closely associated with Florey & Bevan.

Chapter 7.

SOUTHWEST PHILADELPHIA

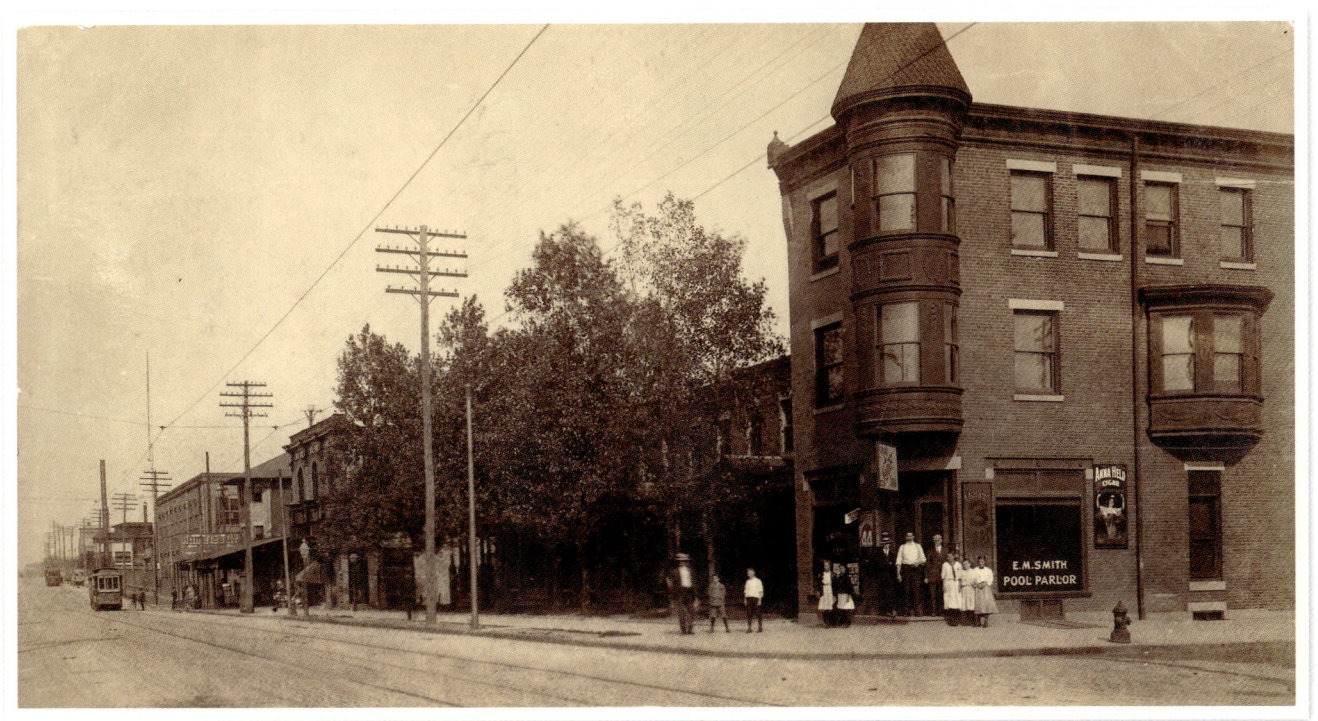

Woodland Avenue east of Sixty-Third Street, 1908

Southwest Philadelphia's history goes back to the early settlement of Kingsesse, then a part of New Sweden (1638–1655), the oldest European settlement within Philadelphia's current boundaries. The Swedes occupied parts of what are now Cobb's Creek and Tinicum Island. Virtually nothing of New Sweden remains in Southwest Philadelphia, but other historic sites of note remain. Historic Bartram's Garden (Fifty-Fourth Street and Lindbergh Boulevard) is the well-preserved home of two of America's preeminent colonial-era botanists—indeed, two of the greatest natural botanists in the world, John Bartram (1699–1777) and his son, William Bartram (1739–1823).[1]

Technically speaking, Southwest Philadelphia is that part of the city west of the Schuylkill River and south of Baltimore Avenue. The northeastern part of this section falls under the University City heading as well. Cedar Park and Squirrel Hill were designed as upper-middle-class suburbs during the late Victorian era. Trolley lines running along the neighborhood's major thoroughfares such as Woodland and Baltimore Avenues made living here convenient. As with much of the city, development took off around 1900. Row houses quickly overtook the southern portion of Southwest Philadelphia. Neighborhoods such as Paschall consist of narrow brick houses, although front porches were pretty much de rigueur. The completion of the Market Street Elevated through West Philadelphia was also a driving force for expanding neighborhoods into previously unoccupied territory.[2]

Paschall

The village of Paschallville was named for Thomas Paschall (1635–1718), who purchased 500 acres from William Penn before coming to America in 1681. The Paschall plantation of Pleasant Prospect was located from present-day Seventy-First Street to Cobbs Creek south of Woodland Avenue. Dr. Henry Paschall laid out Paschallville in 1810, with Paschall Avenue as the main street through the village. Paschall Mill on Cobbs Creek was the primary employer, but in the nineteenth century, other industrial giants, such as Passmore Mill and Fels & Co., found a home near the old village. Paschall Avenue was extended northeast as the demand for new homes grew.[3]

The houses built in Paschall and other parts of Southwest Philadelphia during the boom period were typical of those being built in West Philadelphia. The densely packed row houses featured desirable elements such as projecting master bedrooms and front porches, both of which were designed to alleviate summer heat. The fancier row homes were accented with gables and crests.

Kingsessing

Kingsessing was once a township that included all of present-day Southwest Philadelphia. Swedish settlers chose the name from the native Lenni Lenape language, meaning "bog meadow" or "place of large shells." It referred to a stream that emptied into Bow Creek, an extinct waterway that once connected Cobbs Creek to the Delaware River. The name lives on as a subsection of Southwest Philadelphia, an avenue, and several place names (e.g., Kingsessing Rec Center, Kingsessing Library). Kingsessing's housing stock is a mix of row houses and twins, most of them built between 1900 and 1910. Many now feature unsightly renovations such as aluminum siding and enclosed front porches.[4]

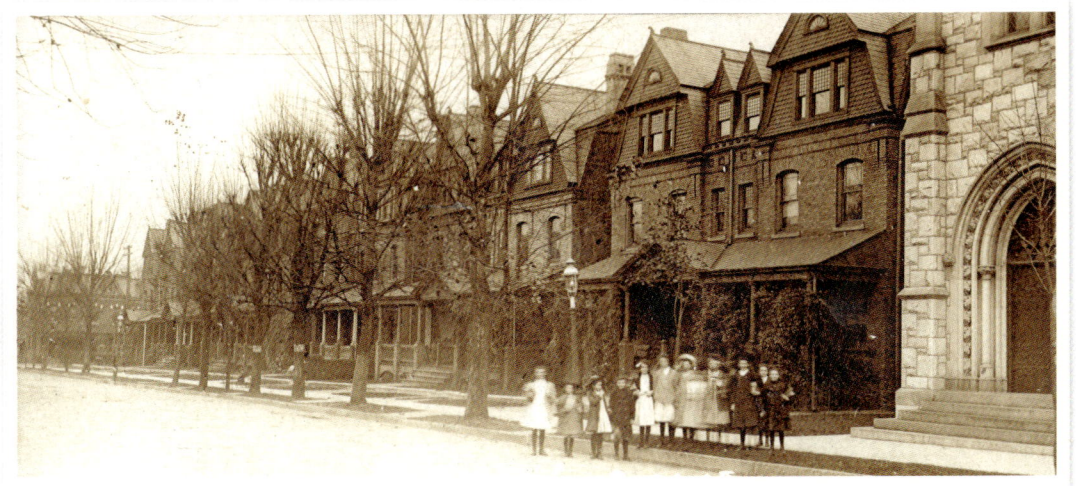

Kingsessing Avenue west of Forty-Seventh Street, ca. 1910. Twin homes were all the rage in this part of Southwest Philadelphia, especially if they had a front porch. Six of these houses were built in March 1891; the other six were built in March of the following year. Fourth Presbyterian Church (1902) is on the far right.

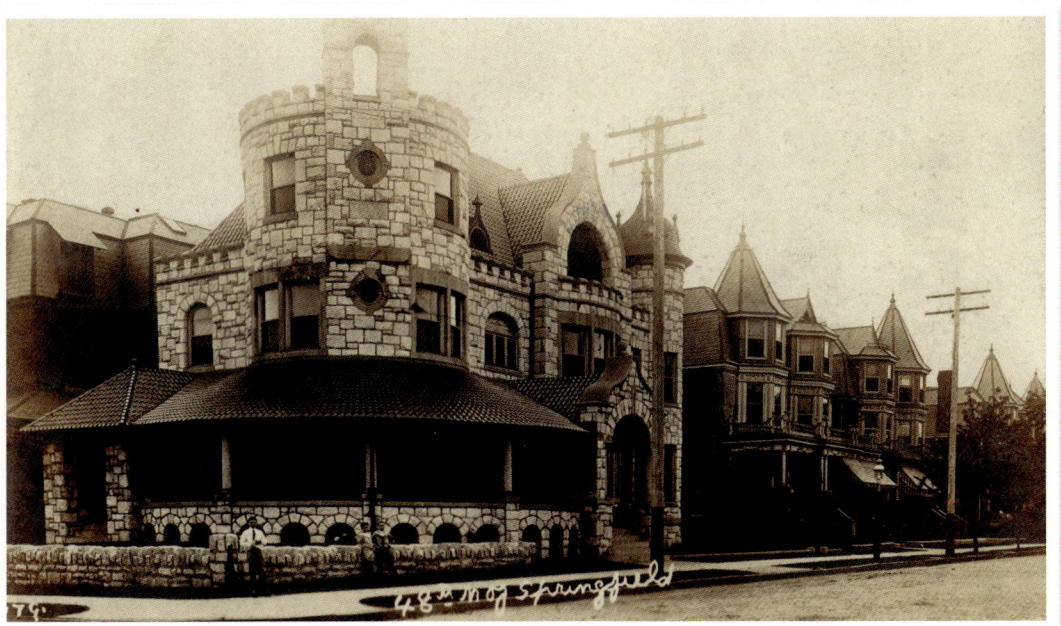

Forty-Eighth Street and Springfield Avenue, 1907. Cedar Park had been an affluent area for quite some time before this photograph was taken. Elegant Queen Anne twin houses (*at right*) are on Forty-Eighth Street, while the main focus of the picture is the unusual stone mansion of Hansom H. Haines, designed by architect Charles Balderston. Construction on the castle-like residence began on May 13, 1903. The Haines house has changed ownership several times during its century-plus existence, undergoing many alterations to the historical interior. Luckily, the right owners came along and lovingly restored it.

Forty-Ninth Street south of Warrington Avenue, ca. 1907. Construction of twin houses on Forty-Ninth Street south of Warrington began in April 1895 on land belonging to John McCoach. In June 1900, Charles W. Budd & Co. built more houses to the south.

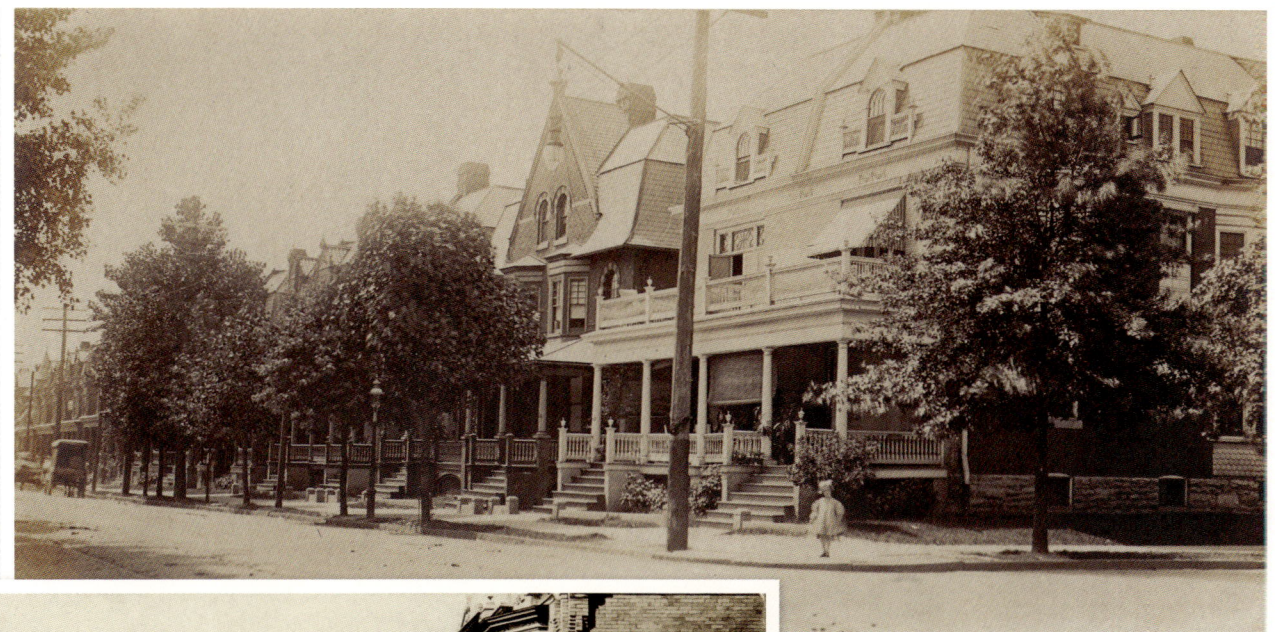

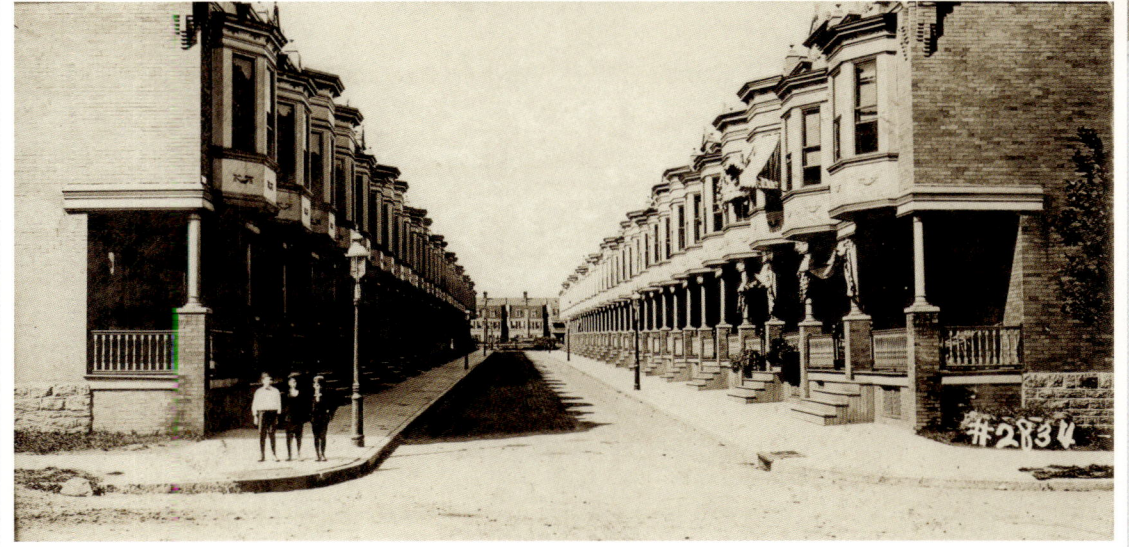

Paxon Street north of Greenway Avenue, 1911. Uniform row homes such as those on Paxon were becoming a common sight in the ever-increasing density of Southwest Philadelphia. They were designed by architect Helena Lukens, one of Philadelphia's earliest female architects. Both sides of Paxon Street were built by Charles G. Henderson in March 1905.

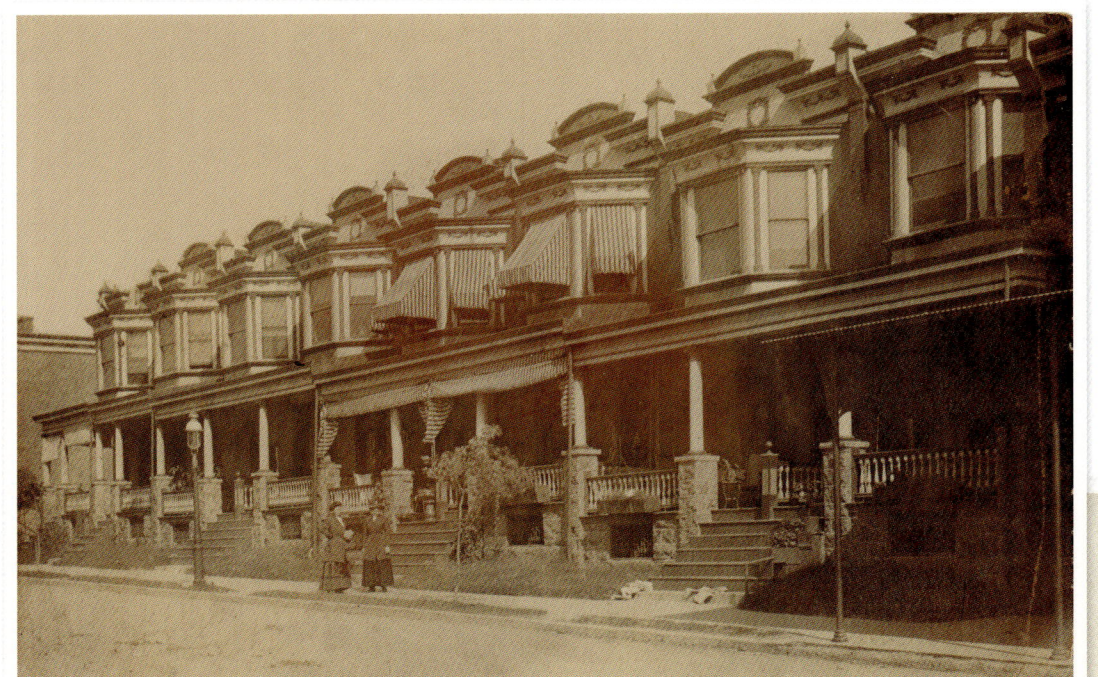

Fifty-Fourth Street north of Greenway Avenue, ca. 1910. Fifty-Fourth Street in Kingsessing features spiffy houses with front-bedroom bay windows and ornamental crests. Construction began in March 1906.

Fifty-Third Street south of Kingsessing Avenue, ca. 1910. Joseph R. Summers built these porch-fronted row houses on Fifty-Third Street. Construction began in early 1905.

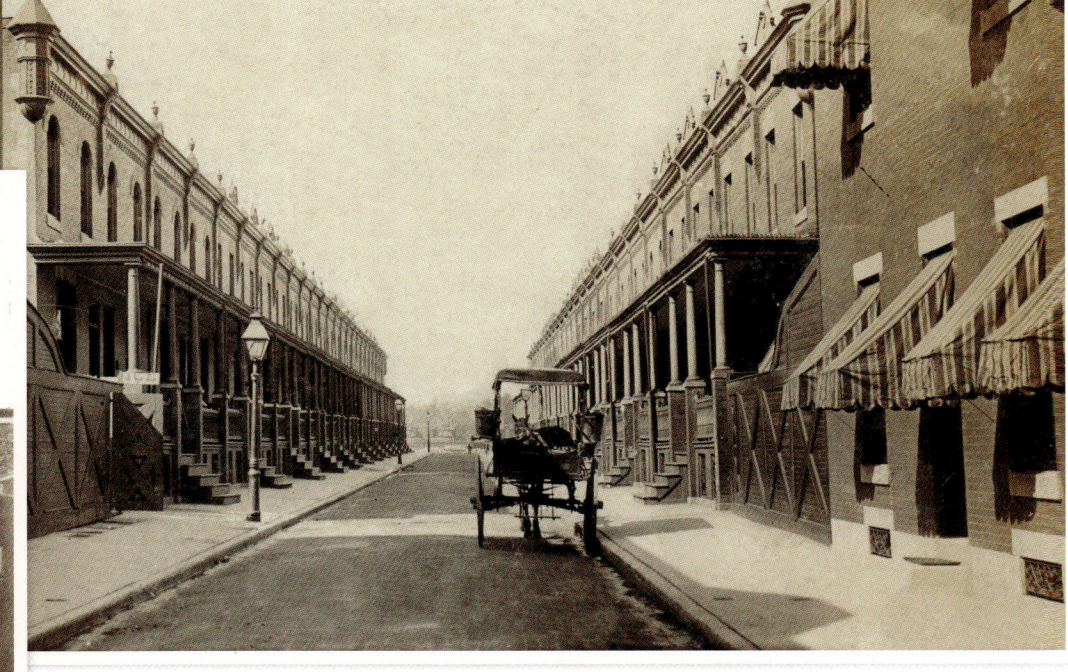

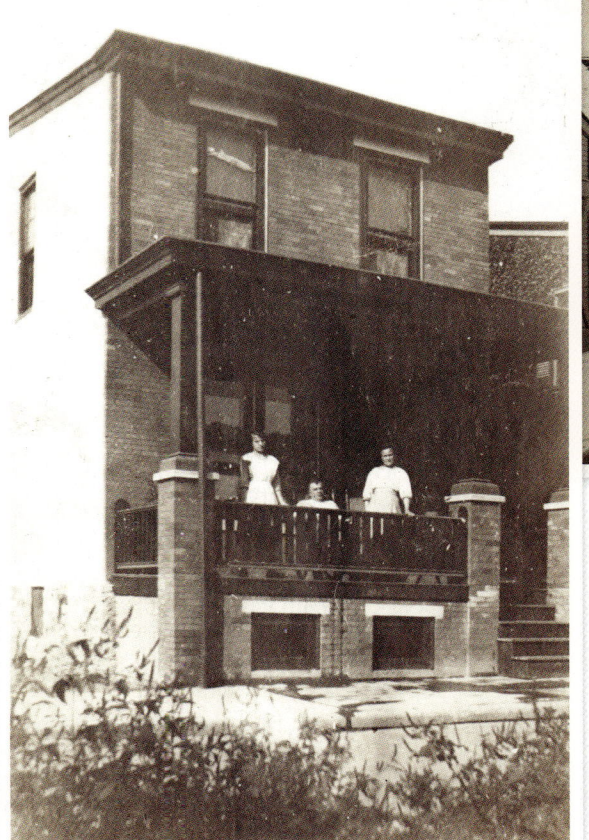

Cecil Street north of Woodland Avenue, 1907. These two-story row houses on Cecil Street were less than a decade old when this photo was taken. This block of Cecil Street extended from Woodland Avenue to Greenway Avenue, just east of Fifty-Eighth Street. Architect James B. Campbell designed and built the modest dwellings in April 1898, for about $2,000.

1838 South Vodges Street, ca. 1910. Family residents pose for a photograph on their front porch on Vodges Street, formerly known as Gibsons Lane. The 1800 block of Vodges, an elbow-shaped street, lies between Woodland and Paschall Avenues west of Fifty-Fifth Street. The vegetation in the foreground is the as-yet-undeveloped east side of Vodges.

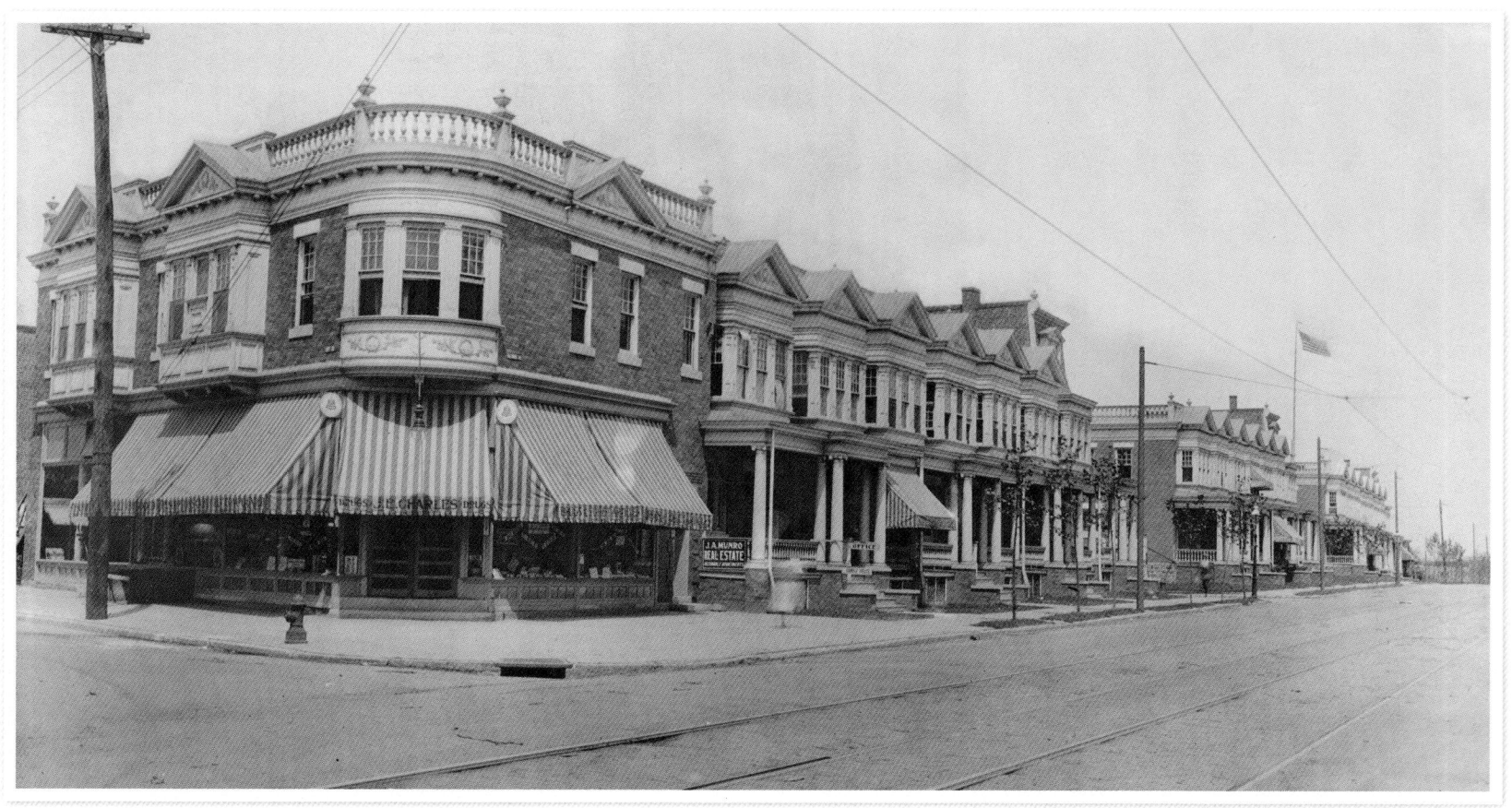

Baltimore Avenue looking east from Fifty-Eighth Street, 1913. The prominently featured corner store, owned by Jacob E. Charles, featured "toilet articles" and "prescriptions carefully compounded." The building is still standing minus its ornamental balustrades and finials. The colonial revival–style row houses were for rent by real estate agent John A. Munro, whose office was next door to Charles's apothecary. These houses were new when this photo was taken, having been built in late December 1911. Transportation to Center City was easily accessed by trolley lines along Baltimore Avenue and by the Angora Station of the West Chester Branch of the Pennsylvania Railroad.

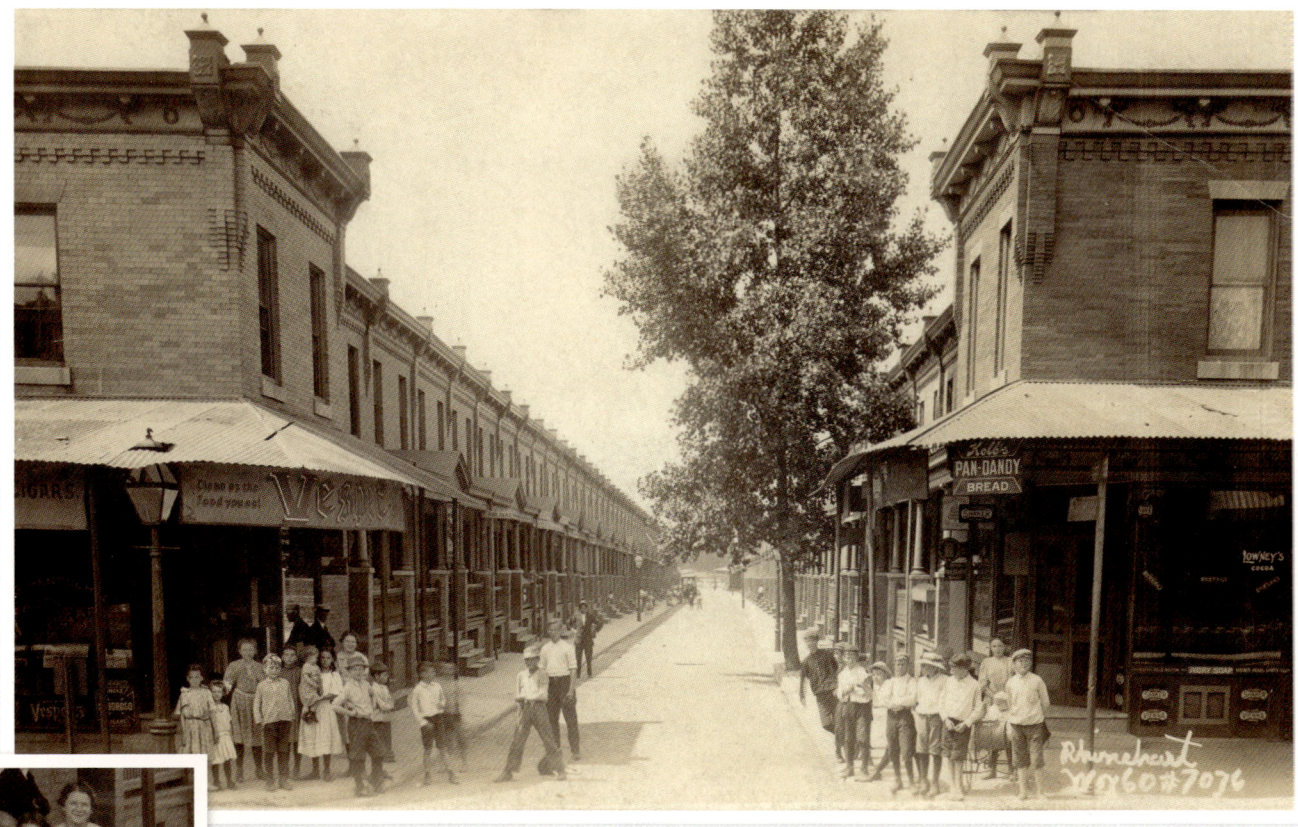

Sixtieth and Reinhard Street, ca. 1910. This view of Southwest Philadelphia shows Reinhard Street (spelled "Rhinehart" on this postcard) at Sixtieth Street, with two corner store / dwelling combinations on opposite sides of the street. The store on the left was a tobacco shop. The grocery on the right side proudly sold Kolb's Pan-Dandy bread, a popular Philadelphia brand. The houses on Reinhard Street were plain but had front porches. The houses on the north side (***left***) were built in late March 1897.

Sixty-First Street and Greenway Avenue, ca. 1910.
Looking east along Greenway Avenue from Sixty-First Street, this intersection was located about halfway between Mt. Moriah Station and Sixtieth Street Station on the Baltimore & Ohio Railroad, making it ideal for residential development. Built in August 1898, the homes have a prominent gabled parapet crowned with a finial. Many have since been altered.

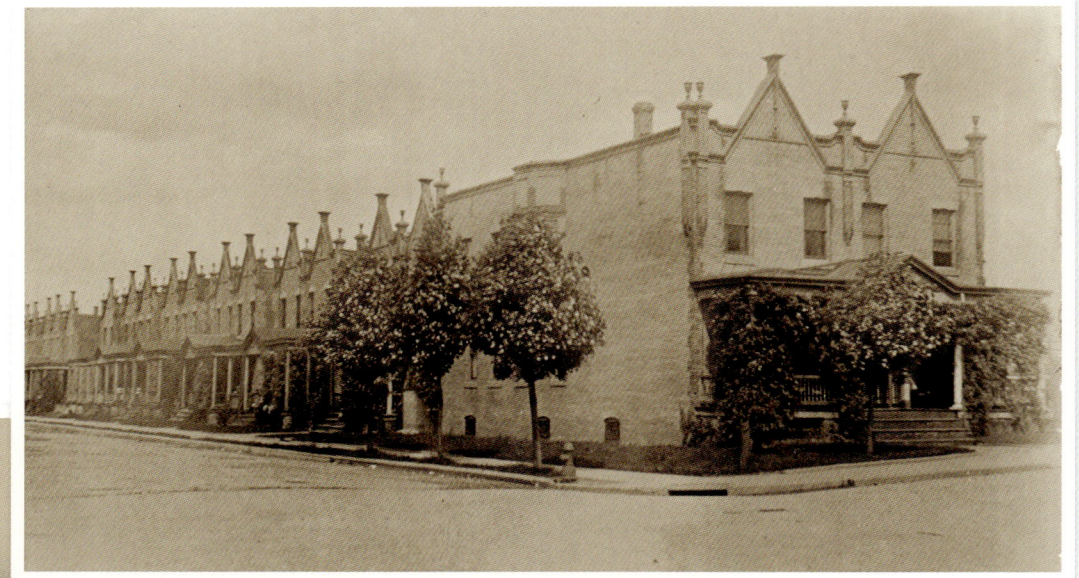

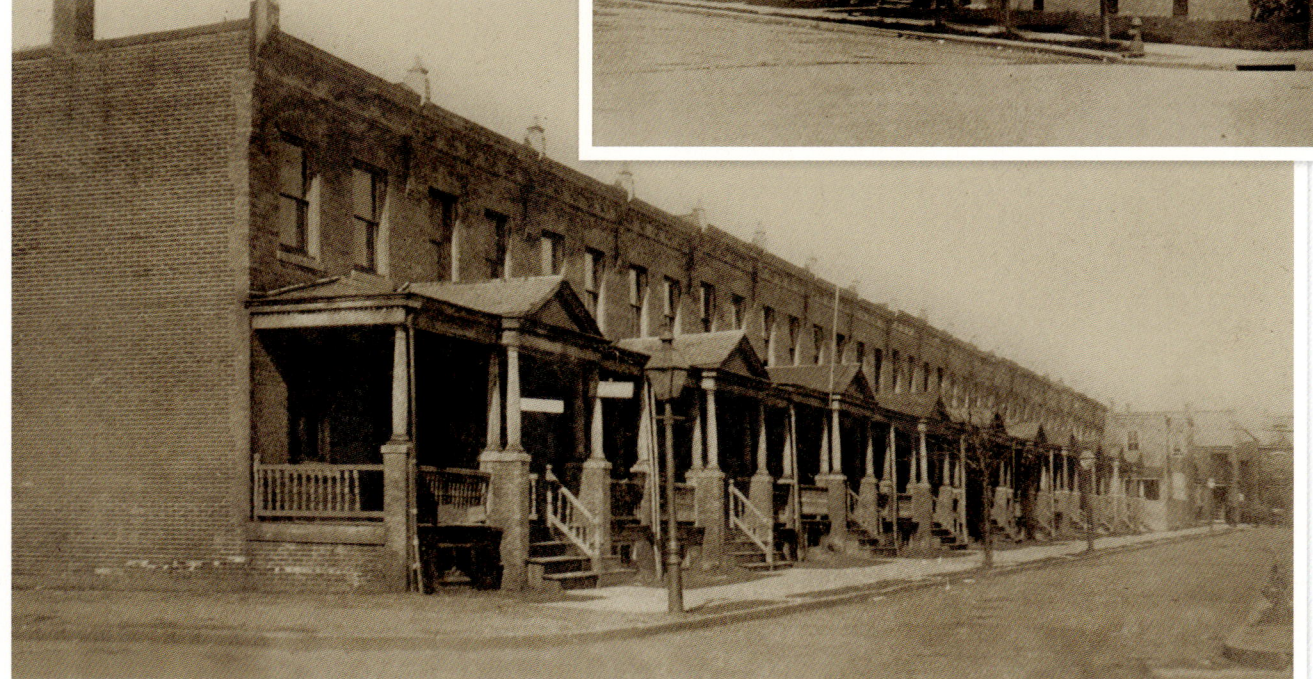

Felton Street north of Paschall Avenue, ca. 1907.
Harry D. Beaston built this block in 1896, when parts of Southwest Philadelphia were still sparsely populated.

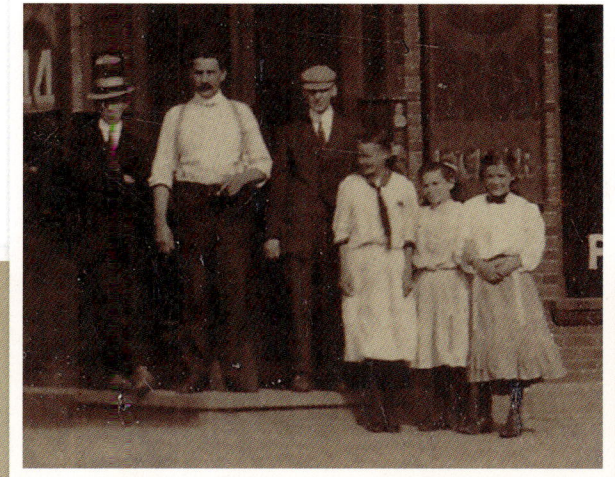

Woodland Avenue east from Sixty-Third Street, ca. 1907. The pool parlor of Emanuel M. Smith at the corner of Sixty-Third and Woodland Avenue was likely the focal point of this neighborhood's manly entertainment. In addition to a lively game of billiards, a gentleman could get his choice of cigars here. The row houses and the corner store were built in April 1896. It's probable that some of the homeowners on this block worked at the J. G. Brill Car Works across Woodland Avenue.

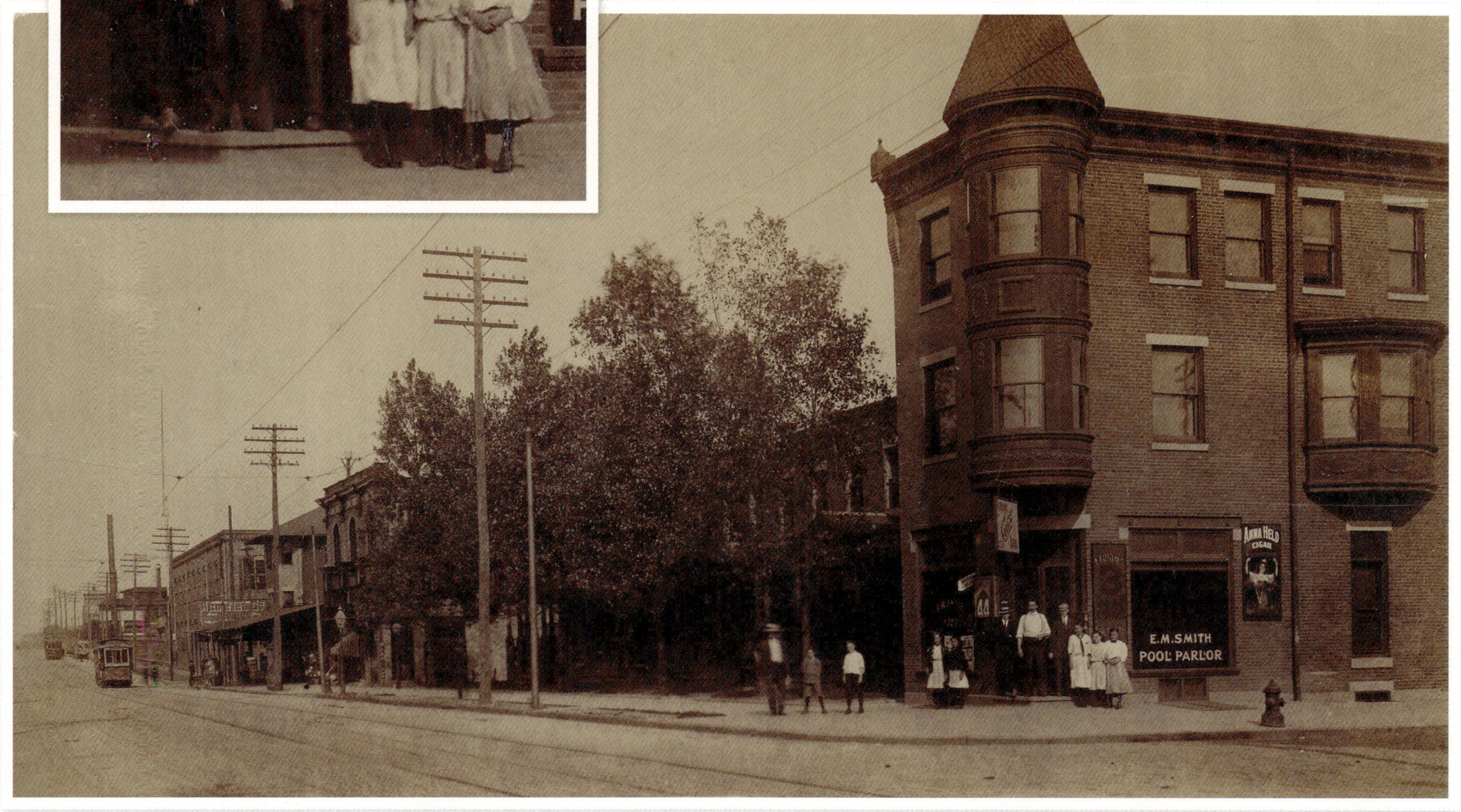

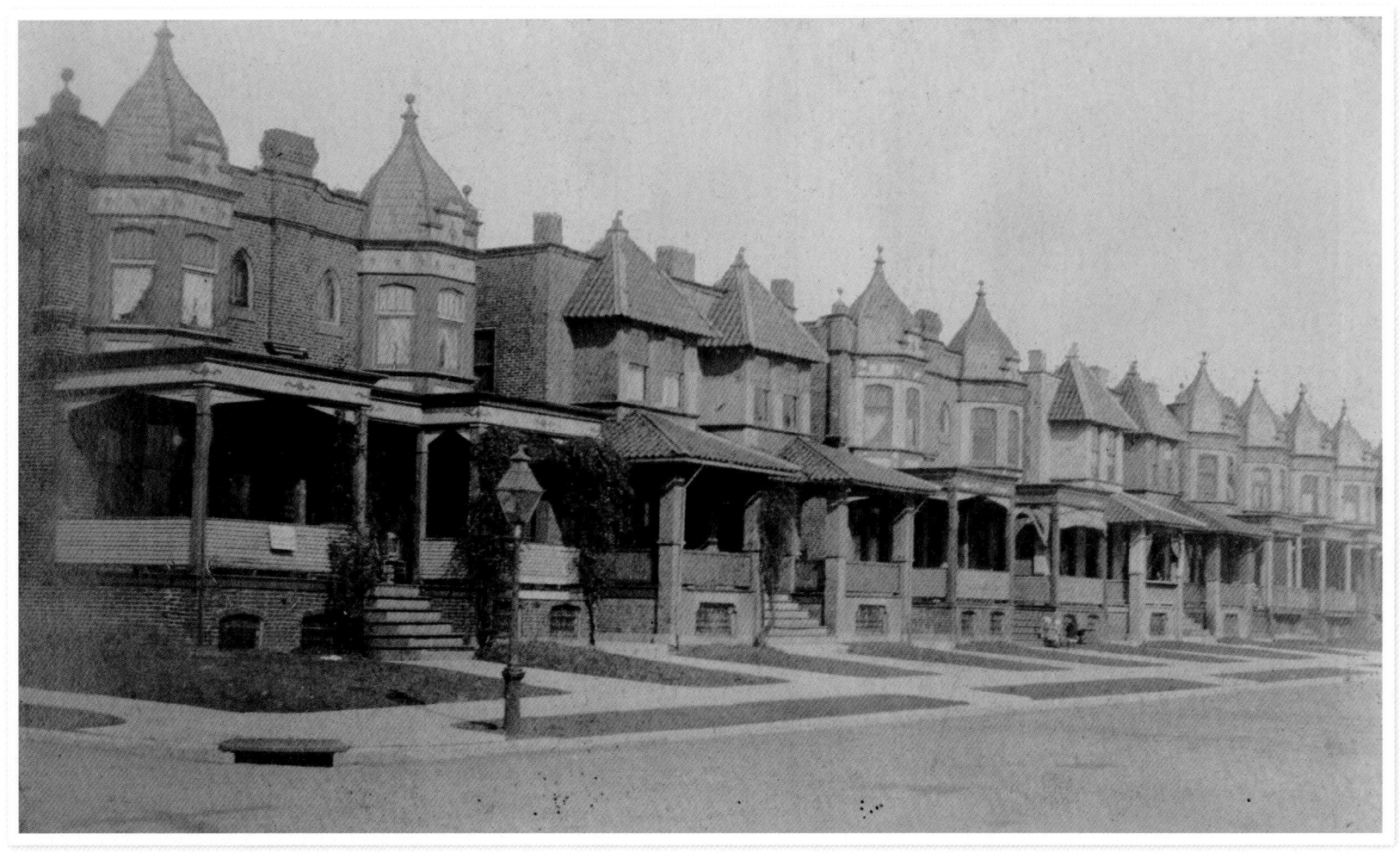

Paschall Avenue east of Sixty-Fifth Street, 1907. These attractive twins on Paschall Avenue were built in July 1899 and designed by architect E. Allen Wilson, who produced plans for houses all over West and Southwest Philadelphia and eventually became a real estate developer. Their Spanish tiles and exotically domed bay windows evoke a Mediterranean style. The builder and developer was S. F. Kemon, of whom little is known.

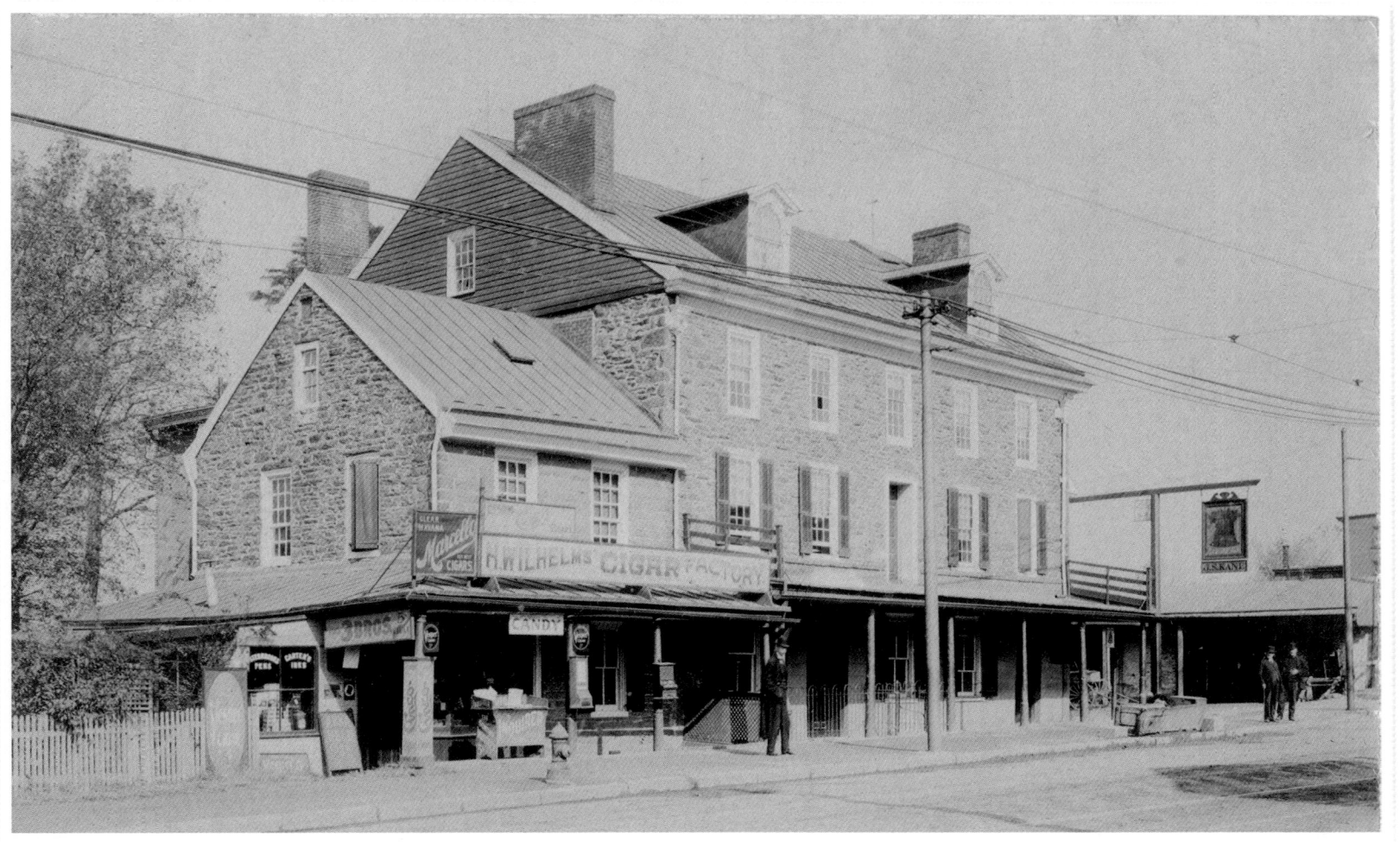

7307 Woodland Avenue, ca. 1908. The Blue Bell Tavern (*on left*) was built in 1768 by Henry Paschall. According to legend, it was here that the gallant and dashing General Washington kissed the landlord's daughter upon overhearing her youthful and enthusiastic desire for him. The Blue Bell was no stranger to Washington, welcoming him on his many trips to and from his Mount Vernon home. In 1801, a three-and-a-half-story addition was built, which was demolished around 1940. At the time of this photo, innkeeper John S. Kane owned the venerable old tavern and used the older portion as a general store. The city purchased the Blue Bell Tavern in 1909 and added it to the Fairmount Park system.

Chapter 8.

NORTHWEST PHILADELPHIA

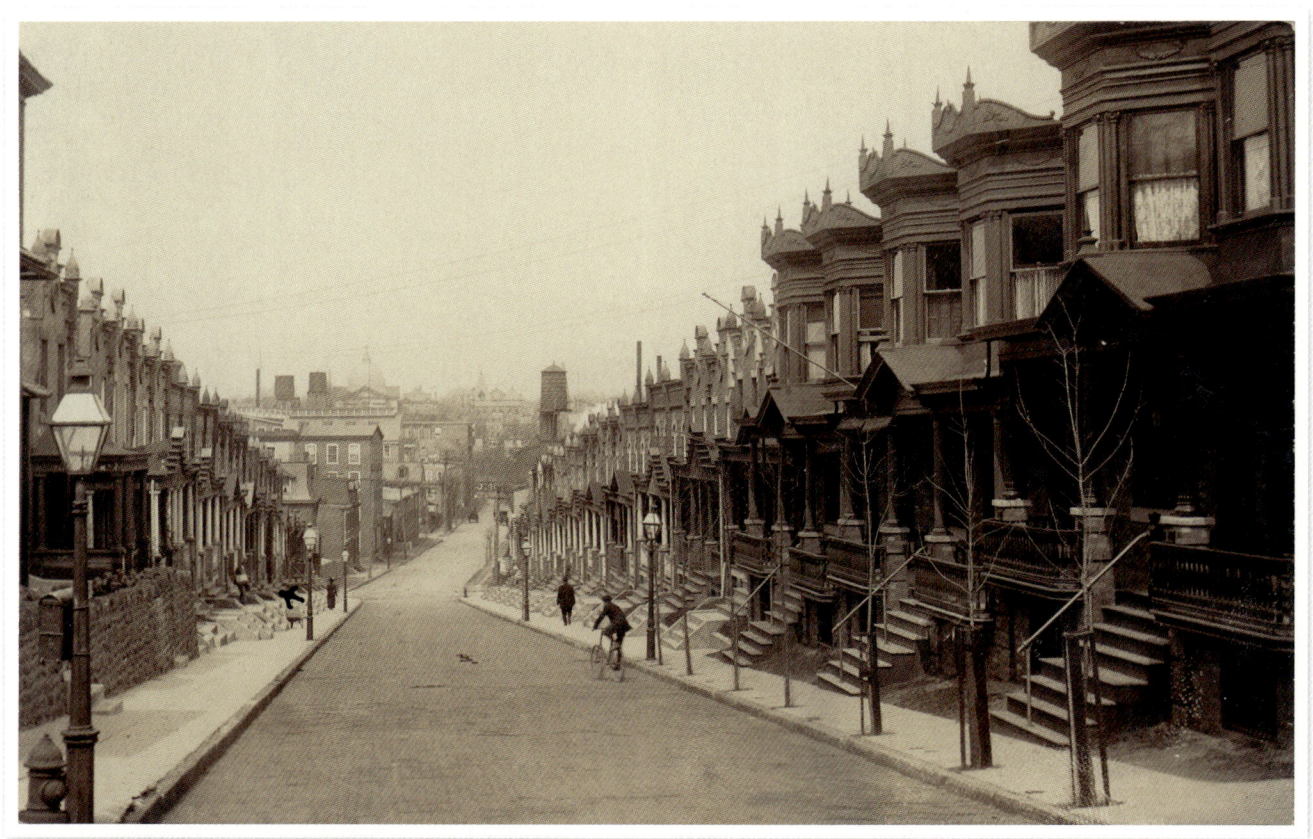

Lena Street looking north from East Penn Street, 1909

The Northwest section of Philadelphia has several unique features. From Germantown to Upper Roxborough, the buildings, whether humble cottage or grand cathedral, are constructed primarily of local Wissahickon schist. And the terrain is rolling, compared to the relatively flat Northeast, South, and Southwest Philadelphia. Northwest Philadelphia is culturally different too, being the location of the earliest permanent German settlement in the New World.[1]

On the other side of the Wissahickon Valley are the sprawling neighborhoods of Roxborough and the once-dynamic industrial community of Manayunk. The style of residential architecture varies, from the dense row house blocks of East Germantown, East Falls, and Manayunk to the sprawling single homes of Roxborough, Mount Airy, and Chestnut Hill.

Germantown, Mount Airy, and Chestnut Hill

A settlement almost as old as the city of Philadelphia itself, Germantown began as a colony for persecuted German Mennonites seeking to worship freely. Within a short period of time, Germantown grew to a highly venerated community and incorporated as a borough in 1844. With the coming of the Philadelphia, Germantown & Reading passenger railroad and subsequent railways, Germantown grew into a suburb of tranquil, tree-lined blocks and attractive Victorian-era homes.[2]

Germantown is lined with cottages and villas, surrounded by neat grounds, trees, shrubbery and flowers, many of them costly and handsome, all comfortable and pretty. . . . They are the results of the railroads which enable anyone to enjoy the pleasures of country life and at the same time attend to business in town.[3]

—Sidney George Fisher, 1859

Additional commuter rail lines allowed for further development near new transportation hubs such as Tulpehocken Station on the Philadelphia, Germantown & Chestnut Hill Railroad. Carpenter Station on the same railroad facilitated the development of Pelham on the old estate of Samuel Carpenter. Mount Airy Station on the Chestnut Hill branch of the railroad helped grow the fashionable neighborhoods of Gowen and Sedgwick Farms.[4]

Chestnut Hill was also well served by the city's passenger railroad system, with exclusive residences built east of Germantown Avenue near the Chestnut Hill Depot on East Chestnut Hill Avenue and Summit Street in the 1850s and 1860s. Wissahickon Heights Station was the brainchild of Henry H. Houston (1820–1895), who was instrumental in creating the Wissahickon Heights suburb on the west side of lush and verdant Chestnut Hill.[5]

By the 1890s, Germantown and Mt. Airy had access to horse-drawn streetcars, and then in 1894 electrified streetcars attracted an even-greater number of new residents. In time, parts of Germantown and Mount Airy began to resemble other parts of Philadelphia, with rows of middle-class households close to factories and mills. Even the popular Wissahickon schist building material was eschewed for Philadelphia's quintessential red brick.[6]

Germantown Avenue, known as Main Street for many years, was served by the #23 trolley, which held the record for the longest-known route in the world at a little over 25 miles. The trolley was discontinued in 1992, but the tracks remain.

Wissahickon

The neighborhood of Wissahickon began developing in the latter half of the nineteenth century, spurred by the Pencoyd Iron Works. The homes, mostly twins, were built in the 1880s to early 1900s. Many of the builders used stone exteriors, but there is a fair amount of red brick in this small yet attractive section of the city. Proximity to beautiful Fairmount Park and the wild Wissahickon Creek was a key selling point for suburbanites looking to escape the crowded urban center.[7]

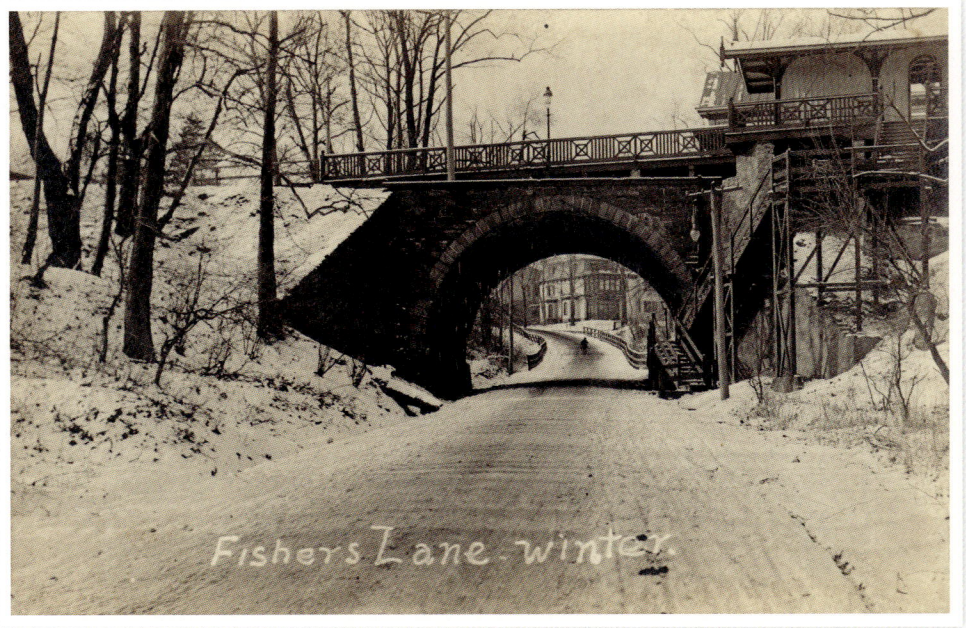

Fishers Lane Station, ca. 1909. Fishers Lane (now East Logan Street) was one of the best sledding hills on snowy winter days. Great sledding parties were held there, and sledding teams had colorful names such as Little Hinton, the Clippers, the Jack Jumpers, and the Cheese Boxes.

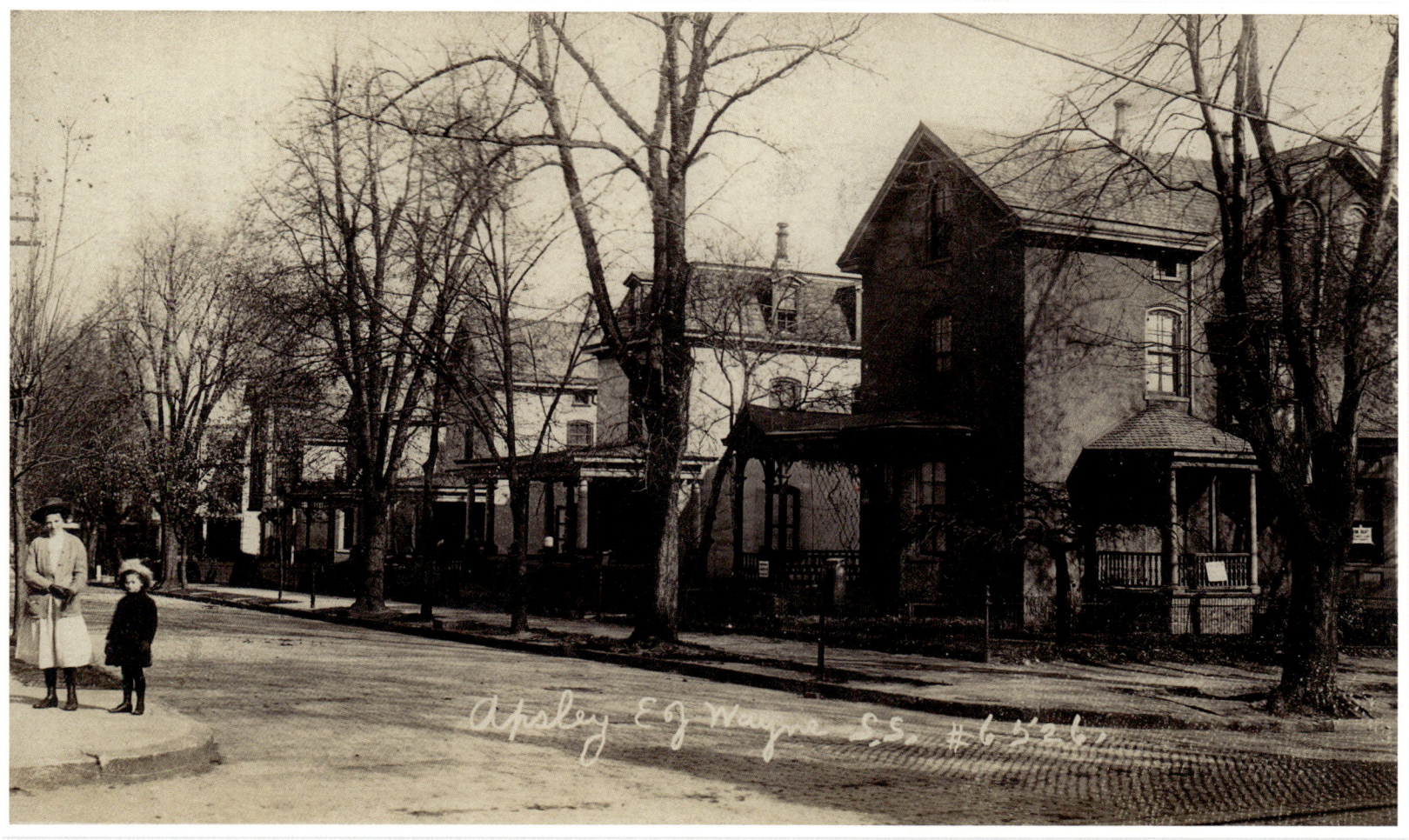

Apsley Street east of Wayne Avenue, ca. 1908. The twin houses in this postcard photo are located near the traditional eastern boundary of Germantown, Wayne Junction. They are faced with stone, a common practice in Germantown and other parts of Northwest Philadelphia.

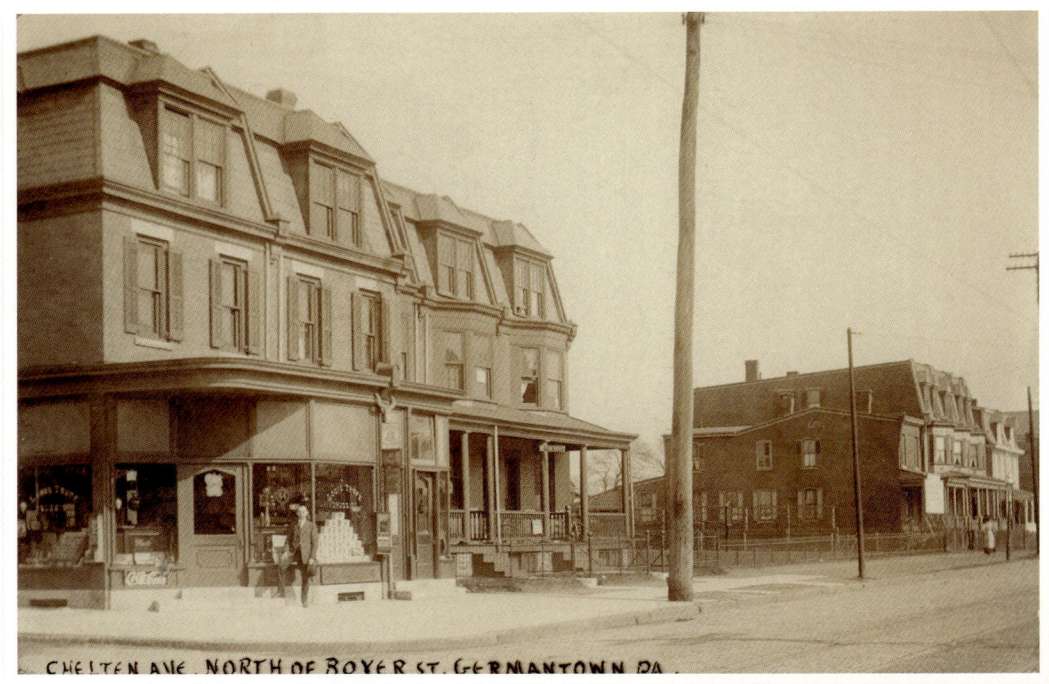

CHELTEN AVE. NORTH OF BOYER ST. GERMANTOWN PA.

Chelten Avenue north of Boyer Street, 1910. These five houses, which include the pharmacy of Louis Trupp at 901 East Chelten, were built by Harry Wetherstine in 1906. They have since been demolished.

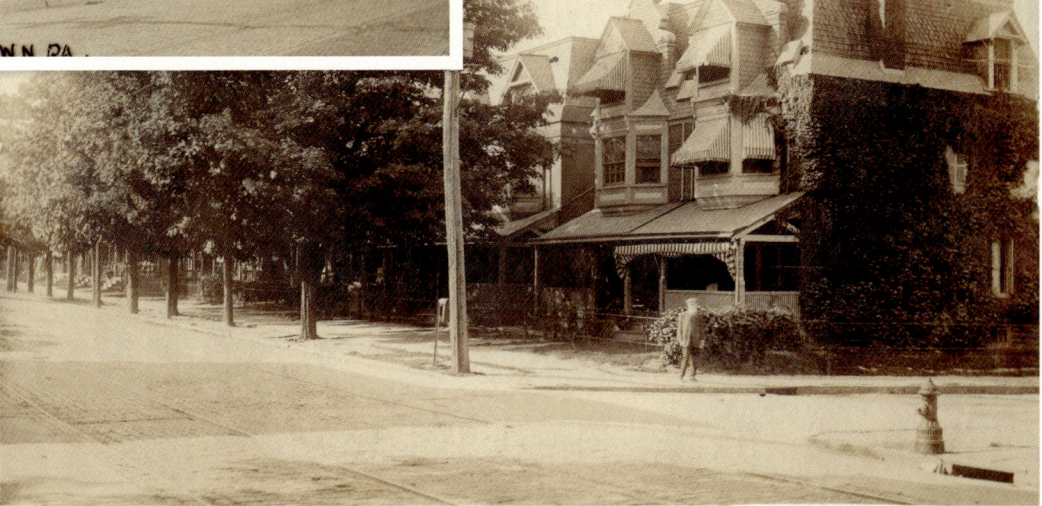

Chew Avenue north of Church Lane, 1908. Chew Avenue was one of East Germantown's major thoroughfares, with a lovely residential block shown here. These houses were twins designed in a combination Queen Anne and Second Empire style.

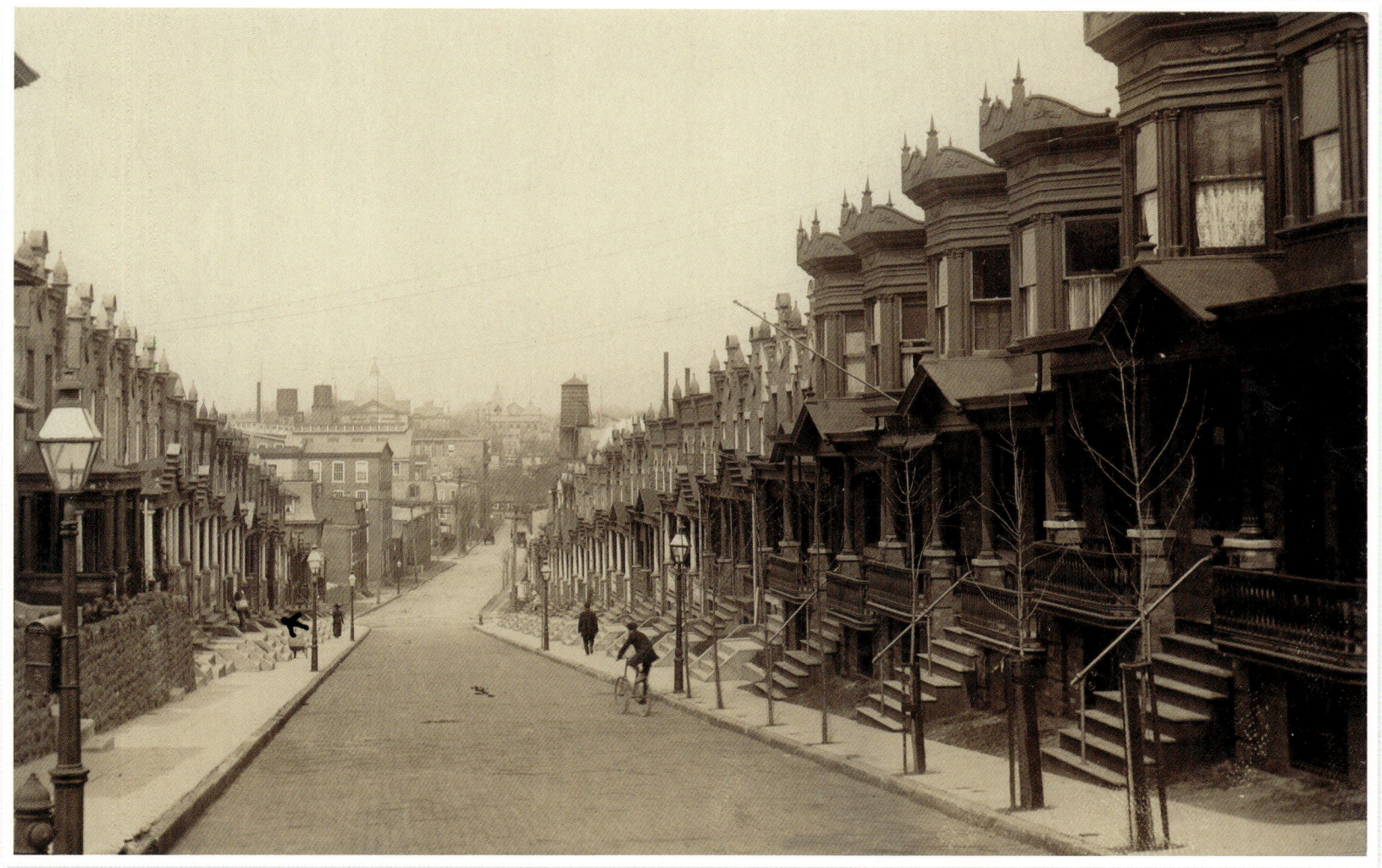

Lena Street north of Penn Street, ca. 1909. Lena Street (formerly Cumberland Street) is an interesting study in changing tastes in residential architecture. The east and west sides of the street were built in June and July 1896 by C. A. Heinke in the High Victorian style. Homes on the far right were built in May 1906 in the more practical but less picturesque bay-and-porch style. Peter Kuhn was the architect of these later homes. The dome of St. Vincent DePaul Roman Catholic Church (1857) can be seen on the horizon.

Rittenhouse Street east of Crittendon Street, 1909. The row houses shown here were constructed for economy rather than sophistication, perfect for a factory worker looking for an affordable family home close to his job. Both sides of the 1300 block of East Rittenhouse were built in October 1901 by Solomon Greenberg, a big-time Germantown developer.

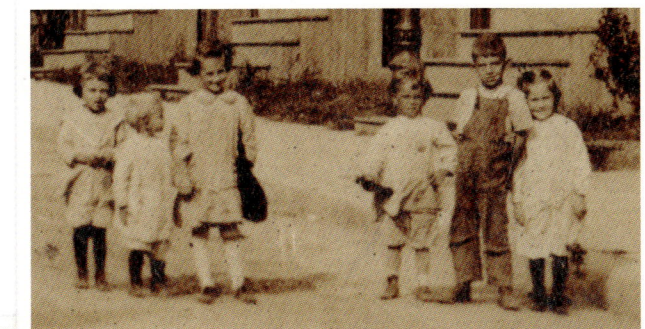

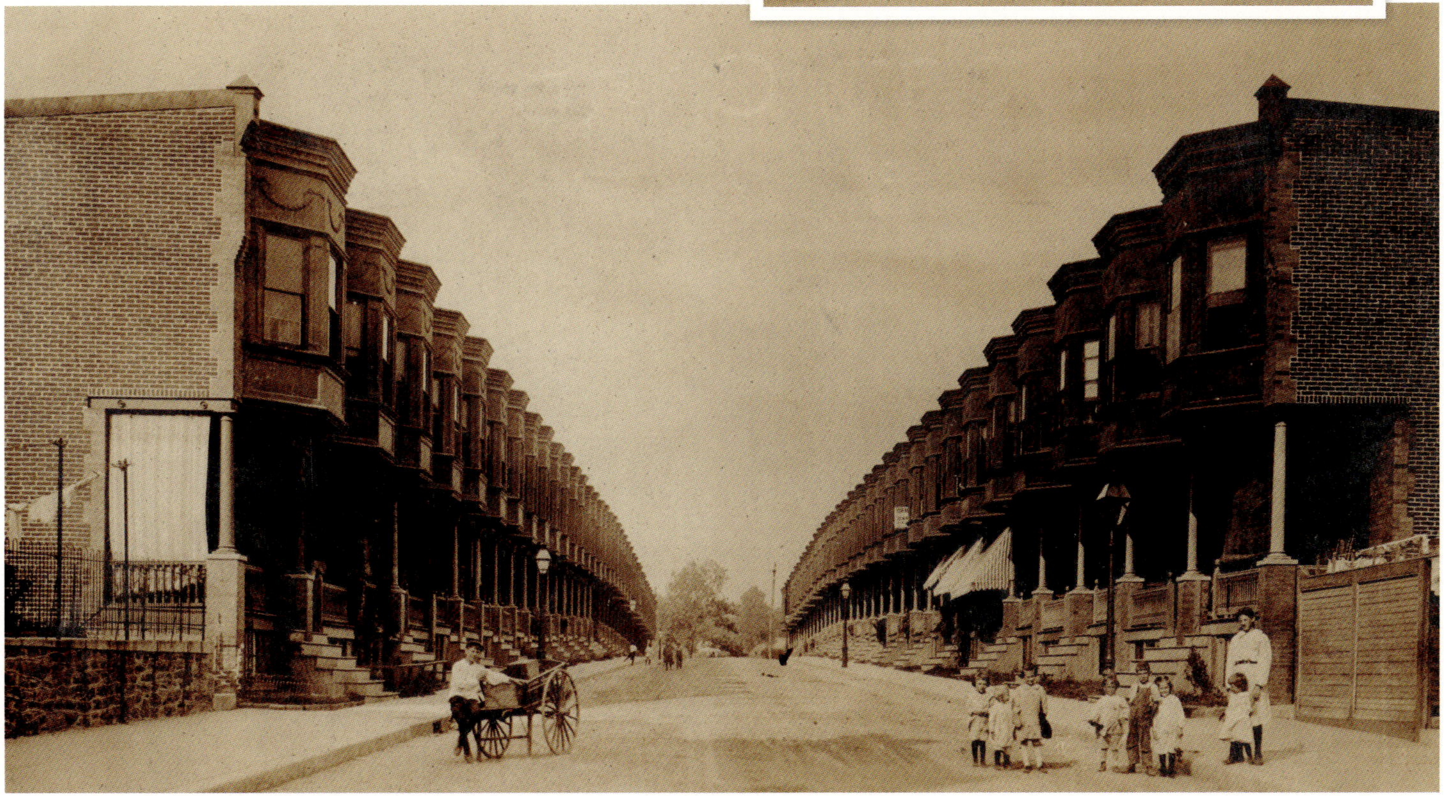

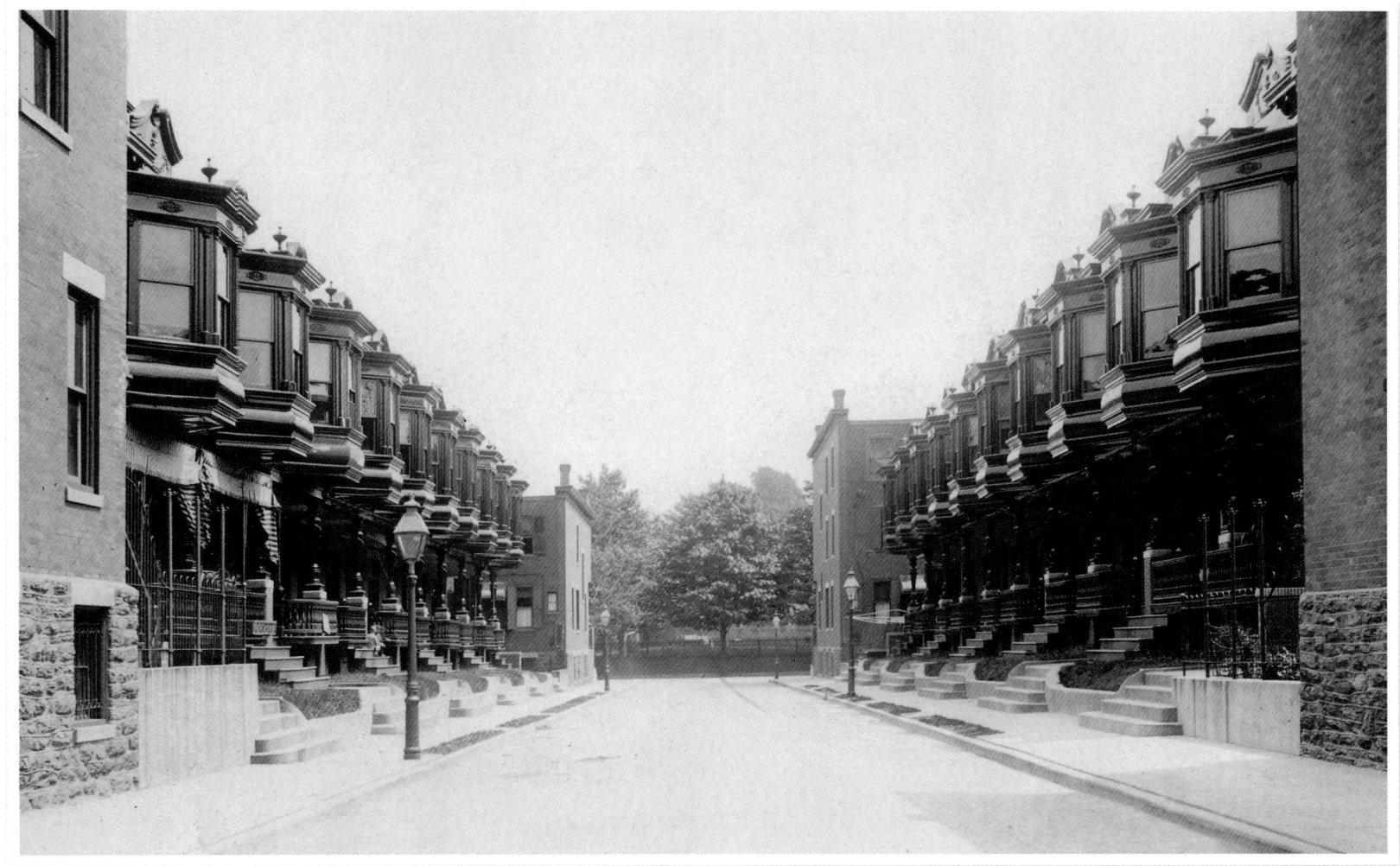

Stokes Street east of Woodlawn Street, ca. 1910. Stokes Street is a tiny street in East Germantown, running only one block between Woodlawn and Locust Avenue. Its twenty row homes were built in June 1906 and feature bay windows supported by neoclassical columns. East Locust Avenue can be seen in the distance before its development with twin houses.

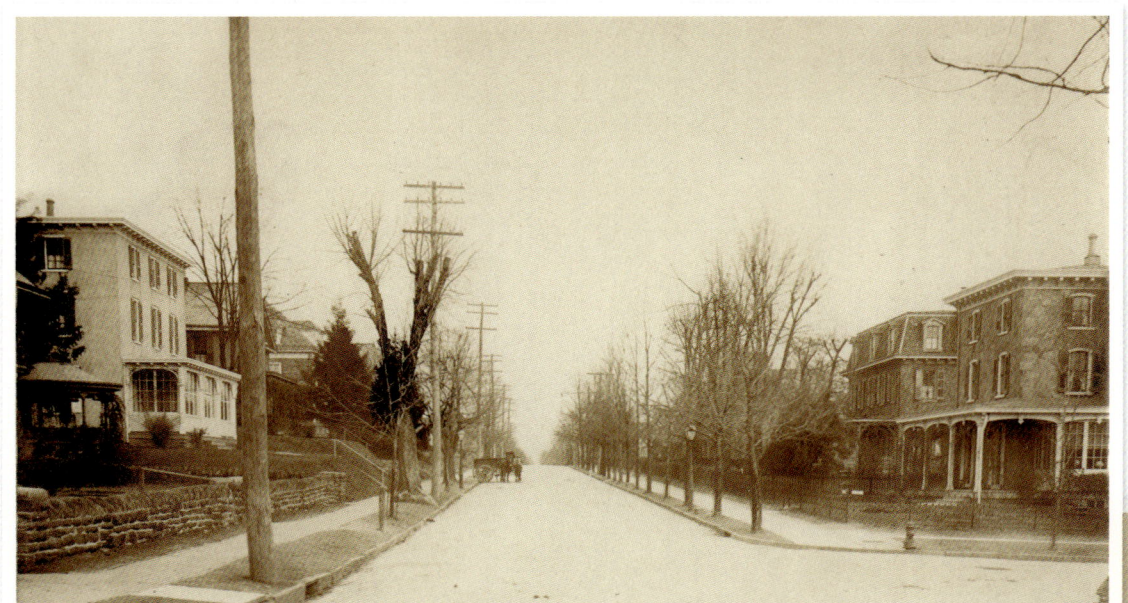

Mount Airy Avenue east from Chew Avenue, 1914. A companion to the photo below, this view shows Mt. Airy Avenue looking east from Chew and depicts homes from the late 1800s. The intersection of Mt. Airy Avenue and Chew Avenue is east of Germantown Avenue and close to the Mt. Airy Station of the Philadelphia & Reading Railroad.

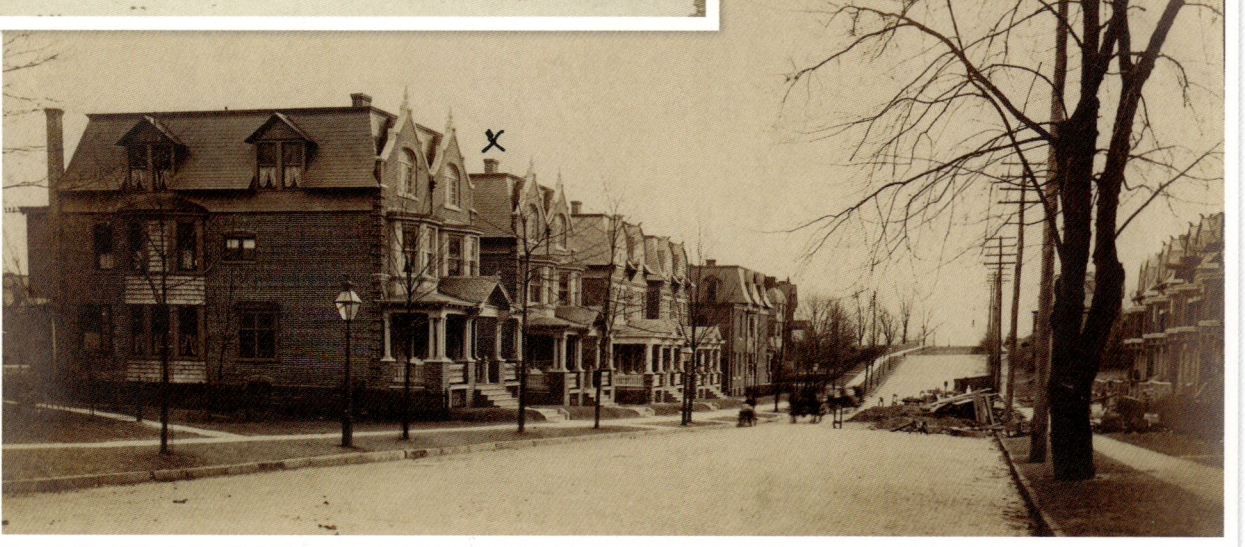

Chew Avenue south from Mt. Airy Avenue, 1907. These twin homes shown here were very new when this photo was taken, built in March 1906 by A. B. & C. F. Millett. The sender of this postcard marked his house (7137 Chew Avenue) with an "X."

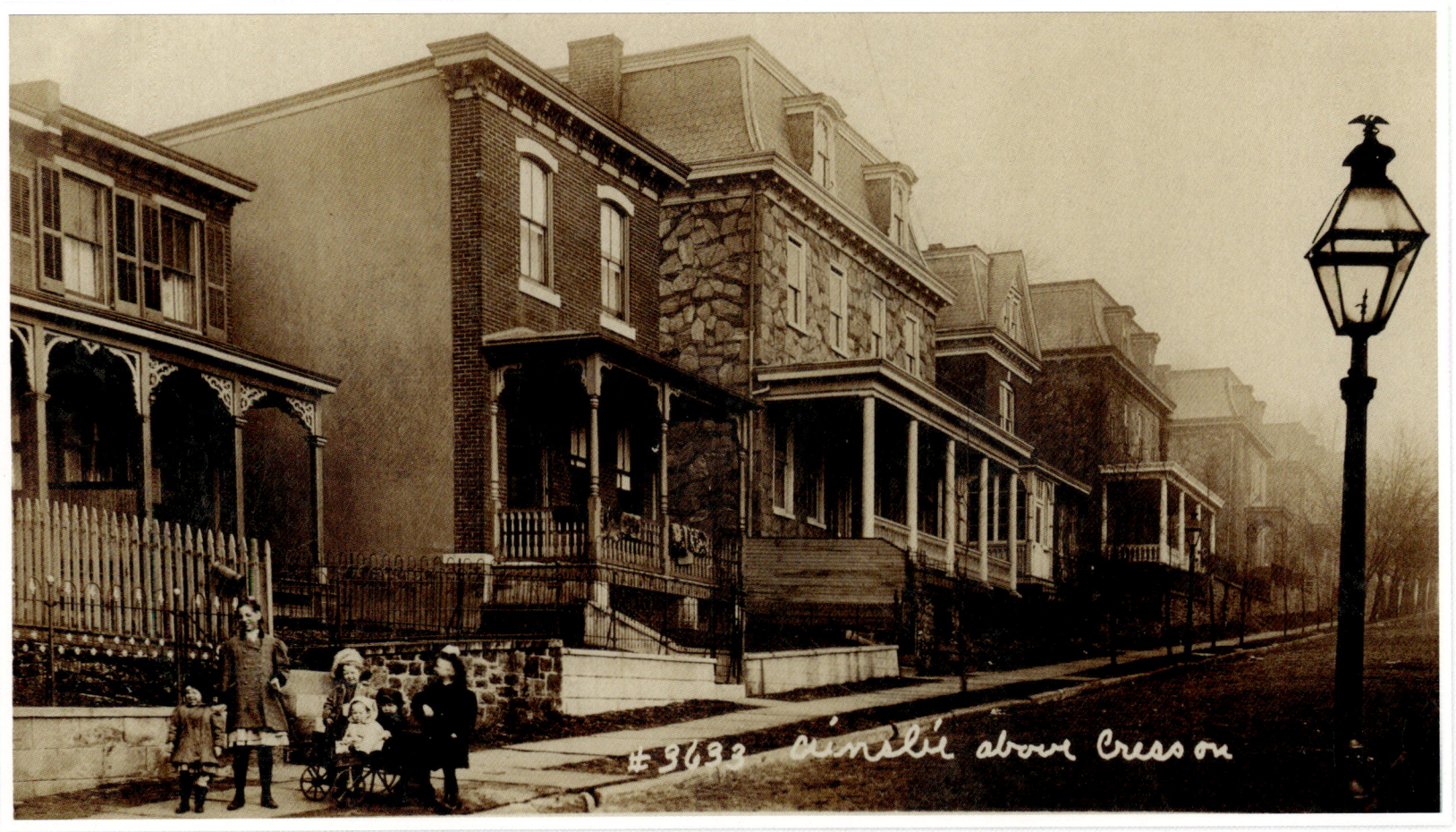

#3633 *ainslie above Cresson*

Ainslie Street north of Cresson Street, 1907. Children gather at the foot of Ainslie Street in East Falls. At the time, the neighborhood was known as the Falls of the Schuylkill. On the north side of the steeply sloping street is an eclectic mix of nineteenth-century houses, all of which are still standing.

Righter Street north of Kalos Street, 1906. These attractive row houses were built by William H. Wright between 1896 and 1897.

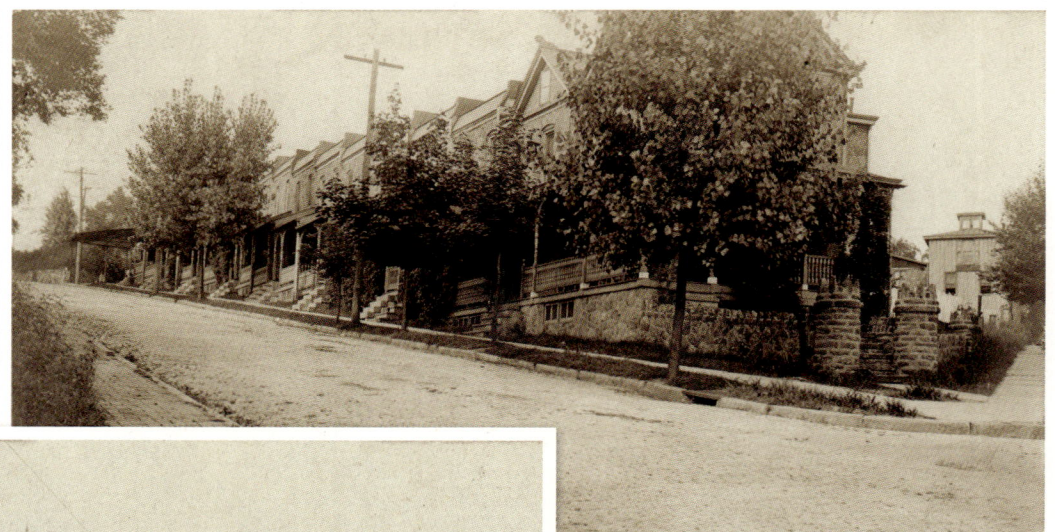

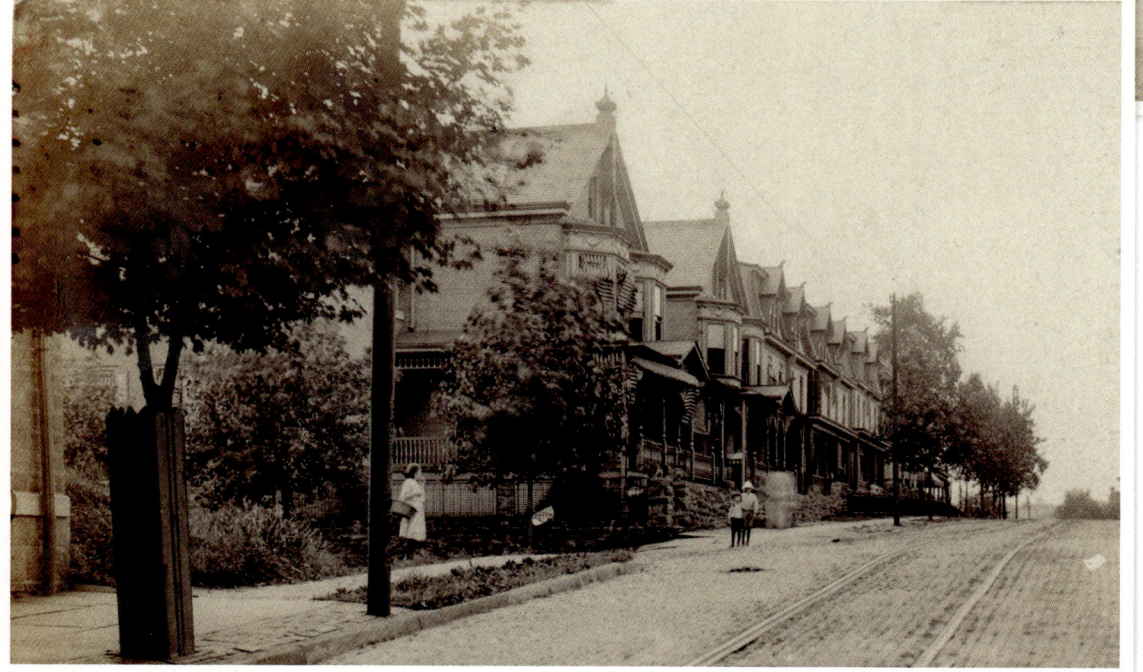

Manayunk Avenue north of Osborn Street, 1906. Attractive twin houses populate the Wissahickon neighborhood. The houses on the left were built by Dr. James Sibbald in 1899. Howard R. Yocum built the others on the block a few years earlier, in 1895.

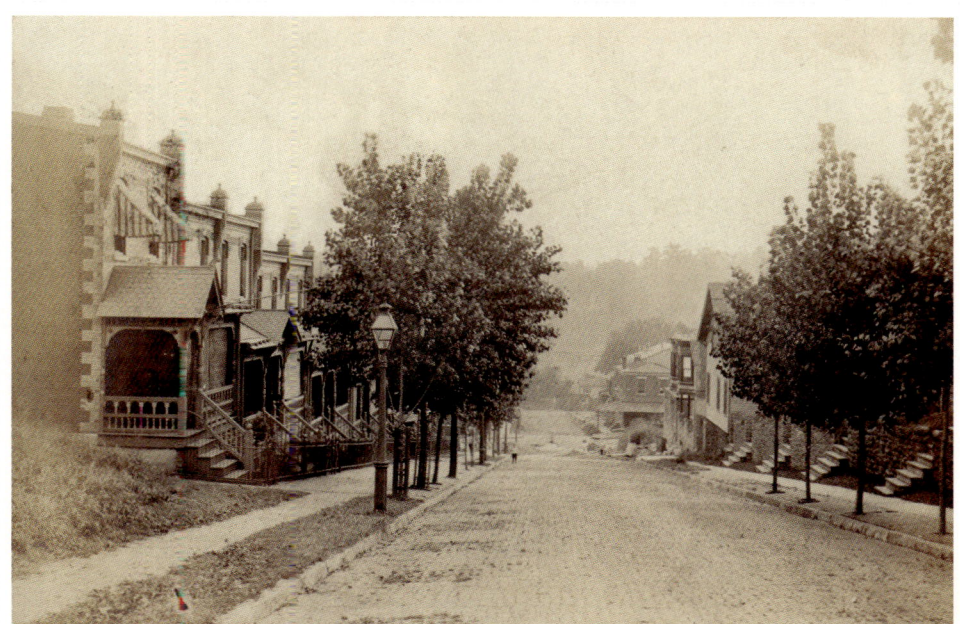

Osborne Street west of Manayunk Avenue, 1906. Br ck-paved Osborne Street descends rapidly toward Ridge Avenue. John Simpson built the row houses on the left in April 1890.

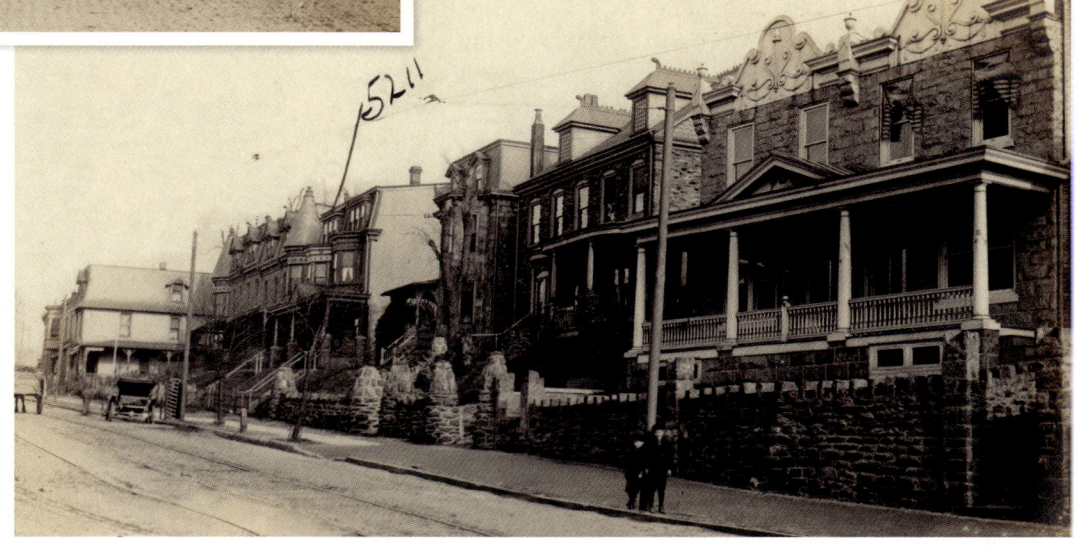

Ridge Avenue north of Osborne Street, 1906. Ridge Avenue was always the main thoroughfare in Roxbcrough. By the early twentieth century, expensive dwellings began to appear on the old road. The stone facades and retaining walls are typical of the region.

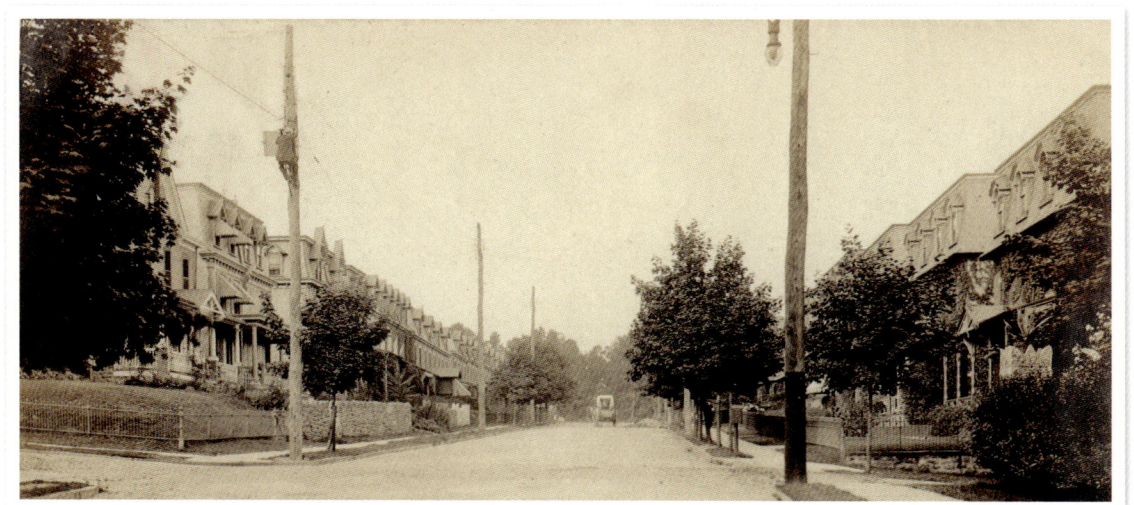

Rochelle Avenue east of Freeland Avenue, 1906. The Wissahickon section of Philadelphia was known for upscale living, with tree-lined streets and fine dwellings. This block of ca. 1885 twin houses is typical of the neighborhood. Note the utility worker at the telephone pole at left.

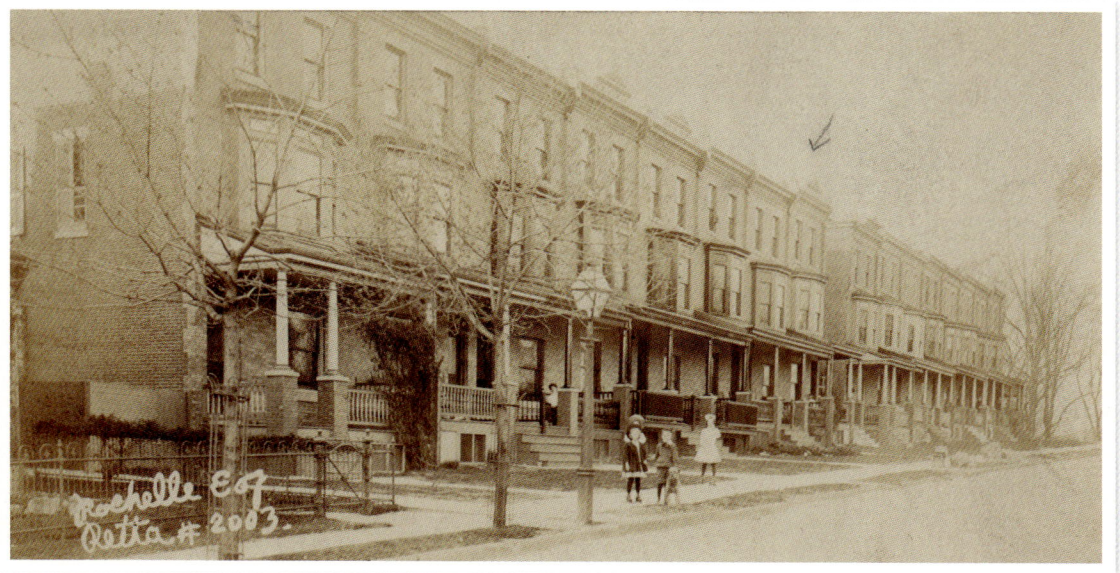

Rochelle Avenue east of Retta Street, ca. 1907. Bell & Kershaw built these sixteen row houses in 1899 at a cost of $2,500 each.

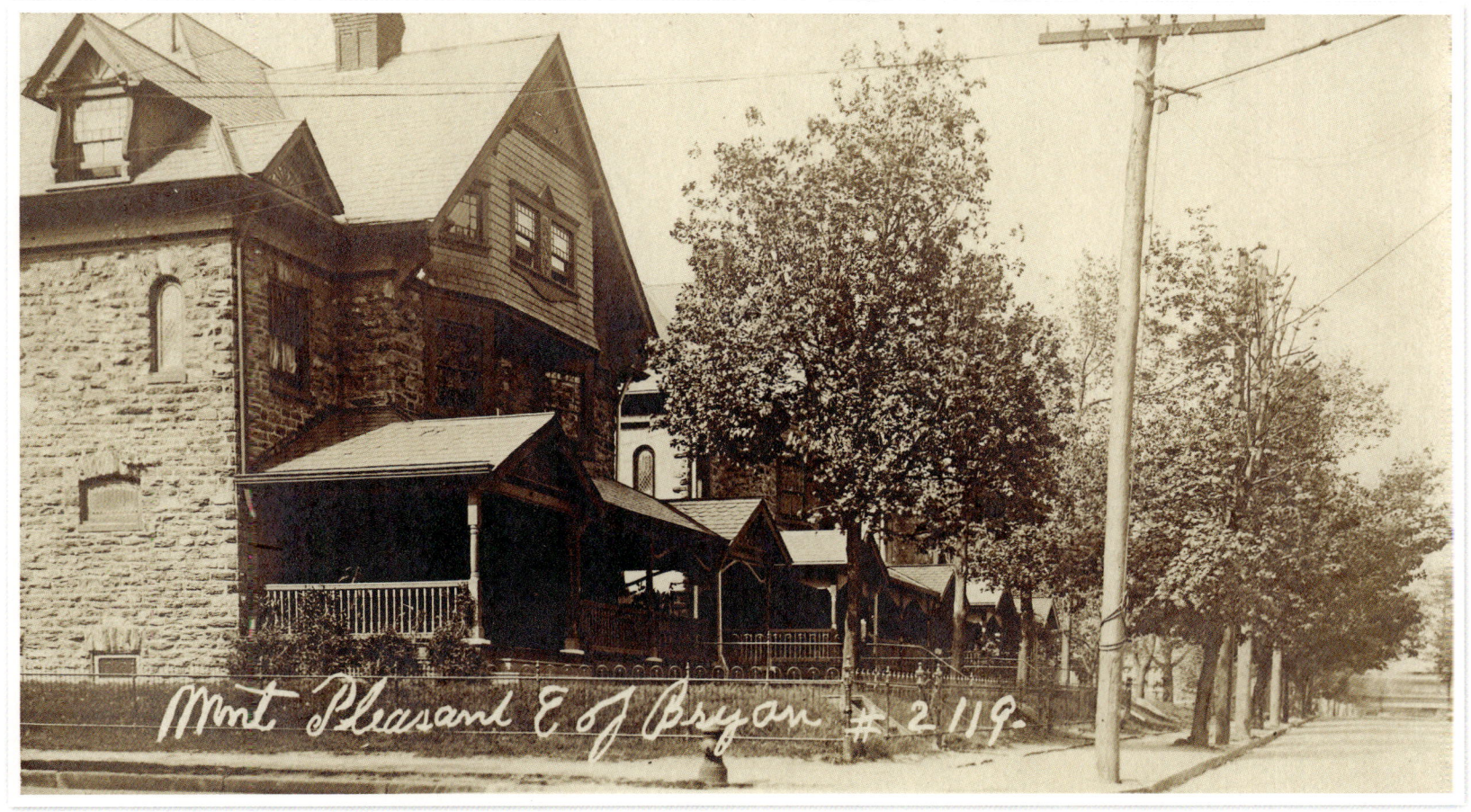

Mount Pleasant Avenue east of Bryan Street, ca. 1907. The three twins on the left in this genteel suburban setting were built in May 1892 by C. R. Kohl & Brother, a construction firm active from 1891 to 1896.

Chapter 9.

THE PEOPLE

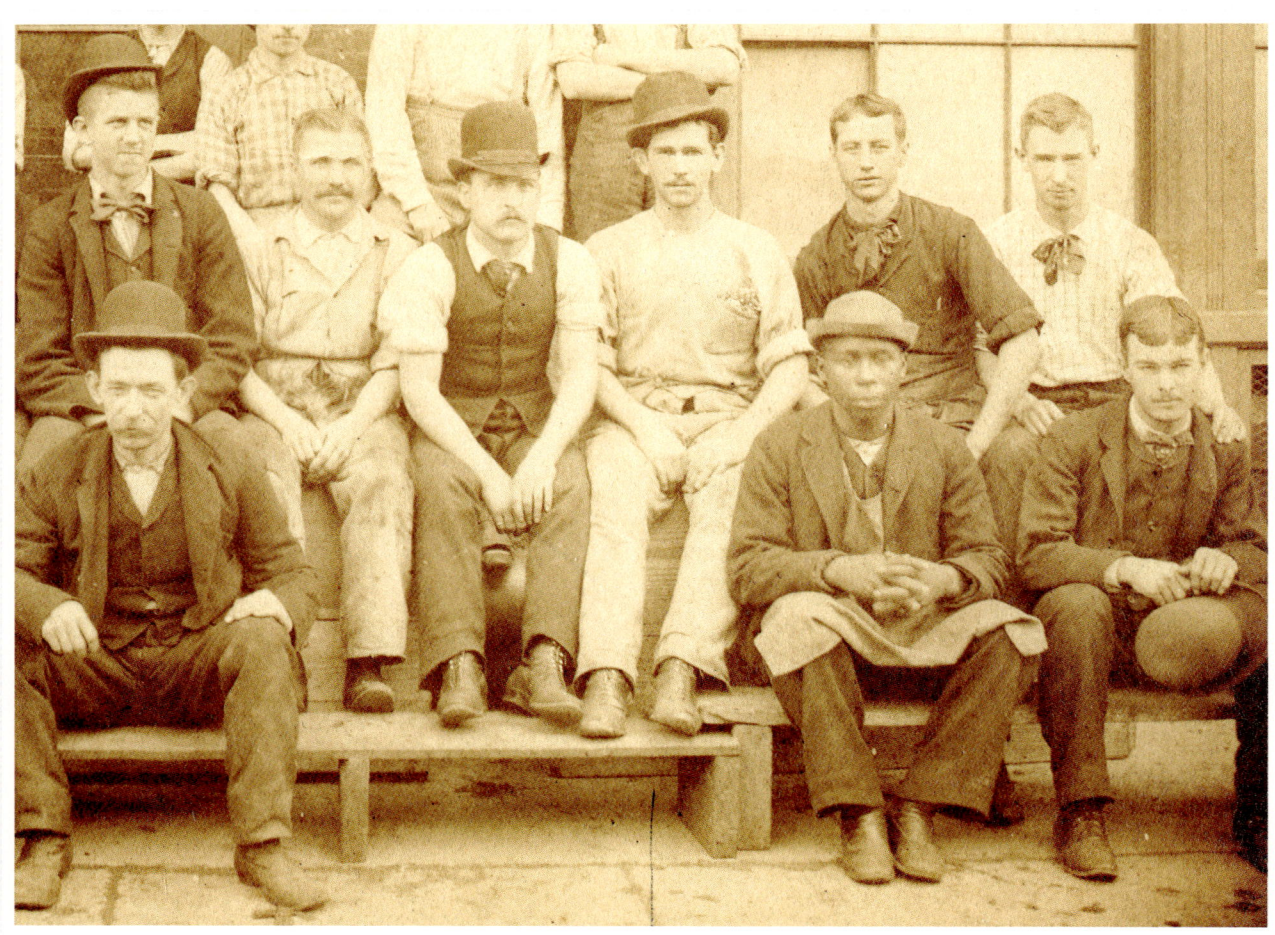

**Workers at Historical
Publishing Company, ca. 1895**

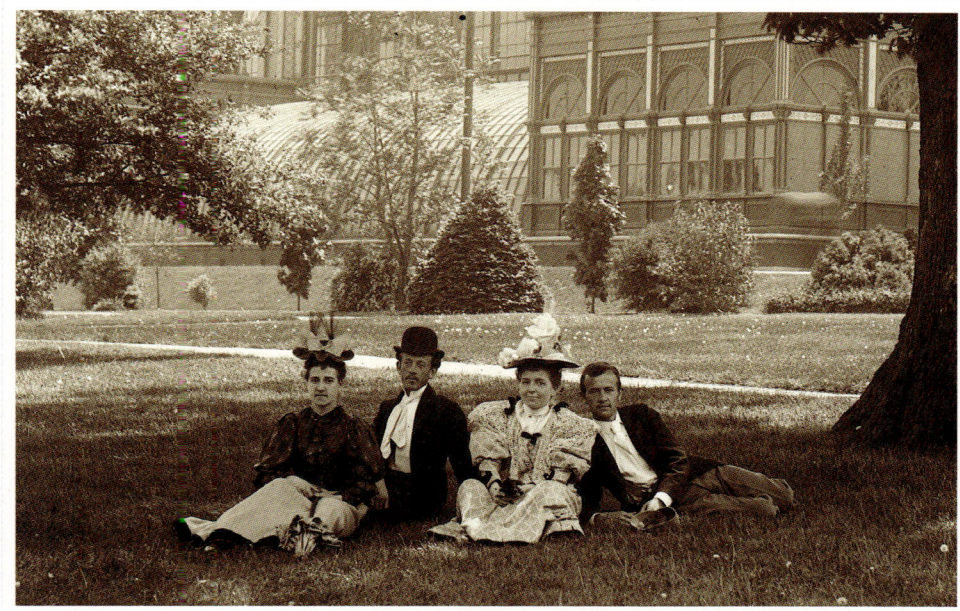

Philadelphia couples near Horticultural Hall, 1890. Two young couples relax on the grass under the shade of a tall tree in Fairmount Park in May 1890. Their fine attire suggests they were "proper" Philadelphians. In the background is Horticultural Hall, built for the 1876 Centennial Exposition. It was torn down in 1955.

When Philadelphia's City Hall was completed in 1901, it was run by the infamous Republican Machine, composed mostly of "proper Philadelphians," many with familial ties to the city's colonial past. Together with the city's wealthy industrialists and bankers, they represented Philadelphia's Gilded Age aristocracy. They picnicked in Fairmount Park and in the summer vacationed at the Bryn Mawr Hotel. A great concentration of the wealthy elites lived on or near the very fashionable Rittenhouse Square. In 1890 there were more than 120 single-family dwellings in the Rittenhouse Square area (five decades later, the number dwindled to just three). The areas north of Market Street and certain parts of West Philadelphia were not considered "fashionable" by the Victorian beau monde.[1]

Unlike their peers in other northeastern US metropolises, proper Philadelphians avoided the spotlight of national politics, preferring instead the pursuits of gentlemanly club life. Alexander Van Rensselaer (1850–1933), for example, who built one of the finest houses on Rittenhouse Square in 1896, was the commodore of the Corinthian Yacht Club and an avid tennis and cricket player.[2]

The next rung down on the ladder of success was the emerging white-collar class of professional workers. They began buying up impressive homes on the fringes of Center City and farther afield, if they were financially able. By the late nineteenth century, Philadelphia was thoroughly connected by hundreds of trolley car lines, allowing for upwardly mobile office workers to travel to and from their jobs through, as one writer put it, "bourgeois corridors." The housing choice for the new upper-middle class was the semidetached or twin house. Twins began appearing all over the city, particularly in West Philadelphia, which had easy access to electrified streetcar lines.[3]

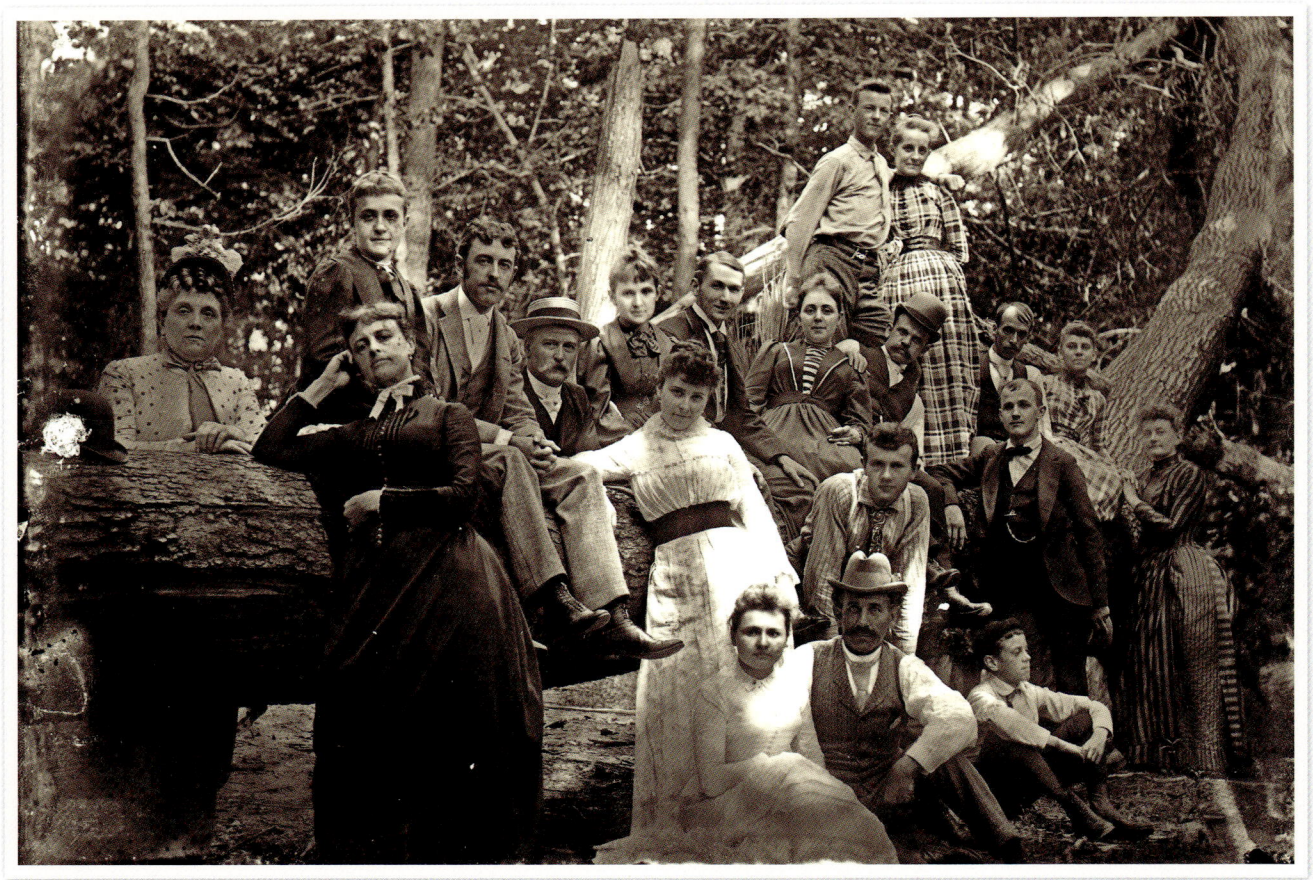

Picnic to Chamounix, 1889. A gathering of well-heeled
Philadelphians posed for a merry picture (some even managed to
crack a smile) on a June day in 1889. Apparently they were on their
way to a picnic at Chamounix, the 1802 house of George Plumstead in
Fairmount Park.

Porch scene near Lancaster Avenue and Fifty-Second Street, 1888. As Victorian fashion dictated, these three women were covered up to the neck and down to the wrist, even in the August heat. Having a front porch where one could catch the occasional summer breeze was a luxury some Philadelphians enjoyed.

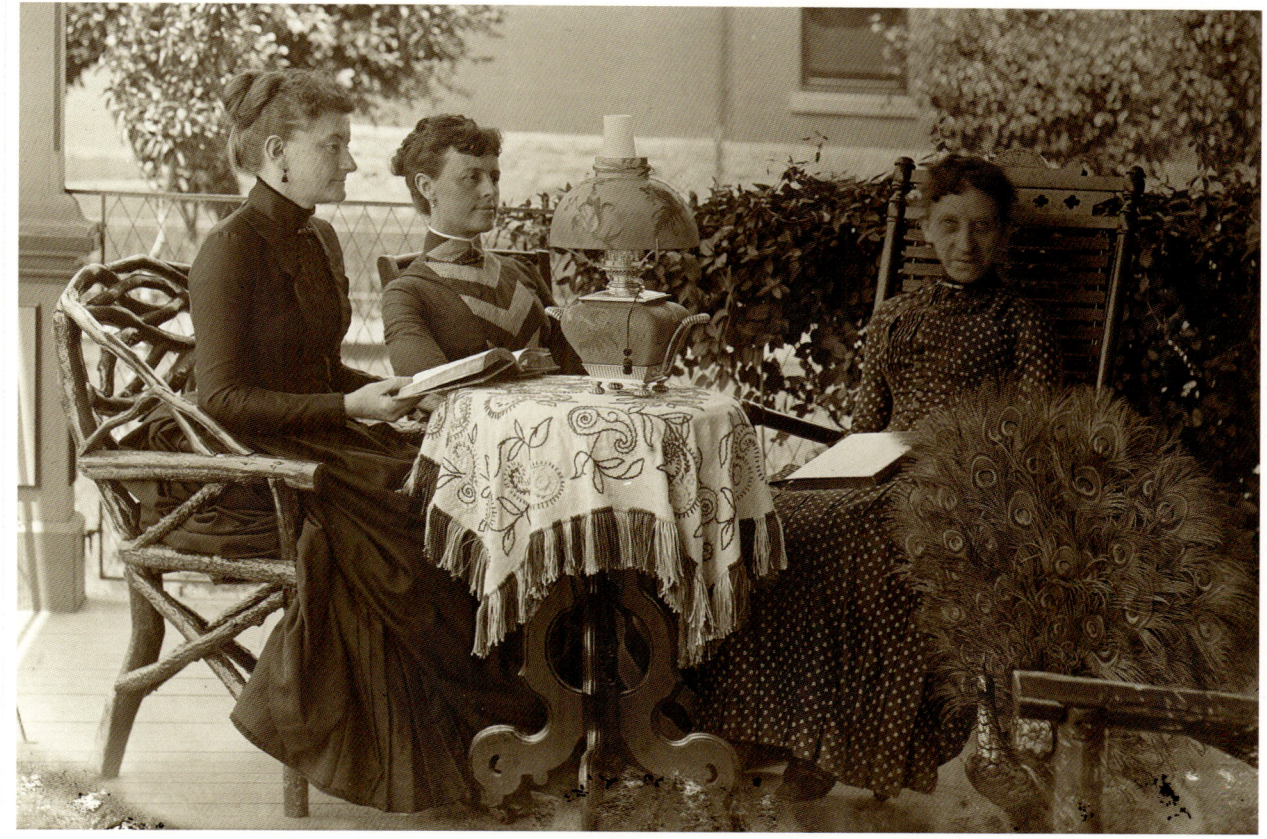

Immigrant Groups

The Irish came to Philadelphia in large numbers following the Great Famine (1845–1849) and settled in Southwark and northern Moyamensing Township. The Irish were frequent victims of violent attacks, mostly from the anti-Catholic Know-Nothing Party. The Philadelphia Nativist Riots of May and July 1844 resulted in thirteen Catholic churches being burned and dozens killed or wounded. The Irish also doled out their fair share of abuse. There were frequent skirmishes between the Irish and African Americans, resulting in injuries, deaths, and extensive property damage.[4]

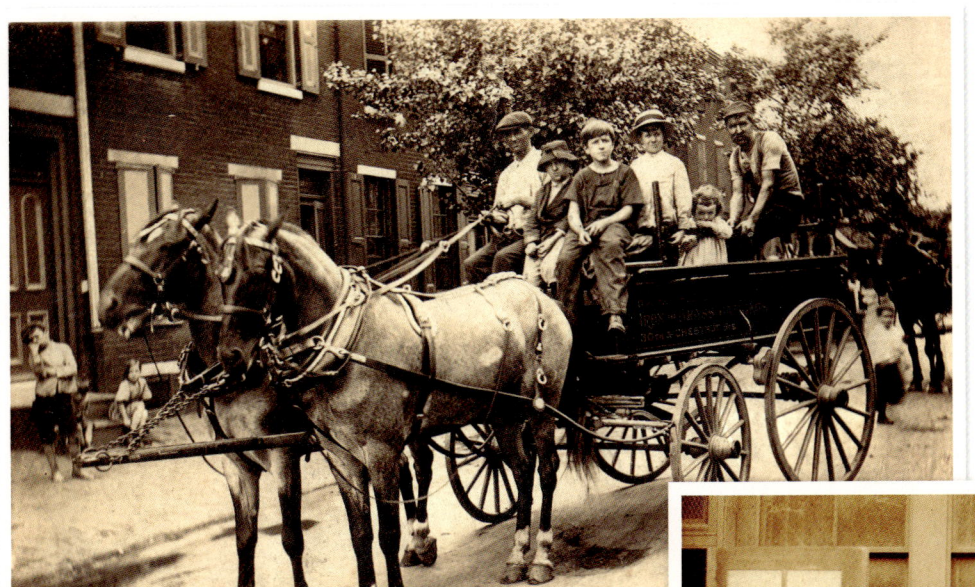

H. A. May Wagon and children, ca. 1900. A delivery wagon for the H. A. May Company of Thirtieth and Chestnut Streets stopped for a cameraman around 1900. Local children stepped into the picture too.

Historical Printing Company, ca. 1895. Twenty-two workers of the Historical Printing Company of 3941 Market Street pose for a group photograph.

Corner market, ca. 1895.
"The place to save your hard earned money" was the slogan of this food market. The proprietor and some of the workers stood out in front with the family dog.

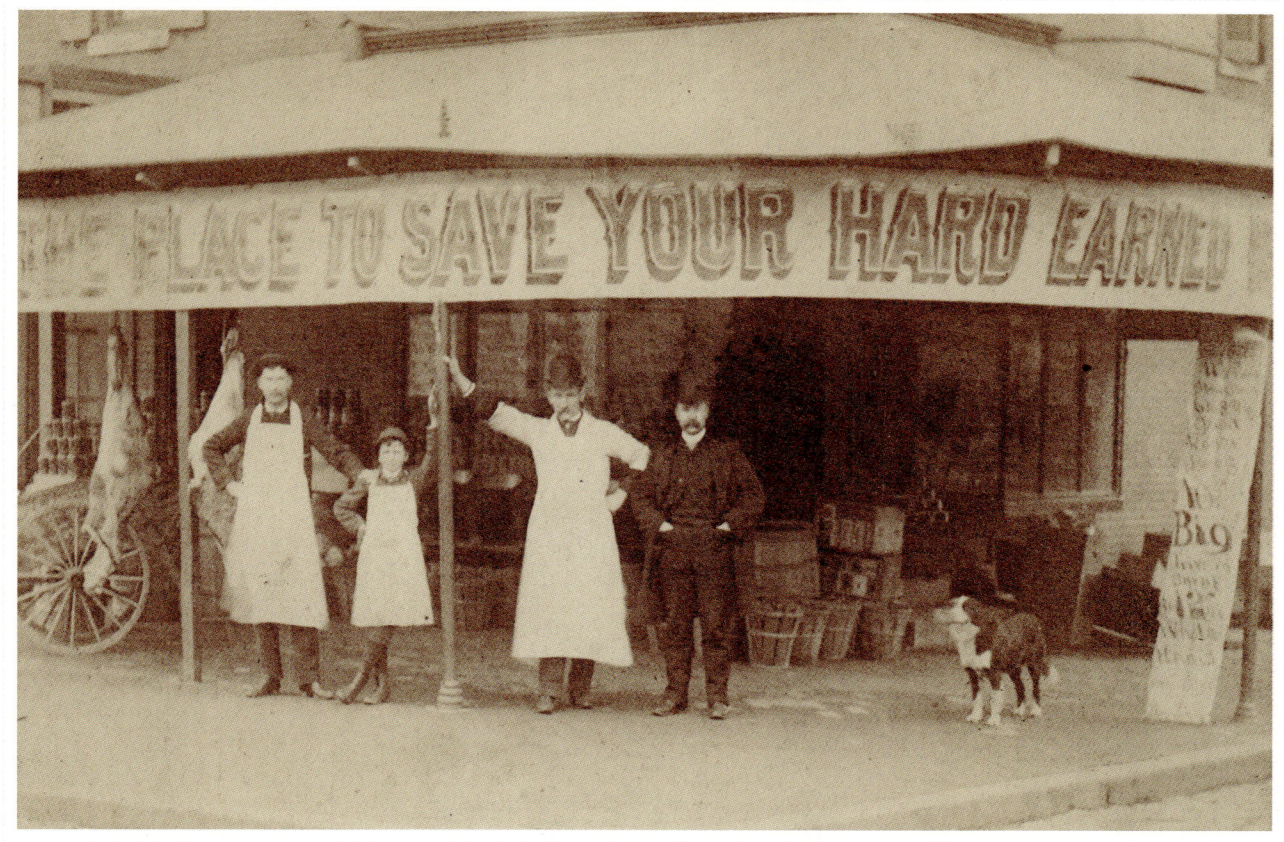

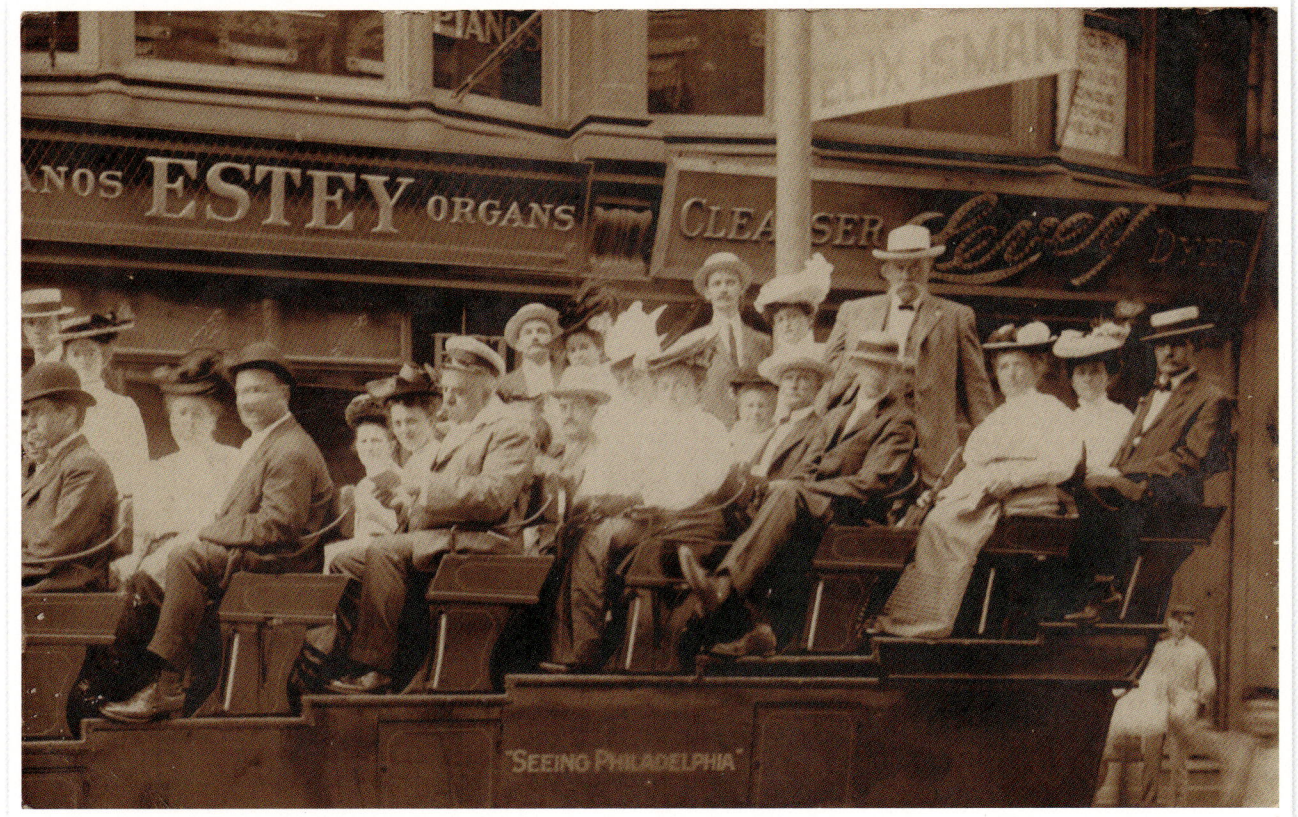

"Seeing Philadelphia," ca. 1906. Philadelphia has been a popular sightseeing destination for a long time, as this open-air tour bus attests.

Pacific Street east of Twenty-Second, ca. 1907. Young boys and girls pose on the 2100 block of West Pacific Street. The houses on this block were about two years old at the time of the photo.

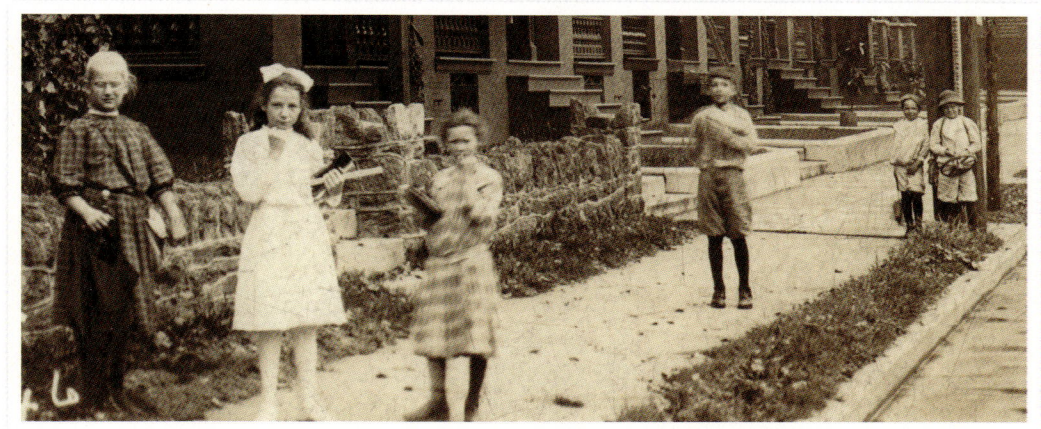

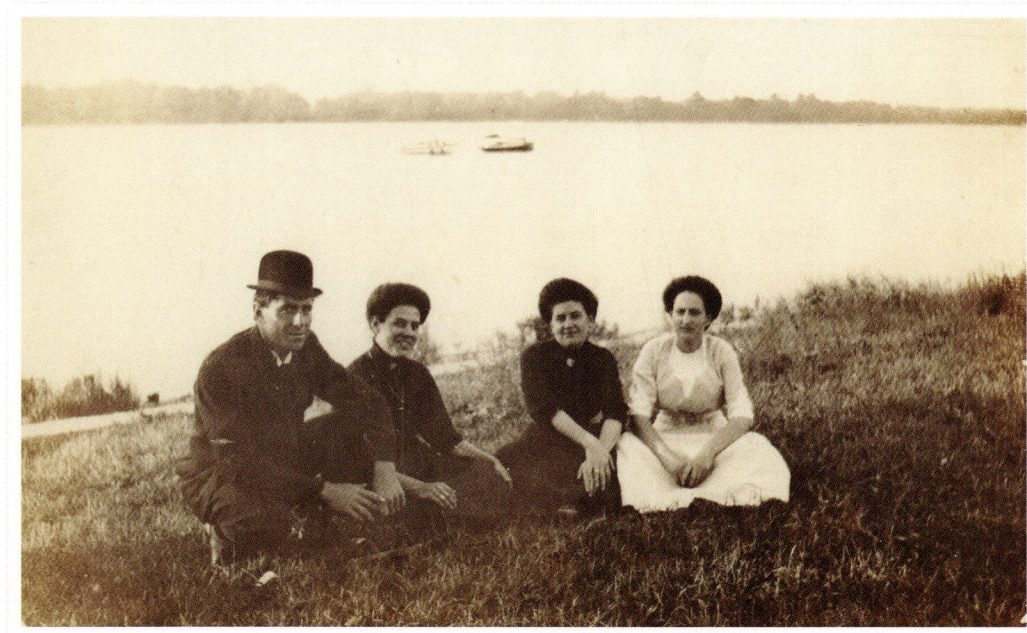

Delaware River at Bridesburg, ca. 1910. Four young friends from Bridesburg relax on the banks of the Delaware River on a late-summer afternoon. The sender of this postcard indicates she has just started a night job.

By 1860, nearly 95,000 foreign-born Irish were living in the city, most of them concentrated in South Philadelphia, Kensington, and Port Richmond. Still later there were large Irish communities in North Philadelphia (Swampoodle) and Germantown (Irishtown).[5]

Immigrants from southern and eastern Europe arrived in the latter half of the nineteenth century in ever-increasing numbers. Some were fleeing persecution, while others were escaping the crushing poverty of their homelands. But whatever the reason for leaving, they came to Philadelphia because that is where the jobs were to be found.[6]

These immigrant groups settled in a section of South Philadelphia just below South Street. The eastern part of the new immigrant haven was the Delaware waterfront, not far from their point of debarkation. Once there, the new arrivals found themselves in close quarters with an established Irish neighborhood close to the docks, and an African American district just to the north.[7]

Jewish people began flocking to the city's ports of entry beginning in March 1882, following the Warsaw Christmas Massacre of 1881. A small group of Jews were already living in a poor section of South Philadelphia just below South Street, and they welcomed their compatriots. The Jewish Quarter, as it was known, extended from Spruce Street to Christian Street and from Second Street west to Sixth Street. Jewish immigration numbers saw a huge increase between 1881 and 1892. By the early twentieth century, some 55,000 Jews lived in South Philadelphia. "Oh, it was like Jerusalem then" was the recollection of one old-time resident of the old Jewish Quarter. It was a time when Philadelphia may well have laid claim to being the Jewish capital of the United States.[8]

The city's Jewish Quarter reached its peak population in 1920 at around 100,000. Eventually Jews from South Philadelphia resettled in other sections of the city such as Brewerytown, Strawberry Mansion, Logan, Mount Airy, West Philadelphia, and Northeast Philadelphia. In the twenty-first century, the scant reminders of Jewish life in South Philadelphia are slowly fading away.[9]

Italians were also arriving in steadily increasing numbers, rising dramatically by the early 1900s. In South Philadelphia, the Italian District was a narrow area bounded by Eighth Street and Ninth Street and Christian Street to Catherine Street. The heart of the district was the famous Ninth Street Italian Market. The new arrivals found spartan living conditions in Little Italy. A housing advocate in 1904 noted that 15 percent of families shared a toilet with six other families.[10]

But as one Sicilian immigrant said, "It is better to be a poor man in South Philadelphia than to be a rich man anywhere else."[11]

Italian District residents were subject to poor wages, long working hours, and substandard housing, but some outsiders viewed the situation with perfunctory enviousness.[12]

One saw a secret pathos in the effort to reproduce in the flat dull streets of a foreign city something of the color and mirth of Mediterranean soil.[13]

—Christopher Morley

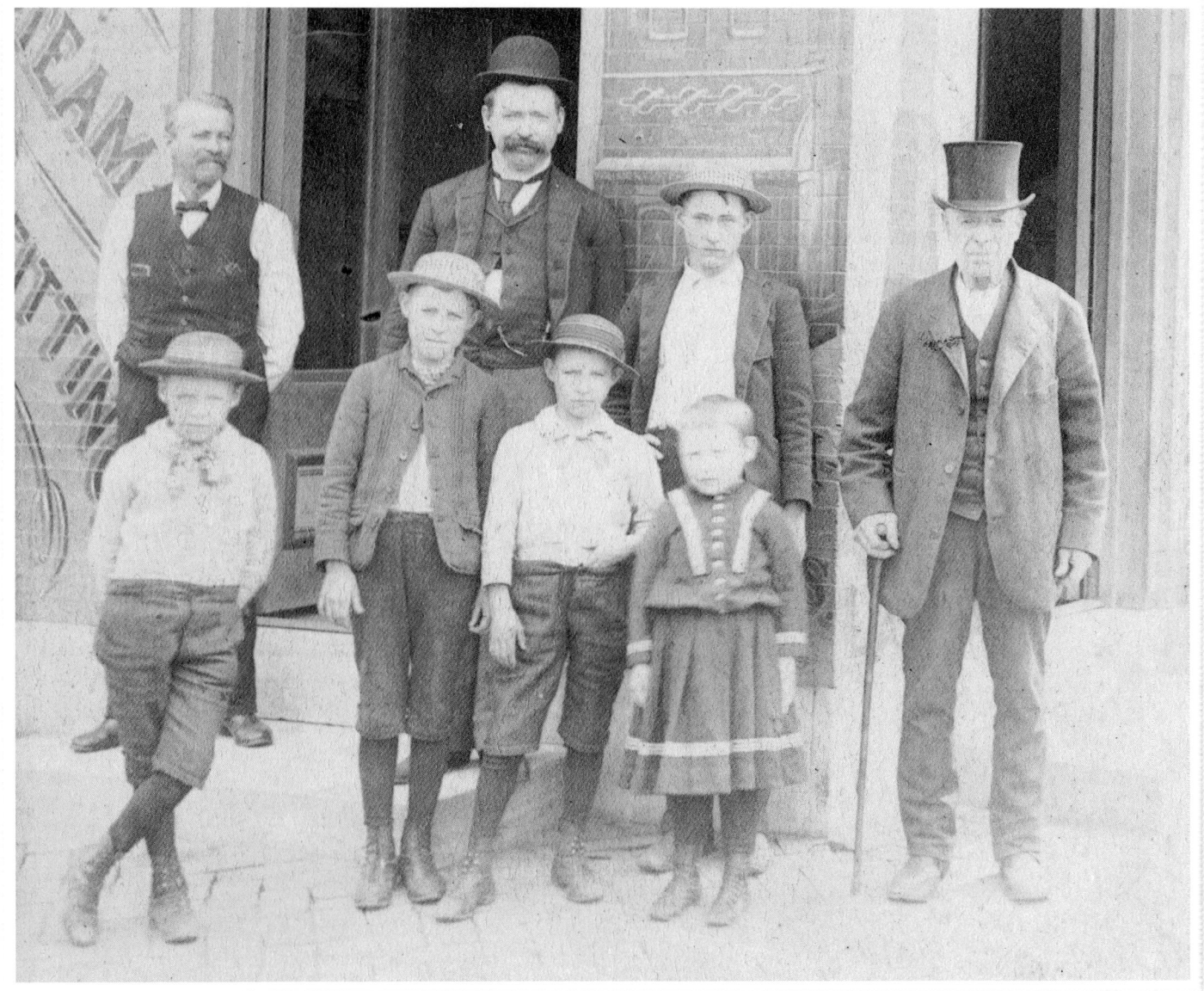

The Kelly family, ca. 1890. Three generations of the Kelly family are posed outside their beer pump business. Irish families such as the Kellys were important to the Philadelphia economy.

In 1890 there were 6,799 Italian immigrants living in Philadelphia. By 1900 that number had swelled to more than 17,830, and by 1910 to more than 45,308, making Philadelphia's Italian settlement second only to New York's at 340,770.[14]

Like the Jewish people of South Philadelphia, the Italians relocated to other parts of the city. By 1902 there were Italian communities in Manayunk, Germantown, Chestnut Hill, Frankford, Mayfair, North Philadelphia, and West Philadelphia.[15]

African Americans are part of this rich immigrant history too. Philadelphia has the oldest African American community in the US, which included luminaries such as Richard Allen (1760–1830) and Octavius Catto (1839–1871). By the mid-1890s, the city's African American population was relatively small compared to its overall population, but it was still the fourth largest in the US, exceeded by Washington, DC; New Orleans; and Baltimore, respectively. At the beginning of that decade, the African American population stood at 39,371. By the end of the decade, the black population had increased 63 percent, to 62,613. By 1910 the number had risen to 84,459, with the highest percentage residing in Center City's Seventh Ward between Sixth and Eighth Streets and from Pine to South Street. The number of African Americans moving to Philadelphia increased even more dramatically in the coming decades, accelerated by the Great Migration Northward (1916-1970).[16]

In his 1896 book *The Philadelphia Negro*, W. E. B. Du Bois (1868–1963) painted an overall negative picture of the Seventh Ward as "uncared for rather than dilapidated, bordering on Jewish and Italian slums to the east." Beyond Eighth and Lombard Streets, his assessment improved considerably.

The residences are good-sized and pleasant. Here some of the best Negro families of the ward live. Some are wealthy in a small way, nearly all are Philadelphia born, and they represent an early wave of emigration from the old slum section.[17]

Du Bois went on to note some well-off black families living beyond Broad Street out to Eighteenth Street, with the area of Seventeenth and Lombard being one of the best African American sections in the city.[18]

Outside of Center City in the 1890s, South Philadelphia and North Philadelphia had the second- and third-largest black populations in the city, respectively.[19]

Although African Americans faced more housing discrimination than other groups, some were living in neighborhoods that were mostly white before World War I.[20]

But all Philadelphians, whether rich or poor, took a great deal of pride in their homes and communities. Philadelphia truly is a city of homes and a city of neighborhoods.

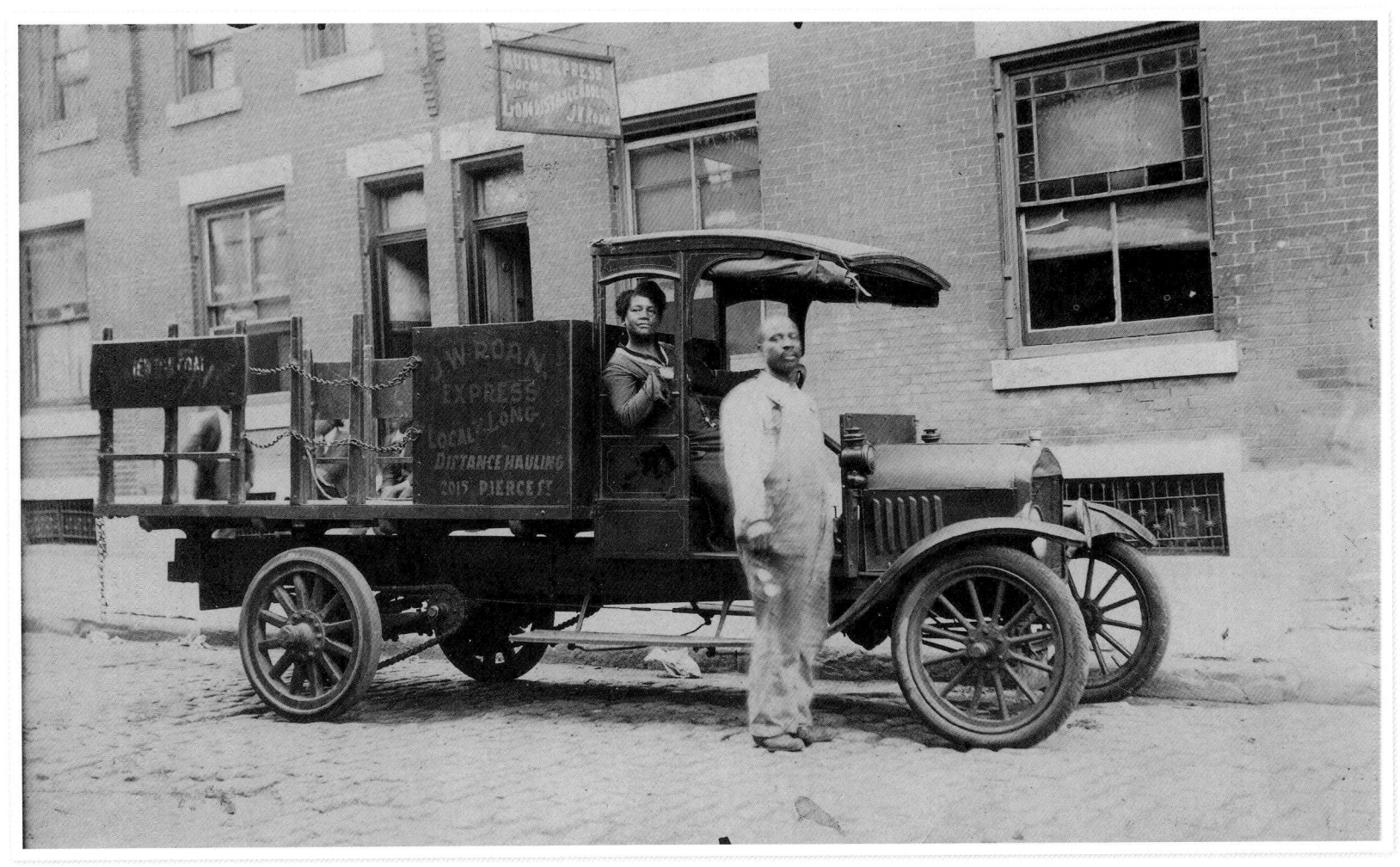

John W. Roan, ca. 1907. John W. Roan, listed in city directories alternately as a driver and laborer, stands in front of his delivery truck. The photo was taken in front of Roan's home at 2015 Pierce Street in South Philadelphia.

NOTES

PREFACE

1. Fred Miller, *Still Philadelphia: A Photographic History, 1890–1940* (Philadelphia: Temple University Press, 1983), 119.

2. United States Census, 1890, 1900, 1910.

3. Conversations with Barry Grosbach and Elizabeth Stegner, two longtime residents of West Philadelphia, both active in civic affairs.

4. Metropostcard.com/History (www.metropostcard.com).

INTRODUCTION

1. William Bucke Campbell, *Old Towns and Districts of Philadelphia* (Philadelphia: City History Society of Philadelphia, 1942), 94–96.

2. Ken Finkel, "The Quintessential Object of Industrial Philadelphia," *The Philly History Blog*, October 25, 2012.

3. *Philadelphia Real Estate and Builders' Guide*, vol. V, no. 6 (February 12, 1890): 65.

4. *Philadelphia Real Estate and Builders' Guide*, vol. VI, no. 1 (January 7, 1891): 3.

5. Miller, *Still Philadelphia*, 73.

6. Ibid., 224.

7. City-issued building permits on file at the Philadelphia City Archives.

8. Miller, *Still Philadelphia*, 71. See also Harold E. Cox, *The Road from Upper Darby: The Story of the Market Street Subway-Elevated* (New York: Electric Railroaders Association, 1967), 16.

9. Frank H. Taylor and William B. McManus, *The City of Philadelphia: As It Appears in the Year 1894* (Philadelphia: George S. Harris & Sons, 1894), 84.

10. William John Murtagh, "The Philadelphia Row House," *Journal of the Society of Architectural Historians* 16, no. 4 (December 1957): 8.

11. Ibid., 12.

12. Ibid.

13. Finkel, "The Quintessential Object of Industrial Philadelphia."

CHAPTER 1. LOWER NORTH PHILADELPHIA

1. Miller, *Still Philadelphia*, 22, 77.

2. Campbell, *Old Towns and Districts of Philadelphia*, 100–101.

3. *Brewerytown Historic District Inventory*, National Register of Historic Places (Washington, DC: United States Department of the Interior, National Park Service, 1991).

4. Shannon Ullman, *Philadelphia Weekly*, May 23, 2018.

5. Rakhmiel Peltz, *From Immigrant to Ethnic Culture: American Yiddish in South Philadelphia* (Stanford, CA: Stanford University Press, 1998), 15.

6. Tom Fox, "Swampoodle's Days of Yore," *Philadelphia Inquirer*, March 29, 1977, 1-B.

7. Eric Enders, *Baseball Parks Then and Now* (San Diego, CA: Thunder Bay, 2007), 12. See also *Millennium Philadelphia* (Philadelphia: Camino Books, 1999), 229, for an excellent photo of the illicit right-field bleachers.

CHAPTER 2. UPPER NORTH PHILADELPHIA

1. George W. Bromley and Walter S. Bromley, *Atlas of the City of Philadelphia: Complete in One Volume* (Philadelphia: G. W. Bromley, 1910), plate 39.

2. S. F. Hotchkin, *The York Road, Old and New* (Philadelphia: Binder & Kelly, 1892), 40–41.

3. Ibid., 33.

4. Campbell, *Old Towns and Districts of Philadelphia*, 127.

5. Bromley and Bromley, *Atlas of the City of Philadelphia*, plates 39–40.

6. Miller, *Still Philadelphia*, 172, 181.

7. Campbell, *Old Towns and Districts of Philadelphia*, 128

8. Bromley and Bromley, *Atlas of the City of Philadelphia*, plate 39.

9. Hotchkin, *The York Road, Old and New*, 110.

10. Adam Levin, "From Creek to Sewer: A Brief Overview of the Topographical Change in Philadelphia," PhillyH2O.org, 2018.

11. Hotchkin, *The York Road, Old and New*, 71.

12. Ibid.

13. Bromley and Bromley, *Atlas of the City of Philadelphia*, plate 39.

14. Campbell, *Old Towns and Districts of Philadelphia*, 125.

15. Marita Krivda Poxon and Rachel Hildebrandt, *Oak Lane, Olney, and Logan* (Mount Pleasant, SC: Arcadia, 2011), 104–105.

16. Dennis DeBrandt, *My Oak Lane Avenue* (Dennis DeBrandt, 2012), 39.

CHAPTER 3. NORTHEAST PHILADELPHIA

1. Natalie Pompilio, "Secede? The Idea Is Faint, but Not Yet Dead," *Philadelphia Inquirer*, November 17, 2004.

2. Miller, *Still Philadelphia*, 225.

3. Guernsey A. Hallowell, *History of Frankford* (Philadelphia: Frankford Business Men's and Taxpayers' Association, 1912), 8.

4. Ibid., 74.

5. Herman LeRoy and Wilfred Collins Jordan, *Philadelphia: A Story of Progress* (New York: Lewis Historical Publishing, 1941), 284–285.

6. Cox, *The Road from Upper Darby*, 16.

7. Anna Bustill Smith, "A Communication," *Journal of Negro History* 10, no. 4 (October 1925): 645–647. See also Hotchkin, *The York Road, Old and New*, 433–434.

8. Bromley and Bromley, *Atlas of the City of Philadelphia*, plate 51.

9. Hotchkin, *The York Road, Old and New*, 442.

10. Ibid., 433.

11. Interview with William Hansell, a longtime resident of Fox Chase, Center for Northeast Philadelphia History, 1994.

12. Campbell, *Old Towns and Districts of Philadelphia*, 111.

CHAPTER 4. GREATER KENSINGTON

1. Oliver Evans, Chapter of the Society for Industrial Archeology, *Workshop of the World* (Philadelphia: Oliver Evans Press, 1990), 5-3, 5-4.

2. Jean Seder, *Voices of Kensington: Vanishing Mills, Vanishing Neighborhoods* (Ardmore, PA: Whitmore, 1982), 19.

3. Ibid., 5.

4. William Beatty's Mills, "Workshop of the World," www.workshopoftheworld.com.

5. Katherine Flynn, "Light Industry," *Preservation* 69, no. 3 (Summer 2017): 41.

CHAPTER 5. SOUTH PHILADELPHIA

1. Henry D. Paxson, *Where Pennsylvania History Began* (Henry D. Paxson, 1926), 26–27.

2. Campbell, *Old Towns and Districts of Philadelphia*, 102, 115.

3. Christopher Morley, *Travels in Philadelphia* (Philadelphia: David McKay, 1920), 174.

4. Peltz, *From Immigrant to Ethnic Culture*, 15.

5. Anonymous, *Press*, October 25, 1891.

6. Peltz, *From Immigrant to Ethnic Culture*, 6. See also Historical Society of

Pennsylvania, "Vitality of Immigration Lives on in the Italian Market," HiddenCity.org, January 22, 2019.

7. Frederick A. McCord, "Tragedy Renews Cry to Out Squatters—but Nobody Knows How," *Sunday Bulletin*, May 8, 1955, S1.

8. Ibid.

9. Campbell, *Old Towns and Districts of Philadelphia*, 96–97.

10. Ibid., 114.

11. Maurice F. Egan, "A Day in the Ma'sh," *Scribner's Monthly* 22, no. 3 (July 1881): 347–348.

12. Philadelphia Historical Commission, *Girard Estate Historic District* (Philadelphia: Philadelphia Historical Commission, 2008), 3–4.

13. Kevin C. Shelley, "Devil's Pocket Neighborhood Fading Away," *Philly Voice*, August 27, 2015.

14. Campbell, *Old Towns and Districts of Philadelphia*, 102.

CHAPTER 6. WEST PHILADELPHIA

1. "Great Improvements Made in Beautiful Part of West Philadelphia," *Philadelphia Inquirer*, November 6, 1895, 7.

2. Robert M. Skaler, *West Philadelphia, University City to Fifty-Second Street* (Mount Pleasant, SC: Arcadia, 2002), 55.

3. Cox, *The Road from Upper Darby*, 12. See also Skaler, *West Philadelphia*, 8.

4. Campbell, *Old Towns and Districts of Philadelphia*, 102, 105.

5. Ibid., 108. See also Skaler, *West Philadelphia*, 95.

CHAPTER 7. SOUTHWEST PHILADELPHIA

1. Paxson, *Where Pennsylvania History Began*, 15, 26. See also Campbell, *Old Towns and Districts of Philadelphia*, 119,

2. *Brewerytown Historic District Inventory*, National Register of Historic Places (Continuation Sheet, Section 7), 2–3.

3. Campbell, *Old Towns and Districts of Philadelphia*, 118.

4. Ibid.

CHAPTER 8. NORTHWEST PHILADELPHIA

1. Naaman H. Keyser, *History of Old Germantown* (Philadelphia: Horace F. McCann, 1907).

2. Campbell, *Old Towns and Districts of Philadelphia*, 108.

3. Harry M. Tinkcom, Margaret B. Tinkcom, and Grant Miles Simon, "Historic Germantown," *Memoirs of the American Philosophical Society* 39 (1955): 56.

4. Bromley and Bromley, *Atlas of the City of Philadelphia*, plates 35, 38.

5. David R. Contosta, *Suburb in the City: Chestnut Hill, Philadelphia, 1850–1990* (Columbus: Ohio State University Press, 1992), 2.

6. Edward W. Hocker, *Germantown, 1683–1933* (Edward W. Hocker, 1933), 226.

7. John C. Manton, *Bygones: A Guide to Historic Roxborough-Manayunk* (John C. Manton, 1990), 160.

CHAPTER 9. THE PEOPLE

1. E. Digby Baltzell, *Philadelphia Gentlemen: The Making of a National Upper Class* (Philadelphia: University of Pennsylvania Press, 1979), 175–176, 185–186.

2. Ibid., 131.

3. John Henry Hepp IV, *The Middle-Class City: Transforming Space and Time in Philadelphia, 1876–1926* (Philadelphia: University of Pennsylvania Press, 2003), 40.

4. Sam Bass Warner, *The Private City: Philadelphia in Three Periods of Its Growth* (Philadelphia: University of Pennsylvania Press, 1968), 144–147.

5. Ibid., 139.

6. Richard N. Juliani, *The Social Organization of Immigration: The Italians in Philadelphia* (Philadelphia: University of Pennsylvania Press, 1971), 164, 188.

7. Warner, *The Private City*, 127.

8. Murray Friedman, *Jewish Life in Philadelphia: 1830–1940* (Philadelphia: Temple University Press, 1983), 3, 6. See also Harry D. Boonin, *The Jewish Quarter of Philadelphia: A History and Guide, 1881–1930* (Philadelphia: Jewish Walking Tours of Philadelphia, 1999), 6, 10, 25; and Peltz, *From Immigrant to Ethnic Culture*, 15.

9. Peltz, *From Immigrant to Ethnic Culture*, 15.

10. Historical Society of Pennsylvania, "Vitality of Immigration Lives On in the Italian Market," https://hiddencityphilly.org, 2019.

11. Juliani, *The Social Organization of Immigration*, 229.

12. Ibid., 226.

13. Morley, *Travels in Philadelphia*, 13.

14. Robert F. Foerster, *The Italian Immigration of Our Times* (Cambridge, MA: Harvard University Press, 1924), 328–329. See also United States Census Records for 1890, 1900, and 1910.

15. Bianca Arcangeli, *The Italians in Philadelphia, 1880–1920: Origins, Geographical and Occupational Distribution* (Bianca Arcangeli, 1974), 8, 11. See also Juliani, *The Social Organization of Immigration*, 122.

16. W. E. B. Du Bois, *The Philadelphia Negro: A Social Study* (Philadelphia: University of Pennsylvania Press, 1899, republished 1967), xxvii, xxix, xxx (1967 introduction by E. Digby Baltzell), 53, 58.

17. Ibid., 58.

18. Ibid., 61.

19. Ibid., xxx, table 2.

20. Miller, *Still Philadelphia*, 31.

Adams, Henry P. *One Hundred Years in Philadelphia, 1847–1947: The Evening Bulletin's Anniversary Book.* New York: Whittlesey House, 1947.

American Philosophical Society. "Historic Philadelphia: From the Founding until the Early Nineteenth Century, Papers Dealing with Its People and Buildings with an Illustrative Map." Philadelphia: American Philosophical Society, 1953.

Blumenson, John J. G. *Identifying American Architecture: A Pictorial Guide to Styles and Terms, 1600–1945.* Nashville: American Association for State and Local History, 1982.

Boonin, Harry D. *The Jewish Quarter of Philadelphia: A History and Guide, 1881–1930.* Philadelphia: Jewish Walking Tours of Philadelphia, 1999.

Boorse, J. W., Jr. *Philadelphia in Motion: A Nostalgic View of How Philadelphia Traveled, 1902–1940.* Bryn Mawr, PA: Bryn Mawr Press, 1976.

Burke, Bobbye, Otto Sperr, Hugh J. McCauley, and Trina Vaux. *Historic Rittenhouse: A Philadelphia Neighborhood.* Philadelphia: University of Pennsylvania Press, 1985.

Burt, Nathaniel. *The Perennial Philadelphians: The Anatomy of an American Aristocracy.* Philadelphia: University of Pennsylvania Press, 2007.

Clark, Dennis. *The Irish in Philadelphia: Ten Generations of Urban Experience.* Philadelphia: Temple University Press, 1973.

Cotter, John L., Daniel G. Roberts, and Michael Parrington. *The Buried Past: An Archaeological History of Philadelphia.* Philadelphia: University of Pennsylvania Press, 1992.

Custer, Jay F. *Prehistoric Cultures of Eastern Pennsylvania.* Harrisburg: Pennsylvania Historical and Museum Commission, 1996.

Davis, Allen F., and Mark H. Haller. *The Peoples of Philadelphia: A History of Ethnic Groups and Lower-Class Life, 1790–1940.* Philadelphia: Temple University Press, 1973.

Eberlein, Harold Donaldson, and Cortlandt Van Dyke Hubbard. *Portrait of a Colonial City: Philadelphia, 1670–1838.* Philadelphia: J. B. Lippincott, 1939.

Eisenhart, Luther P., ed. *Historic Philadelphia: From the Founding Until the Early Nineteenth Century; Papers Dealing with Its People and Buildings, with an Illustrated Map.* Philadelphia: American Philosophical Society, 1953.

Faris, John T. *Old Roads out of Philadelphia.* Philadelphia: J. B. Lippincott, 1917.

Foster, Janet W. *The Queen Anne House.* New York: Harry N. Abrams, 2006.

Gallery, John A., gen. ed. *Philadelphia Architecture: A Guide to the City.* Prepared for the Foundation of Architecture, Philadelphia, by the Group for Environmental Education. Cambridge, MA: MIT Press, 1984.

Garvan, Beatrice B. *Federal Philadelphia, 1785–1825: The Athens of the Western World.* Philadelphia: Philadelphia Museum of Art, 1987.

Guinther, John. *Philadelphia: A Dream for the Keeping.* Tulsa, OK: Continental Heritage, 1982.

Hayes, John P. *Philadelphia in Color.* New York: Hasting House, 1983.

Hogarth, Paul. *Walking Tours of Old Philadelphia.* Barre, MA: Barre, 1976.

Jackson, Joseph. *Encyclopedia of Philadelphia, in Four Volumes.* Harrisburg,

PA: National Historical Association, 1933.

Keels, Thomas H. *Forgotten Philadelphia: Lost Architecture of the Quaker City*. Philadelphia: Temple University Press, 2007.

King, Moses. *Philadelphia and Notable Philadelphians*. New York: Blanchard, 1901.

Lawrence, Charles. *History of Philadelphia Almshouses and Hospitals*. Philadelphia: Charles Lawrence, 1905.

Lewis, Michael J. *Frank Furness: Architecture and the Violent Mind*. New York: Norton, 2001.

Lippincott, Horace Mather. *The Colonial Homes of Philadelphia and Its Neighborhoods*. Philadelphia: J. B. Lippincott, 1912.

Looney, Robert F. *Old Philadelphia in Early Photographs, 1839–1914*. New York: Dover, 1976.

Luconi, Stefano. *From Paesani to White Ethnics: The Italian Experience in Philadelphia*. Albany: State University of New York Press, 2001.

Maass, John. *The Victorian Home in America with over 250 Illustrations*. Mineola, NY: Dover, 1973.

Marcus, George H., and David Van Zanten. *The Second Empire and Philadelphia*. Philadelphia: Philadelphia Museum of Art Bulletin, 1978.

Marion, John Francis. *Walking Tours of Historic Philadelphia*. Princeton, NJ: Pyne, 1974.

Mauger, Edward A., and Bob Skiba. *Lost Philadelphia*. London: Pavilion Books, 2013.

Maynard, W Barkesdale. *Architecture in the United States, 1800–1850*. New Haven, CT: Yale University Press, 2002.

Miller, Fredric M., Morris J. Vogel, and Allen F. Davis. *Philadelphia Stories: A Photographic History, 1920–1960*. Philadelphia: Temple University Press, 1988.

Moss, Roger W. *Historic Houses of Philadelphia*. Philadelphia: University of Pennsylvania Press, 1998.

Moss, Roger W. *Historic Landmarks of Philadelphia*. Philadelphia: University of Pennsylvania Press, 2008.

Moss, Roger W. *Historic Sacred Places of Philadelphia*. Philadelphia: University of Pennsylvania Press, 2005.

Myers, Nicholas. *Philadelphia's New Hope: Manayunk*. Conshohocken, PA: Print America, 1988.

Nash, Gary B. *First City: Philadelphia and the Forging of Historical Memory*. Philadelphia: University of Pennsylvania Press, 2002.

Oliver Evans Chapter of the Society for Industrial Archeology. *Workshop of the World*. Wallingford, PA: Oliver Evans Press, 1990.

Pennell, Elizabeth R., and Joseph Pennell. *Our Philadelphia*. Philadelphia: J. B. Lippincott, 1914.

Perkins, G. Holmes, ed. *Philadelphia Architecture*. New York: Reinhold, 1961.

Philadelphia Inquirer. *Millennium Philadelphia: The Last 100 Years*. Philadelphia: Camino Books, 2000.

Repplier, Agnes. *Philadelphia: The Place and the People*. New York: Macmillan, 1898.

Shade, Rachel Simmons. *Philadelphia Rowhouse Manual: A Practical Guide for Homeowners*. Philadelphia: City of Philadelphia, 2008.

Sheldon, Noah, and Richard Guy Wilson. *The Colonial Revival House*. New York: Henry N. Abrams, 2004.

Snyder, Martin P. *City of Independence: Views of Philadelphia before 1800*. New York: Praeger, 1975.

Tatman, Sandra L., and Roger W. Moss. *Biographical Dictionary of Philadelphia Architects*. Boston: G. K. Hall, 1985.

Tatum, George B. *Penn's Great Town: 250 Years of Philadelphia Architecture*

Philadelphia: University of Pennsylvania Press, 1961.

Tatum, George B. *Philadelphia Georgian: The City House of Samuel Powell.* Middletown, CT: Wesleyan University Press, 1976.

Taylor, Frank H., and William B. McManus. *The City of Philadelphia: As It Appears in the Year 1894.* Philadelphia: George S. Harris & Sons, 1894.

Teitelman, Edward, and Richard W. Longstreth. *Architecture in Philadelphia: A Guide.* Cambridge, MA: MIT Press, 1981.

Traub, David S. *Discovering Philadelphia: Places Little Known.* Philadelphia: Camino Books, 2017.

Traub, David S. *Searching for Philadelphia: The Concealed City.* Philadelphia: Camino Books, 2013.

Wainwright, Nicholas B. *Philadelphia in the Romantic Age of Lithography.*

Philadelphia: Pennsylvania Historical Society, 1958.

Webster, Richard W. *Philadelphia Preserved: Catalog of the Historic American Building Survey.* Philadelphia: Temple University Press, 1981.

Weigley, Russell F., ed. *Philadelphia: A 300-Year History.* New York: W. W. Norton, 1982.

White, Theo B., ed. *Philadelphia Architecture in the Nineteenth Century.* Philadelphia: University of Pennsylvania Press, 1953.

Wilson, George. *Yesterday's Philadelphia.* Miami, FL: E. A. Seemann, 1975.

Wolf, Edwin, II. *Philadelphia: Portrait of an American City.* Harrisburg, PA: Stackpole Books, 1975.

INDEX

A. B. & C. F. Millett Construction, 46, 146

Acme Supermarkets, 29, 104, 113, 118

African American community in Philadelphia, 26, 28, 59, 60, 91, 155, 160, 162

All Saints Catholic Church, 66

Allegheny Methodist-Episcopal Church, 83

Allegheny Worsted Mills, 75

Allen, Richard, 162

Allison Mansion, 112

Anderson, Erik A., 98

Angora Station (Pennsylvania Railroad), 132

Annunciation of the Blessed Virgin Mary Roman Catholic Church, 102

Asbury, Thomas Henry, 41

Atget, Eugéne, 8

Baker Bowl, 25

Balderston, Charles, 128

Baldwin Locomotive Works, 27

Bartram, John, 127

Bartram, William, 127

Bartram's Garden, 127

Bayuk Brothers, 33

Beaston, Harry D., 134

Beatty's Mill, 75

Bell & Kershaw, 150

Bella Vista, 92

Belmont, 110, 119

Betsy Ross Bridge, 62

Blockley Township, 110

"Blood-Pit, the", 73

Blue Bell Tavern, 137

Boulanger, Fredric, 43

Branchtown, 18, 42, 43

Brewerytown, 27–28, 30, 32–33, 160

Bridesburg, 16, 22, 62, 65,66, 159

Broad Street Subway Line, 39

Brooke, Charles J., 123

Bryant, Thomas, 98

Bryn Mawr Hotel, 153

Bustill, Cyrus, 60

"Bustling Bess", 60

Bustleton, 18, 57, 59, 60, 69–71

Bustleton Methodist Episcopal Church, 70

Butler, Pierce, 43

Butler Place, 42–43

C. Schmidt's & Sons, 37

C. R. Kohl & Brother, 151

Cameron & Co. Spinning Mill, 88, 89

Campbell, James B., 131

Carpenter Station (Philadelphia, Germantown & Chestnut Hill Railroad), 139

Carpenter, Samuel, 139

Carroll Park, 122, 125

Catto, Octavius, 162

Cedar Hill Hotel, 58, 59

Cedar Park, 110, 127, 128

Center City Philadelphia, 22, 36, 39, 93, 105, 107, 111, 132, 153, 162

Chamounix, 154

Charles W. Budd & Co., 129

Cheltenham Township, 60

Chestnut Hill, 139

Chestnut Hill Depot (Philadelphia, Germantown & Chestnut Hill Railroad), 139, 162

Christmas Massacre of 1881, 160

Church of Gloria Dei (Old Swedes Church), 91–92

City Hall, 9, 57, 153

Clarke, James C., 116

Cobbs Creek, 110, 127

Comly, James J., 119

Consolidation Act of 1854, 10, 18, 57, 110

Cooke, Jay, 41

Coral Street Arts House, 75

Corinthian Yacht Club, 153

Cowper, William, 41

Crescentville, 39

David C. Schuler & Son, 78, 80

DeBenneville, George, 43

Delaware River, 18, 21, 62, 93, 127, 159, 160

DeMoll, Carl, 35

Devil's Pocket, 93

Diesel, Harrison N., 114

Disston, Mary, 66

Divine Lorraine Hotel, 27

Donato, Antonio, 22

D'Ortona, Paul, 92

Drexel University, 112

Drovers Hotel, 43

Du Bois, W. E. B., 162

Eagle Hotel, 59, 71

East Falls, 139, 147

Eddystone, Pennsylvania, 27

Eleven-Gun Battery, 93

Elfreth's Alley, 21

Ellenberg, Harry, Jr., 48

Fairmount (neighborhood), 27

Fairmount Park, 27–28, 35, 110, 123–124, 137, 140, 153–154

Falls of the Schuylkill, *See* East Falls

Father–Son–Holy Ghost house, 21, 73

Fels-Naptha Soap, 51

Felton, John, 51

Feltonville, 51

Fern Rock Building Association, 43

Fern Rock Land Association, 39

Fernald, James C., 22, 114–115

Fishers Station (Philadelphia & Reading Railroad), 140

Fishtown, 73, 75

Fletcher, George A., 123

Florey & Bevan, 125

Food Distribution Center, 92

Forrest, Edwin, 26–27

"Fourteen Chimneys", 21

Fourth Presbyterian Church, 128

Fox Chase (neighborhood), 57, 59–60, 71

Fox Chase Inn, 60

Frankford Creek, 57, 62, 65

Frankford and Southwark Philadelphia Passenger Railroad Company, 59

Frankfort Land Company, 57

Free African Society, 60

Freedom Theatre, 26–27

Frogtown, see Martinsville

Gallagher, John C., 99

Garden City movement, 93, 101

Gentilehommiere, 93

Gentrification, 75

George H. Thomas Public School, 37

German settlements in Philadelphia, 57, 139

Germantown, 9, 18, 57, 73, 139–142, 144–145, 160, 162

Girard College, 27

Girard Estate, 93, 100–101

Girard, Stephen, 93, 101

Gowen, 139

Graduate Hospital, 93

Graff, Frederick, 27

Gray, George, 93

Great Depression, 57

Great Famine (Ireland), 155

Great Migration Northward, 162

Greenberg, Solomon, 22, 144

Greenwich Island, 93

Guenthoer, Otto, 12, 22

Hale, Willis G., 26, 112

Hales & Ballinger, 86

Harnett, James J., 123

Harrowgate, 22, 75

Hartranft, 22

Haviland, John, 21

Heidrich, J. V., 23

Heinke, C. A., 143

Henderson, Charles G., 129

Henry G. Schultz & Son, 37

Historical Publishing Company, 152

Hollander's Creek, 93

Holmesburg, 57, 67–68

Holmesburg and Bustleton Railroad, 60, 70

Horse-drawn streetcars, 20, 59, 140

Houston, Henry H., 139

Howard, Ebenezer, 93, 101

Hunting Park (neighborhood), 45

Huntingdon Station (Philadelphia & Reading Railroad), 25

Ibetson, Bertha, 92

Interstate 95, 62

Iris Theatre, 84

Irish community in Philadelphia, 28–29, 91–93, 155, 160–161

Irvin, Harold C., 46

Italian community in Philadelphia, 91–92, 160, 162

Italian District, 92, 160

Italian Market, 91–92, 160

J. G. Brill Car Works, 135

J. S. Ivins Cracker Factory, 29

Jewish community in Philadelphia, 28, 91–92, 160, 162

Jewish Quarter, 92, 160

John Bromley & Sons Mill, 74

John G. Carruth Endurance Mills, 82

Jolly Post Tavern, 58–59

Jordan, Jacob R., 119

Kemble, "Fanny", 43

Kemble Park, 43

Kemon, S. F., 136

Kensington, 11, 18, 22, 25, 72–89, 160

Kettiman, Herman F., 68

Killough, Robert, 49

Kingsessing, 127–128, 130

Kirkbride, Joseph, 65

Know-Nothing Party, 155

Kuhn, Peter, 143

Lambrecht, Ludwig, 22

Lawnton Station (Philadelphia & Reading Railroad), 41

League Island, 93, 102

Lenni Lenape, 37, 127

Lewis Elkin Elementary School, 86

Lewis, William, 28

Liberty County, 57

Logan, 39, 46–47, 160

Logan, James, 39–40

Logan Station (Philadelphia & Reading Railroad), 39

Loughran, John, 37

Lower North Philadelphia, 22, 24–37

Lukens, Helena, 129

Mack, Connie, 34

Manayunk, 73, 139, 162

Mantua, 110

Market Street Subway-Elevated, 59, 62, 107, 111, 127

Martinsville, 91, 93

Mayfair, 162

McCoach, John, 129

McConaghy, John, 123

McGill, A. C., 120

McKibben, David, 80

McNamee, Frank, 92

Michaelsen, F. C., 115

Milestown, 18

Milnamow, Thomas J., 99

Morley, Christopher, 91, 160

Mount Airy, 139–140, 160

Mount Airy Station (Philadelphia & Reading Railroad), 139, 146

Moyamensing Township, 91, 93, 155

Mt. Moriah Station (Baltimore & Ohio Railroad), 134

Mummers, 91

Municipal Stadium (John F. Kennedy Stadium), 102

National Register of Historic Places, 27

National Trust Community Investment Corporation, 75

"Neck, the", 92–93, 95–96, 102

New Freedom Theater, 26–27

New Kensington Community Development Corporation, 75

New Sweden, 91, 127

New York City, 10, 20, 91, 162

Newell, Robert, 42

North American Lace Company, 37

Northeast Philadelphia, 20, 22, 56–71, 73, 139, 160

Nyce, Jonathan P., 52

Oak Lane Station (Philadelphia & Reading Railroad),

41, 54

Ogontz, 41–42

Ogontz (Lenape Indian chief), 41

Ogontz Manor Apartments, 43

Olney, 16, 22, 39, 41, 51–52

Olney Mutual Land Association, 39

omnibuses, 59

Orr, James W., 87

Overbrook Farms, 110

Oxford Mills, 75

Oxford Township, 57

Paschall, 127

Paschall Mill, 127

Paschall, Henry, 137

Paschall, Thomas, 127

Passyunk Township, 93

Pegg's Run, 27

Pelham, 139

Penn, William, 9, 21, 127

Pennsport, 92

Peters, Richard, 110

Philadelphia & Reading Railroad, 25, 39, 41, 54, 59, 62,
    110, 139, 146

Philadelphia Athletics baseball club, 28, 33

Philadelphia, Germantown & Chestnut Hill Railroad,
    139

Philadelphia Inquirer, 91, 107,

Philadelphia Museum of Art, 27

Philadelphia Navy Yard, 93

Philadelphia Negro, the, 162

Philadelphia Opera House, 27

Philadelphia Phillies baseball club, 25

Philadelphia Real Estate Record and Builders' Guide, 18,
    20

Pitts, Robert A., 22

Pittville, 18

Pleasant Prospect, 127

Point Breeze, 11, 93, 104

Polish community in Philadelphia, 62

Port Richmond, 22, 73, 75, 160

postcards, 8, 15–16

Powelton Village, 110

Prettyman, Charles, 22, 101

Prohibition, 27, 32

Puerto Rican community in Philadelphia, 73

Quaker City Dye Works, 75

Queen Village, 92

Rambler Playground, 67

Reading Terminal, 59

Reading Terminal Land Association, 39

Restaurant School at Walnut Hill College, 112

Richards & Son, 87

Rittenhouse Square, 22, 153

Roan, John W., 163

Roosevelt Boulevard, 22, 41, 57

Roxborough, 11, 60, 139, 149

Schermerhorn & Reinhold, 125

Schmitt, Harry, 54

Schuylkill (neighborhood), 93, 103

Schuylkill River, 18, 21, 27, 107, 110, 127, 153

Sedgwick Farms, 139

Sesquicentennial International Exhibition, 102

Seven Stars, 59

Sherman, George W., 122

Shetzline, Charles H., 96

Shibe Park, 28, 34

Shisler, George W., 87

South Kensington, 75

South Philadelphia, 8, 16, 29, 90–105

Southwark, 18, 59, 92–93, 155

Southwest Philadelphia, 8, 22, 126–137

Sparks Shot Tower, 92

Spencer, Joseph, 43

Spruce Hill, 110

Spruce Street Row, 108

Squatterville, 92

St. Elizabeth Protestant Episcopal Church, 101

St. Mark's P. E. Church, 62

St. Mary's Church, 112

St. Monica's Roman Catholic Church, 99

St. Vincent DePaul Roman Catholic Church, 143

Stafford, John, 22, 32, 35

stagecoaches, 59

Stonehouse Lane, 93

Summers, Joseph R., 130

Swampoodle, 28, 160

Temple University, 24

textile industry, 37, 73, 75–76

Tinicum Island, 127

Tioga Station (Philadelphia & Reading Railroad), 25

Tioga/Nicetown, 11. 25

Townsend's Mill, 42

Trinity Episcopal Church, 85

Trinity M. E. Church, 29

trolley cars, 20, 39, 59, 64, 73, 94, 107, 110, 127, 132, 140, 153

Trumbauer, Horace, 25

Tulpehocken Station (Philadelphia, Germantown & Chestnut Hill Railroad), 139

Union Hotel, 71

University of Pennsylvania, 112

Upper Darby, Pennsylvania, 59

Upper North Philadelphia, 8, 22, 38–55

Van Rensselaer, Alexander, 153

Vancleave, Richard, 22

Waddy, Henry, 57

Waddy's Grange, 57

Wade, Angus, 120

Walnut Hill, 110

Walt Whitman Bridge, 92

Walter, Thomas U., 21

Washington, George, 58, 137

Watson, John F., 27

Wayne Junction (Philadelphia & Reading Railroad), 39, 140–141

Wellens, Jules, 51

West Philadelphia, 9, 16, 18, 20, 22, 106–125, 127, 153, 160, 162

Wetherstine, Harry, 142

Whitman, 93

Wiccaco Church, 91

Widener, Peter A. B., 26

William Steele & Sons, 37

Wilson, Alexander, 41

Wilson, Alexander, Jr., 114

Wilson, E. Allen, 12, 22, 136

Windrim, James T., 93

Windrim, John D., 93

Wingohocking Creek, 39, 41–42, 46, 57

Wissahickon (neighborhood), 140, 148, 150

Wissahickon Creek, 140

Wissahickon Heights (neighborhood), 139

Wissahickon Heights Station (Philadelphia, Germantown & Chestnut Hill Railroad), 139

Wissinoming, 57

Workshop of the World, 10, 20, 73

World War II, 57

Wright & Prentzel, 78–79

Wright, William H., 148

Yoder, Abraham L., 23

Yoder, Rosa (Rosie), 23

Young, George, 22

Young, William H., 87

Yoder, Abraham L., 23

Yoder, Rosa (Rosie), 23

Young, George, 22

Young, William H., 87

Zane, G. W. and J. M., 34

ABOUT THE AUTHOR

Joseph Minardi is an award-winning local photographer and a recipient of the 2007 Preservation Initiative Award from the University City Historical Society and the 2014 Annual Award for Service to the Preservation Community from Save Our Sites. He is a former vice president of the University City Historical Society and editor of its bimonthly newsletter, *On the West Side*, and writer of "History Matters" for the *East Falls Local*. Minardi has also hosted walking tours and lectures about Philadelphia's historic architecture. This is his fourth book about Philadelphia.